MOSAICS

Popular Music History

Series Editor: Alyn Shipton, Royal Academy of Music, London, and City University, London

This series publishes books that challenge established orthodoxies in popular music studies, examine the formation and dissolution of canons, interrogate histories of genres, focus on previously neglected forms, or engage in archaeologies of popular music.

Published

An Unholy Row
Jazz in Britain and its Audience, 1945–1960
Dave Gelly

Being Prez
The Life and Music of Lester Young
Dave Gelly

Chasin' the Bird
The Life and Legacy of Charlie Parker
Brian Priestley

Handful of Keys:
Conversations with Thirty Jazz Pianists
Alyn Shipton

Jazz Me Blues:
The Autobiography of Chris Barber
Chris Barber with Alyn Shipton

Jazz Visions:
Lennie Tristano and His Legacy
Peter Ind

Lee Morgan:
His Life, Music and Culture
Tom Perchard

Lionel Richie:
Hello
Sharon Davis

Mr P.C.:
The Life and Music of Paul Chambers
Rob Palmer

Out of the Long Dark:
The Life of Ian Carr
Alyn Shipton

Rufus Wainwright
Katherine Williams

Soul Unsung: Reflections on the Band in Black Popular Music
Kevin Le Gendre

The Godfather of British Jazz:
The Life and Music of Stan Tracey
Clark Tracey

The Last Miles: The Music of Miles Davis, 1980–1991
George Cole

The Long Shadow of the Little Giant:
The Life, Work and Legacy of Tubby Hayes (second edition)
Simon Spillett

The Ultimate Guide to Great Reggae:
The Complete Story of Reggae Told through its Greatest Songs, Famous and Forgotten
Michael Garnice

Trad Dads, Dirty Boppers and Free Fusioneers: A History of British Jazz, 1960–1975
Duncan Heining

MOSAICS
THE LIFE AND WORKS OF GRAHAM COLLIER

DUNCAN HEINING

SHEFFIELD UK   BRISTOL CT

Published by Equinox Publishing Ltd.

UK: Office 415, The Workstation, 15 Paternoster Row, Sheffield, South Yorkshire S1 2BX
USA: ISD, 70 Enterprise Drive, Bristol, CT 06010

www.equinoxpub.com

First published 2018
First printing in paperback 2022

© Duncan Heining 2018

All rights reserved. No part of this publication may be reproduced or transmitted in any form or by any means, electronic or mechanical, including photocopying, recording or any information storage or retrieval system, without prior permission in writing from the publishers.

British Library Cataloguing-in-Publication Data
A catalogue record for this book is available from the British Library.

Library of Congress Cataloging-in-Publication Data
Names: Heining, Duncan, 1953- author.
Title: Mosaics : the life and works of Graham Collier / Duncan Heining.
Description: Sheffield, UK ; Bristol, CT : Equinox Publishing, 2018. |
  Series: Popular music history | Includes bibliographical references and index.
Identifiers: LCCN 2017025637 (print) | LCCN 2017027734 (ebook) | ISBN
  9781781796504 (ePDF) | ISBN 9781781792636 (hb)
Subjects: LCSH: Collier, Graham, 1937-2011. | Jazz
  musicians--England--Biography. | Double bassists--England--Biography. |
  Composers--England--Biography.
Classification: LCC ML418.C72 (ebook) | LCC ML418.C72 H45 2018 (print) | DDC
  781.65092 [B] --dc23
LC record available at https://lccn.loc.gov/2017025637

ISBN: 978 1 78179 263 6 (hardback)
ISBN: 978 1 80050 293 2 (paperback)
ISBN: 978 1 78179 650 4 (ePDF)

Typeset by CA Typesetting Ltd, www.publisherservices.co.uk

This book is dedicated to Graham Collier and his partner John Gill, who lie buried next to each other in a cemetery on the Greek island of Skopelos.

Graham Collier set great store by education. It transformed his life and he spent many years helping young musicians to study and develop their abilities. In that light, I would like to thank three teachers who have helped me immensely – in the past and more recently.

I owe a particularly great debt to Dr David Dunn, my International Relations tutor at North Staffs Polytechnic 1973–1977. David was the first teacher I ever had who made me analyse my own thinking and question my own assumptions. On a lighter but still important note, I want to thank Bella Rose Manning of the Camena Music School, Essex, who taught me Music Theory, and Natasha Fellowes of the Diamante Dance Academy, Chelmsford, who got me dancing. In their different ways, all three are natural teachers, who know instinctively how to make learning a positive, if challenging, experience. It's been a joy, guys!

Contents

List of Figures		ix
Preface		xi
1	At Home with the Folks	1
2	Berklee with Herb	15
3	Return of the Native	27
4	Down Another Road	49
5	Nil Desperandum – The Jazz Hustler	72
6	'Author! Author!'	90
7	Glad to Be Gay	113
8	The Day of the Dead	131
9	The Eighties or 'Graham Collier – The Wilderness Years'	150
10	Pte. James Collier returns to Hong Kong	174
11	Educating NYJO	188
12	'Not for any jazz use'	205
13	The Last Suites	227
14	Legacy	248
Bibliography		266
Mosaics Interviews and Correspondence		273
Appendix 1: Graham Collier Discography		275
Appendix 2: Compositions		282
Appendix 3: Graham Collier BBC Radio Broadcasts		291
Appendix 4: Royal Academy of Music Collier Alumni		296
Index		298

List of Figures

Figure 1.	Graham and older brother John, circa 1940. Courtesy of Elsie Ashberry.	5
Figure 2.	Jack Collier, 'Drum and Tymps Man'.	8
Figure 3.	Army days: Graham Collier on trombone. Saxophonist, Jack Lancaster – later Blodwyn Pig.	13
Figure 4.	Graham Collier Septet first gig, Hampstead, April 1964.	30
Figure 5.	Barry Summer School 1967.	35
Figure 6.	*Deep Dark Blue Centre* Septet. Photo courtesy of Cuneiform Records.	38
Figure 7.	Graham Collier Sextet – *Mosaics* at the Montreux Jazz Festival 1971. Photo by Harry M. Monty.	80
Figure 8.	Cover of *Lunch* Magazine, May 1973. Ironically titled 'Graham Collier; Gay Jazzman'.	115
Figure 9.	Graham Collier Twelve at The Roundhouse, October 1978. Mosaic Festival. Copyright Jak Kilby.	153
Figure 10.	Jazz Yatra, India, January 1979. Graham Collier, Ed Speight, Geoff Warren.	156
Figure 11.	Graham Collier and Eje Thelin, *Hoarded Dreams* concert, Logan Hall, Camden, March 1985. Copyright Nick White.	167
Figure 12.	Graham Collier Sextet at the British Council circa 1984. Copyright Jak Kilby.	175
Figure 13.	Graham and May Collier following Collier receiving the OBE, February 1987.	184
Figure 14.	Graham Collier 1975. Photoshoot for *Jazz: A Student's and Teacher's Guide*. Courtesy Cuneiform Records.	189
Figure 15.	Graham Collier and students – Israel RAM/Rimon collaboration, March 1995.	215
Figure 16.	Graham Collier, Purcell Room, London Jazz Festival, November 2004. *Directing 14 Jackson Pollocks*.	240

Preface

Graham Collier asked me to be his literary executor around 2005. It was a great shock and sadness that someone so full of life and with so much still to contribute would die so soon after making such a request. I inherited from him six arch-lever files containing magazine and newspaper articles and reviews, correspondence, old school reports, material relating to his period in the Green Howards Regiment, record and book contracts and much besides. Everything was kept beautifully and in chronological order. Work on the material to create an archive soon turned into the writing of a biography.

I interviewed Collier on three occasions – twice for magazine articles and once in connection with a book on British jazz. Many musicians who worked with him over the years, as well as colleagues at the Royal Academy of Music and friends, have been extremely helpful with information and reminiscences about their contact with him. I have also interviewed his partner John Gill on several occasions and we spoke on many others about the project. Fellow author, John Wickes, provided a 22-page typed interview from 1986 that also proved very useful (Interview with Graham Collier 1986, courtesy John Wickes; henceforth Interview Collier/Wickes 1986). When I had almost completed the first draft of the biography, John Gill discovered on Collier's computer a number of 'Timelines' for the decades from 1970–2000. These included extracts from diaries and references to events, his relationships and health issues, including bouts of depression from which he suffered periodically. I refer to these as the 'Timeline'.

It should be noted that Collier had his own website, *Jazz Continuum*, on which he posted reviews of CDs, blogs and opinion pieces on jazz and jazz education. He also used this for a more substantial work, which he called the 'Not A Book…' Project. The idea was that this would develop over time. By the time I reached that point in my research, the *Jazz Continuum* website was out of commission. Although John Gill told me that he was trying to get the site restored to the web, this never happened. Sadly, Gill himself passed in December 2016. As a result, I have not been able to access the 'NOTA' Project.

The reader should note that I have left to one side various comments made in the 'Timeline' about other musicians or jazz professionals, simply on the grounds that it is hard to contextualize these. Most are, in any event, well past their use-by dates. I have also decided against perpetuating arguments between Collier and certain antagonists beyond the grave. People argue and fall out. This is a fact of life. Collier was no different from the rest of us in this regard. On the whole, I have kept references to such matters brief. The exception here involves Collier's relationship with Bill Ashton of NYJO fame. My reason for dwelling on the Collier–Ashton issue is simply due to their respective involvements in and differing views on jazz education.

With this wealth of material, new insights and possibilities for interpretation emerged. Ideally, I would have wished to check out these with Collier himself. It was very sad that John Gill also died in December 2016. He had read and been able to comment on my first draft. However, I was unable to follow up a number of questions that had arisen. I hope that what emerges will still result in a fair, objective portrait of a complex and highly creative individual.

There are many musicians and artists who merit such attention but who will never receive it. On the other hand, there are many lesser figures who attract such favour that their lasting achievements would not warrant but whose lifestyles make them 'interesting'. There is a saying that 'everyone has a book inside them'. Those who quote this and sometimes pursue it are unaware of the corollary – 'and that is precisely where it should stay!'

Graham Collier justifies the tribute of a full biography. Firstly, he, his work, his career, his life and his personality appear as part of one package. It is neither possible, nor desirable in his case to try and parcel off or compartmentalize aspects of his life. This makes him an ideal subject for a critical biography.

Secondly, he lived his life quite openly. He did not use drugs or drink excessively and there were few, if any, instances of riotous behaviour. At the same time, Collier never sought to hide who he was or what he thought. In his case, the biography can legitimately focus on the essentials of the work and what went into its creation, personally and artistically. One writer interviewing Collier for a magazine directed at gay and lesbian students described him as 'the gay jazz musician'. The statement is accurate but inadequate. As he himself would have put it, he was a jazz composer and jazz educator, who was a gay man.

Thirdly, and most importantly, there is the work itself. It was a career littered with firsts – the first British student at Berklee, the first jazz musician to be awarded an Arts Council grant, the founder of the first full-time jazz degree course, and so on. Collier was a pioneer in jazz education. He was a jazz critic, writing reviews for *Gay News* and other publications. He was also a successful jazz author, writing both for the jazz fan and the student musician. In all these areas, he was a high achiever, who set himself high standards. Few in jazz have had such success in these different areas of jazz. In fact, in the British context only the name of Ian Carr springs readily to mind.

Finally, there is a coherent and well-articulated theoretical thread that runs through Collier's work as a composer-musician, writer and educator. His two most recent books written with students and jazz musicians in mind – *Interaction: Opening up the Jazz Ensemble* (1995) and *The Jazz Composer: Moving Music off the Paper* (2009a) – are much more than 'How to Do Jazz Properly' manuals. They reveal a philosophy of music and art, albeit incompletely grounded, that was formed quite early in Collier's career, which brought to bear on jazz an appreciation of art and literature and of their critical underpinnings. This philosophy might not have been stated explicitly but by the time Collier wrote *The Jazz Composer*, these ideas had begun to define an aesthetic of jazz and its performance.

Collier shared with jazz composers such as Jelly Roll Morton, Duke Ellington, George Russell, Gil Evans and Carla Bley in America, and Mike Westbrook, Barry Guy, Roberto Bonati and Geir Lysne in Europe, the fundamental dilemma posed by the relationship between composition and performance in a music where improvisation provides the cornerstone of its architecture. Where Collier differs, from all except perhaps George Russell, is that he theorized that relationship at length and in detail. His approach was not defined, however, so much by a musical theory, as being derived from his own ideas regarding the nature of jazz as an art, which led in turn to his elaboration of, what I refer to as, a 'performance aesthetic'.

* * *

With regard to methodology, *Mosaics* falls into the category of a 'critical biography'. I use the term in the sense used by author, Paul Murray Kendall. Kendall defines the approach in relation to emphasis on research, evidencing, academic standards of referencing, 'proofs' supported by evidence, conjecture 'duly labelled' as such (Kendall 2013). As he notes, 'The biographer...seeks to elicit from his materials the motives for his subject's actions and to discover the shape of his personality' (Kendall 2013; see also Kendall 1973).

I also draw upon my own background in the social sciences and, in particular, on General Systems Theory (von Bertalanffy 1973). GST is not only used in the natural sciences but also in the social sciences. It is not a 'theory' per se. Nor does it prescribe a particular causal model of explanation. Instead, it allows for the kind of multi-causality that best helps us to understand how individuals relate to their world and how different aspects of that world impinge upon and affect them. It is essentially a way of mapping relationships within systems – we are after all biological systems ourselves and part at the same time of many other systems, social and professional. GST enables me to explore the 'hows' and 'whys' of Collier's life and career as much as the 'whats'.

Aesthetic considerations are central to Collier's own view of the nature of jazz and this was reflected in his work as a composer and educator. Indeed, he went to great lengths to explain his ideas both through reference to other jazz composers but also in relation to art and literary criticism. Not only did Collier draw inspiration from these two creative worlds; he sought to inform his own musical practice through his understanding of other artistic disciplines and practices. In examining these aspects of Collier's work and thinking, I draw, therefore, on theoretical approaches where such considerations are themselves central, namely on the ideas of Theodor Adorno and Herbert Marcuse of the Frankfurt School but also on the axiological philosophy of John Dewey and on the work of Abraham Maslow and Carl Rogers, two American humanistic psychologists influenced by Dewey.[1]

In terms of the structure of the book, by and large, I have sought to follow Collier's life and career chronologically. However, at various points I have consciously taken the decision to depart from this and deal with some material thematically. For example, Collier's sexuality and experiences as a gay man in a very male-dominated, heterosexual jazz world are covered at some length outside a strict chronological approach. Additionally, although referred to throughout the biography, I have discussed his work as an educator primarily in one chapter. The same applies in respect of his work in film, theatre and radio. Simply, it seemed to make sense to do so.

My admiration for Graham Collier's work and of him as an individual, though never uncritical, has grown through the process of researching *Mosaics*. It is my hope that readers will come to an appreciation of Collier's rightful place in jazz – as a composer, educator and theorist – but also that those who knew him personally will recognize him from *Mosaics* and also learn something new about him and his work as well.

Note

1. Dewey was not a Marxist and he was also highly critical of Kant, whose writings certainly inform the Critical Theorists. Dewey disputed Kant's dismissal of merely pleasurable cultural experiences (his distinction between 'agreeable art' and its 'passive receptor' and 'fine art' and its 'contemplative, reflexive subject'). However, both Kant and Dewey see the appreciation of culture as something innately human and Kant's 'contemplation' can also be seen as both purposeful and instrumental. Here, I follow Casey Haskins' argument in this regard. In restoring 'desire' to the process, Dewey creates a bridge between himself and Marcuse, if not also to Adorno. In defining Kant as an 'instrumental autonomist', Haskins makes a direct association between Kant and writers in both 'the pragmatist and Marxist traditions' (Haskins 1989: 43, 53 note).

1   At Home with the Folks

> The amazing variety in jazz activity today, against all the odds, is due to the determined efforts of strong-willed individuals to create work for themselves and for others. Bassist Graham Collier, for example, has been able to keep his bands together by sheer strength of character. He has gone out and looked for work, and time after time his band has opened up new places to jazz – new festivals, new establishments, and indeed some key work areas abroad. He was the first British musician to have a concert of his own music with an international band at the Hamburg Jazz Workshop, the first young British composer to be invited to Denmark to conduct a performance of his music by the Danish radio orchestra. And, as I mentioned earlier, he was the first jazz musician to receive an Arts Council grant; this kind of pioneering is typical of him. A literate and articulate person, he can also explain his music to audiences – which, in a verbal culture like ours, can mean the difference between working and not working (Carr 1973: 3).

Composer-bandleader-bassist James Graham Collier was born in Tynemouth, Northumberland on 21 February 1937. His parents had actually moved from Northumberland to Luton in Bedfordshire around 1933–34 and, though born in the north-east of England, Collier was actually brought up in Luton. In fact, it was Collier's mother, Elizabeth May Collier, known to everyone as 'May', who determined that her child should be Geordie born, if not bred, and who decided to return 'home' to give birth. Aside from that, and visits to family, any influence upon the nascent jazz composer of his birthplace was solely spiritual rather than directly experienced!

Collier's childhood and early adolescence were spent in Luton. The only health issue of any note was that Collier was born with a 'lazy eye' or amblyopia. By the time corrective surgery was available, Collier was too old to benefit. Home and family life seem to have been very happy and he had strong relationships with both his parents and with his older brother, John, who was born in 1934. In fact, Collier's love for his parents ran very deep indeed and he was always conscious and grateful for the support and guidance they had given to him.

Collier's cousin, Elsie Ashberry, describes the Collier family as being '*very close*', and she adds, 'They were a very warm family. They were warm to us and they seemed very warm to each other.' She tells how the Colliers would return to Tyneside on holiday, illustrating this with a lovely story that seems to speak volumes about the Colliers and about Jack Collier, the boy's father, in particular.

> They would come back once every two years. I would assume it would be due to lack of money and, of course, transport wasn't as good as it is now and uncle Jack didn't have a car. It was usually train to Newcastle and then train to my grandmother's in Balkwell (North Shields). I do remember one particular occasion meeting them off the bus. My mother and Graham's mother, they were very close and so for weeks before they came I can remember this excitement in the family that they were coming up. And my middle brother and I went to meet them off the bus. I remember it as clear as day, I've no idea why, but they all got off the bus with their suitcases and for some stupid reason uncle Jack got us all singing as we walked towards my grandmother's. I even remember what we were singing. It was totally stupid. Guy Mitchell was in the hit parade at the time with a song called 'She Wears Red Feathers'. We all sang that as we walked along. 'She wears red feathers and a huly-huly skirt' (Interview Ashberry/Heining 2014).

This would have been early in 1953. Collier would have been barely sixteen and, trivial though the incident may seem, it stuck in Elsie Ashberry's mind. It conveys a family who were just as she has described them. There is no sense of awkwardness about them but rather a sense of fun – and music was clearly at the centre of their world.

Jack Collier was a very keen amateur musician. He had played drums in the cinema, probably at Whitley Bay, during the era of silent films and continued to work in amateur and semi-professional bands in the Luton area. Jack was born into a mining family in a small village called Seaton Deleval, which is just up the coast from Whitley Bay (Interview Collier/Heining 2005; Interview Ashberry/Heining 2014). The Collier surname suggests, of course, a longer ancestral involvement of the family in the mines. This was, however, a career that Jack was able to avoid. In fact, Collier told his partner John Gill that his father had refused to go down the mines (Email Gill/Heining 2014).

High levels of unemployment during the depression of the 1930s hit the north-east of England particularly badly. Seaton Deleval is just ten miles north of Jarrow from where, in 1936, 207 people set out with their MP 'Red Ellen' Wilkinson to march the 270 miles to London to hand in a petition to parliament. Wilkinson later wrote:

> At Middlesbrough, I had thought I had known what poverty could mean. But in that town some industry was going on, some people had work. Compared to Jarrow, things on Tees-side were moving. Jarrow in that year, 1932–33, was utterly stagnant. There was no work. No one had a job, except a few railwaymen, officials, the workers in the co-operative stores, and the few clerks and craftsmen who went out of town to their jobs each day. The unemployment rate was over 80 per cent (Wilkinson 1939: 191–92).

'The Jarrow Crusade' continues to be remembered as a major moment in British labour history, which is somewhat ironic as both the British Labour Party and TUC opposed the march (Wilkinson 1939: 204–207). In fact, there were several such marches in the inter-war years, which both served to demonstrate the strength of feeling amongst the working classes at their lot but also their belief that those with power might be able and willing to address their plight (Cockburn 1973: 59–81).

Asked the reason for Jack's move south, Elsie Ashberry replied, 'I think it was pure jobs'. She recalls that her own family had been similarly affected by unemployment in those years, adding:

> I remember being told that my father moved to Cumbria at one stage because he couldn't get a job because he'd worked in the shipyards in the North East and there was very little work and he went down to London at one point and stayed with his brother to try and find work and then he went to Cumberland and back to the North East. I think there were a lot of people moving at the time due to lack of opportunities (Interview Ashberry/Heining 2014).

Jack Collier left the north-east several years before Jarrow, and there is no indication that he was in any degree 'politically' active or conscious. However, his decision to move south and bring up a family there reflects the experience of many working- and lower-middle-class workers in those years. He found work at Vauxhall Motors in Luton, the town's main employer, as a machinist and assembler. Working at Vauxhall did turn out to offer a greater level of security to the Collier family than many in those years could have experienced, and Jack remained with the company for twenty-seven years before taking retirement and a job at the Ministry of Health and Social Security (*Luton News* n.d.). In 1939, however, with the outbreak of the Second World War, Vauxhall Motors became very important in terms of the war effort, switching production away from cars to military vehicles. It also seems likely that Jack's job would have been classed as a 'reserved occupation' and, as a consequence, he would not have been required to serve in a military capacity (Holden 2003).

This would have had important implications for the family. Obviously, they would have suffered the privations of rationing during the war years and afterwards. Nevertheless, they had a secure income and, at least as important, this meant that both John and Graham Collier grew up with both parents living at home during their childhood years. According to Elsie Ashberry, May Collier never went out to work, a fact which, whilst far from uncommon in that period, suggests that the family were sufficiently comfortable financially for this to be unnecessary.

Elsie Ashberry describes Jack as 'a lovely man', and she adds, 'He was a great jokester. He liked things happening around him. He liked lots of noise going on. The thing that both Graham and uncle Jack shared I would say – I mean, you knew Graham – was his twinkly eyes. They both had twinkly eyes. They just looked the same.'

From her comments, and others made by Graham Collier himself, the marriage of Jack and May Collier was a strong one. Whilst the younger Collier certainly took after his father in looks, it seems that he was closer in some ways to his mother. Elsie Ashberry recalls:

> Auntie May had a great sense of fun. She had a wonderful laugh which could go on for ages. And she and Graham were close. I'm not saying she wasn't close to Johnny as well but you could see that she had that...whether it was to do with him being the younger of the two, I don't know but she had that great closeness with him (Interview Ashberry/Heining 2014).

Collier's love for both his parents is abundantly clear from his archive. There are several very touching photographs in his archive but few more so than those taken outside Buckingham Palace of Collier and May when he received his OBE from Queen Elizabeth II in 1987 for 'Services to Jazz'. May looks so very proud – and, frankly, so does her son (see p. 184 below).

There are also many photographs in the Collier archive of the two brothers together that follow their lives from infancy to adulthood. One is rather moving. It was taken at the nearby Whipsnade Zoo with John and some other children riding on an elephant. A very young Graham Collier looks up with an expression of amazement and anxiety. Later in young adulthood, the two brothers are pictured in their military uniforms in the back garden of the family home. John, it seems, was the more outgoing of the two as a child and was perhaps also a little protective towards his younger brother, though the younger boy was certainly not shy.

Figure 1. Graham and older brother John, circa 1940. Courtesy of Elsie Ashberry.

From comments by Elsie Ashberry and also from Collier's partner John Gill, the two brothers drifted apart as they grew older. Interestingly, both Ashberry and Gill put this down to a dislike of John's wife, whom he married in 1965. According to Elsie Ashberry, 'She was a bit a cut above or she thought she was a bit a cut above. I didn't find her an easy person at all. I think Johnny and Graham were just very different people. That's all it was.' There certainly was no animosity between them, more a case that their life paths diverged. Whilst Graham Collier joined the army as a band boy aged sixteen, John remained in Luton and 'went into management at Vauxhall's', with a starting salary of £1000 per annum, much to the amazement and pride of the wider family (Interview Ashberry/Heining 2014).

Yet John, like his brother and their father, was also musical. Like Jack, he was in the Vauxhall band and Elsie Ashberry's brother remembers visiting his uncle and aunt and attending a rehearsal for a production of *Salad Days* (Ashberry/Heining 2014). Jack's obituary notes that he played drums in the Vauxhall Motors Orchestra, that he also played in other local orchestras and dance bands and that, on moving to Luton, he became the 'pit' drummer at the Grand and, occasionally, the Alma Theatre. Two family photos show Jack behind his 'theatrical' drum kit – such drummers provided appropriate percussive sound effects, as well as musical accompaniment. The first shows him in his satin shirt in front of a stage set, whilst the other seems to have been taken at a summer fete. In the latter, Jack is demonstrating drumming to a small group of young onlookers.

Graham Collier clearly shared that musical ability and, though this is speculation, it is worth suggesting that he grew up in a household where music was primarily concerned with performance. Throughout his career, Collier emphasized the spontaneity of jazz, which he would come to describe in the following terms, 'Jazz happens in real time, once'. Though he would later articulate this theoretically and analytically, the sense remained that, for him, music was always immediate and, to a degree, only truly present in the moment of its creation. This perception may well have begun growing up in a family where the emphasis was always on music as something spontaneous and alive.

Interviewed by writer John Wickes (1986), Collier explained that his father, 'encouraged myself and my brother to take up music. My father was very much a semi-pro and he gave that up'. And he continued,

> Well, my father was very much a dance band type musician. There was always that kind of music around the house – there wasn't classical – and I got into Harry James and Frankie Laine when I was a kid and from that I got into Stan Kenton and that end of jazz. It was quite a while before I appreciated what Ellington was doing or Charlie Parker (Interview Collier/Wickes 1986).

The Collier brothers both attended Luton Grammar School in Bradgers Hill, a single-sex school as was the norm for grammar as opposed to other state secondary schools. John Gill recalls his partner saying how proud both parents were that they made it into a grammar school being from a council estate background (Email Gill/Heining 2014). If his musical and other talents had been evident when he was younger, this did not come across to his teachers. At the end of his first term in December 1948, his form master C. W. Parry wrote:

> He has made a satisfactory beginning, and his solid work led me to expect a higher 'place'. He is sometimes inclined to be too laboured over small points, which may impede his progress. In posture I should like him not to keep his eyes so close to his books, this must be detrimental to his eyesight. He is a member of the school choir, and a serious and reliable pupil (Luton Grammar School Report, December 1948).

Other comments suggest a lack of concentration and the young Collier's highest placing in exams was for music, where he came eleventh out of thirty-five pupils in his class. Nevertheless, it should be noted that he was in the 'A' or 'top' stream in his year and, taking this into account, at the end of his first year, he came seventh in history, twelfth in music and fifteenth in art across the year's intake of 130 or so pupils. The general comments emphasize his 'satisfactory progress'. Overall, the pattern of his five years at Luton Grammar can best be described as 'inconsistent'. He might improve one term in a subject, only to fall behind the next. His strongest subjects were music and English, though even here his results fluctuated and, for his final year at the school, he dropped down a class to the 'B' stream.

Most British grammar schools provided an excellent standard of education for their pupils. At the same time, they tended even in the 1960s and beyond to ape the more prestigious public—that is, fee-paying—schools. There were three ways of standing out, aside from rebellion or delinquency, at such establishments. One could be good at sports, excel academically or be both an exceptional scholar and fine rugby player or cricketer. For the rest, each pupil was but one amongst many. Collier clearly fell into the latter category at Luton Grammar. He left with two GCEs (General Certificate of Education or 'O' or Ordinary Grade) in English and Mathematics, the basic essential qualifications for many occupations such as a career in the lower echelons of the civil service. Collier, however, had decided on joining the British Army, as his form master, Mr Woodcock, noted in his final school report in those typical, school-masterly tones that combined relief, exasperated disappointment and pious hope:

> He is leaving this year and hopes to make a career as a military bandsman. He has shown satisfactory ability and application and the standard of his work generally is above average for the form. His conduct has been good (Luton Grammar School Report, July 1953).

Reading these school reports, it is hard to believe that the same Graham Collier would go on to lead one of the finest small groups in British jazz in the sixties and seventies and would become a major jazz composer. Home influences were probably more important in this respect. After all, his father was always a big band enthusiast – cousin Elsie remembers family celebrations accompanied by recordings of big band leaders such as Ambrose. Nor, in those reports, is there a glimpse of the highly cultured and articulate lover of literature and fine art and major jazz educator of Collier's middle and later years. If he could be seen as rebelling against the expectations of the grammar school system, it would have been only quietly so – a kind of, 'It's really not for me, sir!' rather than an ill-mannered refusal. And anyway, as he told John Wickes in 1986, he had already decided when he was thirteen that he wanted to be a musician (Interview Collier/Wickes 1986).

Given his less than stellar performance at Luton Grammar, and his class background, the door to the academies would probably have been closed to him. Joining the army offered both a chance to further his musical education and also a wage, a secure career and the most acceptable way for a young man to leave home and family.

Interviewed for *Jazz UK* in 2005 shortly before a concert at the Purcell Room on London's South Bank, he explained his reasons for joining the army:

> I played trumpet when I was nine or ten and played in little bands. Then, when I joined the army, they told me that having thick lips I couldn't be a trumpeter – one of those stupid army things. By that time, I was interested in jazz and playing string bass, so I was doing that. So, they put me playing euphonium, which I hated, but being in the army you had to do what you were told. I joined the army at sixteen, not to get away from home but from Luton, which was a dreadful place. I went to Hong Kong for three years with the army, went to Germany a couple of times, which really got me into travelling and which I still enjoy (Interview Collier/Heining 2005).

Figure 2. Jack Collier, 'Drum and Tymps Man'.

As an aside, Collier noted every single trip abroad and the number of days abroad in his 'Timeline' between 1970 and 2010, whether these were for holiday or work. At the end of each year, he totalled up the days and finishing off his entries for 2000–2010, he calculated in great detail decade by decade, concluding,

> Away from Base (England, then Spain, then Greece)...
> To end 2009 13 years 4 months (22% of time since I was 16)
> But if I ignore Army and Berklee it's 5 years and 6 months ±10%.

This clearly mattered to him a great deal and probably informed his later decision to move first to Spain in 1999 and then to the island of Skopelos, Greece in 2008.

According to a later article in the *Luton News*, Collier played in both the Luton Grammar School orchestra and the Vauxhall Motors' Brass Band. In many ways, his decision to join the army as a bandboy made a great deal of sense. The standard of musical training in the British forces was then, and is now, very high indeed.[1] Several leading British jazz musicians, who came to prominence in the mid- to late sixties, came up though that route – drummers John Stevens and Tony Oxley, saxophonists Bob Downes and Trevor Watts, bassist Jeff Clyne and trombonists Paul Rutherford and Chris Pyne.

Graham Collier seems to have enjoyed his time in the army. Rather like an army recruitment advert of the time, he appreciated the opportunities for travel and that he was able to make music for a living. In the photographs in Collier's archive, the picture presented seems to be a reasonably contented one. From his period in the services, he gained a knowledge of music and, in particular, of its performance virtues. He also acquired a sense of discipline and structure but also of possibility, of his own potential – something it seems he had not gained from school-based education. Perhaps the army also gave him confidence and resilience. It is not too great a stretch to suggest that these qualities informed his subsequent life and career. The photographs and mementoes in this section of his archive seem to tell that story.

Included there are the certificates Collier achieved, as well as the musical programme of the passing-out parade concert at Kneller Hall, Twickenham. Also in his archive are his certificate of recognition of service in the Green Howards, with its motto 'Once a Green Howard, always a Green Howard', and his 'Regular Reservist's Instruction Book', in case of recall at times of national emergency. Fortunately, despite a number of national emergencies since, none required the services of a euphonium player, so Collier was never recalled.

Yet it must also have been a strange existence for Collier, most particularly in Hong Kong. A fellow bandsman, Pte. Paddy Riordan, remembers him as a 'quiet chap. In fact, if I'm remembering rightly, he was always a little bit snooty' (Interview Riordan/Heining 2014). According to John Gill, Graham's partner, Pte. James Collier, as he was known in the army, saw many of his comrades as 'alien beings' (Email interview Gill/Heining 2015). Not exactly a meeting of minds or souls, then.

Gill remembers Graham mentioning a trumpeter friend, who was more on his wavelength and there is a photograph of two soldiers amongst Collier's effects. They look very close and on the back of the photograph, it states, 'Dave and me! NAAFI Club Singapore'. Gill suspected that 'Dave' was that friend.

> It's unlikely that Graham's army circles overlapped with family. It does, however, seem likely that this is the trumpeter, as I also remember Graham saying he didn't really make any other true friends, as most other squaddies were 'squaddies', whereas his trumpeter pal was into the same sort of music, read similar books, talked about art and philosophy and so on (Email interview Gill/Heining 2015).

Paddy Riordan's description of life in the British Army in the Far East sounds both idyllic and unreal. The bandsmen would perform at many public events such as the Singapore Races, when stationed there, and at the famous Peninsula Hotel in Hong Kong, as well as on public occasions such as the Queen's Birthday or St. George's Day.

> Oh, it was great. We shared a big flat with a chap who joined up with me, as a matter of fact, and his wife and his youngster and we shared the flat with them. We had three servants who did virtually everything... Wonderful cinemas – you all paid a very low price for the top seats, as you were in the army. There were regimental dances, officers' dances. We use to play at them quite often but the dance band always used to play at the officers' mess when they had a dance and things like that... They used to let us in if you were bandsmen but we didn't used to go to officers' dances too often because they were too posh (Laughing).

And,

> Taxis, we used to get cheaply and things like that and one I remember...we had the old rickshaws, we had a rickshaw race up and down the road outside our place. We had a prize of about twenty dollars for the one who won it.

Paddy Riordan's comments also indicate the perception held by serving soldiers in Hong Kong, both of the reasons why they were there and of the potentially precarious nature of their position.

> Hong Kong was then right on the border with Communist China. If there had been trouble, you know real trouble with China, we were expected to be wiped out. We would have stayed there. We wouldn't have been withdrawn. We would have stayed there and fought it out until whatever happened. That was how on an edge it used to be.

Paddy Riordan added that, whenever tensions increased, his wife would be ordered to pack a small bag ready for evacuation to Australia. There was, in fact, one occasion in October 1956, which could have escalated and resulted in an international incident between Britain and China. The disturbances, known as the 'Double Tenth' riots in reference to the date they broke out, took place primarily in Kowloon and were provoked by a paid network of Nationalist agents provocateurs and catalysed bitter political tensions that had crossed over from China during the civil war in the late 1940s, and steadily grew in Hong Kong from the early fifties. The unrest left sixty dead and five hundred injured and caused widespread damage to property.

> It was a tension that could have burst at any time, like when we had the riots. Because we had to go in between the Chiang Kai-Shek lot and what they called the October Party, which he backed up from their place on the island off China, Taiwan. It was something that blew up, which we didn't expect and the British Army had to go in between them. That was the idea of it. But that was about all that ever actually happened.

And he continued,

> [O]n the first day, when a lot of the Chinese Communists were murdered and things like that by Chiang Kai-Shek's crowd, if we didn't sort it out… I think there was about three days or a week given us to do it [or] the Chinese Army would take over instead. We knew what that meant. That meant us having to fight them – and they had thousands and thousands and still have in their armies – and being killed. But we did. We sorted it out. We were stationed with the Ghurkhas. Them blokes didn't let anything go wrong (Interview Riordan/Heining 2014).

Hong Kong's leftist press attacked the colonial authorities for their failure to protect their 'compatriots' and issued veiled threats that Chinese troops would be sent in to do what the Hong Kong police seemed unable or unwilling to do. The British Army was eventually called out in support of civil power, and soldiers patrolled the streets of Kowloon for several nights (https://tinyurl.com/2025663-riots; see also Webb 1994: 455–57; Carroll 2007: 146; Wordie 2016).

It is unclear whether or not Collier was involved in quelling the riot but this does seem unlikely. He did, however, speak to John Gill of a similar incident.

> Graham did tell a story about the army band being ordered into downtown Hong Kong to play in a military march, only for them to arrive in the middle of a riot and be sent back to barracks by a furious general or commander, with much 'effing' and blinding from the officer class (Email interview Gill/Heining 2015).

On the whole, Collier's photographs tell a simple and largely undramatic story of army life. Other photographs from the archive, taken in that period, seem to reflect the most important aspects for him – music and friendship. There are photos taken in the garden at the family home, on his own but also with brother John, who was undertaking national service. These emphasize again the significance of family attachments for Collier. One photograph of note, however, was taken at the Foreign Correspondents' Club in Hong Kong. It features tenor saxophonist Jack Lancaster. Lancaster went on to gain fame as a founder member of Blodwyn Pig and is now a successful session musician and film and TV composer based in Hollywood.

It was whilst serving with the army that Collier started playing the double bass, though he also played the trombone as one photograph in his collection reveals. As well as playing in various army bands, he also played in jazz bands, which he and fellow soldiers formed. It seems that an idea of his future as a musician was beginning to form, as is suggested by the correspondence course in writing and arranging music he undertook. By the early sixties, he had decided to leave the army, as explained in 2005:

> I had to put up with the military stuff but I enjoyed playing danceband music and writing music. I started to do transcriptions and things like that. Then, towards the end of that time, a mate encouraged me to go in for a *Down Beat* competition for a scholarship to Berklee. So, I did and got a very small scholarship but because I'd never lived in London, it was a way of going somewhere to learn rather than go to London and starve and scuffle. So, I went to Boston and starved and scuffled while I was learning! (Interview Collier/ Heining 2005).

Collier told John Wickes that he had to send in a tape of either himself playing or of a composition he had written. He received one of the three third-place prizes of 200 dollar scholarships. First prize of $850 went to Heinz Bigler, the Swiss saxophonist, with second prize of $400 going to British composer-pianist Richard Rodney Bennett.[2] Collier's success was trumpeted in *Jazz News* in its 25 February 1961 edition (McLean 1961), whilst the *Luton News*, no doubt

1 At Home with the Folks   13

Figure 3. Army days: Graham Collier on trombone. Saxophonist, Jack Lancaster – later Blodwyn Pig.

contacted by Graham's proud parents proclaimed, 'Graham (jazz arranger) is set for states'. The newspaper described him as a 'Luton musicman-of-many-instruments' and quoted Jack Collier:

> 'He plays the cornet, valve trombone, euphonium and double bass', explained Graham's father, himself a musician – drum-and-timps man in the Vauxhall Orchestra. 'But his main interest is modern

jazz arrangement', added Mr Collier, who lives at 50 Derwent Road. 'Graham has just completed a long correspondence course on arrangement with Bill Russo, Stan Kenton's musical arranger', he went on (*Luton News*).

The article also mentions that, whilst in Hong Kong, Collier had broadcast on Hong Kong Radio with 'Philippino' (*sic*) musicians. It added that the *Down Beat* competition was not his first such award and that he had reached the finals of a *Melody Maker* contest with an arrangement of the Woody Herman tune 'Early Autumn'.

The *Jazz News* piece is as much about Berklee as it is about Collier. It does quote him, however, discussing the Schillinger method quite succinctly: 'It is a method of composition based on mathematics. It enables you to write quicker and is ideal for dramatic music such as film scores. Glenn Miller apparently studied it.'

The article also notes that Collier's favourite arranger was Gil Evans and that he counted Gerry Mulligan, Miles Davis and Paul Desmond 'amongst his favourite musicians'. It finishes in bold type: 'One thing is certain that, while the course is long, the training is thorough, **when Graham Collier returns in 1965, he will be an arranger to watch!**' (McLean 1961, emphasis in original).

The tune Collier sent in to the competition was called 'Macau Interlude' and he told John Wickes in 1986, 'I had a listen to it the other day and I thought it was dreadful!' However, it was enough to impress the *Down Beat* judges and, in 1961, Graham Collier was Berklee bound.

Notes

1. An acquaintance of mine studied clarinet in the army with the virtuoso Jack Brymer – described in his *Times* obituary as 'the leading clarinettist of his generation'.
2. It is often noted that Collier was the first British student to attend Berklee or, in other accounts, the first British jazz musician to win a scholarship to the college. Clearly, this needs qualifying, as Richard Rodney Bennett also won such a scholarship. Nevertheless, it appears that Bennett never took up the offer.

2 Berklee with Herb

Collier set sail for Boston on the *RMS Newfoundland* around the middle of February 1961. It was apparently an eventful journey, lengthened by several days as a result of storms, with a drunken captain and a stopover in Nova Scotia where Collier and some other adventurous passengers got off and climbed a mountain! (Email correspondence Gill/Heining 2015). Amongst his papers, he kept the menu for Sunday 19 February. He chose the mixed fruit cocktail, crème pompadour, roast Long Island duckling with apple & savoury sauce with a side of cauliflower cream sauce and boiled potatoes. He finished with ice cream and coffee. He would make the return journey in October 1963 with his Berklee diploma in his hand. On that occasion, he travelled on the *Queen Mary* and, although he retained one of the menus, sadly what he ate on that occasion has been lost to posterity. He arrived in Boston on 1 March 1961.

In 1986, Graham Collier told John Wickes that going to Berklee College of Music in Boston 'was one of the best moves I've ever made' (Interview Collier/Wickes 1986). This was no doubt true but one theme that runs through Collier's life was his ability to capitalize on opportunities and experiences. If he seemed to gain little from formal secondary education at Luton Grammar, this was certainly not the case either with his army years or his time at Berklee – perhaps because there was a different kind of learning involved. Some pupils thrive in classroom situations; others do not but can derive great benefit from the chance to learn by doing. It was not that Collier was incapable of learning from books or dealing with abstractions – his love of modern literature and abstract art, as well as his own theorizing on jazz, give the lie to any such suggestion. Rather, Collier seems to have focused his attention – both as a student and as an educator – more on the outcome than on learning as a value in itself. If one imagines this as a continuum, Collier learned in order to do rather than to know.

Asked by Wickes what he learned from his time at Berklee, Collier replied:

> Two things. I was always interested in composition – though the bass was relevant to my playing, of course. What I learned in composition terms was the easiest ways to do conventional writing. Plus – because there were opportunities with bands there, about two rehearsal bands a day – I formed my own band that used to rehearse one evening a week. So, I could always write something on

> a Wednesday and Thursday and copy it over the weekend, do it on a Tuesday, then start again (Interview Collier/Wickes 1986).

At a guess, the reference to 'the easiest ways to do conventional writing' refers to the Schillinger method. Collier does not seem to have referred to Schillinger in any other context and either absorbed what it had to teach or else left it behind as his own approach developed. Otherwise, the emphasis seems to have been on learning by doing, of discovering what worked and what did not through the feedback offered by the rehearsal situation. The second thing that he gained from Berklee focused on the remarkable and much-revered Herb Pomeroy, perhaps the most influential figure in Collier's life – after his parents.

> [T]he main planks of Herb's philosophy were that...he was interested in showing you the possibilities and, of course, the obvious role model is Ellington. Ellington's work is partly for the composer and partly a way of using and involving [and] interacting with your musicians in the band. This is the real lesson that he taught (Interview Collier/Wickes 1986).

The point, for Pomeroy, was not to teach his pupils a methodology or strategy for composition. If the individual had the talent, they would find their own method or approach. There was and is no single way of 'doing jazz'.

> And by doing this to people like me, Mike [Gibbs] and Gary [Burton] he gave us a tremendous amount of encouragement and showed us that we had some talent and, if we were properly fed, as it were, we would grow and we did (Interview Collier/Wickes 1986).

Berklee was founded by composer-arranger-pianist Lawrence Berk in 1945 as Schillinger House. It was originally established to teach Joseph Schillinger's system of harmony and composition but over the years broadened its educational focus, its intake and its influence. From the outset, Berk offered training in jazz and commercial music for radio, theatre, television, and dance. In 1954, when the school's curriculum had expanded to include music education classes and more traditional music theory, Berk changed the name to Berklee School of Music, after his son Lee Eliot Berk, to reflect the broader scope of instruction (Hazell 1995). Vibraphonist Gary Burton studied at Berklee between 1960 and 1962, his time there overlapping with Collier's, and he recalls,

> The school was a small, privately-run music school with the mission of providing a college-level music education for students not in the classical/traditional category. The school was launched in 1945, and

during the early decades, until the mid-80s, that meant careers in jazz, Broadway pit orchestras, studio musicians, lounge and cruise ship musicians, etc. Even by 1960, the enrolment was still quite small, around 150 students when I was there. We had come from all over the world, for one simple reason – Mr Berk, the founder, loved to travel, and as he went abroad with his wife, he always took a bag full of brochures to hand out to local musicians wherever they visited. So, of those 150 students, we had guys from Africa, Britain, most European countries, Japan, South America, India, Australia, etc. I say guys, because there were practically zero female students. The only one I remember was a drummer, who didn't play very well (Email Burton/Heining 2014).

Collier began studying at Berklee in February 1961, graduating in 1963. During those years saxophonist John LaPorta, guitarist Jack Petersen and trumpeter Herb Pomeroy were key faculty members, and Arif Mardin, later to become one of the top record producers of all time, was briefly on the faculty during Collier's first year. Amongst Collier's other fellow students were trombonist Mike Gibbs, saxophonists Heinz Bigler from Switzerland and Sadao Watanabe from Japan, Yugoslavian trumpeter Dusko Gojkovic, bassist and songwriter Jay Leonhart and saxophonist Steve Marcus. Surprisingly, neither Mike Gibbs nor Gary Burton have any particular memories of Collier as a person from that period, although he remembers them. As Mike Gibbs notes, 'I know Graham and I were there at the same time but I have no visual recollection of him there at all. We had no social life together. We only knew each other in the school' (Interview Gibbs/Heining 2014).

In fact, Collier played bass in the 1962 version of the Berklee International Jazz Octet. Gibbs had been a founder member of the International Jazz Sextet in 1959 and was also a member of the 1962 group as well, along with Bigler, Gojkovic, baritone saxophonist Jack Stevens from the USA, pianist 'Dizzy' Sal Saldahna from India and tenor saxophonist Conrado Gregorio from Hong Kong (Hazell 1995: 66–67).

Gibbs does, however, remember being part of the Recording Band at Berklee that recorded Collier's composition, 'The Barley Mow'. Gary Burton also barely remembers Collier from his time at Berklee:

> In terms of other students, I was close to at Berklee, Michael Gibbs was my best friend and he became a star arranger/composer during his years there. I continue to collaborate with him still, on occasion. It was Mike who told me that Graham was openly gay, this was around the time that I also had come out and I was contacted by John Gill, Graham's partner, for a book he was writing about gay musicians (Email Burton/Heining 2014).

Mike Gibbs confirms that Collier was not 'out' – in that sense at least – whilst at Berklee: 'I doubt it because the subject never came up. Later, when I knew him in England, it emerged that he was gay' (Interview Gibbs/Heining 2014). It was, however, in Boston that Collier had his first gay sexual experience. He told Keith Howes in 1976 for a *Gay News* article that he was 'knocking on people's doors collecting information for a city directory and met a "very camp Englishman"'. He was invited back for a drink and the man 'as it were, seduced me'. Collier said that he was horrified and it took him six months before he 'returned to the man for more' (Howes 1976). He would have been twenty-four or twenty-five at the time.

Perhaps Collier simply failed to make much of an impression on his fellow students. However, there are two other possible explanations. Firstly, Gibbs started at Berklee two years before Collier, and Burton one year before. Secondly, Collier started the course late and finished his diploma in quite unusual and somewhat truncated circumstances. As he explained in an interview in 2005, 'I spent two and a half years there. They allowed me to start the course late because I was older than a lot of the students there' (Interview Collier/Heining 2005).

And, as he told John Wickes,

> [B]ecause I'd done a lot before, they allowed me to start late, in about the third semester, and then I had a bad car accident before I left, and they allowed me to finish early, as it were. So, I got through in two years, probably stole a year at the beginning and a few months at the end (Interview Collier/Wickes 1986).

One student who did have one particular and interesting memory of Collier was Dusko Gojkovic.

> I can only remember that first 'rehearsal orchestra' at the school when Graham brought his first arrangement for the big band. I was amazed with such a mature and very modern sound of his voicings! Excellent!!! I thought, 'What the hell is Graham doing here at the arranging course, if he ALREADY can write like this?' I think it took me half a life time to even get close to understand what he was doing (Email Gojkovic/Heining 2014; emphasis in original).

Collier later recalled the incident in his book *Inside Jazz* (1973). The piece had been written in 7/8 time, an unusual signature for jazz then and now. The first soloist, an American student, struggled with the tune: 'The second sailed through it. He was Dusko Gojkovic from Yugoslavia and such "strange" times were part of his folk music – as familiar to him as four beats in the bar is to an American or Englishman' (Collier 1973a: 36–37).

As noted, Collier was that bit older than many of the students; he was twenty-four years old when he started at Berklee, had been a working musician since he was sixteen, albeit in the army, and had played in dance and jazz bands during his soldiering years. But Berklee offered a rare opportunity for Collier and for other would-be jazz musicians at that time, as Gary Burton explains:

> You have to also realize that there wasn't any place like Berklee anywhere else. When I completed high school in the spring of 1960 and looked around for a college, there were only two possibilities in the USA – North Texas State University and Berklee. No other schools offered jazz instruction. I was not only a jazz musician but I also played the vibraphone, which wasn't even a recognized instrument then. I chose Berklee because it was located in a major city [Boston] and I figured I would get more chance to meet other players and become part of a lively music scene. And that was exactly what happened. Berklee attracted students from all over the USA, as well, and the main drawing power was the opportunity to pursue jazz. Fortunately, jazz education exploded starting in the '70s as many school music programs in colleges and high schools added jazz music to their offerings. It's a very different array of choices for today's new students (Email Burton/Heining 2014).

By all accounts, Herb Pomeroy towered over Berklee like a colossus. Not only were there opportunities to study with musicians such as Pomeroy, John LaPorta and Jack Petersen but also to work with them on the stand, a point that for Gary Burton is essential to a young musician's development.

> The great thing about Berklee of that era was the interaction between students and faculty. The teachers were mostly local musicians who played gigs at night, and taught during the day. So, if you were a decent player, you would find yourself in classes and ensembles with a teacher in the day and then share the bandstand with him at night. A terrific educational experience. Many of the teachers were very, very talented players and gifted teachers as well. You mentioned Herb Pomeroy, a legendary figure in early Berklee. Herb played trumpet and had a big band that was playing very adventurous music for the time. And he was part owner, along with two other local musicians of the main local jazz club called 'The Stables'. The big band played there twice a week and Herb held forth with a quintet the rest of the nights. I got to play in his small group quite often, which is still memorable for me. He was such a charismatic leader and teacher, that we came to kind of jokingly refer to him as the George Washington of Berklee – the founding father, as it were (Email Burton/Heining 2014).

According to Collier, Pomeroy considered this to be a 'golden age for Berklee'.

> We were the cream of it in one sense. We got on the recording band and were recognized as having the skills. We all had to work hard – except Gary Burton (Laughing). Gary was so big-headed then. He was 16/17 and a great vibes player. We were in the audition band and I was the house bass player. There'd be fifty or sixty new students and Herb would say 'trumpets?' and half a dozen people would stand up. 'Trombones?' Another five or six. Vibes? No-one. Herb said, 'I'd think not with *that* around' (Laughing). Herb was a great teacher and a very great influence. People like Mike Gibbs, he's still a great mate of mine (Interview Collier/Heining 2005).

Collier was fortunate in being able to study with Pomeroy at all. Not all students at Berklee were granted that valuable educational opportunity. Students had to meet high standards and prove themselves and there were certain courses that had to be completed successfully first. As Mike Gibbs points out, 'Many students even with those who completed never got the chance to study with him, so full was...you know he limited each class to fifteen students'. And he adds, 'He was very much sought after but it also became difficult to get to him' (Interview Gibbs/Heining 2014).

Gibbs, Burton and a few other students were so taken with Pomeroy that a little clique formed around him. It was all a little silly and perhaps elitist too but also a little touching, as they called themselves 'Herb's special people', and gave each other nicknames – Pomeroy was 'The Walrus' because of his grand moustache. Collier was not a part of that group. Nor does he seem to have been part of any clique or group at Berklee.

Pomeroy taught two particularly significant writing courses, the Music of Duke Ellington and Line Writing, as well as his basic arranging class. This was a fresh approach to big band orchestration that focused on writing melodic lines for each instrument instead of thinking of vertical voicings for the instruments to play. As noted, he also led the main student band at Berklee. But he also taught, or perhaps modelled in his own practice, the virtues of discipline and economy. Mike Gibbs recalls:

> In all the years he was there, he had three classes and he was an ensemble coach and he was an amazing ensemble coach. He was very strict about people turning up on time. When they brought music in, it had to be written on only one side of a page. He had this discipline he instilled in us. But the three classes – basic arranging – but it was very much with his musical stamp on it – a class called composition, which in my day was done in private lessons and Duke Ellington music (Interview Gibbs/Heining 2014).

In subsequent years, as Berklee and its student intake expanded, Herb Pomeroy was rationed still further and he no longer offered individual or small group tuition. As Gibbs says he, Burton, Collier *et al.* were fortunate indeed.

> Graham and I were lucky being there earlier and having him on a more one-to-one level. When I was in England and working with Graham, we would often say, if something came up in a piece of music, we would together recognise that that was a Herb Pomeroy connection to what we were hearing, and remembering our instruction from Herb.

It is worth pointing out that both men went on to teach jazz to young jazz musicians, Collier at the Royal Academy of Music and Gibbs at Berklee, alongside his friend Gary Burton. Gibbs explains:

> Herb was an extraordinary person and an extraordinary magnet. I had something he recognised as developable, that I had a potential, Herb did. So, he was a special teacher to me, as well, and I know Graham and I in later years in England, in the later part of our time together, talked about our time with Herb and the influence he was. Herb was an equal influence on both of us. We both loved Herb immensely (Interview Gibbs/Heining 2014).

Among Herb Pomeroy's innovations at Berklee was the introduction of an annual recording by the pick of the students, nicknamed the 'Recording Band', often featuring compositions or arrangements by the students as well those by established jazz composers. In 1957, Pomeroy and Robert Share, the school's provost, approached Lawrence Berk with the idea of a series of albums featuring the best compositions from amongst Pomeroy's students. The recordings would be accompanied by scores and would serve as educational tools demonstrating jazz writing and performance. Interviewed by Ed Hazell, Pomeroy recalled:

> Larry [Berk] immediately saw the merit of it and okayed it. It tied in nicely with what the school was about – teaching jazz music. At that point, I am not aware of anywhere else you could get a record and the corresponding score.

And he continued:

> We did one per school year at the end of the fall semester in December […] Bob Share did the administrative work and took charge of the liner notes and album design. He also took a great deal of pleasure being the A&R man. I was in the studio, and he was in the booth,

> making any number of major decisions on which solos were the best, which take was the best (Hazell 1995: 58).

In 1991, as Head of Jazz at the Royal Academy of Music, Collier would implement an annual student recording, albeit without the addition of the musical scores. Nevertheless, in an article he wrote for *Crescendo* in 1963 on his experiences at Berklee, Collier suggests that less time was available for performances of student compositions and arrangements than for works by established jazz composers.

> The normal ensembles will play any student arrangement which is brought in, as well as scores from the library, which features arrangements by many well-known professional writers, as well as outstanding student scores. Unfortunately for the student, time and ensemble ability rarely permit a good reading of his arrangement, except in one or two choice ensembles.

And he concludes:

> [T]here is still insufficient time adequately to perform all the submitted arrangements and still give the student a fair crack at the professional scores in the library (Collier 1963: 35).

For a student, who had already decided that his path in jazz lay in the direction of composition, this must have been frustrating. At the same time, Collier was full of praise for Herb Pomeroy as an ensemble coach.

> He has a wonderful command of an ensemble, plus the very uncommon knack of making a band play a 'too-difficult' piece well. In other words, he makes the whole greater than the parts. Allied with this is excellent musicianship, his wonderful sense of humour (his description of a dissonant ending chord in an arrangement by a Yugoslav student as a 'Kremlin' chord is a classic). He also evinces a warm personal interest in a student's problems both musical and non-musical (Collier 1963: 35–36).

In the article, Collier also notes a number of other British students who had arrived at Berklee by that point, including Paul Betjeman, son of the later Poet Laureate. Betjeman recalls sharing an apartment with Collier:

> I remember Graham and I shared a basement apartment on Commonwealth Avenue for a semester or so. There was one other student, a guitar player there also who I only remember as having his guitar stolen by a gypsy player in the building and him not resent-

> ing it that much because the thief played the instrument so much better than he did – one of those sad little music stories that just about all of us remember, I think. Graham, I remember as very serious about his writing – he'd been at the school at least a year longer than me and he was in the Herb Pomeroy circle, or admired him anyway. Pomeroy ran the top band in the school at the time and something that I picked up from him which I have retained all my life is a liking for tucking dissonances on the insides of chords with softer intervals outside – Herb said it came from Duke Ellington – whether Graham C found that important or not I don't know. I remember him saying to me in the apartment once 'not before time I'm sure', when I was sharpening a pencil. Mildly irritating but not importantly so – one of those oddities one remembers. I do remember vividly the very large, approaching cat size, rats frequently visible at face level because it was a basement apartment outside the back of the building among the garbage cans (Email Betjeman/Heining 2015).

In the *Crescendo* article, Collier also discusses Pomeroy's 'sole command' of the Recording Band, noting that the 'unified approach from record to record' is justified but can lead to the omission of 'some otherwise good arrangement because it is not in the right "bag"' (Collier 1963: 36).[1] Spoken from the heart, perhaps! Nevertheless, *Jazz in the Classroom Vol VII* featured Collier's 'The Barley Mow', alongside other student compositions including two from Mike Gibbs. Gibbs also wrote the liner notes on this occasion and he wrote of 'The Barley Mow',

> A member of the International Group at Berklee, Graham Collier is a talented English writer whose native folk music is evident in this composition. The modal melody is first stated and then subjected to several variations over pedal points. Of special interest are the excellent solos by Sadao Watanabe, flute, and Dick Iannitelli, alto (Gibbs 1962).

The following year, *Jazz in the Classroom Vol VIII*, a record devoted to Ellington and Strayhorn, featured Collier's arrangement of Duke's 'Star-Crossed Lovers'. Unlike the previous occasion, Collier did not play bass on the session but the liner notes from Milt Freiberg comment:

> This very beautiful tune comes from the Ellington suite *Such Sweet Thunder*, a tribute to Shakespeare, and is done what may be called poetic justice in this very dramatic arrangement by English arranger Graham Collier. This is a very interesting score to contemplate and a very difficult one to play, as it contains many individual lines and

> complimentary solos, and demands extremely delicate playing from everyone. The soloists are Mike Gibbs on trombone and Ford Winner on tenor (Freiberg 1963).

Leonard Feather reviewed *Jazz in the Classroom VII* for *Down Beat*. Commenting on 'No Man's Land' by Gary Burton and trombonist Chris Swansen, Feather writes, 'It is debatable whether, as the notes state, "a folk-like quality characterises this piece", unless this means there is a hummable melody and such a quality is folksy'. He then continues, 'The same comment can be made regarding 'Barley Mow' by British composer Graham Collier, a dramatically impressive piece with fine work by Dick Iannitelli on alto and Sadao Watanabe on flute' (Feather 1964). Meanwhile, Steve Race, writing in *Crescendo*, was more convinced that 'The Barley Mow' reflects the 'folk idiom' of Collier's homeland, though he notes that the performance suffers from 'Student pitch problems'. However, he adds, 'it bears something of a composer's fingerprint and after hearing only this one score I think I would recognise his work again'. Fine praise indeed and Race continued thereafter to be supportive of Collier's work (Race 1963).[2]

Bill Mathieu attended to *Jazz in the Classroom Vol VIII*, the Ellington record, for *Down Beat*. The review is rather nay-saying, as Mathieu chides the students for their lack of adventure, whilst simultaneously praising their execution of the charts. However, he singles out a number of aspects for favourable comment:

> A few musical highlights: Sadao Watanabe's fine alto saxophone solos on 'Upper (Manhattan Medical Group)' and 'Falling (Like A Raindrop)'; the familiar playing of trombonist Mike Gibbs on 'Blue (Serge)', a fine arrangement by Emil Findikoglu; the coloristic, orchestral writing by Graham Collier on 'Star Crossed (Lovers)', (jazz is not being written better than this) (Mathieu 1964).[3]

Emin Findikoglu is a very well-known musician in his homeland of Turkey. He still remembers recording the record, which he points out also included his arrangement of Mercer Ellington's 'The Girl In My Dreams Tries To Look Like You'.

> I started to attend Berklee in summer 1962. Right off, I made friends with Mike Gibbs and Graham. My mentor Arif Mardin had told me to look these two cats up as soon as I get to Boston. They were on their last year as I was starting. Mike did not write for *Jazz in the Classroom Vol VIII*, only played on it. Graham's treatment of Strayhorn's 'Star Crossed Lovers' was classically influenced, in that sense kind of different from the rest of the album. We weren't close friends – not really. They were friendly to me because they knew I was Arif's friend (Email Findikoglu/Heining 2015).[4]

Collier's time at Berklee, in many respects, established the basis for his future career and, in terms of his sexuality, it also seemed to offer a more personal sense of release. Not only had he grown as a composer and arranger but also in his self-confidence and emotional development, as an artist and as a person. During a break between semesters at Berklee in the spring of 1963, he took a gig with the Jimmy Dorsey 'ghost' band, a fact that was announced proudly in the *Luton News* (1963). The article also noted that once his studies were completed at Berklee, Collier planned to return to the UK and 'set up his own school in London to teach arrangement techniques to jazz musicians'. Now twenty-six years old, he was already clearly thinking that his future would involve a contribution to jazz education.

His tour with the Dorsey band was, however, brought to a sudden and dramatic end. After a gig in Wyoming one night, one of the other musicians – Paul F. Anderson – offered Collier a lift back to the hotel. The driver crashed the car with disastrous results for Collier. This is how he told the story in 2005.

> From there I had a bad car accident in Wyoming touring with the Jimmy Dorsey ghost band. We were in a late night place drinking with the locals. Somebody said, 'Oh, I'll take you back to the hotel'. He crashed his car and I went through the windshield. So, that finished that tour and, in a way, finished me with America because it's that thing of where do you get the money to pay the hospital. The insurance paid finally but it was all... so, I came back to England in late '63 and they allowed me to finish the course – I was almost finished anyway – then I started my first band in 1964 (Interview Collier/Heining 2005).

In fact, from the legal correspondence amongst Collier's papers, it is clear that Collier was fortunate indeed to survive. The account given in a letter from E. E. Birchby, Attorney at Law in Sheridan, Wyoming, refers to the accident taking place in May and the letter, though undated, was probably written around June 1963. It states:

> After playing an engagement twenty-two miles south of Sheridan, Mr Paul Anderson, Jr., invited Mr Collier to ride with him back to Sheridan instead of having Mr Collier return in the bus used by the Orchestra. Approximately seven miles south of Sheridan Mr Anderson left the main highway, in order to save a short distance, by turning off on a State Secondary Road. Mr Collier was dozing at the time and apparently the driver, Mr Anderson, had likewise fallen asleep. There were no witnesses to the accident, but the evidence showed that Mr Anderson had driven off the road in the barrow pit (an irrigation ditch), which threw Mr Collier into the windshield. Mr

> Anderson then stated to Mr Collier that he would go for help, but instead of doing this he went on home and went to bed, stating to his wife and others the following day that he was so confused he didn't know what he was doing. Mr Collier finally attracted attention, two hours later, by sounding on the car horn and then was brought to Sheridan Hospital.

According to a local newspaper report, Graham Collier suffered 'multiple lacerations of the face and forehead'. The report noted his condition as 'fair'. Collier did not retain the details of the actual newspaper or date with the cutting. However, on the other side of the clipping, there is a report of astronaut Gordon Cooper's Project Mercury flight. This took place between 8.00am on 15 May and 6.00pm on 16 May 1963. So, assuming the report appeared on 16 May, the accident probably occurred on 14 or 15 May.

The legal correspondence describes the tortuous process Collier went through to obtain compensation. This was made more problematic by local Wyoming law, known as the 'Guest Statute', which states that a guest rides at their own risk. The matter was finally settled by the time Collier was due to return to the UK in October. He received his Professional Diploma with a Major Department in Arranging and Composition on 30 August 1963 and was ready to begin his career as a jazz musician and composer.

Notes

1. Collier also notes in the article a number of other 'Englishmen' at the school – Paul Betjeman (tenor and baritone) from Wantage, Berkshire; Clive Stevens (alto and baritone) from Bristol; Steve Duro (piano and organ) from Nottingham and Glyn Bower (trombone) from Bradford. In fact, prior to the publication of the *Crescendo* article, Collier had also contributed 'discordant interpolations' to a review of Stan Kenton's appearance at the Odeon, Hammersmith on 16 November 1963. This may be his first post-Berklee foray into print (see Fahey and Collier 1963: 4–5).

2. John Gill released 'The Barley Mow' on the wonderful Collier retrospective CD *Relook*. His notes indicate that, despite considerable efforts, he was unable to track down saxophonist Dick Iannitelli.

3. 'Falling Like A Raindrop' was arranged by Gene Perla, whilst 'Upper Manhattan Medical Group' was arranged by Al Feeny.

4. Amongst Graham Collier's personal effects is a card from Arif Mardin, written probably late in 1963, or more likely early 1964, which comments on Graham's contribution to the album. 'Dear Graham, Happy to hear you are settled in London and are in business. We would love to visit London – who knows? One day, maybe. I heard your arrangement on the Berklee LP – your aural sensitivity is truely (*sic*) remarkable. Congratulations for a beautiful chart. Regards from both of us, Arif.'

3 Return of the Native

Returning to the UK in October 1963, Collier could look back on a number of experiences that were to prove significant in his development as an individual and as an artist. Family life had been rich in love, support and encouragement and his childhood and adolescence had been filled with music. As John Bowlby, a renowned child psychiatrist of the time might have put it, Collier was secure in his attachments (Bowlby 1967). That is to say, he had developed a sense of who he was as a person and acquired a capacity to form and sustain relationships. Relationships, professional and personal, and the ability to manage these are obviously crucially important for someone such as Collier, who chose from the outset of his career to lead his own band. In fact, he was acutely aware of what his parents had given him. A letter written as he was about to turn twenty-one is touchingly honest:

> Dear Mother and Father,
>
> I'm writing this to you on the eve of my 21st Birthday, the day when one is supposed to become a man and capable of making one's own decisions. Of course, I've been deciding things on my own for a little while now, but you've always been there for guidance.
>
> What I'm really trying to say is a big thank you to you both for being such grand parents to me. I know it can't have been easy for you clothing and feeding two growing lads and you probably had to make many sacrifices to put us both through Grammar School.
>
> We never had as much money as some, or as nice a house as some. We did have two things though that are far more precious than many or a flashy house – a HOME and parental love, and after seeing some people in the army I realise what tremendous things these can be in shaping a man's mind and character.
>
> I feel I've expressed myself badly, but I hope enough of what I feel is understandable to you both.
>
> Believe me, I've never been more sincere than when I say to you, thanks a million for everything.
>
> Your devoted son,
> Graham.

It seems a remarkably mature and tender letter for a twenty-one year old. But then his years in the army seem to have been a period of emotional growth as well. He seems to have been quite remarkably self-assured. Back in 1963, people from Graham's background would only visit such far-flung places as the USA, if they had relatives there. To go to Boston to study was a far bigger deal then than now. Of course, he was a little older than some students – he was twenty-six when he graduated – but that also meant that in jazz terms he was something of a late starter. One suspects that the army and the opportunities to travel had helped build that sense of self-reliance. It also gave him a sound musical education, the opportunity to begin to play jazz and a love of travelling that stayed with him throughout his life.

The British Army once had a recruiting slogan that went, 'If you've got it in you, we'll bring it out'. One may doubt that what was brought out in Graham Collier was quite what the army had in mind but it seems true nonetheless. But then that slogan would also seem to apply to what Berklee and Pomeroy brought out in Collier. That was the desire and confidence to make his own music in his own way and his career would always be marked by a questing, searching approach to his art.

As he told Charles Fox in 1967 in an interview for the sleeve notes of his first album *Deep Dark Blue Centre*,

> I knew that all I wanted to do was compose jazz, so the only sensible thing seemed to be to form a band of my own. It was a septet because seven instruments was the smallest number that would get the sound I wanted, and the largest I could afford economically. At that time I was reacting against what I considered to be wrong with jazz – those never-ending blowing sessions, the idea that jazz was just a matter of theme and variations. In fact, I swung too far the other way, and the music we played was too tight, too much like West Coast jazz. We've loosened up a lot since then (Fox 1967).

The quote reveals several key issues. Firstly, it indicates a continuity of concern about the relationship in jazz between composition and improvisation – Collier would continue to develop his own strategies for addressing this question. Secondly, it shows his intolerance of the second-rate in jazz, as in all things. Finally, it reveals a musician who was constantly seeking to open up the artistic potential of the music.

Although he knew few people on the London scene at the time, one item of correspondence from critic and musician Steve Race indicates that he was already personally acquainted with Collier. Race wrote, 'I hope you will soon be able to establish yourself as an arranger and teacher, though you will not need me to tell you that it is virtually impossible to make a living out of what you and I would call good music'.¹ A hand-written note on the typed letter adds, 'Write if starting new club or lunchtime thing'.

Collier's plans to start his own school for arrangers mentioned previously in the *Luton News* never materialized but Collier's interest in and commitment to jazz education was evident. In fact, like so many jazz musicians in this early period of his jazz life, income from private lessons was more significant than that from gigging (Interview Collier/Wickes 1986). Collier advertised his services regularly in *Crescendo*, a magazine for which he had written articles since his Berklee days:

> Arranging/Theory/Bass – Berklee Graduate. Experience Jimmy Dorsey/Herb Pomeroy Orchestras – Graham Collier. Phone Museum 1318.

The first such advertisement appeared in the November 1963 issue of the magazine and the last in May 1966. The old London phone system code of Museum 1318 indicates that Collier was living at that time in Bloomsbury. However, by the time of the later adverts, going by a change of number, he was living in Paddington. Drummer Jon Hiseman was one of Collier's early pupils. Hiseman had six lessons on music theory with Collier (Interview Hiseman/Heining 2016). It is not clear where exactly Collier lived in Bloomsbury but pianist Geoff Castle, who met Collier through his involvement with the London Schools Jazz Orchestra, also studied with him, at his basement flat in Seymour Place, Paddington in 1966–67.

Collier's new septet had its first rehearsal on 12 February 1964 and began playing gigs around London in April that year. Its debut was at the Woodstock Gallery in the West End. Barbara Moore was on vocals, with Colin Bradfield and Joe McLear, reeds; Dave Lowe, trumpet; Terry Johns, French horn; Mike Beck, drums; Phil Lee, guitar and Collier, bass. Phil Lee would later play on *Deep Dark Blue Centre* and *Songs For My Father* (1970).

Les Tomkins reviewed the performance favourably in *Crescendo*, noting in particularly Collier's 'intriguing potential for musical colour' and singling out two compositions – 'Bard Lives', described as a 'warmly moody theme', and 'a turbulent, impressionistic' piece called 'Spaniard on the Heath'. (This does not refer to a romantic assignation but to a rather fine old inn on the edge of Hampstead Heath.) The composition was part of the four-part 'London Suite' Graham had recently written, which was given one of its first performances (if not its actual premiere) at the Hampstead Festival of the Arts in May 1965. Tomkins (1964) dignified Barbara Moore's singing with the comment that it was 'as good as her looks' (!) The times were what they were.

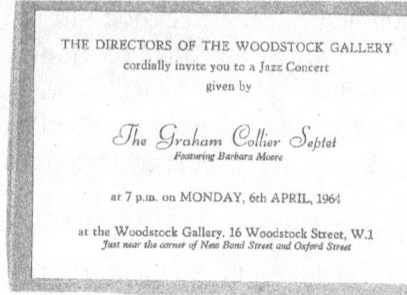

Figure 4. Graham Collier Septet first gig, Hampstead, April 1964. Personnel: Graham Collier (bass), Mike Beck (drums), Joe McLear (baritone), Colin Bradfield (alto), Dave Lowe (trumpet), Terry Johns (French horn), Phil Lee (guitar), Barbara Moore (vocals).

Of more significance was Tomkins' remark about the playing of guitarist Phil Lee, who 'made his presence felt strongly – chording, blending and soloing'. One might say that this was essentially the role of any guitarist, or even any chordal instrument, in a jazz ensemble. However, Tomkins was perhaps reaching for something more in his review concerning the way Collier used the instrument in a variety of ways to create a more diverse range of colours within the music. Similar comment might later be made in relation to guitarist Ed Speight's work within Collier's small and large bands.

Another review also made an intriguing remark about one of the numbers, an arrangement of 'Three Blind Mice', 'which allowed at one point the musicians to "collectively improvise" – they had three notes to play over one section and while the order was fixed, they could play them at any time and at any speed. An interesting group – well worth hearing' (Date/periodical unavailable). In fact, the reviewer is describing how Collier would continue to use motifs in his music throughout his life to maintain a freshness and spontaneity in his music. The other review that Collier had retained was less fulsome in its praise. Ian Christie[2] commented:

> It is difficult to assess the merits of Collier's compositions from Monday's concert because they were so ineptly played that one could only get a rough idea of the composer's original intentions... The written passages were murdered rather than executed and the soloists, with a couple of exceptions, showed an embarrassing lack of ability to improvise. However, one did occasionally get a dim glimpse of some original musical thinking laying dormant on the manuscript paper and one would like to have the opportunity of hearing it brought to life some time by a more capable bunch of musicians (Christie 1964).

A gig sheet from 1964 details four gigs between April–June 1964, all of which were played for free and which included the Woodstock Gallery and two heats of the National Jazz Federation competition for 'amateur jazz bands'. The Graham Collier Septet was one of fourteen bands who made the final, which was held at the 4 National Jazz Festival at Richmond Athletic Ground in August 1964. This was the first NJF festival to extend an invitation to the new white British R&B bands with the Rolling Stones playing on Friday night and Georgie Fame, Graham Bond and the Yardbirds on Sunday evening.

The group's main source of work in this period, however, was its weekly residency on Sundays at the Camden Head in Islington.[3] This accounted for sixteen of the group's remaining eighteen performances in 1964 and was clearly a door-money gig.[4]

Details of the intervening period are somewhat sketchy. However, the year ended with the septet's most prestigious outing to date opposite the New Jazz Orchestra at the Marquee Club in Wardour Street on Sunday 29 November 1964. The group also played the Green Man in Blackheath on 20 December. The take for the former was £7.00; from the latter, £6. Their fortunes were obviously on the rise! 1965 was marked by a BBC *Jazz Club* broadcast on the Light Programme on Monday 13 September opposite Joe Harriott's Quintet and the Mike Carr Trio and by a performance at the Hampstead Arts Festival in May. At Blackfriars Hall in Hampstead, the septet performed two sets, mixing standards and Collier tunes. Much of 1966 appears to have continued in a similar vein, albeit with a slight increase in work, as Collier's response to John Wickes suggests:

> You ask about the places we played. Hampstead Arts Festival 1965, the Marquee 1964, opposite the New Jazz Orchestra, J. Walter Thompson's boardroom... BBC. It was that kind of slowly trying to find places to play.

This was the period when many former jazz clubs in London and other large cities had switched to rhythm and blues and rock music (Heining 2012a; Wickes 1999), and Collier added:

> We were all of us struggling then. And I don't think the Old Place made any difference financially because no one made much money there but it made a difference in that we all got to know each other and got a regular place to play (Interview Collier/Wickes 1986).

There is no doubt that both Ronnie Scott's Old Place in Gerrard Street and the Little Theatre Club, which was run by John Stevens, played remarkably important roles in the development of British jazz in the late sixties (Heining 2012a; Wickes 1999). Nevertheless, the fortunes of British jazz were somewhat mixed in this period. As opportunities to play live became increasingly limited with the rise of rhythm & blues and rock music, the remaining gigs were now being divided between two or even three generations of modern jazz musicians. At the same time, the arrival on the scene of composers and musicians such as Collier, Mike Westbrook, Chris McGregor, Kenny Wheeler, John Surman, Norma Winstone, Harry Beckett, Mike Gibbs, John Stevens, Howard Riley and others, coupled with increasing connections between jazz and rock, did promote a degree of interest amongst rock fans and record companies.

For Collier and his group, 1966 provided several new opportunities to work and develop their repertoire. The first of these was at the Little Theatre Club, where the septet performed late on Thursday nights between April–June 1966. This seems to have been separate from the activities of drummer John Stevens and his cohorts in the Spontaneous Music Ensemble at the venue. *Crescendo* commented on the group's performance at the club in its 'Round and About', noting also that trombonist Mike Gibbs had replaced their French horn player: 'Having heard the present personnel on one of their regular Thursday nights at the Little Theatre Club, we'd say it's a more virile, hard-swinging sound than previously' (*Crescendo* 1966). Another short residency took place on Tuesday lunchtimes at the Cochrane Theatre in Holborn in September and the early part of October.

However, it was The Old Place which would prove most significant during its short life for Collier and others of the new generation of British jazz musicians. In an interview from 2008, Harry Beckett described articulately the experience of playing at the venue and what it meant to those who played there.

> The playing during those days wasn't about making money. It was about enjoying working with each other in different situations, trying out new compositions from Mike Westbrook or from

> Graham Collier. All of these different people were experimenting with new compositions and arrangements. It was like a family situation that developed into this big thing with us making albums. The financial aspect wasn't a big thing – so long as you had some money to live on. Enjoying each other's playing for Ossie [Mike Osborne], myself and a lot of musicians, that's what it was all about (Interview Beckett/Heining 2008).

The Old Place opened under that name – having previously been Ronnie Scott's main club, which now relocated to Frith Street – on 9 September 1966 and closed on Saturday 25 May 1968. The Collier Septet's first performance at the venue seems to have been on Tuesday 13 December 1966 and its last on Friday 17 May 1968. During this period, Collier went from playing The Old Place monthly to fortnightly to weekly.

Drummer John Marshall worked with Collier on and off throughout the bandleader's life and recalls a process where the group gradually built up opportunities to play thanks to Collier's persistence and efficiency in terms of promotion. Marshall had depped in the original septet and was recruited by Phil Lee late in 1965. The group used to rehearse at the Troubadour coffee house in Earl's Court, which was renowned as a folk venue in the sixties and seventies.

> I'd heard the band on BBC *Jazz Club*, I think, and thought it was a bit sort of arranged really. But the thing is I quite like doing gigs like that rather than blowing gigs, like special last minute things, because the music would be organised and it would be reading and it would be an interesting gig. And I was quite surprised because it was a mixture of quite detailed parts and quite open parts. The thing is I was very into Charlie Mingus at that time, which was a hangover from the music I liked when I was at the University at Reading and so it was kind of a pleasant surprise because it was the kind of thing I like which was structured overall but with plenty of freedom and openness within it. I kind of felt comfortable within it straight off.

And he continues:

> [I]t's funny, I don't remember Graham on it in the sense that the only person I really remember is Phil Lee. Maybe he was sort of deputed to liaise (Laughing) and I think at the end of it he said, 'Do you fancy joining the band?' I said, 'Well, sure' and I think basically nothing much happened apart from rehearsals because it was still early days for the band, not for the band I mean he'd got it going but it was before Graham had really got...was becoming successful in generating work, which, of course, was one of the things he was really good at.

Marshall had been gigging on the scene for some years but he notes that, 'Graham's was the first kind of regular jazz group in the sense that it had arrangements and a regular personnel'. As he explains, work built slowly and though he was not aware of it at the time, 'it became obvious that Graham was beavering away because we'd get gigs in all sorts of unusual places'. And he adds, 'I mean it was good to get into a band that I felt comfortable in but there was a lot to learn because Graham was starting to use different time signatures and stuff like that. It was sort of important in getting on the scene and getting seen' (Interview Marshall/Heining 2014).

There was another significant event, however, in 1966. Under the initiative of school teacher and musician Pat Evans,[5] a jazz summer school began under the auspices of the larger Barry Summer School. This latter organization offered a wide range of creative arts courses, including photography, drama, fine art, pottery and, from 1966, jazz. Professor Heike Roms of Aberystwyth University has researched the summer school and other arts-educational programmes in South Wales. For her, it was not just the individual courses in different subjects at Barry that were important but the ways in which students from different areas of the arts came and worked together at the school.

> What I have been particularly interested in is the many stories of stuff happening between the different courses – there are lovely accounts of jazz and embroidery collaborations, of jazz musicians playing at happenings by the fine art students and jazz concerts in the swimming pool involving structures made by the textile students or jazz musicians improvising in response to large wind-affected textile works. Although I should add that Collier's name is never mentioned in relation to these – it's always Ian Carr who is credited for this kind of collaborative venture (Interview Roms/Heining 2015).[6]

In 1966, Collier was one of the tutors along with Evans, saxophonist Don Rendell, Leslie Evans and Peter Sander (Ian Carr joined the staff in 1967) and would return to teach at the school over the next few years, in fact finishing in 1970. Collier's ambitions in this direction had long been apparent and he was clearly moved by the experience, as this quote from a *Melody Maker* article on the school reveals:

> These people are just hungry for knowledge. The free afternoons have been swept aside, and some of them would go on all night if you let them. The spirit here is just unbelievable (Bird 1967a: 6).

Figure 5. Barry Summer School 1967. Collier centre, second row from back.

The importance of the Barry Jazz Summer School in the development of jazz education in Britain is sometimes overlooked. However, a number of students who went on to significant careers in jazz attended the school including Keith Tippett, Elton Dean, Nick Evans, Mark Charig and Karl Jenkins. Trombonist Nick Evans recalls the summer school as a turning point in his musical life:

> My musical career seriously all began there. I am not sure of the exact year but I suspect it was either 1967 or 1968 that I first went. It was run by a wonderful bloke called Pat Evans and Graham was one of the tutors there. I went to the two-week course on my own, being encouraged to do so by my father who suggested that because I was mad keen on jazz I went to Barry and learned something about the music including whether I was ever going to be any good at it.
>
> It so happened that Elton Dean, Mark Charig and Keith Tippett also decided to enrol for the school that year, although it was only Elton and Mark who knew each other (through their work with Bluesology and Long John Baldry). I had not met nor heard of any of the three before I arrived at the school.

> The Summer School at Barry was a wonderful thing. The location was far from the impersonal city. It was held in a low-key and informal atmosphere with time to socialize in the bar that was made available to all students and tutors. The two weeks were crammed with creative improvisation from morning until evening. Graham and the other tutors (Don Rendell being one) were on hand to offer technical advice, inspiration and teach chord theory throughout the day. In the evening, the students would present the results of their day's efforts in the Jazz Club overseen by Graham and the other tutors.
>
> Although over the years Barry acquired a fine reputation throughout the country, it had quite a low profile in its first few years. I don't think education authorities really saw jazz as a viable occupation or even an acceptable hobby. I believe it was Graham's musical qualifications and personal critical acclaim that was instrumental in bringing the 'powers that be' into accepting the legitimacy of the music and the jazz course itself. As a consequence, within a couple of years of its humble beginnings, Barry had become the place for budding jazzers to go in order to advance their ideas and possibly forge a jazz career. I do not think that would have happened without Graham's dedication to the project (Email Evans/Heining 2014).

Collier frequently recruited new members for his band through his educational work and, in 1966, he recruited multi-instrumentalist Karl Jenkins and, a year or so later, Nick Evans joined the Collier group.

By late 1966, Collier and his septet had become fixtures on the British jazz scene. Even if the personnel still fluctuated to some extent, the core of the band was now in place, as Collier noted:

> It's hard to remember. It was almost the *Deep Dark Blue Centre* band. Dave Aaron on alto, Terry Johns, the French horn player, but then people float through as you go on and you finally discover Harry Beckett or Kenny Wheeler and they were both on *Deep Dark Blue Centre* with Dave Aaron, Phil Lee, Mike Gibbs, John Marshall and me (Interview Collier/Heining 2009).

Collier was referring to his debut recording, *Deep Dark Blue Centre*, one of the finest records of the period and unusual at that time for its approach to structure and the scales used.[7] These were detailed in broadcaster and critic Charles Fox's informative notes. The record came about because towards the end of 1966 Collier was approached by the sons of dance band leader and broadcaster Jack Jackson.[8] John and Malcolm Jackson had their own recording studio in London, heard the septet and suggested a recording. Once this was done, they took the tapes to Deram, Decca's 'progressive' off-shoot.

3 Return of the Native

The personnel on *Deep Dark Blue Centre*, its title a reference to a quote from Hoagy Carmichael about the essential element of jazz, is as listed above. Wheeler and Beckett did not play together on the record but at separate sessions. With the exception of Charlie Mariano's 'Blue Walls', the other five tracks were written by Collier, though John Marshall apparently chided Collier jokingly that he did not know how he had the cheek to claim he wrote the title track. It was more or less a series of fragments that had emerged in rehearsal and then been developed during the recording of the piece. The album was favourably reviewed in *Melody Maker*, *Jazz Monthly*, *Jazz Journal*, *The Times*, *The Sunday Times* and the weekly newspaper of the Labour Party's Tribune Group, *Tribune*. Both *Melody Maker*'s Bob Houston and *Jazz Monthly*'s Jack Cooke referred to Gil Evans and George Russell in their reviews, while Derek Jewell in *The Sunday Times* noted:

> Collier's septet plays mostly Collier's music, which is brilliantly constructed in the Gil Evans manner. Could any recommendation be higher? Collier has a great ear for melody, for new ways of jazz counterpoint, for interesting instrumentation – using flute, oboe, flugelhorn *et al*. He's like a 1967 version of those renowned Miles Davis' Capitol tracks ('Jeru' etc) of the late 1940s. Five star (Jewell 1967a: 41).

Of the soloists, trumpeters Kenny Wheeler and Harry Beckett were almost universally singled out for praise. However, with hindsight, two comments – one from Alun Morgan and the other from Jack Cooke – seem particularly pertinent. Morgan picked out 'Hirayoshi Suite' and remarked, 'it is sometimes difficult to tell where writing ends and improvisation begins, which is some measure of the close bond between Collier and his musicians' (Morgan 1967). Cooke's comment, on the other hand, looks forward.

> How the band will develop in the future is hard to say; the ideal of course would be a loosening up of the solos, and at the same time a tighter control of the group style, so that the individual playing grows into as well as out of what is written, but failing this a little more life in the rhythm section would probably help (Cooke 1967).

Listening to the record, one feels sure that Cooke is not referring to John Marshall's highly sensitive and responsive drumming, which is one of the joys of *Deep Dark Blue Centre*. Bob Houston, for example, writing in the *Melody Maker* was rather disparaging about Collier's instrumental skills, noting that 'His bass playing is functional' (Houston 1967). However, in Morgan's comment, we have what would prove to be Collier's musical intention as a composer clearly defined. And in Cooke's remark, we see foretold how Collier would seek to achieve this.

Figure 6. *Deep Dark Blue Centre* Septet. Personnel: Karl Jenkins (oboe), Mike Gibbs (trombone), Harry Beckett (trumpet), Dave Aaron (flute), Graham Collier (bass), John Marshall (drums), Phil Lee (guitar). Photo courtesy of Cuneiform Records.

But perhaps the most perceptive review came from Miles Kington writing in *The Times*. Kington noted, 'The only shortcoming of the first LP by the Graham Collier Septet [...] is that it does not entirely suggest the warmth present in the group's live performances. Otherwise it very successfully captures the way the leader's writing spins loose but logical structures out of sparse modal material, the intelligence with which his soloists build on his written ideas, and the amazing variety of textures he produces from such a small instrumentation' (Kington 1967b). Kington's remark about the warmth of the live performance might have something to do with the fact that the majority of copies were issued in mono. A later CD reissue in stereo does offer a much warmer sound (see n. 7 below).

The record opens with Mariano's 'Blue Walls'. The performance here is lent a slightly modal, Moorish feel by Karl Jenkins' oboe and there are fine solos from guitarist Phil Lee and Dave Aaron on alto. However, of most interest compositionally is the rich textural background that Collier develops behind Aaron from the other horns and guitar and its tonal shifts between C minor and F major. 'El Miklós', a reference to Mike Gibbs' nickname at Berklee,[9] follows and features what must be Gibbs' longest continuous performance on trombone on record. Gibbs is often disparaging about his abilities in this regard and there is perhaps a hesitancy in his playing. However, there is also a quiet sensitivity to his work on the track that is quite touching. Contrast is effected in the piece through the counterposing of long and short notes from different instruments and by the sharp shift in tempo – slow to medium-paced – at various points. The atmosphere, unsurprising perhaps given its title, is Spanish and the use of oboe, flugelhorn and flute behind the lower register of the trombone is highly affective, evoking a kind of sweet sadness. The piece is also noteworthy for the way Collier encourages the horns to improvise alongside the main soloist, 'thickening' as he would later describe it, giving them the freedom to do so either through the scale of the tune or from motifs derived from it. More than this, Phil Lee's solo *cadenza* towards the close gives a first glimpse of a device that Collier would favour throughout his career.

Collier's 'Hirayoshi Suite' was first premiered at the Hampstead Festival in 1965. Again, it is the way that Collier deploys his resources that is so impressive. Harry Beckett is the main soloist, here on flugelhorn, and his capacity to colour the music and create surprising dynamic possibilities within it by the use of a few notes – subtle, crisp, almost at times choked in the moment of their expression – is quite wonderful. The tune is constructed from a simple five-note scale and yet results in great jazz. There is some fine accompaniment from Marshall, seemingly using his hands rather than sticks or brushes, and the use of a softly-voiced, improvising brass chorus behind Beckett's solo provides a sense of harmonic richness.

'Crumblin' Cookie' is perhaps the first indication of Collier's ability in using rock rhythms in his music but then in John Marshall he had one of the finest exponents of the art. Marshall's drumming has always been marked by that ability to give the impression of a solid backbeat but one that emphasizes a rhythmic suppleness and sense of movement rather than simply one of propulsion. Once more the tonal centre of the tune is not fixed and the piece modulates between keys, often seemingly between bars. Karl Jenkins' baritone solo reminds one what an exceptional saxophonist he was (or is), as he lends exactly the right emotional weight to the composition. Halfway through, Beckett takes over on flugelhorn and, as on 'Blue Walls', the horns offer a counterpoint to his solo, here primarily using a simple riff built from the scale. 'Conversations' is structured around a duet between Kenny Wheeler on trumpet and Dave Aaron on alto saxophone. This is a quintessential piece of British jazz of the period, yet one also has the sense that Collier is already finding ways of giving his musicians the space to express themselves, whilst retaining the substantial elements of the composition itself. This seems most evident in the way that Aaron and Wheeler spark off each other. First one plays mainly long notes, while the other uses short, staccato notes in response. Then places are switched. Wheeler's descending melody lines are simply gorgeous and Collier uses the changes in tempo to fine effect. Aaron, a player hardly known outside his association with Collier, shines during the brief ballad section and his flute playing throughout the record is quite lovely. The piece resolves beautifully to the tonic.

That leaves the title track, which closes the album but is in another sense, at seventeen minutes in length, its centrepiece. Charles Fox, in his liner notes, describes it as 'the most episodic of Collier's compositions, a sort of musical equivalent of a picaresque novel' (Fox 1967). It is constructed from the slightest of materials, proof perhaps of one of the lessons Collier took from Miles Davis' *Kind of Blue* that less could in the right hands be more. At one level, the track is a modal showcase for the individual talents in the septet. It is constructed upon a number of solos, duets, trios and quartets that are interspersed with episodes of group playing. These, in turn, are contrasted both in mood – at one point almost funereal, at others frantic and wild – and in tempo. At one level, the music derives its character in large measure from the personalities of the musicians. At another, 'Deep Dark Blue Centre' is an essay on the virtues of economy. It is essentially constructed from a number of motifs, another compositional device that Collier would continue to favour. It is episodic, as is much of Collier's music. However, his use of cadenza here – most notably when after eight minutes Karl Jenkins' bluesy baritone precedes a return to the theme and then when Phil Lee's guitar leads to a slow march section – and in subsequent compositions, is much more than just an opportunity for a musician to strut their stuff but is used carefully to presage changes of mood and/or tempo. In his later work, this would also be used to create jazz that 'happens in real time, once' and to 'move music off the paper' (to use Collier's later descriptions of his musical aims). Here, however, the aim is more modest in that it gives a sense of the music unfolding, albeit in a cyclical sense. The recurring use of thematic material also lends the piece a certain fugue-like quality. Finally, Collier's bass playing is more than functional throughout.[10]

Graham Collier had every reason to be very satisfied with his first recorded effort and with the contribution of his musicians to it. Shortly before his death, interviewed by Clifford Allen for the *New York City Jazz Record*, Collier acknowledged that, because it was his first record, he 'may have wanted to play it safer' (Allen 2011). His response, however, in 2009 mixed satisfaction and self-deprecation in equal measure, 'There were, I'm pleased to say, some good reviews, and they helped us find gigs and fans. The favourable review of the CD reissue in 2000 suggests also that we must, as the saying goes, have been doing something right' (Interview Collier/Heining 2009).

If 1967 began well for Collier, his career continued its upward trend. To begin with, he achieved recognition as a composer and arranger from a number of writers in the *Down Beat* International Jazz Critics' Poll, including Charles Fox, Bob Houston of *Melody Maker* and Val Wilmer, and even made it into the main category of 'talent deserving of wider recognition' as a composer. The following year in February, he came fourth in the 'Arranger' category of the *Melody Maker* Readers' Jazz Poll British section, after John Dankworth, Harry South and Mike Westbrook, whilst *Deep Dark Blue Centre* came fifth in the LP of the year category. This proved Collier's only appearance in the readers' poll, though he continued to appear in the paper's Critics' Poll in the 'Composer' category (Farbey 2010: 161–62).[11]

Then on Saturday 12 August 1967, the new Collier Septet made its first and only appearance at the National Jazz Federation's '7th National Jazz Pop Ballads & Blues Festival' at Windsor in Berkshire. The group performed alongside Yusef Lateef, the Zoot Sims–Al Cohn Quintet, Harold McNair, the Mike Carr Trio and others. By this time, jazz was already being squeezed out of this festival, just as it had been elbowed out of London clubs such as The Flamingo, Klooks Kleek and The Marquee (Heining 2012a; Wickes 1999). At this point, however, it was still one of the more prestigious UK gigs. Miles Kington wrote of the performance in *The Times*:

> The Graham Collier septet played as well as ever, but his intricate music really needs more intimate surroundings than the open expanses of Balloon Meadow. It has been said recently that his soloists are not strong enough; on the contrary, I think he has cleverly found musicians who can improvise well without so much individuality that they obstruct his basic concept. His brilliant new vibraphone player, Frank Ricotti, is a case in point (Kington 1967a).

But of most significance – for him and his peers – was Collier's successful application for an Arts Council grant. His success was celebrated throughout the 'jazz community' of the time. *The Sun*, previously known as the *Daily Herald* in 1964 and at this point a broadsheet owned by IPC (it was sold to Rupert Murdoch's News Limited group in 1969), ended a short article with the words, 'Three swinging cheers, then, for this minor milestone', summing up what seemed to be the prevailing mood amongst critics, musicians and fans (*The Sun* 1967; see also Kington 1967c; Jewell 1967b). By this point, it is evident that Collier's talent was receiving wider recognition, as was clearly acknowledged in Christopher Bird's *Melody Maker* article 'How I learned to stop worrying and live with the avant garde' from December 1967 (Bird 1967b).

The Arts Council grant was for the composition of a new suite and a two-date tour. The composition, *Workpoints*, was written for a twelve-piece jazz orchestra, featuring past and present members of Graham's band, along with several key players including saxophonist John Surman, trumpeter Henry Lowther and vibraphonist/percussionist Frank Ricotti, the latter being one of the stars of the show.

Performances took place in March 1968 in Southampton and at the Purcell Room in London's South Bank complex. At least three further performances took place subsequently, one at the Bull's Head in Barnes, another in Birmingham and the other at the Institute of Contemporary Arts and, perhaps, also one at Cambridge (see Clayton 1968; Blain 1968; Interview Dean/Heining 2014). Reviews were universally favourable and included pieces by Derek Jewell in the *Sunday Times*, Miles Kington in the *Times*, Thomas Laurence in *Melody Maker* and Val Wilmer in *Down Beat*. Of particular significance was a BBC Third Programme (later to become Radio 3) broadcast of *Workpoints*. A tape of the Southampton performance was finally released by Cuneiform in 2005, along with a sextet gig from 1975 recorded in Belgium.

Collier also got to write some notes for the *Radio Times* describing the work prior to its broadcast on the Third Programme on 10 July 1968. He wrote:

> The title *Workpoints* expresses very basically my credo as a jazz writer – that the composed parts are purely starting materials from which the soloists derive their solos and from which the remainder of the band can create their backgrounds. The division between what is written and what is improvised becomes very blurred at times and it is for this reason that each member of the band must be a strong soloist in his own right. The overall form of the piece was determined by myself as the composer, but what happens within that form will be very dependent on the interaction between the musicians on each performance.
>
> Thus it is hoped that each separate performance of *Workpoints* and, in fact, much of my recent output, will be different. Ideally my compositions should, while remaining *my* music, become, by the changes the band impose by their use of the given material, very much the musicians' music – and thus it is hoped that the compositions will retain the freshness and spontaneity of jazz along with some of the more organized aspects of more formal musics (Collier 1968b: 41).

Collier had formed his first group early in 1964. Here, barely four years later, he is already articulating what is in essence a performance aesthetic for his music. Whilst this would be refined in subsequent years, these few words express what became, as he put it, 'my credo as a jazz writer'.

Val Wilmer concluded a long *Down Beat* review:

> Collier's music manages to be out front and avant garde (terrible expression), yet easily assimilable by anyone who has ever listened to jazz. It's also, probably because it's British, rather more *gentlemanly* than Mingus' writing while being just as exciting in its own way (Wilmer 1968: 36; emphasis original).

Peter Clayton, writing of the Third Programme broadcast, felt that the music that followed the baritone duet between John Surman and Karl Jenkins was something of an anti-climax for, 'strong as the trumpet, trombone and rhythm section are, they never quite match the emotional power of the two baritones'. At the same time, he noted the award that had led to the piece: 'This new liberalism on the part of the Arts Council can lead to nothing but good; it's part of that much needed pocket money for jazz that I was pleading for a few weeks ago' (Clayton 1968: 8).

Even Benny Green, never since the late forties a jazz radical, wrote in the *Observer* of this first Arts Council grant to a jazz composer, that 'Collier, aware of the significance that official patronage could hold for British jazz, has struggled heroically to produce something worthy of the occasion'. He ended the review:

> *Workpoints* may be summed up as a composition adventurous in form but conventional in procedure, even down to the long drum solo towards the end. For a long time now, there has been growing in British jazz a strong groundswell of reaction against the old methods of improvisation, and it is a good thing that Collier has been given the chance to express this impatience in positive form with a skilful group, held together by the virile drumming of John Marshall (Green 1968: 32).

Inevitably there were slight differences of opinion, or taste, over certain specific aspects of the music. Miles Kington felt that 'texture, too, was sometimes made soggy by Frank Ricotti's over-active vibraphone work behind the soloists' (Kington 1968: 11). For Charles Fox, John Marshall's drum solo overshadowed the final movement for vibes, bass and drums, though as a solo he thought it 'a gripping piece of virtuosity but a bit too rhetorical in this particular context – as almost *any* drum solo would be' (Fox 1968: 392; emphasis original).

The three most pertinent comments regarding the composition itself came from Benny Green: '*Workpoints* may be summed up as a composition adventurous in form but conventional in procedure' – and from Charles Fox and Brian Priestley. Fox compared Mike Westbrook and Collier, noting,

> Mike Westbrook adopts what might be called the Ellington manner, parading the personalities of his musicians, making a virtue of their aesthetic quirks. Graham Collier seems more concerned with the texture of the instruments themselves (Fox 1968: 392).

Whilst Collier would see this point slightly differently – he would argue that he, too, sought to emphasize the musicians' own individual characteristics – the point about instrumental timbre is a valid one. Perhaps this distinction might owe something to the fact that Westbrook was self-taught as a composer, whilst Collier had studied composition and arranging formally.

Priestley, on the other hand, pointed out:

> [I]t is Collier's achievement to have let his soloists have their say for long stretches where there was obviously nothing written, while contributing to rather than detracting from the character of the music. We have been told time and again that this is what the paradoxical phrase 'jazz composition' really means, and *Workpoints* is perhaps the first important evidence for Graham Collier's claim to be a true jazz composer (Priestley 1968: 13).

As a slight correction to the remark about passages where there was 'obviously nothing written', it may not have been apparent that the musicians did have a number of written elements from which to draw their improvisations, be this a motif, a riff or a scale. That said, Priestley could almost have taken his words from Collier's own, very articulate mouth.

The first set on the tour also featured another new piece, 'Indefinite Relationships', plus 'Deep Dark Blue Centre' and 'The Barley Mow', with the second set devoted to *Workpoints*. In the notes for the Cuneiform release of the concert, Collier pointed out that he had taken the title from Lawrence Durrell's 'use of the word to sum up his starting points' in *Justine*, the first volume of his *Alexandria Quartet*. Ironically, two years earlier Collier had asked for Durrell's permission to use two brief extracts from *Justine* in a work he planned to write. The reply from Durrell's agents, Curtis Brown, was unequivocal:

> [H]e has instructed us to inform you that he would not under any circumstances be prepared to allow you to use these quotations and that you have no authority to use the names of his books or his own name in any way in connection with your composition (letter from Curtis Brown, 16 June 1966).[12]

Collier's use of the term was intended to describe how the motifs, riffs, scales and other devices used in the composition were essentially starting points for the musicians, who would then use their own creativity and skill to develop the composition itself. It is also an early example of how he would use ideas and practices from other art forms to inform his own compositional practice – or, as he put it to New York jazz writer Clifford Allen in 2011, to provide 'a background hum which you work within'.

The work is split into four movements, each of which is structured around a different section of the twelve-piece orchestra, known at the time as Collier's Dozen. It begins with the saxophones of Dave Aaron, John Surman and Karl Jenkins, moves on for Part Two to the trumpets of Kenny Wheeler, Harry Beckett and Henry Lowther, to the trombones of Mike Gibbs, Chris Smith and John Mumford for Part Three and then focuses on the rhythm section of Frank Ricotti on vibes, Collier himself on bass and John Marshall on drums. Whereas in a more conventional big band setting, each soloist might take their turn, in *Workpoints* the musicians continued to improvise around each other and the lead instrument. Similarly, some space was given over to collective improvisation by the whole orchestra, albeit with the musicians utilizing Collier's compositional devices. There is a parallel here with early jazz and the way the frontline would interact and embellish the melody simultaneously and independently at certain points. Collier would later refer to this approach in New Orleans jazz favourably in a number of contexts (Collier 1995: 43, 67; Collier 2009a: 60, 62, 100–102). The procedure might in these senses, as Benny Green pointed out, be 'conventional' but the form and structure of the piece remained 'adventurous'.

Workpoints opens with the rhythm section before the horns pick up a simple three-note riff and a second answering riff. Dave Aaron's alto is the first featured instrument set against a repeated but later fragmented riff. The horns drop out leaving just sax and rhythm playing the riff but return picking up a new seven-note motif. Collier creates further musical interest and contrast by varying tempos and backing, allowing space for a brief cadenza on alto or allowing sections of the orchestra to improvise freely. To take Clayton's point, the high point of the first section is the baritone saxophone duo of John Surman and Karl Jenkins, who seem to force their way out of the orchestra into what builds to a Latin-tinged groove with Ricotti on bongos. At the same time, the ensemble and support playing, from Ricotti and Marshall in particular, is quite magnificent with that 'dancing on the edge' excitement of Mingus' best work.

Anti-climax or not, the trumpet trio of Harry Beckett, Kenny Wheeler and Henry Lowther – soloing in that order – offers a rare glimpse of three of Britain's finest trumpeters improvising together. The section shifts between collective improvisation, either from the whole band or just from the trumpets, to more structured playing set first against a military, marching pulse and then to something with an almost Spanish feel to it. These shifts are interspersed with solo trumpet plus rhythm passages. The section builds in volume briefly as the rest of the horns return; the trumpets and rhythm then pick up the pace before fading for the entry of the trombones for the third section.

In the third section, Collier seems unwilling to allow anything to settle for very long and this section has a rather fragmentary feel to it. It is here, however, that Charles Fox's comment about Collier's use of texture seems most pertinent. There is a greater clarity to the orchestral sound, even when the band rises to a crescendo and freely improvises. For example, there is one passage that runs from around six minutes into Part Three to about eight minutes into the section, where one hears Collier the composer most clearly. There are little touches, as when one of the baritones joins a solo trombone and, when Collier brings the whole orchestra back in, each horn seems to exist simultaneously in its own sonic world but retaining reference to the music as a whole. It is also in this section that one senses most obviously the cyclical nature of the composition. This is in part because of the use of recurring riffs and motifs throughout but also because its form is built upon the variations between solo, duo, trio and ensemble playing.

The final, and longest, section is in some ways the most interesting from a textural point of view given its focus on the rhythm section. Although there had been brief snatches of piano earlier in the work, Karl Jenkins adds some highly effective keyboards to the rhythm trio at various points, whilst the horns offer brief interpolations from two previously unheard riffs into the conversation. John Marshall's long, dramatic but very musical drum solo sits somewhat oddly here, though given the drummer's sterling efforts in anchoring the piece, it would have been churlish not to allow him the spotlight. Nevertheless, as Benny Green seemed to suggest, it does serve to locate *Workpoints* within the jazz big band tradition and the pleasure from hearing this wonderful musician at length is undeniable. Again, the cyclical nature of the composition is emphasized in its closing moments, as some of the instruments seem to reprise and echo their previous solos, duos and trios over the main theme or riff. It builds to a brief crescendo, slows briefly, picks up tempo and finally flutters to a close, its last seconds left appropriately to John Marshall's drums.

The Cuneiform release also included a fine take on 'The Barley Mow', with Harry Beckett excelling even by his standards, and a less episodic, more robust take on 'Deep Dark Blue Centre'. Here the solo spots of the recorded version are replaced with a series of contrasting and attention-seizing duets. Unfortunately, the other piece, 'Indefinite Relationships', seems to have been lost to posterity.

The importance of *Workpoints* for British jazz lay in the fact that it represented a minor breakthrough for British jazz in opening the coffers of the Arts

Council, as others including Mike Westbrook, Keith Tippett, Evan Parker and Ian Carr were to discover over the next few years. The gates were hardly flung wide but a precedent for future opportunities was set. It demonstrated Collier's understanding of the need to hustle for work as a bandleader and composer. Amusingly, Graham kept his hand-written budget for the tour, detailing what he had paid the musicians – £6 for London, £14 for Southampton, which included their expenses – and the amount he was out of pocket, £36.14s.5d. Thirty-six pounds, at that time, would have been enough for a person to live on, covering most of their bills, for at least a couple of weeks.

With regard to Collier himself, we can see in both the composition and the context in which it was created, the composer and the man. Obtaining the grant in the first place required effort, determination but also the ability to speak in a language that was understandable to the arts establishment. It required confidence in his own capacities as an artist and a belief that jazz deserved not only a seat at the table but the chance to partake in the feast and not just the scraps.

For pianist Roger Dean, who would work with Collier from 1974 onwards and who heard the work in Cambridge, this was a breakthrough composition which heralded later works such as *New Conditions*:

> I think that *Workpoints* and *New Conditions* are the ones where the modular structure, the expanded timbre, the expanded tonality, the changed role of the soloist, the multiple soloists, the juxtaposition of soloist with changing modules of composed material – all those things came into play... And also the web-like resequencing of the units of the piece (Interview Dean/Heining 2014).

Workpoints, therefore, revealed certain of Collier's musical strategies in terms of his approach to structure, writing for improvisers and what we might call contextual free improvisation. Finally, in its reference to Lawrence Durrell, the piece revealed how Collier would draw on literature and, subsequently, fine art as a means of informing his own creative practice.

Notes

1. Letter from Steve Race, dated 10 December 1963. At the time, Collier was living in Dyne Road, NW6, which is off Kilburn High Road.
2. It is unclear whether this is the same Ian Christie who played jazz clarinet with his trombonist brother Keith in the Christie Brothers' Stompers and later with Humphrey Lyttleton.
3. The Camden Head is still there but is now a 'stand-up' comedy venue.
4. The differing amounts taken varied from £1.10 shillings (£1.50) to a maximum of £4.14 shillings (£4.70). Whether this was to be divided between seven band mem-

bers or Collier's own take is unclear. Given that admission was 3 shillings for members and 4 shillings for guests, £1.10s would be a maximum of ten in the audience and a minimum of seven. £4.14s would be a minimum of thirty-three and a minimum of twenty-three. If we assumed that the amounts were Collier's own take and that the other band members received the same, we would have to multiply those numbers by seven, which would mean that on a good night the band could expect an audience of as many as two hundred. That seems highly unlikely for a new band.

5. Pat Evans was originally the driving force behind the London Schools Jazz Orchestra.

6. Dr Roms interviewed Wyndham Heycock, the vice-principal of the Barry Summer School, on 29 April 2010. He told her that he received a call from Pat Evans in London to ask if he could start a jazz summer school. Heycock had some reservations because of 'the mythology of jazz and wild nights', as he had to submit the whole programme to Glamorgan Educational Committee every year. But no one ever questioned why jazz was being included at the school. The Don Rendell–Ian Carr Quintet gave a 'celebrity' concert in 1966, with Ian Carr joining as tutor for the 1967 school. Ian Carr joined the tutors in 1967 and both the Rendell-Carr Group and Graham Collier's Septet performed for the summer school students that year. Pianist John Burch joined the faculty in 1968 along with John Marshall, whilst Bryan Spring replaced Marshall as drum and percussion tutor in 1970.

7. One point of note is that the record was thought, including by Collier himself, to have been solely issued in mono. In fact, when Beat Goes On records brought out a second reissue (the first being by Disconforme in 2000) as part of a set with *Portraits* (1972) and an unreleased and very different version of *Mosaics*, they remastered the release from an original stereo copy loaned by fan Bob Bastow. It must be said that the stereo version enhances still further the importance of *Deep Dark Blue Centre*. The record was also significant in introducing the great Barbadian trumpeter Harry Beckett to a wider audience.

8. Jack Jackson was a highly influential DJ on the Light Programme and later on Radio 2. His show *Record Roundup* ran from 1948 to 1977. His methods of presentation included punctuating records with surreal comedy clips and using quick cutting of pre-recorded tapes to humorous effect.

9. Gibbs was christened Miklós Schwalb by Ray Santini, one of the Berklee tutors, after the classical pianist of that name.

10. Collier was well aware of criticisms of his bass playing. See Walters 1971.

11. The other successful LPs were (1) Tubby Hayes *100% Proof*, (2) Joe Harriott–John Mayer *Indo Jazz Fusions*, (3) Mike Westbrook *Celebration*, (4) Don Rendell–Ian Carr *Dusk Fire*, (6) Mike Taylor *Trio*. *Melody Maker* abandoned the Poll in 1974.

12. Despite the snub, Collier and his partner John Gill remained undiminished in their enthusiasm for Durrell's work.

4 Down Another Road

With *Workpoints*, Graham Collier had tapped into a certain shift in cultural circles in Britain. We may debate how far the opening up of Arts Council and other state funding to jazz has really assisted this 'music outside', as musician and broadcaster Ian Carr described the position of jazz in Britain in the late sixties/early seventies. Some may suggest, with justification, that funding for jazz has always lagged far behind that granted to opera and classical music. However, Collier's breakthrough had come in the context of the wider cultural pluralism that had emerged in the sixties.[1]

For Collier himself, once he had found a way inside the doorway to funding, he would push it for all he was worth and, if one possibility was closed to him, he would often find another that lay open. In this, he has been nothing but consistent throughout his career, whatever one might think of his music. Yet it seems somehow important to remind oneself of Collier's own position in a music noted for its maleness and sexism towards women (Heining 2012a: 273–302). Collier was a gay man and, in a 'music outside', he was clearly an outsider. We will see that heterosexism certainly did raise its ugly head in Collier's direction. However, by the time he returned to Britain from Boston in 1963, Collier was making no secret of his sexuality. Perhaps it was not the case that the British jazz scene was devoid of such prejudice, so much that its denizens were simply uninterested, as he suggested to Keith Howes in 1976:

> It is true it is basically a heterosexual world – in fact, I can't think of anybody that I've suspected of being gay in jazz! But jazz musicians as a race aren't inquisitive about your personal life and even before 1967 I'd never bothered to hide my gayness if the subject came up. When I've had affairs I've taken them along with me at odd times (Howes 1976: 19).[2]

It is difficult to know how to read this. On the one hand, it is encouraging to know that Collier found ways of existing within the blokey culture of British jazz and even more that he did not, generally, meet prejudice from musicians or fans. On the other hand, one wonders how much this was due to Collier himself being comfortable with his own sexuality and in his own skin by this point. Given his comment about the absence of other 'gay jazz musicians', we might wonder if the very heterosexual maleness of the scene discouraged interest or participation on the part of gay men. What is clear is that Collier was not discouraged, and more than that he moved with relative ease within the world of British jazz in these years. As John Gill put it shortly before his death,

> As to the treatment of his sexuality, while we both know he was a complex individual, I think he largely ignored 'homophobia' unless it stepped into his face, which it was usually too cowardly to do. I think you and me may be making more of this than there is. He largely got on with life, without much public complaint. He certainly never complained about homophobia to me in the 35 years we were together, and expected to be judged on his achievements, not who he slept with. I do remember Alan Jackson, the drummer, getting a little lairy on the booze once, but GC put him in his place (Email Gill/Heining 2016).

Just a couple of months after the *Workpoints* tour, and seeking new opportunities for his music, Collier was in contact with Ronald Snoad, the organizer of the Harlow Festival in Essex. Harlow was one of eight 'new towns' created after 1945 to relieve population pressures on Britain's larger cities, which had been damaged by German bombers during the Second World War. Harlow's architect was Frederick Gibberd and, from the outset, his plans for the town included an emphasis on culture and fine art. As a consequence, Harlow New Town began in 1953 to commission and acquire works of sculpture, which were then positioned in the town's parks, streets, housing estates and shopping centres. The collection now stands at some one hundred pieces of very important and beautiful sculpture by artists including Barbara Hepworth, Henry Moore, Elizabeth Frink, Auguste Rodin and Lynne Chadwick.

In 1968, Harlow Festival wanted to commission a new work from Graham Collier for its festival. Collier visited the town and, taken by its collection of sculptures, selected five examples – Henry Moore's *Upright Motive No. 2: Bronze Cross*, Sally Doig's *Wrestlers*, Will Soukop's *The Donkey*, Lynne Chadwick's *Trigon* and Barbara Hepworth's *Contrapuntal Forms* – as the inspiration for the piece, Hepworth's piece providing the title for the commission. His enthusiasm is evident in his letter to Ronald Snoad and he visited the town at least twice looking for a theme for the piece.[3]

He requested a fee of £70–£75 to cover his writing of the piece, rehearsal time for the sextet – Collier, Frank Ricotti, John Marshall, Harry Beckett, Karl Jenkins and, new recruit, saxophonist and flautist Stan Sulzmann[4] – and other expenses. Collier had met both Ricotti and Sulzmann (and also saxophonist Alan Wakeman, who would join later in 1969) when he was working as a coach/tutor on a voluntary basis with the recently formed London Schools

Jazz Orchestra, which eventually became the National Youth Jazz Orchestra (see Heining 2012a: 87–90). In the event, the festival agreed to a fee of £85.

Stan Sulzmann, a fine saxophonist and composer in his own right, was very young when he joined Collier. Initially, Sulzmann was reluctant to be interviewed for this book because, as he says, he was never really a fan of Collier's writing and felt awkward about saying so in print. It will be clear later that he was not alone amongst Collier alumni in this respect. But like, for example, saxophonists Art Themen and Pete Hurt who have similar feelings, Sulzmann's remarks lend balance to the account. They also confirm the sheer professionalism and commitment that jazz musicians often bring even to situations outside their preferred modes of musical expression.

> Like many other musicians, I had an uneasy relationship with Graham's music. Looking at my career over the years, I think it's probably clear that Kenny Wheeler, John Taylor and Mike Gibbs were the musical approaches that I followed and which excited me. Having said that Graham was responsible for me getting regular gigs and playing and meeting, in fact, the players on that recording – for example, Karl Jenkins, Harry Beckett, John Marshall. But, sadly, I can't in all honesty endorse his music. Let's just say that he was an important person in my early attempts at playing and I'm very grateful for that.

As well as working in the group that would make *Down Another Road*, Sulzmann played in the *Workpoints* twelve piece and visited Hamburg with Collier to perform on West German television.[5]

> Yes, I was in the group including the twelve piece which had John Surman and Kenny Wheeler in it. That was where I got to play a piece of Kenny's called '25 Blue', which later became part of the legendary *Windmill Tilter* record with John Dankworth's band. That piece was the first time I had played Ken's writing, which really drew me in. And I was also part of the group that went to Hamburg for the legendary Hans Gertburg jazz programme *Jazz Workshop*. Ted Curson on trumpet and Pierre Cavelli on guitar were added to this line-up as well as Tony Roberts saxes/bass clarinet from the UK (Email Sulzmann/Heining 2015).

Contrapuntal Forms was never recorded, though a section of it was performed for a BBC broadcast in July 1968 (Jewell 1968). It is hard to know how successful Collier was in creating what was clearly intended to be a programme work. He was not the first composer in British jazz to produce such a work. Both John Dankworth and Kenny Graham did so – the eight tracks of Dankworth's

$1,000,000 Collection, also inspired by works of art, had come out in 1967. Graham's *Moondog and the Suncat Suites* (1956) drew on the work of New York street musician/composer Louis 'Moondog' Hardin, as well as Graham's own compositions to create a musical picture of Moondog and New York. Nor was Collier alone in his desire to open up jazz in terms of its potential subject matter or belief that jazz could and should concern itself with worlds outside its immediate domain – one thinks immediately here of Mike Westbrook, Michael Garrick and Stan Tracey.

Collier's notes for the composition describe a day in the town using the five sculptures as staging points. He writes:

> Contrapuntal Forms is, of course, the name of the statue by Barbara Hepworth, which is situated in Glebelands, Harlow. I have used it as the title for this suite not only for that reason and the obvious musical connotations but because of the counterpoint between sculptures and their environments in Harlow. Both the sculpture and the situation can exist separately but when placed together they complement each other and make something larger than the separate parts (Collier 1968a).

Collier was clearly using another art form both to reflect upon his own ideas about form in composition and on the contrapuntal relationship in his music between written music and improvisation. This was the second example – the other being the reference to Durrell in the context of *Workpoints* – where Collier explained his approach to composing in such a way. A pattern was already established that he would continue to develop in his later work.

The agreement with the Jackson brothers for *Deep Dark Blue Centre* went no further than that recording. In July 1969, Collier concluded a deal with what was then the Dutch-owned Phillips Record Company. This involved a deal for one recording with an option for a further two-year contract, meaning in effect two further releases should artist and record company pick up the option. Between 1969–71, Collier would record three albums for the company – *Down Another Road* (1969), *Songs For My Father* (1970) and *Mosaics* (1971). They are all remarkable and different albums, albeit clearly from the same pen. The first two of these came out on Phillips' subsidiary, Fontana – home of Dankworth, Cleo Laine, tenorists Tubby Hayes, Dick Morrissey and Ronnie Scott. In 1970–71, Phillips dropped the Fontana imprint when it introduced its 'progressive' label Vertigo, so *Mosaics* came out on the main Phillips imprint.

Down Another Road is perhaps Collier's most accessible release, which might explain why one number, 'Aberdeen Angus', featured on the rock group Babyshambles' CD of their favourite tracks, *Back to the Bus*. Frank Ricotti had moved on by this point and the group, still a sextet, now included trombonist Nick Evans. Prior to joining the group, Evans had depped for Chris Smith in the *Workpoints* band at one of the later London gigs in 1968 and, with that and the Barry experience behind him, was a 'shoe-in'.

According to Evans and John Marshall, the sextet was gigging reasonably regularly and on *Down Another Road* the impression is of a band that knows the material and understands fully Collier's *modus operandi* as a composer and bandleader. The album was recorded over two days in March 1969 and seems drenched in Collier's love of the blues but coupled with a sensibility that accommodates the new sounds and rhythms of rock. According to Collier, Harry Beckett had suggested to him that, 'I was one of the first to use rock rhythms in jazz...' (Interview Collier/Wickes 1986) and there was already some evidence of this on *Deep Dark Blue Centre*, notably on 'Crumblin' Cookie'. However, *Down Another Road* emphasized this still further on the title track, 'Aberdeen Angus' and 'Molewrench'. In fact, the feel of these numbers – and that of Karl Jenkins' compositional contribution to the set, 'Lullaby for a Lonely Child' – is not unlike that of Ian Carr's Nucleus, with whom both Jenkins and Marshall would later play.

For John Marshall, Collier brought change into the group and the fabric of the music by changing the musical personalities:

> That was definitely a case of people coming out with different approaches. The groove, the rock thing on 'Aberdeen Angus' was something to do with me, I think. 'Barley Mow', I remember trying to think of something different, not playing it like a normal ballad, so I used those wind chimes. It was that kind of thing. It was a feeling of trying to get something a little bit different and I think there was probably that kind of feeling for everybody in the band at that time (Interview Marshall/Heining 2014).

The title track is a twelve-bar blues, which shifts between 5/4 and 4/4 but with a bar of 3/4 before it returns to 5/4. This tendency to move between time signatures, not entirely uncommon in modern jazz, is a regular feature of Collier's writing, at this point – and it makes it hard sometimes to be precise about the time signature of particular numbers. Marshall's drumming is perfect in this context, going far beyond the use of the backbeat to mark the second and fourth and then adding fills, more a case of *perpetuum mobile*. Nick Evans solos first, with Beckett and Sulzmann playing the theme behind him. Sulzmann follows on tenor – amazingly just twenty at the time – backed by the rhythm section, with Jenkins seeming to channel Herbie Hancock in his comping behind the solo. What strikes the listener immediately is the confidence and swagger of both Evans and Sulzmann. It makes for a fine opening statement.

'Danish Blue', the most 'out' and longest piece on the album, follows. Collier's original sleeve notes state that the tune was 'written' for the Danish Radio Jazz Group in 1968, when he was invited to work with the band for a series of broadcasts of his music, the first British jazz composer to do so. He points out that very little of the material was scored, adding that the 'overall form is controlled, the inner form is left to the players at the time' (Collier 1968c). In a way, it plays a similar role here to that played by 'Deep Dark Blue Centre' on the previous record, acting as an opportunity for the musicians to 'show their stuff'. Collier makes extensive use of his much-loved cadenzas here, first with Nick Evans, then Beckett, each cadenza serving to introduce the next phase in the performance of the tune. The weighting of each solo is crucial here and the impression of the musicians listening intently to each other is palpable, as if one slip in concentration and its flimsy fabric would unravel. Despite its free opening and brief snatch of collective improvisation, the piece is essentially a slow-moving ballad. Evans' solo is stately and graceful, reflective and just the right side of mournful. A wild duet between Jenkins (on oboe) and John Marshall lends the piece a strong North African feel before Collier joins on bass and the pace increases dramatically. Beckett's solo here is a classic of melodic ingenuity filled with fluttering semi-quavers. There is a lovely moment towards the end of his solo where Jenkins' oboe joins Beckett's flugelhorn with an accompanying counter-melody. Again, the reference point is Miles Davis' *Kind of Blue* – not in terms of its sound or vibe but in terms of the lesson that Collier took from the record that less can sometimes be more.

'The Barley Mow' is Collier's pastoral ode to England written whilst far from home in Boston and evokes perfectly Collier's memories of English pubs and real ale. In his notes for the reissue of the album on Beat Goes On Records in 2007, Alyn Shipton mentions both Elgar and Vaughan Williams in relation to the track, referring perhaps to the mixture of timbral and harmonic palette that makes the piece so redolent of these composers (Shipton 2007).

Shipton's point is well-made and, indeed, one hears elements of these same composers – and Gustav Holst – in much British jazz of the period and since. Here such thoughts are perhaps also evoked by the interlocking melody lines, the way sax and trombone play sustained, bar-length notes behind Beckett's flugelhorn, the part played by the bass in maintaining a steady pulse without ornamentation and, finally, in the contrast between the timbres of brass and woodwinds, notably in the duet between Jenkins' oboe and Beckett.

'Aberdeen Angus' is something else again. The staccato notes from the frontline over the rhythm sections vamp create an impression of speed over what is actually a moderate underlying tempo, with Jenkins' chord voicings adding further musical interest. Yet the impression given by both Harry Beckett and John Marshall is ferocious indeed, with Marshall's drum solo a masterclass of controlled violence.

Karl Jenkins' 'Lullaby' represents one of the last occasions on which Collier would record a piece by another composer. Jenkins' tune is interesting for the intersection throughout of two melody lines, a lead line played by the horns and followed by the drums and second line from the piano and bass. The pace is, given that it is a lullaby, slow whilst the accompaniment to Stan Sulzmann's heartfelt tenor solo is poised and flowing. Finally, there is 'Molewrench'. Again, the comparison with early Nucleus seems apt. A steady, strolling pace is sustained throughout. Bass and drums combine well with nice cymbal work from Marshall. Jenkins solos first on oboe, stretching the instrument towards its higher register and beyond. Nick Evans follows, offering an immediate contrast by replacing the serpentine sounds of the oboe with something more like a minotaur in full cry. The volume builds as Jenkins adds short, stabbing chords from the piano, as the other horns return and the track fragments to a close.

Down Another Road garnered even better reviews than its predecessor. Bob Dawbarn writing in *Melody Maker* commented, 'In many ways, Collier's music is the perfect link between the older established forms of modern jazz of the 1950s and early '60s and the more free things of today'. He referenced both Mingus and Ellington in the review but added, 'But onto such influences he has granted a definite personality and style of his own and his arrangements give plenty of scope for his musicians to express their own selves' (Dawbarn 1969: 19). That doyen of jazz critics Charles Fox wrote of the sextet, 'These are the men Collier is used to working with, and around whose unique talents he composes his music, involving their identities within a larger more significant whole. It goes without saying that I warmly recommend this record' (Fox 1969b).

Mention above of Mingus and Ellington and the reference above to Miles Davis' *Kind of Blue* are reminders that Collier was always quite clear on his musical influences. Herb Pomeroy had been a profoundly significant figure during his time at Berklee and would continue to influence Collier throughout his career, not least in his role as a jazz educator. However, as a jazz composer, the influences are quite specific and we can identify the parts played by Duke Ellington, Miles Davis, Charles Mingus, Gil Evans and perhaps even Count Basie in the development of his music. One can also hear the influences of New Orleans jazz in Mingus' interest in collective improvisation and in Collier's use of the same technique. We can hear, as well, the way the Basie band used background riffs and the inspiration of Ellington in Collier's interest in orchestral textures (Collier 2009a: 239–40).

It is almost impossible to imagine what jazz composition might have been without Ellington. 'Ellingtonian' is a much used adjective in many a critic's vocabulary. With regard to Ellington, Collier did not see his work and that of his close colleague Billy Strayhorn as being separate entities but rather two bodies of interlinking work, each corpus informing the other. Collier admired Strayhorn greatly as an artist and as an individual. There are many specific references to him in *The Jazz Composer* (2009a). Strayhorn brought fresh colours to Ellington's music, apparently introducing him to Ravel and Debussy.

Like many other jazz composers, Collier took from Ellington a sense of how the jazz orchestra sounded, of how different instruments could be combined to create new and exciting colours and moods, an understanding of how individual voices might be used to achieve particular musical goals and might become the means for transforming what was written on the paper into something fresh and spontaneous. Time and again, one hears in Collier's music passages that are distinctly 'Ellingtonian'. However, any reasonably skilled composer can imitate. What Collier took from Ellington was not just a 'what' but a 'how' and one that Collier realized needed always to be approached critically and self-critically. Finally, Collier saw in Ellington's music the epitome of jazz as an art form deserving of the same respect accorded to European art music but, and this is crucial, according to its own distinctive set of musical values.

The influence of Miles Davis is more indirect perhaps on Collier's own music. One can certainly hear this in the first two albums, *Deep Dark Blue Centre* and *Down Another Road*, and to a lesser extent in Collier's other small group recordings. If *Kind Of Blue* was for Collier quintessential Miles, we can hear echoes of this less in terms of Collier attempting to follow Davis' exploration of modes but more in relation to his deployment of his resources and in terms of the way musical moods are created. There is also, particularly in respect of *Deep Dark Blue Centre*, a similar sense of detachment, of understatement, of reflection and of music emerging organically. This is something that Collier clearly took from *Kind of Blue* and the later quintet records with Herbie Hancock, Ron Carter, Wayne Shorter and Tony Williams. More importantly, Collier also realised that the notion of 'less as more' meant taking risks in the studio and on the stand. This realization would lie at the heart of Collier's dictum that 'jazz happens in real time, once'.

In relation to Davis and *Kind of Blue*, Collier notes in *The Jazz Composer* that the record is 'both literally and figuratively' at the 'heart of this book'. The record was, for Collier as for others, the watershed between what had been and what could be in terms of jazz. Not only were musicians 'empowered to transform the tune away from being solely a starting point for improvising', but what was possible in terms of how the music could be structured was changed utterly. Before *Kind of Blue* what passed for arrangements in jazz terms related to the 'practical function of many large groups as dance bands'. This, in turn, 'led to formalised methods – essentially block voicings in the various sections or the whole ensemble that are still in use today'. Now however, 'post-*Kind of Blue* arrangers have, as with the tune, been empowered to change the parameters' (Collier 2009a: 8–9). What this would mean for Collier, in terms of his own compositions, was that the whole notion of arrangement changed from the singular to the plural. A composition could be rearranged time and again to, in effect, make it anew.

Similar points could arguably be made in respect of Ornette Coleman – and here in the UK with Joe Harriott. Collier never acknowledged Harriott's work and, in *The Jazz Composer*, is disparaging of Coleman's later work but complimentary when it comes to the saxophonist's late fifties/early sixties records. One would also argue that George Russell and Gil Evans – and others such as Gerry Mulligan, Eddie Sauter (earlier) and Gary McFarland (later) – challenged the notion that 'the practical function of many large groups' by 1959 and afterwards was that of 'dance bands'. Russell, after all, was a major influence on Miles Davis' thinking with *Kind of Blue*. Collier admired Evans and Mulligan. However, he had a number of quite strong musical prejudices and, at times, was lacking in the capacity to be objective when it came to certain other composers. Collier acknowledged this when he wrote of Russell and Thelonious Monk, 'This has, obviously, been a personal look at jazz and jazz composition. I have had some harsh things to say about other jazz composers. Some, because like Thelonious Monk and George Russell, because, no matter how hard I try, I cannot like what they do' (Collier 2009a: 313; see also p. 252). Indeed, one of the most serious criticisms of *The Jazz Composer* is that it ignores far too many significant 'jazz composers' in its 300 plus pages.

What Collier gained from listening to Count Basie was quite simple. It was both the idea that jazz could be created on the stand by musicians sympathetic to the leader's aims and, sonically, it was the effortless way the early Basie band was able to create 'a constant series of riffs behind the soloists' (Collier 2009a: 32). In fact, reviewing Basie's 1965 LP, *Basie Picks the Winners* for *Crescendo*, Collier makes a further valid point about what he gained from the bandleader:

> One of the most revealing moments I've had listening to jazz came at the Newport Jazz Festival in 1961. Basie sat down at the piano... and within *three notes* the band was swinging. I'm still not sure *how* he does it (although I think Freddie Green may know), but he can *always* do it – and he doesn't need noise or several choruses to get into it. He arrives...and it happens (Collier 1965: 15; emphasis original).

Like Basie, when Collier wanted something to happen in his music, he just did it without preamble. Given how much the Basie band directly influenced much contemporary big band music, Collier's appreciation of Basie offers a certain paradox here. However, he was clearly making a statement about what he saw as valuable in Basie's approach, whilst rejecting what he saw as its ossification by some composers. For example, he was critical of Thad Jones and even more so of Jim McNeely and Sammy Nestico, whom he saw as aping with much formality music that was created spontaneously by Basie and his musicians (Collier 2009a: 1–2, 66–67). A matter of those 'block voicings' continuing past their use-by dates, referred to earlier.

When it comes to Gil Evans, Collier was inspired by the ways in which Evans changed the parameters of what might be considered jazz. In *The Jazz Composer*, Collier examines in detail two compositions – 'Saeta' from the *Sketches of Spain* album and 'Zee Zee' from the Gil Evans' records, *Svengali* and *Live at the Public Theater New York 1980 Volume II* – but also references the version of Gershwin's 'Summertime' from the Davis/Evans' collaboration, *Porgy and Bess*.

'Saeta' drew on flamenco and Spanish religious song. The *saeta* itself is sung by a woman during the processions of Holy Week and tells of Christ's passion. Evans created in the piece a sense of the processional but also uses Davis as the improvising soloist to convey that same sense of piety and passion. Collier writes: 'What we hear in "Saeta", as well as Arabic scales, fascinating textural backgrounds, and evocations of something "Spanish", is jazz composition being moved into new realms of possibilities.' What was new here was that Evans had created a composition 'that has different aims than the integration *within* accepted jazz traditions of what's written with what's improvised. A composition in which composer and soloist combine to portray an idea *outside* jazz' (Collier 2009a: 227; emphasis original).

With 'Zee Zee', Collier notes, there is very little to the composition 'on paper, or conceptually, but there is just enough for these two great jazz performances to be created' (Collier 2009a: 259). In terms of 'Summertime', the key element for Collier was the way Evans found 'a simple riff' and then repeated this 'almost always with different orchestration' under 'Miles's theme statement and solo' (Collier 2009a: 210).

The frequent Spanish tinges that one hears in Collier's music, often provided by the guitar of Ed Speight, drew upon Evans' love of those Arabic scales and 'evocations of something "Spanish"'. Even without his translation of the second movement of Rodrigo's *Concerto de Aranjuez* on *Sketches of Spain*, it would be hard not to think of Rodrigo and Ravel listening to Evans' music at times. Though it must be added here that Mingus also loved those Spanish colours. There are also textural qualities in Collier's music that echo Evans' work. But the main influence from Evans, as with Ellington and Mingus, was of what was possible in jazz, that there was simply a better way than block voicings and theme-solo repetitions. And jazz might also be about something outside its own self-referential terms.

With Mingus, the obvious starting point is the fact that Collier was inspired by Mingus' example that a band could be led from the bass, rather than the piano or lead horn. Mingus heard Ellington's music in a totally fresh and distinctive way and perhaps listening to Mingus aided Collier in hearing Ellington afresh. Mingus' biographer, Brian Priestley, is well aware of the *ex parte* dialogue that went on between the music of Mingus and that of Ellington. Quoting Martin Williams from *The Jazz Tradition*, Priestley writes:

> The parallel with Duke is illuminating in another way: the critic Martin Williams has written: 'As [Ellington's] message of form began to take effect, revolutionary improvisers arrived. The maturing of Ellington's sense of form was followed by Parker's innovations, but Ellington had a lot to do with planting the seeds'. At the time, however, this fact was hardly very widely recognised and, while Mingus is clearly the only pre-'free'-jazz composer of whom the equivalent could be said, even the musicians whose freedom he had licensed tended to ignore his role in stretching the conventions of the time (Priestley 1982: 71).

Later in the book, Priestley makes an intriguing point about Mingus' *The Black Saint and the Sinner Lady*. He notes,

> *The Black Saint and the Sinner Lady* is not only the most monumental of Mingus' works but the one which most nearly combines his various compositional approaches in a convincing whole. It is also at the same time his most Ellingtonian piece and his least Ellingtonian.

Priestley points to the various direct references to Ellington and draws attention to Mingus' intention from the outset to create a coherent and unified work of LP length and his use of overdubbing in its creation. However, the key differences for Priestley were:

> [T]he basic simplicity of the materials and their polyrhythmic development, the structural use of passages with accelerating tempo or with no tempo, the fact that *all* the improvised solos are modal (many of them based on the favourite 'Spanish scale')[6] – these show how far the work is a product of Mingus' own experience and experimentation (Priestly 1982: 145–46).

Collier also saw *Black Saint* as a seminal composition, as he noted in *The Jazz Composer*: '*The Black Saint and the Sinner Lady* is a work that typifies Mingus' methods. In six movements, and thirty-eight minutes long, it is one of the most successful longer works in jazz' (Collier 2009a: 232).

There is a direct correspondence between what Priestley describes with Mingus as 'the basic simplicity of materials' and 'the structural use of passages with accelerating tempo or with no tempo' and Collier's work. Collier had read Priestley's biography of Mingus and refers to it several times in *The Jazz Composer*, in which he makes it clear that Priestley's perspective on Mingus accorded with his own. Most significantly, he quotes a long passage from the biography where Priestley points out how Ellington had taken key elements from the vocabulary and syntax of New Orleans jazz and swing styles and applied this in the development of his compositional approach. Priestley adds that Mingus took this further still in applying it to 'the more rigid and complex language of bebop, and to the more insistent virtuosity of its players' (Priestley 1982: xi). Billy Strayhorn once remarked that Ellington's achievements could be summed up as, 'Duke simply thought of a better way'. To this, Collier adds a corollary, '[B]ut Mingus went further, allowing the musicians to think for themselves, to add their individuality to what he had written. He was willing to trust his musicians, and accept the consequences' (Collier 2009a: 138). This offers a neat summation of Collier's own approach.

One other technique that Collier took from Mingus – though he also refers to Miles Davis' use of this on 'Walkin'' and 'Nefertiti' – is what he calls 'shadowing', that is, 'when more than one soloist interprets the melody in his or her own way, adding their own textures and timing to the written notes'. He continues, 'Mingus, too, used this technique, what critic Andrew Homzy called "loose togetherness", as part of his music. Something similar was seen in early New Orleans jazz, where it could have been due to a lack of musical skills in playing together' (Collier 2009a: 276–77). One suspects that Archie Shepp also borrowed in this respect from Mingus in his mid-sixties recordings. Finally, Collier was inspired by Mingus' ability to juxtapose effectively beautifully lyrical, gentle passages of music with freer, wilder interludes. In fact, when one hears a Basie-like section – certainly in works such as *Hoarded Dreams* and *Charles River Fragments* – one also hears the way Mingus would intersperse the sound of a traditional jazz big band with charts more akin to the 'new music' of Coltrane, Shepp, Coleman and others. It is worth recalling here Val Wilmer's insightful comment from her review of *Workpoints*: 'It's also, probably because it's British, rather more *gentlemanly* than Mingus' writing while being just as exciting in its own way' (Wilmer 1968: 37, emphasis original).

Four of these artists (I do not include Basie here), who inspired and influenced Collier had something else in common. They were all concerned with texture in music. There are many improvisers in jazz, whom we may recognize for their distinctive *imprimatur* but far fewer jazz composers, or in Davis' case *auteurs* perhaps, whose sound is as instantly recognizable as Ellington, Davis, Mingus and Gil Evans. We recognize the tonal qualities of their music, the colours and timbres, that is, those things that create musical texture. This was always important to Collier as well. One hears it as early as *Deep Dark Blue Centre* but perhaps less so with later/mid-period albums such as *New Conditions* and *Symphony of Scorpions*. However, the concern with texture really came into its own with later albums such as *Bread & Circuses*, *The Third Colour* and *Winter Oranges*. Finally, here, we should note Collier's developing notion of what he would call 'jazz form', a form that could and should be determined by the almost dialectical relationships between the composer and the individual personalities of his musicians, between what was written and what was improvised and which could and should be fluid and spontaneous.

* * *

Keeping a band together is a perennial problem for bandleaders. The nature of the business is such that there is never enough work to sustain a jazz group, so musicians take work in other settings and play regularly in other bands. For groups playing mainly standards, this is less of a problem, which is why so much live jazz draws on 'The Great American Songbook'. With composers like Collier, Westbrook, Mike Gibbs or Michael Garrick, this becomes much more of an issue. As John Marshall explains, with typical ingenuity, Collier came up with a simple solution:

> He was a kind of problem-solver. The way you survived on the scene then was nearly everybody did all sorts of gigs and were in several bands. So, obviously you got clashes and it could have been a big problem and it potentially was. But Graham at one point solved that to a large extent by designating gigs as 'A', 'B' or 'C' (Laughing). 'A' that meant you really had to do that gig. 'B' was negotiable and 'C', if you got someone else to do it that would be okay (Interview Marshall/Heining 2014).

The same ingenuity extended to finding new ways of funding tours and out-of-town gigs. One favoured method was to take jazz into schools, as Nick Evans remembers:

> I also recall the mornings which the sextet spent in UK secondary schools as we toured round the country playing clubs and colleges in the evenings. Graham set up mini-lectures for school children during the empty days when the sextet would demonstrate various jazz styles and answer questions from the floor. I recall Harry Beckett playing a short piece in the style of Louis Armstrong, whereas I had to play a Mingus piece as if I were Jimmy Knepper! However, the additional wages provided by these morning school lectures made the tour financially viable. Tours in the UK came up quite regularly and they were enjoyable with Stan Sulzmann, Karl Jenkins and myself having many laughs (Email Evans/Heining 2014; see also Collier c. 1967).

It was pianist/bandleader Michael Garrick who first had the idea of taking jazz into school, when he formed his 'Travelling Jazz Academy' in 1965.[7] Both he and Collier also saw this as an essential aspect of the promotion of jazz to future generations. And as Evans says, it clearly had the added advantage of subsidizing his band. According to an article by Dave Kennard in *Peace News* in 1968, the anarchist and pacifist weekly newspaper, Collier began writing to local education authorities proposing the idea of 'educational jazz concerts' in schools in 1965. The first such concert took place at a school in Barking in July 1966. By the time of Kennard's article, Collier's group had notched up some twenty concerts in London, Buckinghamshire, Sussex, Suffolk and Yorkshire. The template that Collier had devised involved a lecture on jazz, as well as a concert performance (Kennard 1968). It was this model that would later provide the basis for an innovative package that Collier devised comprising an educational book on jazz, coupled with two LPs – one a jazz concert and the other a record demonstrating different jazz styles and approaches – and a backing tape, with which students could play along.

Alan Wakeman would replace Stan Sulzmann in the band and also remembers that, at the time, the group had plenty of work – subsidized by the school lectures and concerts.

> I remember him giving me this itinerary and it was about three months' work, which is quite amazing now you think back. Three months' work for a small jazz group in and around the country and abroad...he used to take jazz to schools. We'd go up North and do a couple of schools in the day, when Graham would talk about jazz and we'd play and that would subsidize the visit to a Newcastle jazz club or somewhere like that.

And he adds, (laughing), 'I remember saying to Tony Oxley one time, "How come Graham gets all this work?" Tony said, "Because no-one else could be bothered with it"' (Interview Wakeman/Heining 2014).

Collier, as noted, also worked with the London Schools Jazz Orchestra and later when it became the National Youth Jazz Orchestra. When NYJO came to record its first LP in 1971, Collier contributed the tune 'Gay Talk'. Its title was actually inspired by the sound of pigeons in his loft, as Geoff Castle, one of the original pianists with LSJO/NYJO explains: 'He actually took this pattern down and used it. I've got this feeling it might have been in 6/4. Not the most common signature' (Interview Castle/Heining 2014).

As well as those we have mentioned already – Stan Sulzmann, Frank Ricotti, Alan Wakeman – Collier also recruited a number of other musicians through LSJO/NYJO, including saxophonist Bob Sydor, trumpeter Dick Pearce and pianist Geoff Castle, just as he had recruited Karl Jenkins and later Nick Evans from the Barry Summer School. Bob Sydor remembers Collier being there 'more or less at the beginning of the band' (Interview Sydor/Heining 2017), that is the LSJO, and Geoff Castle also recalls him as one of a number of musicians who gladly gave their time to the youth orchestra from its inception onwards:

> [I]t was very helpful and I think Graham over a period got quite involved in rehearsing the band. He always had a very good approach to leading the band and you thought when you were working with him it was very clear what he wanted. There were certain people who were very good at leading the band, Graham was one, Neil Ardley was another one who also came and there were a few other people as well who were also really excellent up front with the band. So, we were quite fortunate to have all these very skilled arrangers, composers and other people leading the band as guests, you know when they would bring their charts along for us to play. It was quite an education in itself... (Interview Castle/Heining 2014).

Collier's commitment to jazz education came from a conviction that jazz deserved its place in the academy and in the concert hall as an art music in its own right. This was clear in a brief article on jazz education he wrote for *Jazz Journal*, which included a photo of Collier rehearsing the London Schools Jazz Orchestra:

> We feel that Jazz is an important part of 20th-century culture and that certain forms of jazz should be accepted as an art form. There are signs that this is slowly happening – many newspapers, for example, which up to recent times confused jazz with pop music

> and cared little for either, now feature intelligent, well-written jazz articles in their columns. Not all that is presented as jazz should be written about in *The Times*, or discussed in schools, but it is important that the whole of jazz should be judged from an informed viewpoint and that the best of it be recognized as part of a current creative art form (Collier, citation unknown).

These three core beliefs – his almost evangelical commitment to jazz education, his belief in jazz as an art form and his dedication to proselytizing on behalf of the music he believed in – shaped his career in jazz. Each of these would be filtered through his own understanding of the role of the composer in jazz. These elements, in turn, combined into a performance aesthetic of jazz, not in the sense this might be used in Performance Studies with its emphasis on semiotics, but in relation to the musical content and the place of improvisation in all aspects of the jazz performance.

* * *

Collier's third album, *Songs For My Father*, was recorded in February 1970 and represented a refinement on its predecessors and also an advance in terms of Collier's objectives, which he defined in the sleeve notes:

> The new material is a series of musically connected pieces which can, by judicious use of linking cadenzas, be played in any order. Although the order was pre-determined for the recording, in performance we 'choose' as we go along.

He recognized that, 'these freedoms...could lead to embarrassing moments', but that when they worked, they enabled the writer/bandleader to retain overall control 'while still allowing the musicians their own freedom and to allow the occasion to dictate some of the content' (Collier 1970a). The record represented a departure in several other respects. Firstly, the sextet or septet would henceforth be called Graham Collier Music. Collier defines the reason for this in terms of his 'desire to free myself from the necessity of *having* to work with six people because of the associations of the word "sextet"', and to allow him, as on *Songs*, to bring in guest musicians.

Secondly, the cover states that the music is by 'Graham Collier Music featuring Harry Beckett', a mark of respect and gratitude on Collier's part to the Barbadian-British trumpeter. In January 1970, Collier had also contributed three tunes to Beckett's debut LP, *Flare Up* – 'Go West', 'Third Road' and 'Rolli's Tune'. Beckett, however, had mixed feelings about the tribute Collier was paying him. As he explained, he found it something of a tie:

> What happened with Graham was that he respected what I was doing because he played trumpet as a young man. So, he understood what was involved with the instrument. The people that use me do so because they like what I'm doing on the trumpet. He started featuring me and the problem with that was when he did it and started putting that out to the media that's dangerous because I'm a freelance musician. You can't do that and expect me to be at every gig (Interview Beckett/Heining 2008).

Thirdly, the record featured a number of guests, including saxophonists Alan Skidmore and Tony Roberts, trombonist Derek Wadsworth and guitarist Phil Lee. Finally, aside from Collier and Beckett, the otherwise wholly new six-piece group now included Bob Sydor on alto and tenor, Alan Wakeman on tenor and soprano, John 'Chick' Webb on drums and John Taylor on piano.

John Marshall had left the group and had taken Karl Jenkins with him (Interview Collier/Wickes 1986). As Marshall tells the story, 'He wasn't too pleased, when I said, "Look, I quite fancy doing Nucleus, as the main band". He just said to me, "If it was anybody else I'd be mad". (Laughing) Because we always got on pretty well' (Interview Marshall/Heining 2014). Nick Evans' leaving was also amicable, prompted by an increasing range of offers from Keith Tippett, Chris McGregor and Soft Machine. In fact, there is a strong thread linking Collier and Nucleus and Soft Machine. Collier alumni who would play with Nucleus included Marshall, Jenkins, Evans, Geoff Castle, Alan Wakeman and saxophonist Brian Smith,[8] while Evans, Marshall, Jenkins and Wakeman would all play with Soft Machine.

The track titles run from 'Song One' to 'Song Seven' and Collier helpfully noted most of the time signatures on the sleeve. The record title was a dedication to Collier's father Jack, who had died in 1969, aged just sixty-five. Alan Wakeman tells a story about the recording session, which says something about the kind of banter on the scene but also about Collier's standing as a bass player:

> Yeah, it was an interesting experience. I can remember that my track was done in one take. I remember feeling quite pleased – the one that featured soprano. It was one that we'd played on gigs. It's always a bit nerve-wracking in studios, hoping you don't have to do anything again. That went off quite smoothly. The silly things being said. Alan Skidmore was on it. I think the trio – Graham, John Taylor and Chick Webb were playing at one point and we were listening in the studio. This was a bit derogatory but Skidmore said to me, 'That sounds like McCoy Tyner, Elvin Jones and Graham Collier' (Laughing) (Interview Wakeman/Heining 2014).

Actually, the rhythm section sounds pretty good and holds to the complex time signatures and the sometimes furious pace well. Several musicians, fond of Collier and respectful though they were of his music, have expressed doubts about his bass playing. Collier stopped playing bass in his groups around 1977, from that point on conducting or directing his groups or playing additional keyboards. Guitarist Ed Speight's working career included stints with songwriter Ian Dury. He joined Collier in 1972 and, on the subject of Collier's bass playing, remarked,

> I think it was kind of a relief when he decided to give up playing the bass to concentrate more on writing. There was certainly a lot of relief from the drummer. Chick Webb – sometimes, I don't know how he survived, if you like. So, there was a generally shared sense of, 'Ah!' (Laughing). But I'm sure I'm not the only person to have mentioned that (Interview Speight/Heining 2014).

John Marshall is a little more generous:

> To be frank, he wasn't the greatest bass player in the world. But, you know, he was okay. A lot of the things were odd time signatures. They were his things which he was comfortable playing. And you know, in a sense, it made me a stronger player because you had to be stronger to make it work. But it was fine, I got on with him personally. He could be grumpy and all that – a lot of people didn't like that all that much – but he was fine. Musically it worked out. Sometimes people's limitations force things to become creative in a different way. I didn't find it a very great problem. I've worked with some of the great bass players and he wasn't the most fabulous bass player but for his music it worked (Interview Marshall/Heining 2014).

When interviewed, John Webb offered a different perspective again:

> As far as Graham's bass playing was concerned, I can only recall one occasion, when the bass speaker was right behind me, and the time was <u>VERY</u> questionable. Whether it was always like that and I couldn't hear it, or just an off night? But on the records it sounds okay to me (Email Webb/Heining 2015; emphasis in original).

Any such difficulties are unlikely to be immediately apparent on *Songs*. If anything, the sheer power and force of the music on these seven cuts is what strikes the listener most. There is less of an emphasis on rock rhythms here – a consequence perhaps of Marshall's departure – and a greater rhythmic flexibility. In fact, Marshall had recommended Webb to Collier as his replacement, as Webb explains:

> I was playing opposite John at an open air festival. When I came off the stand I overheard John saying something like, it was refreshing to hear someone playing in the style of Elvin. At the time I was also playing with an American rock band called Formally Fat Harry, who were experimenting with odd time signatures, as was Graham. As regards John and my styles at that time, I was trying to play more freely. But really what probably made our styles a bit different at the time, was the amazing John Taylor! And, of course, I was playing with another amazing player, the great Harry Beckett.

As an aside, Webb recalls a degree of self-doubt at the point when he joined Collier.

> Just before joining Graham, I was going through a bit of a crisis, both musically, and personally. I seemed to be losing some of my technical facility, after reaching a high. I tried to explain this to some of the musicians but I think I just seemed to piss them off, particularly Harry, who gave me a few pep talks, but really couldn't understand what I was on about (Email Webb/Heining 2015).

Such remarks make Webb's contribution to the group all the more remarkable. Perhaps those doubts pushed him even harder as a player. Despite Webb's apparent lack of confidence, there is no faulting his performances on *Songs For My Father* or on later recordings. Perhaps Collier's approach to composing, with his individual musicians very much in mind, helped settled any such nerves. As Webb explains,

> I think as a drummer you can only do so much with certain people. One of the great things about Graham's writing, in the earlier days anyway, was his appreciation of his players and he tended to write with our styles in mind. Later on, maybe it got a bit self-indulgent, but Graham, I think, always wanted to experiment, maybe [he was] a frustrated classical composer? (Email Webb/Heining 2015)

Once again, with *Songs For My Father*, it is extremely hard to distinguish what might have been written and what was improvised. That said, several of the tracks use quite lengthy introductions. For example, 'Song One' sets out the thematic material in the first two minutes, as the rhythm section plays a riff that is repeated at numerous points and the horns play a four-note motif and variations upon it before solos from Phil Lee, Harry Beckett and Alan Skidmore on soprano.[9] The sense is of a jazz that is modern, demanding of concentration but also accessible. 'Song Two' is a feature for Alan Wakeman on soprano, his sound and tone more North African than Skidmore's on the instrument.

Described by Collier as a ballad, the tempo in 4/4 has the feel of a slow march. The piece and Wakeman's performance is one of the high spots of the album. Wakeman solos against a simple motif from the other horns of six notes which rise and fall, whilst John Taylor's piano plays a succession of cascading, trilling notes. The piece is simple in form but also highly effective. 'Song Three' takes off at a lively pace. Whilst the listener is at first drawn to the solos of Derek Wadsworth on trombone and Harry Beckett on flugelhorn, it is the playing of the rhythm section that is crucial to the success of the piece. A blues in 9/8, 'Song Three' works because of the way the three rhythm players interact. Collier's task is to hold the pulse, a kind of walking bass with a skip at the final step. Taylor's role is freer. He is able to work around the rhythm, whilst offering harmonic support to the soloist using the basic chord sequence of the tune but also inverting the chords repeatedly to give a sense of a shifting harmonic base. John Webb, in turn, holds the pulse but is allowed to do so in ways that provide supple, loose-limbed but dynamic support to both his rhythm colleagues and to the soloist. John Taylor's own solo is powerfully rhythmic but rich in harmonic interest.

On the sleeve, Collier describes 'Song Four' as a waltz in 4/4 time. One presumes that he was being playful here, knowing full well that waltz time is 3/4. Nevertheless, it does sound remarkably like a waltz.[10] Collier's love of the cadenza surfaces once more with both Beckett and Bob Sydor on tenor given the spotlight. Taylor's chords stab away over polyrhythmic drumming from Webb. There is a contrast between the ways in which Beckett and Sydor work with the rhythm of the piece. Sydor essentially plays with the rhythm, albeit at times quite freely, whereas Beckett plays against the rhythm section. Webb's drum solo provides a wonderful release of tension before the theme returns, interpreted loosely by the horns. 'Song Five' is rhythmically the loosest piece here. The theme is stated at some length before Roberts solos briefly on tenor and is then joined by both Wakeman and Skidmore for an extended passage of free improvisation. Webb and Taylor are also given free rein here and Webb, in particular, seems to relish the freedom. The theme returns almost as abruptly as it was discarded, with Beckett's trumpet soaring above the other instruments. It is one of the most dramatic moments on the record.

Collier's sleeve notes describe 'Song Six' as a dirge. It opens with a brief solo from Beckett on flugelhorn before the piano and bass enter playing the theme softly. Beckett and Wakeman duet with the saxophonist on soprano before Sydor joins on tenor over a simple left-hand figure from Taylor. Musical interest here derives in part from the contrasting colours offered by the three horns and the melodies they each weave but also from the delicacy of the rhythmic accompaniment. The final piece, 'Song Seven', begins with a simple riff played by piano and bass and then moved up a tone. The horns briefly state the theme before a short solo statement from John Taylor. The horns then return working around the theme. Bob Sydor takes the first solo on tenor, his tone slightly acerbic and keening in the higher registers. This is one of the most straight-ahead sections on the whole record with something of a classic Coltrane quartet feel about it. The other horns, including Skidmore, pick up the original riff, whilst Sydor solos freely and briefly against that riff. John Taylor's solo is beautifully lyrical and strongly rhythmic, the parallel perhaps being McCoy Tyner, to take up Skidmore's barb about Collier's bass playing. The impression of Coltrane is increased inevitably by Skidmore's entry on tenor. Few saxophonists can do this sort of thing as well as he does. He has always been a strong rhythm player but he couples this with a highly inventive melodic sensibility. His solo here is packed with musical ideas that just seem to pour out of his horn. The return of the theme is brief and the piece ends abruptly to close the record.

Once more the critical response to the new record was largely positive. Steve Voce singled the record out for praise on Peter Clayton's BBC radio show *Jazz Notes* on 23 August 1970, and Charles Fox featured the album as his review record on his own BBC radio programme *Jazz Today* on 16 June 1970. Fox began by emphasizing how the 'best jazz composers' allow their soloists 'their head while still imposing a shape, an identity on the total performance'. Fox mentioned Jelly Roll Morton, Ellington and Mingus and made a direct link to 'the school of young British jazz composers that we've got in our midst, including the man whose new LP is our review record today, Graham Collier'. There were good reviews too from Richard Williams in *Melody Maker*, despite its apparently nay-saying title ('Strong solos on Collier's slight themes', Williams, R. 1970) and from Ron Brown in *Jazz Journal* (Brown 1970). One dissenting voice came from Jack Carter writing in *Crescendo*. Carter hoped that, 'under the able direction of as fine a musician as Graham Collier, the experiments presented here will eventually bring forth jazz music with heart to balance the brain' (Carter 1970: 29). There was also a rather strange review amongst Collier's papers by Michael James. This rather missed the point and noted that *Songs*, 'whilst of mixed quality should be heard as an intelligent approach to the problem of enclosing *currently fashionable solo styles* within musically cohesive structures' (my emphasis). Essentially James was chiding Collier for placing too much emphasis on allowing his musicians their head (cf. Charles Fox's comment) and placing too little on the written aspects (James 1970: 12).

If Carter found *Songs* lacking in emotion, then he would surely never see his wish fulfilled in Collier's developing musical aesthetic. In a way, Collier was already moving on to the next phase. He was determined to keep working and writing and was prepared to follow unusual avenues to achieve that goal. One of the most unusual examples of this was a commission in 1969 by Universal Pictures to write and record the music for a documentary on the QE2 Cunard Liner launched that year. The fee, which included paying the studio musicians, the *Down Another Road* band plus bassists Ron Rubin and Chris Laurence on one session, came to £350. Sadly, despite several similar commissions, the film studios of Hollywood did not open to Collier, though he would later work on a number of film and documentary projects with producer/director/author David Cohen.

He was also proving successful in obtaining commissions for new compositions. In May 1969 the *Down Another Road* band performed *London Cryes* at the Collegiate Theatre in Gordon Street as a commission from the Camden Festival. Stan Tracey's Quartet and Marian Montgomery with the Laurie Holloway Quartet provided the other jazz interest at the festival. For this performance by Collier, Adrian Harmon was added on voice and guitar. The following February, the Graham Collier Music (this time the *Songs* band) performed *Smoke Blackened Walls and Curlews* at the Bradford Arts Festival. The thirty-minute work featured poems and readings from poets and authors including Ted Hughes, J. B. Priestley, Mrs Gaskell and socialist and early gay activist Edward Carpenter. All had connections to Yorkshire – Priestley with Bradford itself, Carpenter with Sheffield (where he had lived for several years with his partner George Merrill), Ted Hughes with the country around Halifax and Mrs Gaskell with Howarth through her biography of Bradford-born novelist, Charlotte Brontë. The readings were by actor John Carbery, who would narrate other similar Collier projects. Also on the bill was classical guitarist John Williams. The piece would go unreleased as a recording, though it was broadcast on BBC Radio Three in July 1971, though apparently under the title *Smoke-Blackened Walls and Purlieus*. Surely, some mistake!

Bearing in mind that this was essentially an example of programme music, a point not lost on Collier, his comments on the piece are instructive:

> One is often asked about the role of improvising in 'pictorial' music such as *Smoke Blackened Walls and Curlews* or indeed music for films and the theatre. In this kind of situation the improvising must, of necessity, be subordinate to the overall composition. The soloist's individual styles and personal mannerisms should be used simply as another part of the composer's technique. The composer must choose the improvising soloist very carefully for what he can add to a given situation and, if necessary, place verbal controls on that improvising. Then the work becomes a composition by a jazz composer –

a piece which utilises the devices of jazz, but, because of its subject matter, lets them colour – not dominate the whole (Collier 1970b).

This is interesting because it appears to go against much of what we have been saying about Collier's compositional methodology. Here, he seems to be making a distinction between the jazz composition, where its content is just the music, and jazz composition as part of a multi-media work. It is a distinction that makes most sense and would operate in later Collier works involving texts, as well as in his later work in theatre but which may also say something more general about his music and some musicians' reactions to it.

Notes

1. In terms of the Arts Council itself, this really took off, firstly, under Jeannie Lee, the first Minister of the Arts and who served in the post throughout the Wilson government from 1964–70 and later under Hugh Jenkins in the second Wilson government from 1974–76. Other incumbents have been distinctly less inspiring (see Hollis 1997; Jenkins 1979; Heining 2012a: 356–58). However, following the Second World War, pressures from below in all areas of social, political, economic and cultural life had driven widespread change. Alongside greater demands for fairer distribution of social and economic resources came demands for a democratization of culture.

2. Homosexuality was decriminalized in England and Wales with the passing of the Sexual Offences Act 1967. It was not, however, until 1980 in Scotland and 1982 in Northern Ireland that similar legislation was introduced.

3. Letter from Collier to Ronald Snoad, Harlow Festival, 26 May 1968.

4. The sextet performing at the Harlow Festival was Harry Beckett, Frank Ricotti, John Marshall, Karl Jenkins (misspelt in the programme notes as 'Lenkins') and newish recruit Stan Sulzmann (again misspelt as 'Sulzman') on tenor and alto saxes and flute. The set included *Contrapuntal Forms*, 'Deep Dark Blue Centre', Karl Jenkins' 'Lullaby for a Lonely Child', 'Down Another Road' and 'Danish Blue'.

5. See quote from Ian Carr's book *Music Outside* (1973) used at the beginning of Chapter 1.

6. In terms of tones and semi-tones, the Spanish 'Phrygian' scale or Phrygian dominant scale follows the distinctive pattern on 1-3-1-2-1-2-2, where 1 is a semi-tone, 2 is a tone and 3 is a whole tone plus an additional semi-tone. 'C' Phrygian dominant would be C - D♭ - E - F - G - A♭ - B♭ - C.

7. In fact, Michael Garrick did a great deal of work in schools and viewed this as a key element in creating new audiences for jazz (see for example Vacher 2011).

8. Brian Smith never recorded with Collier but was in the group at the time Alan Wakeman joined.

9. The sleeve notes for the Fontana LP and the BGO CD reissue have the soloist down as 'Alan Skidmore (tenor)' but it is clearly a soprano rather than tenor saxophone. 'Skid' is only credited on tenor, whilst Alan Wakeman is credited on both instruments. Alan Wakeman confirms that 'Song One' features Alan Skidmore on soprano.

10. I played it for my dance teacher and she is still trying to make sense of it!

5 Nil Desperandum – The Jazz Hustler

By the end of 1970, Collier's three recordings to date had conveyed the sense of a developing musical vision. At the same time, each album had, and has, a very different feel to it. This was something that Charles Fox remarked upon at the time (Fox 1970). If, however, Collier's previous albums had each in their own way broken new ground, his next – *Mosaics* – offered an even more clear statement of compositional intent. Alyn Shipton expressed this point very clearly in his sleeve notes for the BGO Records reissue of *Down Another Road, Songs For My Father* and *Mosaics*:

> By the time we come to *Mosaics*, conceived as two discrete but complimentary sides of an LP album, the idea of separate pieces as part of an extended composition had gone. Instead, Collier overtly chose a long form in which fluidity and change were the order of the day. From the fairly fully composed themes and forms of *Down Another Road* he had moved via 'connected pieces' to 'musical fragments', and an even more open decision-making process than in *Songs For My Father* (Shipton 2007).

Collier fought quite hard to persuade Phillips to agree to a live recording of the group playing this new composition (Interview Collier/Wickes 1986). In 1970, the cost and logistics of live recordings were far more of an issue than is the case today. The record was recorded at The Torrington pub in North Finchley[1] in December 1970, having been given its first performance in July at Wansfell College in Epping. The band members remained the same as for *Songs* but with the young Geoff Castle replacing John Taylor on piano. As mentioned, Castle had met Collier through the London Schools Jazz Orchestra and had paid for private lessons with him, as Castle recalled:

> This friend of mine and I both shared arranging lessons with Graham. So, Steve and myself used to go to Graham's flat in Seymour Place, basement flat in Seymour Place, and he would teach us some of the Berklee syllabus – arranging for horn sections, things like this, close harmony, the voicings that he used, stuff like that and how that worked. I think we were both about seventeen at the time.

> It was quite a help. We probably went to him for about three or four months for a weekly lesson. We split the cost between us. I think it was about seven shillings (35p). It was about 3/6 (17.5p) each (Laughing).

According to Castle, it was actually Harry Beckett who recruited him, albeit at Collier's request:

> My parents used to live in Newton Green, North London. Harry Beckett was a local chap who talked to my father outside his photographic shop and then one day, Harry Beckett says, 'Oh, Graham Collier is thinking of asking you to join his band' (Laughing). Then a couple of days later Graham phoned me up and said, 'Would you like to come for a rehearsal down at the Troubadour in Earl's Court?'

The *Mosaics* recording took place some six months after Castle joined the group. His description of how the music was organized explains Collier's developing approach:

> The way the music worked on *Mosaics* was that the actual compositional element was very minimal really, probably only two pages of manuscript for the whole thing but there were a lot of motifs. The idea was that the players would bring in the motifs and we would actually improvise on them and we would set up the structure at will. The idea was that it was a group improvisation that incorporated Graham's motifs, so it was quite a free approach to composition in that there was input but we had these little themes that were going to be played as part of the piece at some point (Interview Castle/Heining 2014).

As to how it was decided who would play at a particular point or when a specific theme or motif would occur or re-occur, Bob Sydor offers an explanation:

> Graham would call whichever number we were doing or which motif. Then, perhaps he would indicate to a player – a nod or wink – or the players and somebody would move to the mike. They would play and that was it. When you're on stage, you don't want to make a big deal about it. You don't want the audience distracted by the players chatting in the middle of a number about who was going to play next (Laughing). It worked very well. Graham would be nearer the piano and drums, so he could communicate with them and the rest of us would just follow. At other times, he would just go into something. We would recognise it – we had the music in front of us – and take it from there. The more you do it, the easier and more automatic it becomes.

Sydor left Collier after Mosaics to join the Maynard Ferguson Orchestra, touring all over America and beyond. It was not surprising given Collier's strong views about jazz that he was not impressed with Sydor's decision. 'He wasn't very happy about that', he said. 'He couldn't understand why I would want to join Maynard's band and do something like that' (Interview Sydor/Heining 2017).

Pianist and composer Roger Dean would play in various Collier small and large ensembles from the *Midnight Blue* album onwards. In his book *New Structures in Jazz and Improvised Music since 1960* (1992), he notes that *Mosaics*, and the next album *Portraits*, utilized a form that was increasingly modular. This means that the order in which the different modules were played could be varied from one performance to the next. Whilst the relationships between these different elements were often slight in comparison with later large-scale works, Dean points out that 'further links were created by the improvised cadenzas by individuals in the group, who then chose the subsequent section to be performed' (Dean 1992: 165). Therefore, by the time of *Mosaics*, Collier was already allowing the musicians a significant, if controlled, role in how the composition developed.

With the live recording, the band got to play two sets on successive nights, each one featuring *Mosaics* and with each set producing a remarkably different performance. The second set was not released at the time, eventually appearing in 2008 on a second BGO box set, which also included reissues of *Deep Dark Blue Centre* (from a recently discovered stereo master tape) and *Portraits* from 1972. There were apparently eight of the short, linking motifs but 'Theme 7', for some reason, was left out of both performances. It will be seen that the themes are performed outside their numerical sequence.

On the original album, Castle introduces 'Mosaics Part One: Theme 1' with a solo piano cadenza with trills from both hands leading into a series of arpeggios before bass and then drums enter.[2] The opening is essentially *rubato* but with the clear statement of the six-note theme, the piece settles into a 4/2 time signature, which shifts to a slow walking pace. The horns enter with John Webb roaming freely around the pulse. Harry Beckett solos first with just the rhythm section and the modal scale of the piece becomes increasingly clear half-way through the section. Over the remaining minutes of 'Part One', the dynamic of the piece begins quietly and softly before a crescendo/decrescendo. Beckett signs off 'Part One' with shrill upper-register notes. He opens 'Part Two' with a duet with Alan Wakeman on soprano sax. Wakeman picks up the beginning of 'Theme Four', his cadenza leading into the ballad section with 'Theme 2'. The tune resembles somewhat Young and Heyman's song 'When I Fall in Love' and at one point Wakeman appears to quote from Lerner and Loewe's 'On The Street Where You Live'. However, as he points out,

> I listened to the thing on *Mosaics* and I can hear me doing something that sounds like 'On the Street Where You Live' (but not quite) and the bit that sounds like 'When I Fall in Love' must have been Graham's theme because it crops up at the start of the in tempo section and at the end – pure coincidence. I don't think Graham would have suggested quoting someone else's tune during his composition (Email Wakeman/Heining 2015).

There are also several rather effective out-of-time passages during Wakeman's solo, notably at a third and at two-thirds of the way through the piece, which also serve to indicate how strong the rhythm section is here. Drummer John Webb picks up 'Theme 3' with a fine, free-flowing solo, which builds in intensity, as a cry from one audience member confirms, before a rapid shift in pace as piano, bass and horns pick up the theme. 'Theme 3' ends abruptly before Beckett reprises 'Theme 4' to open 'Part Three' of *Mosaics* with a fractured cadenza punctuated by high register squeals and slurs. It is hard to be sure but at certain points Beckett seems to refer back to motivic material from previous themes. A brief and rather lovely flugelhorn and bass duet follows as first Collier, then Beckett pick up the 4/4 Latin rhythm of 'Theme 6'. Webb joins on drums and piano and horns return, with the horns weaving complementary lines around the melody before the other horns drop out and Bob Sydor solos on tenor. Sydor's tone is quite dry and vibrato-less and his rapid-fire arpeggios, swing and timing are quite perfect for the loose feel that Collier seems to be aiming for here. Both Sydor and rhythm slow the pace slightly and bring the volume down. A brief tenor sax cadenza is followed by a duet with Wakeman, also on tenor. Wakeman's tone is broader and with more vibrato and this provides a neat textural contrast. The section ends gently and quietly to loud applause.

'Part Four' begins with 'Theme 2' but also echoes the beginning of *Mosaics*, opening as it does with an arpeggiated piano cadenza marked by a series of unresolved cadences. With the entry of the bass the theme is fully articulated with delicate accompaniment from Webb using brushes. This is one of the most lovely sections of the whole piece, even in its short *rubato* passage, as Castle draws every ounce of tenderness from the ballad. Castle then introduces 'Theme 8', which sounds like a very slow blues in 4/2. Harry Beckett comes in on trumpet squeezing choked, half-swallowed notes set against the long notes of piano and bass and march-like drumming from Webb. The two saxophones pick up the theme, which echoes 'Theme 1' in mood. The dynamic here is driven by increases and decreases in volume and the way the two saxes and trumpet move between higher and lower registers. As with other Collier compositions mentioned earlier, there is a distinct Spanish feel to this section, whilst Beckett's solo features a series of slurs and *glissandi*. A short free passage presages a further rise and fall in volume before an astonishingly long, low note from Beckett brings *Mosaics* to a close.

For a composition involving so little actual writing, *Mosaics* has a unity that extends easily across its four movements. What emerges into view is that elusive and rare creature in jazz – a fully-realized extended composition. According to Alan Wakeman, the piece came together quite easily and almost naturally:

> He kind of let us take the direction. We could move from one piece to another at our discretion rather than his. That was where the title came from, I think. It was like a patchwork of sounds. Anyone could solo on anything and could lead into one of the other sections.

In other hands or at other times, this could easily have produced music that seemed frantic, fractious and chaotic but Collier:

> ... enjoyed that challenge of not knowing quite which way it would go. He was quite open. He never actually stipulated what to do during anything, during the solos. He just gave you the vehicle and you did it. I think because the three frontline [players], because we'd learnt the stuff, it was easy to pick up on a direction that someone was taking (Interview Wakeman/Heining 2014).

It is as if the musicians somehow contained within them a sense of the architecture of the piece but were able to rebuild it in new forms at each performance. There is clearly a very different process involved from the free improvisational approach which Derek Bailey called 'non-idiomatic free improvisation'. In the latter, the musicians build a structure from materials that they bring but which are only made available in that performance and essentially for that performance. With Graham Collier's *Mosaics*, and in later compositions, the structure exists in embryonic form but its final shape is only arrived at in performance. Geoff Castle describes this process well:

> I think for the main part it was from the musicians but I think that Graham was also in there doing stuff as well. So, we were all contributing to where the things were played. The idea was to have a loose structure but there were some elements where everybody would play together...
>
> [The idea] was to integrate these motifs in with the improvisations so that it wouldn't necessarily be obvious but you would find, if you referenced the two evening sets, recognizable patterns that were there in both. But the whole idea was that there was no set

> pattern of where these motifs came so that the performances would be totally different.

And he continues,

> Graham really wanted everybody to express themselves in their own individuality. That was what he used to say. He wanted to have a band of individuals who were all expressing themselves directly inside the music and contributing to the overall composition (Interview Castle/Heining 2014).

Although sections of the second take had already been released by Italian mover-shaker Claudio Bonomi on the British jazz compilation *Elastic Jazz* in 2005 (Auditorium AUD02705), the BGO CD of the whole piece made it possible to see how this approach to open form worked in practice.[3] It is hard to imagine that the *Alternate Mosaics* did not involve some form of additional direction from its composer. Yet this seems not to have been the case. Both versions begin with 'Theme 1'. However, where the first version contains themes one to eight (minus seven) and reprises several of these during the performance, the second just uses themes one, six and eight and then only one in each section.

The *Alternate Mosaics* begins without the piano cadenza of its partner. The horns enter much earlier and state the theme before Wakeman solos with just rhythm accompaniment. There is an increase in volume after two and a half minutes and the band pick up a much faster tempo than on the original version. The feel is not unlike that of the classic Coltrane quartet and the accompaniment by Castle is quite magnificent with a selection of chords that is totally apt but also surprising and imaginative. A *rubato* passage towards the end signals a change in mood and Wakeman ends on one long note.

Castle begins 'Part 2: Theme 2' with a piano cadenza, which could be described as a fantasia on the theme. Beautifully poised, limpid notes and trills lead to descending and ascending lines with a strong blues feeling. The bass enters for a duet that is one of the most lovely moments in Collier's recorded career. Bob Sydor's tenor picks up the ballad after five minutes and there is some fine brush work from Webb. Sydor's tenor cadenza is joined by bass and drums and the trio pick up a quicker tempo before Castle joins with short stabbing chords. There is a moment here of about a minute in length (9:50–10:50) that shows just how good and underrated a musician Sydor was. His solo stands out for its rhythmic and melodic invention. 'Part 3: Theme 6' begins with a trumpet cadenza. As on the original release, the piece is based around a Latin rhythm and feel. The bass enters for a brief duet with Beckett before the bass states the theme. Piano and drums join and then the horns, Wakeman on soprano and Sydor on alto, weaving intersecting melody lines from the thematic material. Beckett then delivers one of those crackling solos that were his trademark, with rhythm accompaniment. The horns return before a short drum solo ends the section. 'Part 4: Theme 8' starts abruptly with the rhythm section and Tynerish chords from Castle. The pace is quite frantic but slows around three minutes in for a brief out-of-time piano cadenza before Collier and Webb join the piano. The pace is now funereal – even slower, it seems, than the first version. After a brief passage with all three horns, Beckett squeezes out a solo against the rhythm section marked by some very free drumming from Webb. The two other horns state the theme as the music builds to a crescendo followed by a sudden decrease in volume which leads to a free section with all three horns pushing ever higher before Beckett closes with a short phrase and a single note.

Several things will strike the listener. Firstly, certain aspects of the architecture recur. For example 'Theme 2' begins as a ballad in both cases before shifting to a much quicker tempo, whilst 'Theme 6' is on both versions built upon a Latin 4/4 rhythm. It is recognizably the same set of themes in both takes. Secondly, not only are different instruments featured soloing on the themes in *Mosaics* and the *Alternate Mosaics* but on the latter they do so at greater length. Thirdly, the two are different dynamically. Obviously, the use of cadenza, crescendo and decrescendo and changes in tempo are Collier's main tools in this regard but the points at which these are deployed vary between the two versions. There is also less use on the *Alternate Mosaics* of ensemble horn passages or shadowing of soloists. Finally, and this is perhaps the most interesting comparison, the second version issued in 2008 is a more straight-ahead take – if one can use that term in relation to Collier's music – on the thematic material.

There is something almost operatic about Collier's use of the cadenza in this context. It works dramatically but is also a reminder that Louis Armstrong developed his remarkable technique and helped create the role of the soloist in jazz through listening to and accompanying operatic arias. There are, of course, other examples in jazz of the use of the cadenza. Sonny Rollins was a master and George Russell used it on occasions, for example with Bill Evans on *Jazz in the Space Age* and with Eric Dolphy on Monk's 'Round Midnight' from *Ezz-Thetics*. Matthias Ruegg uses it sometimes with the Vienna Art Orchestra, notably on the album *The Minimalism of Erik Satie* (1990). But no other musician or composer in jazz has used it so extensively, not only as a bridge between movements but as a dramatic device. In fact, saxophonist and flautist Geoff Warren, who joined Collier around 1979, recalls being 'interviewed' by Collier on the subject before joining the group.

> As a compositional device and being very cynical, it's very, very useful, because Graham could just point to the guy. He does his thing and then everyone organizes themselves around that for what happens later... The freedom is absolute. You will see an empty bar with a rest sign over it saying 'cadenza' and that's it. Graham used the cadenza as a sort of interlude between one movement and the next. It sets up the atmosphere. You could if you wanted, quote what was going to happen but there was no obligation whatsoever. It's just, 'Cadenza, off you go'. Quite often, these cadenzas seem to be a fresh start to a new chapter... Interestingly enough, when I went out for that drink with Graham Collier – it must have been December '78 or January '79 – one of the first questions he asked me was, 'What do you feel about solo cadenzas?' (Laughing) There was I, a spotty youngster saying, 'Yeah, interesting. I can do that'. Good job I said, 'Yes'. If I said, 'No', it would have been, 'I'm crossing this guy's name off the list'. He wanted to know if I was happy doing a solo cadenza. Perhaps some people weren't or thought it wasn't necessary but for him in the late seventies it was an important part of his compositional way of working (Interview Warren/Heining 2014).

Richard Williams in *Melody Maker* suggested that Collier was becoming 'less of a "writer" and more of a "director"'. After years under the thrall of film critics, we might now use the term '*auteur*', but Williams' insight is a helpful one. He saw *Mosaics* as 'a considerable improvement over *Songs For My Father*, his last album and the first in which he used this approach to jazz composition' (Williams 1971: 11). Other reviews from Ron Brown in *Jazz Journal* and from Alun Morgan in *Gramophone* were just as insightful and still more enthusiastic (Brown 1971; Morgan 1971).

Mosaics came out in 1971 and that same year, the Graham Collier Music were chosen by Britain to represent Britain at the Montreux Jazz Festival, following in the wake of the Mike Westbrook Sextet, the Alan Skidmore Quintet and Nucleus. Geoff Castle recalls the experience vividly:

> I remember on the last day of my finals, I had my suitcase outside the door, they wouldn't let me take it into the exam room, went to Heathrow, took the flight to Geneva and then we played that evening at the Montreux Jazz Festival. I'd already toured with Graham. We played the *Mosaics* set at Montreux, which we'd recorded just before, I think (Interview Castle/Heining 2014).

The sextet won the press prize for best group, and came second to the Tuohi Group from Finland in the *Grand Prix*, much to the annoyance of an uncredited reviewer in *Melody Maker* (*Melody Maker* 1971). Hopefully, any sense of disappointment that Collier might have felt was assuaged by the Certificate of

Honour he received for jazz composition in relation to *Songs For My Father* as part of the annual Ivor Novello Awards.

Figure 7. Graham Collier Sextet – *Mosaics* at the Montreux Jazz Festival 1971. Personnel: Geoff Castle (piano), Bob Sydor (alto), Harry Beckett (trumpet), Graham Collier (bass), John Webb (drums), Alan Wakeman (tenor). Photo by Harry M. Monty.

Advertisements paid for by Phillips in the music press suggest a record company that was fully behind the Graham Collier Music, as did the fact that its sleeve design was by famous rock cover artist Roger Dean (no relation). However, it was not to be. Few of the British jazz musicians, who had got to record for major labels – these included Alan Skidmore, Harry Beckett, Stan Tracey, Tony Oxley, Howard Riley, Bob Downes, Ronnie Scott, Neil Ardley, and even John Dankworth – survived a sudden lack of interest on the part of EMI, CBS, Phillips, Decca and the rest.

Quite what happened is both complex and easily explained. Britain – and the record industry – was still a year away from the first oil crisis of 1973–74, which would have such major ramifications across the economy, including causing a shortage of shellac from which records were made. However, the optimism of the sixties and some of the values it inspired were beginning to dissipate. Previously record companies had believed in the prestige that came with having a 'catalogue in depth' and had been buoyed in this belief by the expansion of the industry that had followed the success of the Beatles, Rolling Stones *et al*. The late sixties, with its greater emphasis on improvisation in rock, had briefly opened the door to a new generation of jazz musicians such as Westbrook, Surman, Collier, Gibbs, Carr and others. Jazz and rock musicians often played together and guested on each other's records. By the early seventies, however, doors began to close. Perhaps the apparent fact that jazz records simply did not produce the levels of return of rock albums was reason enough. Suffice to say that only one or two jazz artists – for example, Mike Westbrook, who was with RCA, and Ian Carr, who was with Phonogram/Vertigo – survived the cull. *Mosaics* would be Collier's last release on a major label.

Jazz might have been shoved to one side in a lot of arenas, festivals and clubs in Britain by rock music, but a great deal of cross-fertilization between jazz, blues and later progressive rock music continued to take place. The college circuit continued to support jazz into the early seventies, though even there gig opportunities for jazz groups declined. Perhaps rock gave its audience some of the same sense of adventure that their older siblings had found in jazz. But rock, even in its growing attachment to elements of improvisation, was still largely song-based and was therefore also more accessible than jazz. An audience amongst young music fans for jazz remained, however, directed more towards bands such as Soft Machine, Nucleus and American acts such as Herbie Hancock, Weather Report and Mahavishnu than towards local artists playing largely unamplified, acoustic music.

There were a number of initiatives aimed at combating these difficulties that came from within the jazz part of the music business such as the formation of the Jazz Centre Society, the Musicians' Co-operative and, later in 1975, the London Musicians' Co-operative. Nevertheless, the nature of the jazz business of would-be bandleaders and self-employed, gun-for-hire musicians rather militates against self-help organizations or activism. To make matters far worse, the recording industry, in Britain and elsewhere, was changing. It would be some time before computers and bean counters would run the show but in the major record companies there was an increasing emphasis on a swift return on an investment. Jazz records sold slowly and they were difficult to market to a jazz audience that was itself hard to pinpoint. By contrast, younger music fans were more oriented to rock or pop music, musical styles that the industry had become quite adept at promoting and selling through a range of youth-oriented radio and television programmes and magazines. The seventies were lean times for jazz in Britain, arguably more so than was the case in continental Europe (see Heining 2012a; Wickes 1999).

It was in this context that Graham Collier once more came into his own. He was not a business man or a 'bread-head' but he understood the importance of a creative approach to finding work or ways of subsidizing it. In an article from 1970, Collier offered a number of insights into the situation facing British jazz and its musicians. He compared the level of critical acclaim for jazz in the UK and abroad with the financial struggles that jazz artists faced in trying to make a living from jazz. He noted that he and his group had played sixty-five gigs in 1969, including recording sessions, four sessions for the film of the QE2 he had been involved with, and two festivals abroad. He pointed out that the amount paid to each musician was £543, out of which each player had to spend a certain amount on travel and food expenses. The article identifies the problem in terms of the failure of record companies to promote jazz and, in particular, British jazz. It also berates British television and radio for not providing sufficient broadcasting opportunities for jazz.[4] However, Collier also draws attention to the need for musicians themselves to be more active in promoting their music. Promotion is, for Collier, the main answer to the audience dilemma faced by British jazz.[5]

Whilst some points were well-made, the problems facing jazz in Britain were arguably more fundamental than Collier allows. However, it was clear that he was not prepared to merely accept the situation and was keen to generate solutions to it. One of these, as we have seen, focused on the pursuit of commissions and other sources of funding. Another 'solution' involved trying to generate new opportunities and new situations in which to perform. One very important innovation was, of course, taking jazz into schools. But the key to this activity was that it needed to be organized and Collier was nothing if not organized.

And Collier, himself, does not seem to have been short of work. Three tunes on Harry Beckett's first album, *Flare Up* (1970) were written by Collier – 'Go West', 'Third Road' and 'The Other Side'. He then provided scores for several pieces for Radio Suisse Romande in June 1970 and January 1971. It is not entirely clear on what basis these were provided but presumably this was for performance by the radio big band. The pieces included 'Aberdeen Angus', 'Gay Talk' (recorded by NYJO), 'Go West' and 'Third Road' (both see above). The other four – 'Trigon Blues', 'Latin Brown', 'Burbling for Bob' and 'Crowley's Carol' – have never been recorded. In addition, in January 1971, his group had played opposite The Trio (John Surman, Barre Phillips, Stu Martin) in Stuttgart for Suddeutscher Rundfunk and toured Holland and Belgium and represented Britain in Montreux in June.

The musician, Ken Hyder, interviewed Collier for *Melody Maker* in 1973. The article was aptly titled, 'Collier: hustler supreme' (Hyder 1973). Hyder described how Collier had employed a part-time secretary to phone, write and generally assist in hustling for work. As Hyder noted, 'If you want to get it on, you've got to get it on yourself. And the sad fact is that many musicians aren't cut out for it.' In the article, Collier describes how he goes about 'hustling' for work:

> I look for gigs in different areas, particularly festivals. A lot of them are run by small towns. I keep my eyes open in the papers and if I see that festival's coming off, I'll write to the organisers. This knowledge is available to anyone who wants to get it. I also do lectures on jazz, and they can pay quite well.

Collier goes on to describe a similar process in relation to film composition and commercials:

> I'm a member of the Composers Guild, and they try to sort out film rights. I've done a few industrial documentaries, writing music for things like Women in Engineering. For seven or eight minutes of music, you get about £200, and for cinema documentaries, you get about twice that much. And for ordinary film scores…well, it's a lot of money (Hyder 1973: 20).

Hyder notes that Collier did a butter commercial for which he was paid £150 for 7½ seconds of music. Such work helped Collier in financing the work that really mattered to him. As he also comments in the Hyder article, earnings from recordings formed a very small part of his income. Life for the modern-day, British jazz composer and bandleader was a struggle but one that required a degree of diversification. He returned to this point in a piece by Michael Walters for *Sounds* in 1971:

> It is really down to the economics of the jazz business. I am trying to find a middle road between starving for the sake of my art, and doing very well. I am sure I could make a better living by commercialising myself. So I go into the film thing at times to make enough money to keep the band going, and to allow me scope to get the band more work.

As a film composer, between 1968–74, Collier provided music for five films for various companies including Cunard, the Midland Bank and Shell.[6]

The term 'jazz hustler' was used again in an article by Ronald Atkins in *The Guardian* in 1976 (Atkins 1976). In a way, it very much described Collier's work ethic. He knew from the beginning that, if he were to make a career out of jazz, he would have to be organized in his approach. Indeed, one can think of few musicians in jazz who have been quite so efficient, disciplined and scrupulous when it came to the business side of the music. He paid his musicians fairly and on time. When it later came to reissues of his recordings, he would always try and ensure that some payment, or at least a copy or two of the reissue, went to the musicians on the record. And he was extraordinarily thorough in chasing recalcitrant record companies or publishers for outstanding royalties. If necessary, he would seek legal assistance in pursuing those unwilling to honour their contractual obligations or do so promptly. No one had ever handed Graham Collier anything in his life. He grew up as a working-class lad in a warm, loving family but lived through times of hardship. What he had, he had earned honestly. He was honest in his dealings and expected others to behave in the same way towards him.

*　*　*

Collier's first major challenge in the early seventies came with the ending of his contract with Philips. The initial solution involved a one-off contract with Cotswold-based record company, Saydisc,[7] but for subsequent releases Collier would follow the route taken by bassist Harry Miller and his partner Hazel Miller (Ogun Records), pianist Stan Tracey (Steam) and free improvisers saxophonist Evan Parker, guitarist Derek Bailey and drummer Tony Oxley (Incus) in establishing his own label, Mosaic. The first release after the ending of the contract with Philips was *Portraits* and that would be followed by a further six LPs by Collier himself and another eight by other artists on his own imprint.

After the ground broken by *Songs*, and more significantly *Mosaics*, with his next three releases, Collier seemed to be retracing his steps as a composer. In fact, he said as much with regard to *Portraits* in the sleeve notes:

> The title was meant to apply to the fact that the piece was written for a new band and that there was a shift in my writing – for the time being anyway – away from the free-structure of *Mosaics*. This more ordered, more orchestrated style could be said to return to the sound of the first band and *Deep Dark Blue Centre*. Certainly using the guitar again has given me more 'orchestral' possibilities than I have had for some time (Collier 1973b).

Portraits does indeed bear comparison to *Deep Dark Blue Centre*, both in its introspective mood and in the way its use of form pushes against the restrictions of more straight-ahead jazz composition without actually transcending those restrictions. *Darius* followed and was recorded live. A distinct improvement on its predecessor, it can be compared to *Down Another Road* in its feel and use of rock rhythms and riffs. Finally, the more complex and intricate *Midnight Blue* partners *Mosaics* as an ensemble record, where thematic development is shared to a larger extent by composer and improvisers. *Midnight Blue* differs, however, from *Mosaics* in what appears to be a greater reliance on compositional form. Here, while *Mosaics* was a live album, Collier chose to go into the studio with *Midnight Blue* 'because it was more intricate music' (O'Reagan 2009). Given both the parallels and differences between these albums and their predecessors, was Collier perhaps examining different ways of achieving results similar to those already achieved but by varying his compositional methodology?

According to his 'Timeline', Collier had planned to start work with his new group, the one that would record *Portraits*, towards the end of 1971. However, in December he was rushed into hospital in severe pain. Following investigation, his gall bladder was removed. The rest of the December and then January 1972 were spent recovering from the operation.

As a result, the start of the new band had to be postponed. Their first performance with Dick Pearce on trumpet and flugelhorn, Pete Hurt alto, Ed Speight guitar, Geoff Castle piano, John Webb drums and Collier on bass took place in March 1972 in Lincoln. Pearce and Hurt were both LYJO/NYJO alumni, whilst Speight was recruited at the suggestion of Geoff Castle. The association with Speight would prove particularly valuable to Collier throughout the rest of his career, mirroring to a degree the role played by American guitarist Barry Galbraith in relation to George Russell's work in the 1950s.[8]

This group, augmented by singer Norma Winstone, Derek Wadsworth on trombone and a cellist, would also perform Collier's words and music project, *Wheel of Dreams*, a Camden Festival Commission in May 1971.

The original vinyl release of *Portraits* was divided between a long suite, 'And Now For Something Completely Different', a reference to the popular, anarchic comedy sketch show *Monty Python's Flying Circus* and the shorter title track.[9] The first part of the suite took up the whole of the first side of the original LP and concludes on side two. The record closes with 'Portraits 1', written for Dick Pearce and the first of a series of compositional portraits of band members Collier planned. In the event, only one of these – 'Portraits 2', for John Webb – was actually completed. It was not, however, recorded.

Portraits is sadly a disappointment given the achievements of the previous four albums. Despite strong performances from Geoff Castle, Ed Speight and John Webb, 'And Now For Something Completely Different' never quite takes off. It sounds like a good enough British jazz record of the period but is hardly exceptional or up to Collier's usual standards. It contains many of the compositional devices that Collier had used so notably on *Songs For My Father* and even more successfully on *Mosaics*. As ever, it features a number of cadenzas, changes of mood and tempo. For example, a ballad section contrasts with a *rubato* passage and later with another towards the end of the first part of the suite that has a rock feel to it. Further contrast is found at the beginning of part 2, which has a distinctly North African, modal character. As with the earlier records, a variety of jazz styles are drawn upon – Pete Hurt's bebop-inflected alto, touches of free jazz, modal playing and jazz-rock. However, it all feels rather flat. It smoulders but never catches fire.

'Portraits 1' is a ballad feature for Pearce. Overall the piece is more successful than the suite, emphasizing Pearce's gorgeous tone on flugelhorn and the strengths of the rhythm section both in the ballad and in two danceable sections, the first a fox-trot and the second more Latin in feel, a rhumba perhaps. The overriding impression is of a lack of clarity in the writing, which *Portraits*' rather congested sound, compared to the Phillips' recordings, emphasizes.

Furthermore, the two frontline players Dick Pearce and Pete Hurt, both excellent musicians, do not seem right for Collier's music.[10] To take Pearce as an example, his great strengths lie in his grasp of harmony and his beautiful tone on trumpet and flugelhorn, strengths to which 'Portraits 1' plays with some success. The problem is not about the quality of his solos. Rather it is one of attack, that ability to seize a note rather than arrive at it stealthily. Such a criticism, here of Collier's choice of musician rather than of the musician himself, could not be made of Harry Beckett, Nick Evans or Alan Wakeman or later Collier alumni such as saxophonist Art Themen or trombonist Malcolm Griffiths.

With regard to Pete Hurt one wonders how comfortable he was in this setting. Interviewed by fellow saxophonist Martin Speake for his website, Hurt makes it clear that he was not a fan of Collier's music.

> [S]ome of it was OK but I wasn't bowled over by it. As a jazz composer, I'm afraid that I'm of the opinion that Graham…his music sounds a bit grim some…most of the time to me. He's never been a favourite of mine as opposed to other British Jazz composers like Mike Gibbs or Kenny Wheeler (Speake 2010).

Pearce, however, found his period with Collier an important learning experience, noting at the same time that his subsequent musical journey took him in a different direction. He wrote in his autobiography:

> Graham gave me my first professional gigs as a jazz musician back in late 1971, just as I was preparing to leave the army. He was one of the first people to give me a feeling of musical worth (improvisationally speaking) and encouragement. I was very happy to explore the various avenues of free music at the time, and his group was the perfect platform for me to stretch in that direction (Pearce 2013: 305).

Several critics expressed a certain ambivalence in their reviews of *Portraits*. In *Melody Maker*, Richard Williams' piece was rich in back-handed compliments:

> Times have changed since Graham Collier and Mike Westbrook were the lynchpins of the younger generation in British jazz, half a dozen years ago. While Westy now leads a vaudeville troupe, poor old Graham has been coming in for stick from a few critics.

Williams draws attention once more to the weakness of Collier's own playing before continuing,

> It's not his fault he's sometimes been overpraised in the past, *notably by writers in the provinces who get little exposure to live jazz and are thus almost pathetically grateful for Graham's visitations* (my emphasis).

Finally, his neck chiming like a bell, Williams concludes,

> While I don't consider Collier to be in jazz's major league, I have never yet failed to enjoy one of his records, and this is no exception (Williams 1973: 42; see also Williams 1972).

John Fordham's review in *Time Out* (Fordham 1973) also succeeded in damning Collier at the same time as praising the record. Describing him as 'a composer of mild, transparent themes', Fordham concludes, 'When he keeps to the middle road, which is most of the time, he proves himself to be increasingly sure-footed; *Portraits*, deceptively enough, stands a lot of listening'. The reviewer for *Coda* was similarly ambivalent, remarking 'This is an immaculate recording of nice music that demands little concentration' (Temperer 1974: 17). Barry McRae was more enthusiastic in *Jazz Journal*, noting that, '*Portraits* reaffirms Collier's feeling for Ellingtonian ideas but the whole record is redolent of the unique Collier spirit' (McRae 1973: 28).

A mixed critical blessing, perhaps. However, Collier's recordings and concerts invariably attracted reviews, and their placing in all the main music magazines and in the broadsheets, coupled with regular BBC radio broadcasts, reveal that Collier was very much in the forefront of British jazz at this time. The sextet was certainly not short of work. Pete Hurt told Martin Speake in 2010, in an interview for Speake's website, that he did a lot of school concerts with Collier – something Collier and fellow bandleader/composer Michael Garrick pioneered – and that 'the band were fairly busy, actually' and worked 'most weeks' (Speake 2010).

Despite that, following the release of *Portraits*, Collier began seeking new outlets for his work and ideas. He noted in his 'Timeline',

> Starting to think of doing without a regular band and concentrating on being a composer and specific projects... Speaking of hiring a

secretary for 50p an hour, needing £20 per week to live on, getting £1000 per annum from PRS [Performing Rights Society] and needing another £1000 from somewhere else...

Such comments and also references to depression in the 'Timeline' suggest a certain frustration on Collier's part, perhaps partly due to the load he carried as bandleader/tour organizer/fund-raiser/composer but perhaps also a certain feeling of alienation and/or lack of appreciation. The latter would be a recurring feature in Collier's life and career and one that could at times lead him to behave in ways that were envious and petty.

Notes

1. The Torrington was a famous London music venue from 1967 until 2004. When its closure was announced in September 2004, Pete Feenstra, an independent promoter, told *The Hendon & Finchley Times*, 'First it was a jazz venue, then it was part of the psychedelic explosion. It survived punk and now caters for enduring rock bands, R&B, American tour bands, blues acts and quality tribute bands. It's featured in about 20 rock biographies, including The Stranglers.' http://www.times-series.co.uk/news/529874.famous_pub_rock_venue_to_shut_down/

2. There is what sounds like a 'fluff' at 1:04 where Collier starts to come in and thinks better of it.

3. *Elastic Jazz – Sketches of Britain* is an intriguing record put together by Claudio Bonomi and Gennaro Fucile that also included the Westbrooks, Mike Cooper, Evan Parker and the London Jazz Composers Orchestra.

4. The article, titled 'Plight of the British Jazz Musician', was amongst Graham Collier's papers. It is dated 10 October 1970 but gives no details regarding where it appeared. The type font looks like *Sounds Magazine*, the first issue of which appeared on that date.

5. In fact, Collier and his group appeared on London Weekend Television's Sunday lunchtime arts programme *Music in the Round* hosted by Humphrey Burton in December 1970. Collier was paid £200 and gave £25 each to his five musicians. It included both a performance by the Graham Collier Music and a discussion with Burton, Collier and the audience ('Timeline').

6. The five films were *Meet the Group* (1968) on the activities of the Midland Bank Group; *The Engineer is a Woman* (1969), which set out 'to explode the idea that engineering is only for men by showing at first hand five women engineers'; *Magic Ride* (1970) on the building and maiden voyage of the *Queen Elizabeth II*; *Diesel* (1973) on 'the many types and applications of diesel engines'; *Acting in Turn* (1974) on 'the history of the gear from its invention 2000 years ago'. Descriptions courtesy of the British Film Library's online catalogue.

7. Saydisc specialized then in recordings of regional interest of Cotswold characters and steam engines but also early jazz. See 'Collier leads local record firm into new fields', *Gloucestershire Gazette*, 9 February 1972.

8. Here, I note again Collier's remark in the sleeve notes to *Portraits*: 'Certainly using the guitar again has given me more "orchestral possibilities" than I have had for some time'

(Collier 1973b). Russell often described Galbraith as his 'orchestra'. In an obituary Russell wrote for Galbraith in 1983, 'From 1950 to the late 1960's, I relied most heavily on Barry to make my music "come off". His guitar became a lead trumpet, or part of a saxophone section, or doubled in octaves with the bass and, at times, the whole orchestra. He was a professional in the true sense of the word.' The description might easily apply to Ed Speight in Collier's various bands.

9. Bizarrely, *Melody Maker* reviewed the record under the title 'And Now For Something Completely Different'. N.B. Pete Hurt declined to be interviewed for this book.

10. Dick Pearce's gifts are well-served by his first CD as a leader, *Big Hit* (FMR).

6 'Author! Author!'

Collier's 'Timeline' is split into different decades and begins in the seventies. Not only does Collier comment on his work, health and social life, he also includes extracts from his diaries. In this regard, he first notes experiencing depression in 1971 but such references continue on and off up to the early nineties.

He notes early in the 1970s section of the 'Timeline', 'Depressions showing up fairly regularly in diaries for the late 60s-early 70s. Mid-life crisis?' Without being able to discuss the issue with Collier himself, it is difficult to know what to make of this or of similar comments in later entries. What seems clear is that these were not simply one-off bouts of reactive depression.

Following this early reference, there is then nothing further until 1984, when he writes, 'June – Severe depression (8–10 weeks)' and '1984 – seeing psycho-therapist about depression and over-emotionalism'. In 1985, he reports, 'During year still some serious depressions and irritations and possibly related stomach illnesses'. Finally, in 1991, he notes, 'Notebooks show a depression through part of '91 because I had little to do and I was trying to come to terms with RAM [Royal Academy of Music] and my commitment to it'. After that, there are no further entries of this kind.

Any individual can suffer from depression but most often this takes the form of a reaction to a life event – a bereavement, divorce, injury, unemployment. This usually passes with the crisis unless, for example, it connects profoundly with earlier losses. Under such circumstances, the illness can pass from being acute, that is intense but of shorter duration, to becoming chronic. Because Collier's bouts of depression recurred over a period of twenty years or more, it seems likely that these bouts were in some degree related and that they did not appear to have triggers in terms of specific life events. It is reasonable to conclude from this that Collier experienced difficulties in managing his mood at various times, perhaps when things were not going well for him or when he was simply under-occupied.

John Gill was certainly aware that his partner suffered from bouts of depression and knew that he had seen a therapist. However, he was surprised on reading the 'Timeline' to discover that these episodes seemed more intense and protracted than he had been aware (Email interview Gill/Heining 2015). Without wishing to suggest that creative individuals are more prone to depression than other individuals – evidence to support such a conclusion is limited[1] – the position of the independent artist is an insecure one and in jazz particularly so. It is reasonable to accept that the levels of frustration must be great indeed. However, in Collier's case, there were aspects of his life and situation that were specific to him as a person, which may shed light on his condition.

Collier was, in many respects, always an outsider. As a working-class boy, he attended a grammar school, an institution modelled on the upper middle-class values of the public (or for non-British readers, 'private') school system. As a serving soldier, he found his interests at odds with all but one of his comrades and, as John Gill has noted, saw his fellow squaddies as 'alien beings'. He was the first British student to attend Berklee, again making him an outsider. Later, he was a gay man in the 'blokey', heterosexual world of British jazz. He was a bandleader and a jazz composer, roles that to a degree set him apart from his fellow musicians. When he later became head of jazz at the Royal Academy of Music, he was taking jazz into a conservative institution, which saw the music as little more than a sideshow to the main event of high-art classical music. Collier held high standards and, for all his desire and strength of character, he set himself enormous challenges. Some did say that he 'bigged himself up' or thought 'he was some kind of genius'. But it would seem that, at times, what he felt inside did not match what he presented to the outside world. Put this way, depression could almost be seen as an occupational hazard.

Despite such feelings and doubts, there is no impression that Collier ever stopped pushing himself. He continued to press his own case – and that of the music he devoted his life to – with incredible persistence. He attended conferences, gave lectures, wrote articles and letters and continually pursued funding for any number of new projects. At one point (autumn 1973), he even tutored adult evening classes in Brentwood and Croydon on jazz history and appreciation. It is not surprising that he fantasized in his diary about 'doing without a regular band and concentrating on being a composer...' Things would change later and allow him to fulfil that fantasy. However, at that time at least, one suspects that his success probably owed a great deal to the fact that it all came as one package – bandleader, recording artist, composer and the rest.

The word 'driven' in this context is both trite and overused. Yet, it was clear, even before he got on that boat to Berklee, that Collier was never going to be satisfied with being a sideman – even if his talents as a bass player would have allowed this. Way back then he wanted to compose and to set up his own school for jazz, as his father Jack had told the *Luton News* in 1960. His writing projects, all focused on jazz and jazz education, which he began and which continued to the end of his life, must be seen in this light. But then, very early on in his career, he was also already committed to a belief in jazz as an art form and to bringing that art form into contact with other arts such as literature, fine art and drama. At times, this latter enthusiasm might overreach itself but there is no doubting Collier's sincerity.

It was not just about generating work. It was about creating the right kind of opportunities. *Contrapuntal Forms*, commissioned by the Harlow Festival in 1968, and *Smoke Blackened Walls and Curlews*, commissioned by the Bradford Arts Festival in 1970, were the kind of creative opportunities Collier was after and, as he told Ken Hyder in 1973, it often took a large number of letters to promoters or festival directors to get even one job (Hyder 1973). A further such commission, *Wheel of Dreams*, was premiered at the Camden Festival in May 1972, with a second performance in June that same year in Kensington. Written between 1970 and 1972, the composer described the work as a 'multi-media self-portrait' and, in his handwritten notes, as 'an autobiography of images, music, words, thoughts that make up me now'. The words were drawn from a variety of sources including Conrad Aiken, Walt Whitman, W. H. Auden, Michelangelo and Collier himself and were projected onto three screens on stage. Such multi-media projects were certainly not unusual at that time – Mike Westbrook's *Earthrise* created with John Fox of the Welfare State theatre group being one example, along with other Welfare State productions with saxophonist Lol Coxhill. Additionally, both saxophonist Bob Downes and S.O.S. (John Surman, Mike Osborne, Alan Skidmore) worked with choreographer Carolyn Carlson at the Opèra de Paris in the mid-seventies.

When and in what circumstances multi-media projects succeed is a moot question. Accusations of pretentiousness or an excess of vanity are as much a matter of opinion as plaudits and praise. However, it is surely valid to examine the goals of any such project and consider how far these might have been achieved.

I have suggested already that Collier's interest in literature and art seemed to reflect a deep concern with the ways in which creative practices in one area might inform practices in another. In order to be clear about what I am saying with regard to the process or processes involved, it is important to note that John Gill did not entirely share my opinion here.

In terms of the abstract art that Collier loved, Gill advised caution in making the assumption that his partner tried to apply specific techniques or theories used in abstract art to his work as a composer. Gill did, however, seem to have a slightly different opinion when it came to the works of literature Collier referenced in his music. In the late 1970s, Collier would draw on the writings of novelist Malcolm Lowry for inspiration, most notably in relation to the records

Symphony of Scorpions (1977) and *The Day of the Dead* (1978). In terms of these works, Gill did acknowledge parallels between Lowry's use of different levels in his novels and his partner's musical goals, 'Not directly, perhaps, but he saw a workable correlation between what was going on in that particular book, *Under the Volcano*, and what he wanted to do with levels of activity in a composition' (Email correspondence Gill/Heining 2015). Whilst noting Gill's strictures, my view is that he was being overly cautious. In his later work, in particular, Collier seems to have been increasingly focused on correspondences between artistic practices in other areas of the arts and his own compositional practice.

What is clear is that Collier did not seek to represent the paintings that inspired works such as *Contrapuntal Forms*, *Midnight Blue*, *Luminosity* or *The Miró Tile* or the work of painters such as Pollock, Rothko and Still programmatically. Yet it was more than a simple desire to present a musical response to such art works. As Gill notes, 'He found a spark there. It made him think'. And he adds, 'There was something about them that got Graham thinking in reading those novels or looking at those paintings and he would be thinking about the way he was working' (Email correspondence Gill/Heining 2015).

And yet, Collier seems to go further than Gill allows in the Disconforme reissue of *The Day of the Dead* (2000), which also included *Triptych* (a work addressing three paintings – one by Mark Rothko, the second by Clyfford Still, the third by Hans Hartung) and *October Ferry*.

> These records were my first attempts to explore larger forms. Some present day critics have talked of my writing 'jazz symphonies', which is flattering (although, not surprisingly, I would disown the word symphony if it is meant in its classical sense). *What I seek to do is integrate the real power of jazz – its use of improvisation and the individuality of the musicians concerned into works which will place these skills on to a large canvas which expresses my ideas about art. Some of these efforts can be seen in these records (several of which are directly concerned with other art forms, specifically painting and literature).* Hidden behind the idea to write longer works was – and still is – a dissatisfaction with the passivity of much jazz, where nothing happens that hasn't happened before a hundred perhaps a thousand times. Why do it? It certainly demeans the word jazz as I understand it (Collier 2000a, emphasis mine).

Collier is clearly discussing aesthetic values here, ideas and values that reflect upon his own beliefs about art and culture and, by extension, their place in a wider context. What is somewhat unsatisfying about this and other such comments is Collier's failure to locate these thoughts in a more explicit social or cultural-political dimension. Without such a dimension, there is a nagging feeling that, like Onan's seeds, such ideas lack the soil to fertilize them and enable them to grow into something that is simultaneously aesthetical and ethical.

Wheel of Dreams featured John Carbery as narrator alongside Collier's *Portraits* sextet, Norma Winstone, Derek Wadsworth on trombone and Timothy Kramer on cello. Reviewing the work in *Jazz Journal*, Ron Brown wrote:

> It was gratifying that one of our leading jazzmen has shown that his thoughts and feelings range far wider than what's thought of as his normal field, but more important perhaps that the unpleasant whiff of a 'jazzman' going 'respectable' was completely absent; music is to be enjoyed first, academically dissected second, and at the Shaw Theatre Graham Collier enjoyed presenting his music and himself in a new way; and I enjoyed hearing him do it (Brown 1972: 15).

Christopher Bird in *Melody Maker* told his readers that *Wheel of Dreams*, 'proved to be one of the most absorbing evenings I've spent in some time; the kind of experience that continues to stimulate the mind, as well as the emotions, long after it is over. Don't shout too loud or you might frighten everyone away, but isn't that what they call Art?' (Bird 1972: 58).

Ronald Atkins, however, dissented from the enthusiastic reviews of Ron Brown and Christopher Bird regarding *Wheel of Dreams*. His comments in *The Guardian*, arguably, serve to highlight some of the hazards with such works.

> The text is based on Collier's credo as a composer and on extracts from writers that he admires. He points out that not all the literary passages are meant to illuminate his own thoughts and here lies part of the trouble. With the music also tending towards the fragmentary, it is doubly difficult for the audience to latch on to anything. Collier is much too sensitive to resort to the gimmicks and the excesses inherent in the form, but I can't help feeling that he has exchanged vulgarity for a kind of polite artiness. If you superimpose words over music you automatically detract from the latter, and this happens consistently... (Atkins 1972: 12).

This passage sounds very negative but it is important to appreciate exactly what Atkins is saying. His argument is that combining words and music is most easily achieved where a musical device, such as a melody or even a riff, is used to accompany or underscore the spoken word. My guess is that Atkins was referring here to other attempts to bring spoken word and jazz together and, though it is not said explicitly in the review, he might have been thinking of the poetry and jazz experiments of drummer Tony Kinsey and poet Christopher Logue, those of Michael Garrick and poets such as Jeremy Robson and Danny Abse or those of Michael Horovitz, Pete Brown and Stan Tracey (see

Heining 2012a: 362–65). Atkins' argument is not that Collier's *Wheel of Dreams* fails because he has chosen not to deploy 'gimmicks' but that, in choosing a different path, he has opened up a different series of potential pitfalls. His final point quoted here is much more complex and relates to how and why we privilege the spoken voice over music in situations. We will discuss this later in relation to *The Day of the Dead*.

Wheel of Dreams was arguably Collier's most ambitious project to date. Other such projects would follow and what is also interesting in this context is that many of Collier's festival commissions came not from 'jazz festivals' but arts and literary festivals. As well as being performed in Camden and Kensington, *Wheel of Dreams* was later performed as a 'song cycle' at the North Monmouthshire Festival of the Arts on 22 September 1972. Collier's abiding interest in literature made him ideally placed to garner such work opportunities and, at the time, his interest coincided with a broader enthusiasm in funding and audience circles for these multi-media or genre-crossing works (see Heining 2012a: ch. 12).

A further commission, this time, from the Southern Arts Association for the Worthing Festival of Literature resulted in *Sea, Sky and Down*, another work combining music and poetry, here that of Sussex poet Ted Walker. The Graham Collier Music performed the piece again with actor John Carbery, and another new work, *Children of Adam*, a setting of Walt Whitman poems from his volume *Leaves of Grass* in Worthing in March 1973.[2] Collier received £180 for the performance and £100 for the commission itself. Going by the letter from the festival's assistant director, the music was a success, even if some aspects of the organization left something to be desired and if the group's performance seemed at certain points – mainly, involving John Carbery – under-rehearsed. The letter notes that the poet, Ted Walker, was present and was pleased with the piece and had 'several ideas' about the composition he wished to discuss with Collier. It is not known what, if any, discussions took place.

All of these diverse projects certainly fuelled Collier's art or 'Art'. Sometimes material would be carried over and reworked. But more importantly, everything he composed was an exploration of his thinking and his musical conception at that point in time. It is fair to state here that Collier constantly experimented in order to consolidate that which worked into his later thinking and practice.

At the same time, the practicalities of maintaining a working band and generating income remained an everyday necessity. As noted in the Ken Hyder article for *Melody Maker*, he did, however, hire a secretary in 1973 and subsequently took on Harry Paton Evans as an agent, both for his work as a bandleader and composer and for a number of book projects that he began around that time.

Collier had written about jazz before for magazines but, early in 1972, he signed a contract with Cambridge University Press to produce both a teacher and student guide to jazz – *Jazz: A Student's and Teacher's Guide* (1975a) – and three accompanying recordings. The first of these would be an LP record to be called *Jazz Illustrations*, which would illustrate various jazz styles and approaches; the second, *Jazz Lecture Concert*, would be devoted to a lecture on jazz history, improvisation and the instruments of jazz; the third would be a cassette of rhythm backings for students to play alongside.

It was a highly innovative idea, not least given the fact that there were no jazz courses, outside of Leeds College of Music, in the UK at the time. The following year, Collier agreed to produce a book for Berklee Press Publications, *Compositional Devices* (1975b), which would examine different approaches to composition in jazz, drawing on his own recorded work. Both reflected Collier's own jazz aesthetic and were informed by his increasingly sophisticated ideas on jazz performance, which he would develop in later publications such as *Jazz Workshop: The Blues* (1988), *Interaction: Opening up the Jazz Ensemble* (1995, reprinted 2000) and *The Jazz Composer: Moving Music off the Paper* (2009a), as well as in his writing for and editing of *Jazz Changes*, the magazine of the International Association of Schools of Jazz. Indeed, with each of these publications, it is clear that Collier was seeking to offer the student/teacher a functional teaching manual, with exercises and suggestions for practice, but that he also aimed to set out his ideas about the nature of the music. His last work, *The Jazz Composer*, is in that sense merely the final elaboration of this dual purpose.

Collier had also landed a contract with Quartet Books to write a general primer on Jazz – *Inside Jazz*. This came out in November 1973, the same month as trumpeter Ian Carr's *Music Outside: Contemporary Jazz in Britain*. These were the first two 'serious' books by practising British modern jazzmen.[3] *Inside Jazz* and *Music Outside* were both different in intention and content but strangely complementary. Collier's was a general survey of the music and how it is put together. Carr's book was more polemical and argued passionately on behalf of British jazz and its musicians. *Inside Jazz* was written at a particular point in the history of the music, in a particular context and with a particular audience in mind. It reflected Collier's proselytizing on behalf of jazz to those, probably younger, individuals coming to jazz for the first time. On that basis, *Inside Jazz* works very well. Its brief portraits of several 'key' artists on the modern era are sharply observed and honest. He is critical of Dave Brubeck, generous towards Ornette Coleman – a musician he admired but whose later music he never enjoyed – and fulsome in his praise of Miles Davis.

Like most of Collier's writing on jazz, it is hard to separate what he writes from who he was as a person. As such, it is at times an amusing read and at others a frustrating one. Anyone reading *Inside Jazz* and then *The Jazz Composer*, published thirty-six years later, will immediately be struck by the continuity of concern on Collier's part – and also by his 'occasional' lapses of objectivity.

Amusingly, *Inside Jazz* contains its share of asides and even little 'digs'. For example, in a reference to his own composition 'Gay Talk', written for NYJO, Collier notes in parentheses, 'written for the NYJO record in 1971 and, though the band enjoyed playing it, unplayed since'. Collier's relationship with NYJO's founder-director Bill Ashton was ever fractious. Elsewhere in the book, he discussed the difficulties experienced by British jazz musicians in persuading major record companies to promote their records. He writes, 'It seemed that every time I was wandering the corridors of Phillips making a nuisance of myself I'd see Bob Downes (saxophonist and bandleader) coming the other way!' (Collier 1973a: 140). Such remarks help to personalize *Inside Jazz* and bring alive the problems and joys of working as a jazz musician.

However, *Inside Jazz* does more than give its readers, jazz neophytes in particular, an idea of jazz, its origins and history, its tenuous position in a market economy and the place of improvisation within it. Notably, it provides a useful distinction between jazz and classical music. This is almost a sub-theme that runs through the book and he is scathing, perhaps too scathing, about what he sees as the kind of arranged marriages between the two. His definition of so-called 'third stream music' differs from my own understanding and, at another point, he makes similarly disparaging comments about 'Indo-jazz'. In fact, Collier's major foray into composition for symphony orchestra, *Plain Song and Mountain Birds* (1987), sounds not that different sonically, timbrally and texturally from other mixed marriages such as Gunther Schuller's *7 Studies on Themes of Paul Klee* (1959) and *Concertino for Jazz Quartet and Orchestra* (1959), Larry Austin's *Improvisations for Jazz Soloist and Orchestra* (1965) or, more recent works by Mark-Anthony Turnage such as *Blood on the Floor* (1993) and *Scorched* (2000). Nevertheless, one would find it hard to disagree with the following:

> Playing jazz is a specific talent as divorced from reading a Tchaikovsky piano concerto as playing football is from playing cricket. People can do both but they are rare and if one is going to write jazz then one must understand the real nature of the music – its human quality – and write for some real live jazz musicians (Collier 1973a: 17).

On the other hand, 'Almost all the "jazz concertos", "jazz symphonies" and "jazz inspired" compositions are overwritten and fail to impart that most intangible of things – the spirit of jazz – to the written notes', might be seen as far too sweeping a statement (Collier 1973a: 17).

John Gill, himself a music journalist, had many discussions with his partner on this and related issues over their thirty-six years together. He explained:

> I think he felt that a lot of third stream music was the jazz equivalent of Emerson, Lake and Palmer playing Mussorgsky, basically not very pleasant and wrong-headed from the moment go. He thought that if there were to be decent third stream music in a jazz context, it shouldn't have these delusions of grandeur. He felt that jazz could do it anyway, had its own sound resources. It didn't need orchestras, except sometimes if a composer wanted to use an orchestra as a sound resource.

He suggested that *New Conditions* might be read as an example of 'decent third stream music in a jazz context' (Email correspondence Gill/Heining 2015).

Many years later in *The Jazz Composer*, Collier would make his point about the differences between jazz and classical music even more sharply. He had noted in *Inside Jazz*, 'Even with a symphony or concerto where a conductor can interpret the piece the basic work of art remains unchanged' (Collier 1973a: 33). Twenty-six years later in *The Jazz Composer*, Collier writes that with the classical symphony or concerto, 'the essential truth is contained in the score' (Collier 2009a: 313). With a jazz composition the essential truth lies in the performance – 'What is exclusive about jazz is that what happens, happens in real time' (Collier 2009a: 30). Each element informs and shapes the other and will (or at least should) result in something different each time it is performed. Collier illustrates this argument in *Inside Jazz* with a quote from Joe Goldberg, author of *Jazz Masters of the Fifties*. Goldberg notes, 'records are an artificial means of retaining that which was never meant to be permanent' (Collier 1973a: 131; see Goldberg 1980: 2). It is not totally accurate to state that a classical symphony 'will sound much the same played by the London Symphony Orchestra under Previn as it would by the New York Philharmonic under Bernstein', as Collier suggests (Collier 1973a: 130–31). But, in jazz, as he rightly points out, the scores are only a guide.

> Even if you have the scores it's no good a band trying to sound *exactly* [emphasis original] like Ellington if you haven't hired Harry Carney and the others. Your musicians are different people. If the individual talent is strong enough then that will come through and enhance the Duke scores – *make them live for you and for now* [emphasis mine] (Collier 1973a: 141).

Collier is again seeking to articulate a particular view of jazz and its aesthetic values, based on a notion of jazz as a music of individuals but one that is essentially relational. That is, that the individual achieves their fullest expression of their individuality in relation to the other members of the group. For example, in *Inside Jazz*, he quotes Charles Fox's description of his approach to jazz composition as 'participatory democracy' (Collier 1973a: 128). Collier championed the individual in jazz and their personal sound and, from the beginnings of his career as a composer and bandleader, he shaped his music to capture those qualities, just like his mentor *in absentia* Duke Ellington (see, for example, Collier 1973a: 33–37). However, he continually contextualizes the individual within the group context. In *Jazz* (Collier 1975a), the book written for students and teachers, he goes so far as to quote Charles Fox from the latter's *Jazz in Perspective*, a quotation that suggests a broader understanding of such relationships, even if Collier never fully explores the implications of the statement:

> It is the blend of the personal and the social, the aesthetic and the economic, that makes jazz reflect our century so faithfully (Fox 1969a: 10).

There is, however, another comment made by Fox with which Collier would surely agree. He writes:

> Another radical difference between jazz and European music has been the way the former lacks architectural shape. Jazz mostly exists as a strip in time, its metaphor the river rather than the cathedral (Fox, op cit.: 9).

Years later, in *The Jazz Composer*, Collier discusses how he fashioned a compositional approach that did not rely on particular aggregations of instruments and notes: 'My answer to this has been to develop methods that are designed to use *the creativity of the group* playing them...' (Collier 2009a: 272, emphasis mine). The key to understanding Collier's jazz aesthetic is that for him the individual creates in a setting, where the creative efforts of the group can aid or hinder the act of creation. The composer's task is to shift the balance always in favour of the former and, referring to Charles Fox's comments above, to create shape.

There is one final point to be made in relation to *Inside Jazz* and Collier's emergent aesthetic. This is, at this stage, implicit. However, his understanding of jazz can be best summed up by a quote from Bill Evans, which he references in *The Jazz Composer*: 'Jazz is not a what. It is a how' (quoted in Collier 2009a: 312). By this token, jazz differs from classical music – and from folk or pop or rock or country music – by virtue of the fact that it is not a style or genre but a way of making music. It is a river rather than a cathedral.

Of the two books, *Jazz* and *Inside Jazz*, both were well-reviewed but the former, with its educational intent, received coverage in eighteen different publications and other media from the *Financial Times* to the *Times Educational Supplement* and *Music in Education*. Kevin Henriques' review in the *FT* sums up the consensus: '*Jazz, a Student's and Teacher's Guide*...provides for newcomers a simple, easy-to-follow introduction to jazz as well as plenty to interest the informed devotee. Apart from explaining the structure of jazz he writes pertinently about its leading musicians and the music itself' (Henriques 1975: 3). *Inside Jazz* did even better in terms of reviews, appearing in a total of twenty publications from local papers such as the *Kentish Observer* to the *Oldham Chronicle* to the *Sunday Times*, *Time Out*, *Jazz Journal* and even *New Society*. Writing in the latter, Bill Lucklin in his review of both *Inside Jazz* and Ian Carr's *Music Outside* for *New Society* summed up one aspect of both books – the parlous and troubled state of jazz in Britain – when he concluded:

> The prospect for jazz in this country may well be depressing, but the business of self-discovery has at least begun; and it will be enriched by studies from within such as these by Carr and Collier. More significantly, this self-discovery will in the long run surely contribute to a committed unearthing of the control of popular culture as a whole (Lucklin 1973: 610).

Lucklin clearly pinned his hopes on a jazz and cultural activism that might have been present at that point but of which there is currently and sadly little evidence. The other review of note came from 'mainstream' clarinettist Sandy Brown writing in *Punch*. Collier was a big fan of Brown and actually featured him in one of his groups, which unfortunately went unrecorded. Collier comments in *Inside Jazz*, 'Sandy's kind of jazz – classified as "mainstream" but, like any good jazz, timeless' (Collier 1973a: 46). Brown's review, which covers both *Inside Jazz* and *Music Outside*, speaks beautifully and wittily about its subject but also adds so much about the author himself. It is delightfully cantankerous. In one passage, Brown corrects the psychiatrist R. D. Laing's description of schizophrenics as people who mentally had their backs turned to you. For Brown, it is the lay 'British public', who in the case of jazz had turned their backs on jazz.

> This is the condition which a creative jazz musician is normally presented by the British public. Almost in self-defence we considered that the public were mad and thus urgently in need of treatment.

> Lacking the appropriate tools of psychiatry, electric-shock therapy and so on, treatment was occasionally administered manually, resulting in musicians arriving home from a tour not only mentally exhausted but physically injured as well.

Brown notes that Collier 'traces jazz history simplistically, which is all he had space to do if he were to get on with his real message'.

> Graham Collier adopts an approach which is ideal for the newcomer to the what-must-be-news-to-many fact that British jazz music, persecuted as it is, leads the world in some of the most vital aspects of the music: stylistic and thematic invention.

And he adds, 'These are kindly books. Treat them kindly. They let the Great British Philistine down gently' (Brown, S. 1974: 141).

Details of the advances that Collier received for these books may be of some interest, not least to present-day authors. The Berklee School book, *Compositional Devices* (1975b), paid $250 in advance, *Inside Jazz* (Quartet) gave Collier £600 paid in three instalments and Cambridge University Press allowed him £250 towards the book, £100 for the use of the music transcripts, £25 for the backing tape and a total of £150 paid in two instalments for the LP and booklet. It is not clear who paid for the actual recording of the LP and backing tape. Including an estimate of the value of the Berklee payment in pounds sterling, this came to £1225. This would amount today to the equivalent of £12,930 in terms of purchasing power or £23,250 in terms of relative income value. That means that the total sum would have covered Collier's living expenses for between six and twelve months.

The calculation reveals several things. Firstly, it shows how the fortunes of jazz – and publishing – have continued to ebb, such advances being rare indeed today. Secondly, it reveals Collier's skills as a negotiator. Thirdly, it indicates a worthy capacity for hard work on his part. Finally, it proves again his ability to diversify within his career.

It seems useful to deal in detail with Collier's relationship with Cambridge University Press at this juncture. As with his dealings with Quartet, Collier's relationship with CUP was not without its issues. We will refer to Quartet later. The first problem with the publisher was over the issue of mechanical royalties for the Collier compositions included on the two LPs and the cassette. CUP didn't initially accept that he had a right to these royalties, despite the compositions being copyrighted to him. Collier involved solicitors to represent him, not for the last time in his career, and the matter was resolved in his favour.

The next problem came in the late seventies, when Collier contacted the publisher regarding the possibility of a new edition of *Jazz: A Student's and Teacher's Guide*. The publishing director of CUP, Rosemary Davidson, gave details of sales to date (1975–79) in her reply (dated 26 March 1979) – a total of nearly 7500, hardback and paperback – and pointed out that the company considered they had sufficient stock to meet future demand. The letter was firm but very reasonable and polite and Collier, somewhat reluctantly, let the matter go.

There was no further correspondence until autumn 1986. Collier had been teaching at Dartington Hall School in Devon in the summer. There he had met the composer and educator, John Paynter, who was at the time the general editor of the *Resources of Music* series, under which imprint *Jazz: A Student's and Teacher's Guide* had appeared. Quite what Paynter said to him is unclear but it led to an angry letter to Ms Davidson from Collier (dated 2 September 1986), basically accusing CUP of failing to continue to maintain sales of the book both in the UK and in its various German, Norwegian and other translations. Looking at the figures quoted for the sales of the translations, these do seem pitifully small, given that the German and Norwegian publishers had wished to publish them. In this, at least, he may have had a point. His letter read, 'Is this all coincidence (bad deals being made everywhere), incompetence in selling from all three of you [author's note: presumably CUP and the German and Norwegian publishers] or some other reason yet unthought of?'

Ms Davidson replied (dated 22 October 1986) reasonably that the book had come out in 1977 and that sales tended to tail off over time. She noted that the environment in which publishers found themselves in 1986 was very different from that which pertained when the book was commissioned. She added in response to comments by Collier in his letter, 'I do not think either that the book is bad or that we have been incompetent in selling it'.

In his reply, Collier (dated 26 October 1986) responded that he had been approached on many occasions by individuals who wanted the book but had had difficulty in 'finding it in the shops'. One suspects that this was the kind of item that most bookshops would be happy to order but not necessarily keep on the shelf. However, Collier was not easily assuaged. Ms Davidson's reply (dated 31 October 1986) was succinct. She wrote, 'I can't think of anything to add in reply to your letter of October 26, so I am afraid all I can do is acknowledge your letter and hope that the translations do better in the future'.

* * *

Two other significant events occurred for Collier in the early to mid-seventies. Firstly, he was invited, as were Ian Carr, Mike Westbrook and Mike Gibbs, to compose a piece of music by the Globe Playhouse Trust for a concert at Southwark Cathedral in honour of Shakespeare's birthday. The purpose of the concert, the second such event, was to raise awareness of the trust and its goal of building an Elizabethan theatre on the banks of the Thames, close to where the original Globe Theatre might have stood.

The music from the four composers was performed by an augmented Graham Collier Music with Dick Pearce and Harry Beckett on trumpet and flugelhorn, Brian Smith and Art Themen on woodwinds, Ed Speight on guitar, Geoff Castle on piano, John Webb on drums and Collier on bass. The second set was performed by singer Annie Ross and her quartet. Of the compositions, only Gibbs' 'Lady Mac' and Carr's 'Ban Ban Caliban' later found their way onto record.[4] Two rather contradictory reviews appeared, one by Charles Fox in the *New Statesman* (Fox 1973) and the other by Ron Brown in *Jazz Journal* (Brown 1973). In fact, so great are the differences, it almost seems like the two writers had attended two different concerts. The acoustics were clearly an issue and, whilst Fox praised Annie Ross for her approach to the problem, Brown described most of her singing as inaudible. It seems likely that how the performance was heard and perceived owed a lot to where in the cathedral the listener sat.

There is mention in the 'Timeline' of another new, extended composition – *Odyssey*, which included the piece 'New Dawn' and which would appear on Collier's next album, *Darius*. This was for an eleven-piece group. Hurt appears to have left by then but the remaining five members of the *Portraits* group were augmented by Art Themen, Brian Smith and Alan Skidmore on saxes, Harry Beckett and Kenny Wheeler on trumpets and a cellist. The piece was performed twice, once at the Institute for Contemporary Arts (August 1973) and then at the Cockpit Theatre in Marylebone (October 1973). Early in 1974, Collier's group undertook a short, six-date UK tour and, ever one to expand his horizons, Collier also refers in his 'Timeline' to working on a musical to be called, 'Postal Order from my Grannie', and also a 'jazz opera' entitled 'World Turned Upside Down' with Mike Naylor. Collier had met Naylor, who was the creative director of a large advertising agency, when he was hired to do a number of jingles for ICI and music for a commercial for South West Gas.

'World Turned Upside Down' was performed once only, at the Institute of Contemporary Arts in August 1974. However, two of the Collier/Naylor songs from it – 'Singing for the Small Change' and 'It's Been So Good' – were performed by Norma Winstone for a BBC Radio 3 broadcast on 17 August 1975. 'Singing for the Small Change', a blues with a strong rock backbeat, was released on the *Trad Dads, Dirty Boppers and Free Fusioneers* compilation on Reel Recordings that accompanied the book of that same name.

'Postal Order from my Grannie', which had nothing to do with a Monty Python sketch with a similar title, was completed but never made it to the stage. Hattie Naylor, Mike Naylor's daughter and herself a playwright with a number of successes to her name, remembers seeing 'World Turned Upside Down' at the ICA. She explained that it was a serious dramatic piece with a woman as its central character and a kind of *Brief Encounter* theme of an illicit affair. Hattie Naylor remembers it was 'quite sassy with gorgeous songs'. 'Postal Order from my Grannie' was built around a 'Joe Orton/Mr Sloan-like' figure. Naylor described it as 'a lovely story, again with strong songs and music'.[5]

Collier, and later his partner John Gill, became close friends of Mike and Barbie Naylor, often visiting them in their Cotswolds home. Hattie Naylor's recollections of Collier are intriguing, conveying something quite affecting about his personality and his lifestyle.

> Graham was really like an uncle to us, which is a testament to how much he was around. He stayed with us and came for Christmas. We were all enormously fond of him. I remember that he had a string of young male lovers before John came into his life. I knew these young men were boyfriends and I knew that Graham was homosexual. They were all, without exception, very kind and patient with my sister and brothers and me and I really loved spending time with Graham and these gentle young men. I stayed with him in his Earl's Court flat, in fact just after he had met John. So, I knew John right from the beginning of their relationship.
>
> Knowing them became an important part of my upbringing and I consequently grew up with an absence of prejudice. This went on to inform my own writing and also my activism. Both John and Graham were marvellous generous men. My parents' last child Ben was a particularly enchanting child and Graham was inspired to write a piece of music for him, which he called 'Little Ben', as a gift not only to Ben but to the whole of our family (Interview Naylor/ Heining 2017).[6]

In March 1974, Collier launched his record company, Mosaic, recording *Darius* with a new frontline at Cranfield Institute in Bedfordshire for its first release. 1974 was one of Collier's busiest years. There was music for a Shell Oil documentary, a further UK tour in November, several teaching situations, including at the Wavendon Allmusic Plan in Buckinghamshire, a BBC Jazz Club broadcast (a tribute to Ellington) and, on one occasion, Collier 'depped' for John Dankworth, teaching at the Royal Academy of Music.

However, the year's other major event came in the form of a three-week tour of Germany, Switzerland and France, sponsored by the British Council, who effectively underwrote the tour for the sum of £3000. This seems to have been the first of several such Collier tours supported by the Council and which would take him and his music to the Far East, India, Greece and Israel amongst other places. This was yet another example of Collier's enterprise and ingenuity and makes an interesting riposte to Tony Oxley's comment in response to Alan Wakeman's question, 'How come Graham gets all this work?', noted earlier.

The tour was not without incident but seems to have been marked by a great degree of resourcefulness by one promoter. A gig in Willisau was missed due to customs and other delays but Bruno Rub, an important figure in jazz and in the history of the Willisau Jazz Festival, succeeded in organizing two extra concerts at very short notice. The first of these was a 'lecture-concert' at a local school 'with an older student doing the translation'. The second took place in Baden, a small town north of Zurich, where the band played for 'Takings less expenses and attracted over 100 people at two days notice'. A concert in Lausanne was also broadcast in part on Swiss radio.

There is a sense of enthusiasm in Collier's report on the tour for the British Council that is quite infectious. On a night off in Corsica, they played a gig for the crew and officers of *H.M.S. Hampshire*, which was moored in Ajaccio harbour. A concert in Bastia followed a 'hair-raising ride' across the island to perform to a small but appreciative audience in a cinema, but the gig in Ajaccio itself saw the band entertain an audience of between 400–500 in near-perfect circumstances: 'good hall, good piano and good audience'. The one that followed in Toulouse was, it seems, a disaster. There was no piano: 'The manager said he'd been told by the British Council in Paris that we didn't need one!' The acoustics were also poor and the band bus was broken into and two cassette recorders stolen. All in all, Collier reflected, 'Musically I feel it was largely a successful tour but in most cases the promotion left a lot to be desired' (Collier 1974).[7]

By the time the tour took place, Collier had released his new album, *Darius*. This saw Harry Beckett return to the fold in place of Dick Pearce. Trombonist Derek Wadsworth joined the group, staying on for *Midnight Blue*, making the sextet the first Collier group not to feature saxophone.

Following the weaker *Portraits*, *Darius* saw a return to form. Released in 1974, it bears comparison stylistically, sonically and texturally with early Nucleus, notably with *Elastic Rock* and *We'll Talk About It Later*. It shares a similar emphasis in terms of pacing, mainly a moderate tempo, slowing into the ballad section of 'Part 2' and with the slow vamp for 'Part 4', but quickening with the opening of 'Part 3'. Generally in small-group jazz, bandleaders prefer to use one brass and one or two woodwinds in the frontline for timbral variety, though obviously the use of trumpet, sax (or in early jazz, clarinet) and trombone is also common, for example with the Jazz Messengers. One parallel, in terms of *Darius*' frontline instrumentation, would be with the Clark Terry–Bob Brookmeyer group of the 1960s and there are perhaps echoes of that 'cool' vibe. Collier's decision to use trumpet and trombone works well here, partly due to the level of empathy between Beckett and Wadsworth, and partly due to the fact that the music was clearly written with both players and instruments in mind. In fact, the backing seems to be built around Beckett and Wadsworth. It is as if the rhythm section enwraps the two brass rather than the frontline soaring over the rhythm. There are parallels here with Nucleus but more in terms of the ensembles written and arranged for Carr's group than in terms of the relationship between soloist and backing. On *Darius*, the solo unfolds almost within the womb of the rhythm section.

Collier also eschews his preference for unusual time signatures and asymmetrical metres. Much, if not all, of the music is in 4/4 and built mainly upon a mode derived from the B flat scale but with frequent uses of flattened notes outside the scale. This is confirmed by Roger Dean in *New Structures in Jazz* (1992) where he notes that *Darius* represented a move towards a greater harmonic freedom. Specifically, he points out that Collier was including in the thematic material a 'limited number of notes outside the main harmonies upon which the improviser can draw offering harmonic contrast' (Dean 1992: 166).

The first section of *Darius* uses a minimal amount of written material and is essentially built upon a number of motifs. The other three movements seem to offer more detailed written instruction in terms of how melody, counter melody and backings intersect. Throughout *Darius*, Collier achieves an intriguing layering effect in the music by allowing the musicians a certain degree of rhythmic freedom and by allowing them to approach the music ad lib using the notes from within and outside the main harmonic structure. John Webb is given considerable latitude throughout. The main written instruction to the drums is defined as 'free rock', an instruction that seems to carry for all four sections. It is a role Webb fills with great skill. Geoff Castle's electric piano adds some lovely colours and his two cadenzas, with baroque-like flourishes, and solo in 'Part 3', by far the piece's longest section, are beautifully weighted.

The dominant voices on *Darius*, however, are Derek Wadsworth and Harry Beckett. 'Part 2' is a ballad feature for Wadsworth complete with characteristic slurs and growls on his trombone. The written instructions on the manuscript paper for 'Part 2' are intriguing and apply to the whole section: 'Very gentle but full *pianissimo* to *mezzo forte* to *pianissimo* start with *rubato* melody, then use of any elements'. Beckett's rhythmic skills are instantly apparent every time he plays and his solos in 'Part 3' and at the beginning of 'Part 4' have that delightfully warm, tender grace that he brought to everything he did. But it is also the way that Beckett and Wadsworth combine that lifts *Darius* to a much higher level than was the case with *Portraits*. It is not just the empathy that they achieve but the way in which they move in and around each other like two dancers, lithe and flowing.

Here, as elsewhere in their work together, Collier allows Speight to shift freely between the rhythm section and frontline. Speight is definitely a group player and his support play is assured and confident. But he is also a strong soloist and his playing on 'Part 3' combines elements of jazz and rock guitar perfectly. At one point early in his solo there is a long pause before he re-enters with a fresh aggression that raises the tension dramatically.

The final piece on *Darius* is 'New Dawn'. It is a rather lovely and very slow waltz in 6/4 with chiming guitar and mandolin-like trills from Ed Speight underpinning gutbucket trombone from Derek Wadsworth with occasional fills from Harry Beckett and some beautifully limber drumming from John Webb. It offers a concise and elegant closure to the record.

Darius was recorded live at Cranfield Institute before an enthusiastic audience. It is beautifully paced and Collier allows the music to shift between a series of moods – slow and stately, quicker and more forceful, lighter and dancing. Some moments do, perhaps, sound a little dated, with touches of seventies fusion. But these are few and detract little from some fine music and strong performances from the sextet, as a group and individually.

Pianist Geoff Castle had made a huge contribution to Collier's music from *Mosaics* to *Darius*, which was to be the final album he made with Collier. Given that the comparison to Nucleus made in terms of *Portraits* and *Darius*, it is worth reminding ourselves that, after leaving Collier, Castle joined Nucleus, another band to which he contributed so much. Castle found the change of groups quite a shock, as he explains:

> [I]t was quite interesting to go from something where it was very hard to put a foot wrong, in terms of the critics, and going to Ian's group who were very appreciated internationally but in this country were just not being treated well by the critics at that time for some reason. But it stood the test of time with Nucleus.

In relation to the differences musically between the two groups, Castle is particularly helpful. With regard to Nucleus, he notes that things were more structured:

> It was much more rhythm based than Graham's stuff. Graham had little riffs in his music as well but...it was a lot looser rhythmically. Ian wanted grooves. So, he wanted this rhythm thing happening.

And he continues:

> But then you had sections with very tricky time signatures. Like Graham's music, it was quite complex in some of the pieces. It was interesting – the contrast there. I actually liked Ian's complexity. I liked the fact that he had much more written on the page than Graham. Graham tended to be more minimalist, whereas Ian wrote a lot of notes. He had problems playing some of them (Laughing) but I liked that and I enjoyed that complexity and the challenge of playing the stuff.

Castle sees the music he made with Nucleus as 'more technically intricate' but adds that both 'were amazing learning experiences'. And he adds, 'Graham's [music] had much more group improvisation inside the ensemble. Whereas, Ian's music tended to have soloists accompanied by rhythm section format. So, there was a lot less improvisation in the group as a whole and over the whole performance' (Interview Castle/Heining 2014).

The first part of *Darius*, or rather another version of it, was released as the second side of the Music Resources LP, *Jazz Lecture Concert*, issued to coincide with Collier's book *Jazz: A Student's and Teacher's Guide*. However, with the *Darius* LP, Collier took the unusual step of making the written music available at the same time, an interesting innovation, which emphasizes Collier's desire to see jazz and his music, in particular, taken seriously. The album garnered a fair span of reviews, which ranged as ever from the highly enthusiastic – Steve Voce in *Jazz Journal* (Voce 1975) and Kevin Henriques (1975) in the *Financial Times* – to the more reserved – John Fordham in *Time Out*, who reviewed both *Darius* and Stan Tracey's *Alone at Wigmore Hall* (Fordham 1974).[8]

The follow-up to *Darius*, *Midnight Blue*, was recorded in February 1975 and released later that year. However, for reasons that are not quite clear, when the Graham Collier Music with a new line-up toured Europe in August, including performing at the Middelheim Festival, they were still performing *Darius* rather than premiering the new album. This is evident from the recording issued alongside *Workpoints* by Cuneiform in 2005.[9] The one change in the band for the new record was Geoff Castle's replacement by Roger Dean.

* * *

In *New Structures in Jazz*, Roger Dean makes a very useful series of points regarding the comparison between Collier's early works and the mid-period, for Dean, represented by *New Conditions* and, to a lesser extent, *Midnight Blue*. He describes how the early compositions would begin with 'slow ballads revolving around maj 7 and min 7b5 chords, or faster pieces with modal bases for improvising'. Although Collier had always used motivic elements as the bases for his improvisers' solos, these were initially restricted to material taken from simple harmonies or scalar motifs. Dean notes in relation to *Midnight Blue* that 'elements of two modes or scales might be combined in a single chord, and there was greater use of "open" sections of improvising in which solo length is not specified' (Dean 1992: 164). Essentially, this opened up greater harmonic possibilities for improvisers and took the music more clearly into areas of polytonality. As Dean suggests, this presaged the next major shift in Collier's writing that would be seen with *New Conditions* (1976).

Midnight Blue also featured Derek Wadsworth's last appearance with the sextet. It is hard to be entirely objective about Wadsworth's playing. Along with Nick Evans and Malcolm Griffiths, he is surely one of the finest modern jazz trombonists to come out of Britain or anywhere else during this period. Wadsworth was also a successful arranger and composer both for film and television, working twice with director Lindsay Anderson on *Britannia Hospital* and *The Whales of August*, and with various MOR, pop and rock acts such as the Rolling Stones, the Small Faces, Nina Simone, Judy Garland and Dusty Springfield. It seems reasonable to suggest that in Wadsworth the skills involved in being an instrumentalist and soloist, on the one hand, and being an arranger of music, on the other, were very closely integrated. This is not to suggest that his playing with Collier is overly formal. In fact, his every solo or ensemble contribution seems spontaneous and immediate in its emotional impact. It is more that Wadsworth seems totally aware of the frame of the music and how to structure his contribution to best effect. Poise and elegance combine perfectly with an earthy, bluesy sensibility.

Midnight Blue was not the first of Collier's compositions to draw upon fine art and he is still at this point using this as a referential or inspirational source, rather than as a way of informing his own compositional practice more directly. All three tracks on the record are responses to paintings by American abstract expressionist, Barnett Newman – *Midnight Blue*, *Adam* and *Cathedra*. Newman was a great proselytizer on behalf of his own work and on behalf of other abstract expressionists, something that Collier could, no doubt, relate to. However, one suspects that there was a great deal in Newman's writings that chimed with Collier's own, developing aesthetic. The American tended to wrap his pronouncements in polemical language. So, 'man's first speech was poetic before it was utilitarian' (Newman 1947a) and the 'basis of an aesthetic act is the pure idea…the pure idea is of necessity, an aesthetic act' (ibid.). Or from an article published in the magazine *Tiger's Eye*, which Newman edited, 'Man's first expression, like his first dream, was an aesthetic one', and 'The human in language is literature, not communication' (Newman 1947b). This is about more than self-belief; it is about a romantic ideal of art and one to a certain extent predicated on Emmanuel Kant's concept of the 'sublime', albeit with a greater emphasis on desire and emotion against Kant's contemplative reflection (Haskins 1989).

Midnight Blue features three tracks: the long title track, which occupied side one of the original vinyl, and the comparatively short 'Adam' and 'Cathedra'. After the jazz-rock of *Darius*, *Midnight Blue* was essentially an acoustic record. It is hard to know precisely what it was that Collier wanted to convey about Barnett Newman's paintings. However, in 1976, he visited Amsterdam's Stedelijk Museum and saw Newman's *Cathedra* for the first time in the flesh. He wrote in his 'Timeline', 'It really sings, very deep, infinite, seems to pulse with life…certainly the best Newman I've seen'. The three paintings chosen by Collier are large canvases featuring fields of colour with a 'zip', a vertical line of contrasting colour, or in the case of *Adam* three 'zips'. The canvases seem to vibrate. One suspects that it is this quality that Collier wished to represent musically.[10]

Whilst Roger Dean has noted that, 'Complete harmonic freedom, permitting tonality, polytonality and atonality was reached by the time of *Midnight Blue*' (Dean 1992: 166), this is accessible music performed by a band that is very tight and disciplined. Inevitably, it features Collier trademarks such as intersecting themes, countermelodies played by the frontline, linking cadenzas, shifting moods and changes of tempo. But each track pulsates, often over a driving rhythm, most notably on 'Cathedra'. New recruit Dean would prove to be by far the longest serving pianist to work with Collier. His arrival certainly changed the group sound and it seemed to acquire at this point something of the feel of the Coltrane Quartet with McCoy Tyner.

Throughout, the confidence, the swing and verve of the group is always matched by strong individual performances. As with *Darius*, its pacing is one of the keys to the record's success. Dean points out that, with *Midnight Blue*, Collier preferred to allow the rhythmic 'feel' for a particular piece 'to be generated and decided during rehearsal' (Dean 1992: 166). Barry McRae in his review for *Jazz Journal* (McRae 1976a) commented on hearing these pieces performed live: 'It is instructive to hear how each player changes from one date to another'. It is clear from such comments, as well as from his own writings on jazz, that, for Collier, jazz was a collaborative art and that he was a composer who trusted his musicians.

Despite being one of Collier's most approachable albums, *Midnight Blue* garnered very few reviews, the most prestigious being that by Barry McRae, while *Music Week* described the album as arguably 'the best British jazz album of 1975' (BGOCD 895 sleeve notes). This was a great shame, albeit one reflecting the increasing difficulties facing British jazz and its musicians at the time. On a more positive note, the Graham Collier Music with the addition of Art Themen were able to promote the album at a concert at London's Queen Elizabeth Hall on Monday 24 November 1975. This time, Collier's sponsors were the Park Lane Group, an organization noted for its sponsorship of young musicians, mainly from classical music. Sponsorship from this source was another Collier coup and Park Lane would sponsor a further concert in 1978 at the same venue, on that occasion featuring *The Day of the Dead*. In November 1975, however, Collier would present 'Midnight Blue' and 'Adam' from the new album, along with *British Conversations*, a commission for Swedish Radio premiered earlier in Stockholm in 1975, with the Swedish Radio Big Band along with Harry Beckett and Ed Speight, and *Café Blues*, a commission from the Park Lane Group based on Carson McCullers' short story, *The Ballad of the Sad Café*. The concert was favourably reviewed in the *Sunday Times* by Derek Jewell (1975).

With Collier busily working on his biography of Cleo Laine and John Dankworth for Quartet Books, a new album and a new band, he was now approaching his fortieth year. He had achieved a huge amount in a short space of time. He was a published author, had recorded and released seven albums as a leader to some critical acclaim and he had done so pretty much on his own terms, as a result of astute self-promotion. Further changes would follow in his music, notably with the next album *New Conditions*, and in his personal and professional life.

Notes

1. There is a study that appeared in the *Journal of Psychiatric Research*, 'Mental illness, suicide and creativity: 40-year prospective total population study', which was much trumpeted in the press (Kyaga *et al.* 2012: 1–8). This was a longitudinal study using a large population sample. However, as the authors note the study had its limitations. 'Limitations include the use of scientific and artistic occupations as a proxy for creativity, patients having higher rates of missing data than their respective controls, different diagnostic systems throughout the study, the narrow definition of scientific occupations as those active solely within the academic arena, and artistic occupations possibly reflecting social drift rather than creativity' (p. 8). To that I would add that any such study deals only with those who report or are reported as having a diagnosable psychiatric illness. There is no way of knowing whether creative individuals suffering depression are more or less likely to report than others in the general population. As a representative of the charity MIND com-

mented at the time, 'It is important that we do not romanticise people with mental health problems, who are too often portrayed as struggling creative geniuses' (http://www.bbc.co.uk/news/health-19959565).

2. *Children of Adam* was first performed at The Bankside Globe on 3 September 1972. This refers to the public house and obviously not to the Globe theatre, which opened in 1997.

3. Trumpeter John Chilton's *Who's Who of Jazz: Storyville to Swing Street* first appeared in 1970 but is an encyclopaedia of jazz.

4. 'Lady Mac' appeared in two guises on Mike Gibbs' album *In The Public Interest* with Gary Burton (Polydor 1974) and again on *The Only Chrome Waterfall Orchestra* (Bronze 1975). 'Ban Ban Caliban' appeared in part only as 'Caliban' on the Nucleus record, *Roots* (Vertigo 1973). The following year, the trust put on another concert this time with contributions from Gibbs, Carr, Neil Ardley and Stan Tracey. It was subsequently released as a double album on the Argo label under the title, *Will Power – A Shakespeare Birthday Celebration in Music* and has been reissued in 2005 by the Vocalion label.

5. Mike Naylor's advertising career was highly successful – the much loved/loathed 'Milky Bar Kid' was his creation. His daughter Hattie is a successful playwright for stage, TV and radio. Her *The Diaries of Samuel Pepys* was nominated Best Radio Drama 2012, while *The Aeneid* was nominated Best Radio Adaptation, BBC Audio awards 2013. In the 'Timeline' Collier also notes writing songs with Naylor for Marion Montgomery. However, her partner, Laurie Holloway, has no recollection of any Collier songs being recorded by his late wife.

6. 'Little Ben' can be found on the 'Live at Middelheim' CD released as part of the *Workpoints* CD by Cuneiform in 2005 (Rune 213–14).

7. It is interesting to note that Collier's contacts and supporters at the British Council were none other than Grayston Burgess, the famous English counter-tenor and conductor, and the composer Barrie Iliffe. The cost for the tour, including subsistence, hotels, travel, administration and payment of the band, came to £7449.30.

8. Rather unfortunately, Fordham chides Collier for his absence of balls, whilst Stan Tracey is credited with 'having several sets to spare'.

9. The Middelheim concert is featured as the second CD released by Cuneiform along with the epic *Hoarded Dreams*, recorded at Bracknell in 1983. It is a good live set, indeed Ed Speight cites it as one of his most enjoyable and satisfying gigs with Collier's Music, but it does live somewhat in the shadows of its partner disc.

10. Collier's notes for the record describe his attempts not as a desire to represent these paintings in musical terms but in relation to his 'subjective reactions to the paintings; supported by the writings by and about the artist in the Tate Gallery exhibition catalogue of 1972'.

7 Glad to Be Gay

Asked in December 2008 about his experiences as a gay man in the predominantly male and heterosexual world of British jazz, Collier's reply revealed both his capacity to negotiate that world effectively and the apparent absence of prurience on the part of British jazzers.

> I don't think it was ever a problem – possibly because I was more of a loner composer/bandleader than a regular gigging musician. The musicians I worked with never bothered if I brought a boyfriend to a gig, probably never noticed until it was someone regular. Although when John [Gill] and I met in 1976, he came on an Arts Council Great Britain tour with me and they certainly knew then, but there were never any problems. I even got my band to play at a Campaign For Homosexual Equality conference for free in Sheffield.

His strategy, he explained, was simple, '[I] was always surrounded by nice people – kind of a vicious circle but if I had suspected any strong anti-feminist or gay vibe, they wouldn't have been there in the first place'. Collier took care to choose people for their musical ability but also because he felt he could work with them as individuals (Email Collier/Heining 2008). As Duke Ellington once suggested in one of Collier's favourite quotes, it was important to 'get to know how they play poker'.

Thirty-five years later, in 2010, the American jazz magazine *Jazz Times* published a piece by John Murph on gay men and lesbians in jazz under the title, 'Rhapsody in rainbow: jazz and the queer aesthetic'. The piece provoked a certain amount of controversy about the use of the word 'queer'. It prompted a response on the magazine's website from Collier that expresses very clearly his own position and experiences in the jazz world.

> Thanks for the article. I am a veteran gay British jazz musician/composer and I'm pleased to say I've been out, with no problems either on the band stand, or in my previous academic teaching post in London. But, of course one knows others – in jazz and elsewhere – who haven't made that move. Which I find sad in jazz where the music is supposed to be honest, and sad elsewhere, when one realises the importance of role models. And speaking of the controversy over the word 'Queer' I should also put a plug in for my partner John Gill's book *Queer Noises: Male and Female Homosexuality in Twentieth Century Music* (1995) (Email interview Gill/Heining 2015).

Collier met John Gill, who was to become his life partner, in 1976 around the time he was working on *New Conditions*. Gill was involved with the Gay Liberation movement through the Campaign for Homosexual Equality (CHE) and was meeting a 'fellow politico' in The Salisbury in Leicester Square, at that time a gay bar. He had recently discovered Collier's album, *Mosaics*, albeit in the first instance due to its cover design by artist, Roger Dean. Gill's colleague introduced him to another man standing nearby, whispering discretely, 'This guy's a crushing bore. I think he works for one of the local CHE organisations', having confused him with someone else entirely. Gill told me:

> Graham introduced himself and it was one of those classic cliché moments. I said, '*The* Graham Collier?' (Laughing) We arranged to meet for a drink a couple of days later, so I went out and bought a couple more of his albums of the early stuff. We went out on a date and it went from there (Interview Gill/Heining, March 2015).

They became friends in the first instance rather than lovers, as Gill explains: 'It started as a friendship actually and developed into a relationship almost by accident'. At the time Gill was living in a squat in Tufnell Park, whilst Collier had a mortgage on a flat in Nutford Place, Paddington. Collier could never really be described as an 'easy-going' individual. He believed passionately in what he was doing and was trying to achieve. As Gill says, he was one of those people whose emotions were always close to the surface. He cried easily and, if something upset him, he would let people know. However, certain colleagues, notably Ed Speight, suggest that Collier seemed more settled in himself after he met John Gill.

Gill's response to that suggestion is measured and reflective.

> We sort of came together by accident but I even thought at the time that perhaps settling down with someone, that is me, may have made Graham more secure because he was still in the process of coming out in some ways. I noticed that he was coming out more as we were together. However, we never sort of set out with any kind of vision of 'let's live together forever' (Email interview Gill/Heining 2015).

Certainly, Collier had made no secret that he was gay. Several years before the Keith Howes' article in *Gay News* (1976), he had been interviewed by Peter Bostrell for another gay magazine, *Lunch*. In a candid and thoughtful interview, Bostrell asked Collier, 'Is your music very tied to your love-life, to your emotional life in general?' Collier acknowledged that perhaps, 'to be creative at all one lives much more off one's emotions', and went on to say:

> Creativity is inevitably erratic but I've found that to stimulate myself requires three things: the external necessity to work, meeting a deadline, fulfilling a commission. I need the freedom to work. I need to have my life organized so that I'm not worried about the business of life while I'm creating. Thirdly I need some kind of emotional relationship. These things all interact.

Collier explained that he could function creatively, if two of the three conditions were fulfilled, 'But just to have one (or at the moment none!) – that makes for a very strange problem'. Asked by Bostrell if he saw that 'strange problem' as specific to him as a gay composer, Collier responded, 'Well, in one way of course it would be identical if I were straight. The problems of gay people are perhaps not as special as gay people would sometimes like to make them sound' (Bostrell 1973: 5).

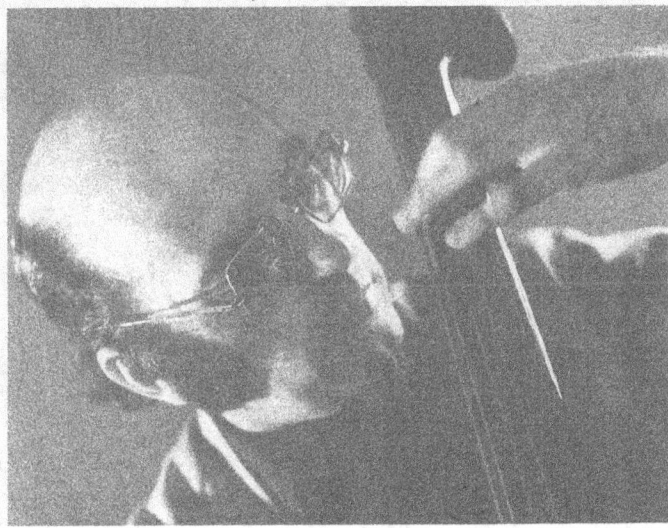

Figure 8. Cover of *Lunch* Magazine, May 1973. Ironically titled 'Graham Collier; Gay Jazzman'.

However, as Gill points out, Collier was 'not a joiner'. Gill, by contrast, was far more politically aware and active and not just in terms of gay issues. Expanding on his earlier point that Collier was still in the process of 'coming out' when they met, Gill adds, 'He was unabashedly "out" but I think it was more a question of...not of self-assertiveness but being more at home in his skin as a gay man, as any gay man would when they found themselves in a settled relationship' (Email interview Gill/Heining 2015). There are discrepancies between John Gill's recollections regarding when he and Collier began living together and Collier's 'Timeline'. According to Gill, this was in the autumn 1976 when he was starting at college studying for a degree in English. The 'Timeline', however, gives the date as May 1977. Either way, they remained together until Collier's death in September 2011.

Collier had, by this point, released just two records on his own Mosaic imprint – *Darius* and *Midnight Blue*. However, in August 1976, he had succeeded in obtaining Arts Council funding for the label and for the recording of a new album, *New Conditions*, to the amount of £4000. This funding source enabled Collier to release records by other musicians as well as his own recordings. In addition, the Arts Council helped fund the Graham Collier Music UK tour in support of *New Conditions*. This was yet another example of Collier's ability to negotiate with 'the suits' and he was as ever scrupulously honest in his dealings with the Council. Collier's skills when it came to the business side were second to none. On the *New Conditions* tour and after, John Gill was able to observe this at first had, as he notes:

> I think he was quite good at the business – full stop! It didn't make him rich by any means, as we both know. But I think you mentioned this before when we spoke – the army background gave him a sense, not just of discipline but, of organisation. I think he realised that it was important to be able to do the business side of things, as well as the music. That was why he set up his own record company. That's why he organized his own tours (Email interview Gill/Heining 2015).

New Conditions was composed early in 1976 and was first performed in Paris on 26 January 1976 and broadcast by Radio France, while Collier and his band – now a twelve-piece big band – were on a tour of France. Collier had noted in his diary earlier in January, 'New found authority. Band working for me'. The comment seems to indicate that he felt he had made something of a breakthrough as a composer and bandleader. The tour itself was not without incident. The band faced a fourteen-hour trip from Paris to Toulouse in heavy snow and, en route to Corsica, 'Derek Wadsworth refused to fly from Marseilles to Corsica at the last minute' ('Timeline'). Quite what the problem was remains a mystery.

Collier had used modular structures in his music before, in terms of the potential these offered to change the order in which different sections of a composition might be performed, as well as in terms of their length or chosen soloists. Now the modular structures themselves contained their own micro-modular structures, which could be further modified and moved around in performance. At the same time, as Collier describes below, he provided the musical elements upon which his musicians would draw in their solos:

> It [*New Conditions*] was composed in order to present the musicians with new challenges in improvisation within a carefully constructed – though seemingly free – compositional framework. Each section contains some new or relatively little used technique to this end, with perhaps the most common being the construction of solos and backing passages from given motifs (shown for example in the piano solo of Part 2). The most difficult technique – and the rarest – is shown in Part 1. Here the three trumpets are asked to incorporate written material – played in unison with other members of the band – into their otherwise freely improvised solos (*New Conditions* original sleeve notes; Collier 1976b).

On the one hand, the use of motifs in his work clearly predates *New Conditions*. In addition, the use of simultaneous improvisations from selected instruments had been a feature of *Workpoints*. On the other hand, Collier seems to suggest here either a return to a device previously used but not since, or that its use in this context is a further development of the technique. The more general point stands, however. His aim with *New Conditions* was to create new conditions for improvisation.

By this point in the fortunes of jazz, reviews and even opportunities to be reviewed were diminishing. Several reviews of *New Conditions*, one from Charles Fox in *Gay News*, another from Yves Thebault in *Jazz Magazine* and another from Barry McRae in *Jazz Journal*, were favourable. The one from Chris Welch in *Melody Maker*, once the musician's bible, attempted to be witty but only succeeded in being smug. Whatever his strengths as a writer, Welch was rather conservative in his big band tastes – Buddy Rich, Thad Jones-Mel Lewis and Kenny Clarke-Francy Boland. Essentially, his review focused on chiding Collier for not producing something along such lines.

> While one loathes to halt the search for new ideas and concepts there is no sense in ditching perfectly valid ones along the way. There's nothing wrong with playing unison, with editing, with re-arranging ideas that don't happen, with bringing a stronger sense of direction to the proceedings (Welch 1978: 18).

In fact, there are many 'unison' passages on the record and there is a strong sense of direction and of organization to *New Conditions*. What Collier provided here was simply not to Welch's taste.

Charles Fox's review in *Gay News* came about, as Fox took delight in pointing out, from a rather obvious ruse on Collier's part, one that he would repeat with Fox when it came to the release of his next album, *Symphony of Scorpions*. He gave his column over to Fox but gave him copies to review of *New Conditions*, Roger Dean's first album on Mosaic Records *Lysis Live* and Harry Beckett's *Memories of Bacares* on Hazel and Harry Miller's Ogun label. Fox clearly enjoyed Beckett's offering greatly and was quick to praise Roger Dean's disc. However, his remarks regarding *New Conditions* were typically astute. Fox realized that the record represented a breakthrough for Collier and concluded:

> It is not some prissy notion of being a well-behaved guest that makes me welcome *New Conditions*. From writing too tightly in the early 1960s, Collier moved to what was perhaps too loose an approach. Now he is striking the right balance, firming up, rather as jazz in general appears to be doing at the moment (Fox 1977a).

New Conditions featured a number of new players – Mike Page and Art Themen on saxophones, Pete Duncan on trumpet, Malcolm Griffiths on trombone and percussionist John Mitchell. Alan Wakeman also returned, as did Henry Lowther, who had played on the *Workpoints* tour. The music is non-programmatic and divided into ten sections that are linked through the melodic and motivic material Collier has provided. These episodes vary according to mood, tempo and degree of apparent freedom. The 'Introduction' and 'Part 4' seem loosely structured and led by John Mitchell's array of percussion, supported by Roger Dean on piano and with added fills from the horns. 'Part 2' involves a long solo performance from Dean, at times using prepared piano. 'Part 3', featuring Mike Page's alto, and 'Part 7', with Ed Speight's guitar, are both ballads, the former suggesting the influence of Ellington and the latter that of Gil Evans. 'Part 8' is a hybrid, fragmentary and episodic, but leading into a ballad section with that great servant of British jazz Malcolm Griffiths on trombone. 'Part 1', on the other hand, is for big band with a simultaneous improvisation from the trumpets of Harry Beckett, Henry Lowther and Pete Duncan.

'Part 5' and 'Part 6' are linked by John Webb's drums with 'Part 6' featuring a duel on sopranos from Alan Wakeman and Art Themen alongside fills from the other instruments. That leaves the rather surprising 'Finale', a jazz-rock ending, with Dean on electric piano, to an album that had shown no previous inclination in that direction. This gives an overarching structure to *New Conditions*, as follows – Open Form, Big Band, Solo/Bridging Cadenza, Ballad, Solo with Fills, Duet/Trio (two sopranos and drums), Ballad, Open Form/Ballad, Big Band/Jazz Rock.

We have mentioned both Ellington and Gil Evans. However, there are also echoes of Messiaen – in the brooding fanfares, sustained polytonal chords across the orchestra and the way percussion is used in relation to the horns and chordal instruments. It is not possible to say whether Collier was in any way influenced, consciously or unconsciously, by the French composer. Yet there are certain similarities, notably in the above respects, to Messaien's *Des canyons aux etoiles* and *Et exspecto resurrectionem mortuorum*.[1]

New Conditions was, as both Yves Thibault and Barry McRae noted, a record that found intriguing ways of integrating solo performance within a compositional structure that was paradoxically predetermined but open. A parallel perhaps, as Thibault noted, with Barry Guy's work with the London Jazz Composer's Orchestra. The last word needs to go to Barry McRae, who seems to have grasped Collier's intention accurately when he wrote:

> [E]very solo sequence is an integral part of the composition that contains it. This is perhaps most apparent during the musical discourse that is conducted on Part Four between Mitchell and various sections of the band. It is an item that fully illustrates Collier's use of space and underlines the point that, in his music, tension is built up by the juxtaposition and superimposition of solo parts and ensemble, rather than by any routine principle of overall development (McRae 1977a: 41).

Comparison with other British big band recordings of the period reveals a number of key composers, all dealing with the composition/improvisation dilemma but all reaching their own distinctive solutions – and yet, in certain cases, drawing on the same influence or inspiration in Duke Ellington.

Mike Westbrook's *Citadel/Room 315* (1975) was originally written for the Swedish Radio Jazz Group but recorded by the newly formed Mike Westbrook Orchestra. While Ellington remained a core influence on Westbrook's work throughout his career, *Citadel* is a contemporary British big band album of the period drawing both on Westbrook's work with the Concert Band but also with the jazz-rock orientation of his Solid Gold Cadillac. In some ways, George Russell's music of the late sixties and early seventies with the Swedish Radio big band offers a parallel, though Duke is never far away, notably on the record's centrepiece, 'View from the Drawbridge'. The music is dense and layered, though differently so from *New Conditions*, making more use of the rock colours available from electric piano, electric bass and guitar. The Westbrook Orchestra was also, of course, a much larger band – eighteen pieces to *New Conditions*' twelve.

There are, however, other immediate points of comparison between the two composers. For example, Westbrook uses pianist Dave MacRae to provide bridging cadenzas on 'Pistache' and 'Tender Love'. This is also one of Collier's signature compositional tools. More significantly, however, Westbrook's use of percussionist John Mitchell focuses more on rhythmic possibilities, where Collier uses Mitchell's percussion on *New Conditions* more for its textural qualities. Finally, comparing the two records, *New Conditions* is certainly the more abstract in its approach.

Stan Tracey had recorded three big band LPs for Denis Preston in the 1960s but by the mid-seventies was working largely with an octet of three saxes, trumpet and trombone, in effect a scaled-down big band. He recorded *Salisbury Suite* in 1976, the same year that Collier wrote and recorded *New Conditions*. The music on the first and final parts of *Salisbury Suite* – 'Peg-Leg Bates' and 'Miff' – is intensely rhythmic, driven by the pianist-composer's percussive approach to his instrument, and emotionally exhilarating. The middle section, 'Ballad for St. Ed', is, of course, a ballad and one characterized by Tracey's gruff romanticism. The music throughout is more clearly harmonic and, unlike *New Conditions*, never strays into atonality. Intriguingly, Malcolm Griffiths, Harry Beckett and Art Themen play on both *Salisbury Suite* and *New Conditions*. There is, nevertheless, a major difference in the way in which their performances on these two records are heard. On the Tracey record, the solos clearly emerge from thematic writing. On *New Conditions*, the sense is precisely as Collier intended – the musicians are placed in 'new conditions'. On both discs, they rise spectacularly to the occasion, though in Themen's case, at least, the saxophonist is more apparently comfortable with Tracey's music.

Other British jazz composers of this period found other solutions to the improvisation/composition dilemma. Neil Ardley, for example, drew on Greek scales on *Greek Variations* and those of Bali on *Kaleidoscope of Rainbows* to create a rich, polyharmonic music full of possibilities for his musicians. Both Keith Tippett and Barry Guy found ways of using the language of free improvisation within semi-formal compositional structures, that also drew on the ideas of Messiaen and Boulez. In fact, two points emerge from any examination of the approaches to composition of these composers. Firstly, there is the sheer stylistic breadth of the music they produced. Secondly, we notice how very individualistic the solutions they arrived at were in practice.

* * *

It is not easy keeping track of all of Graham Collier's activities in this period. His involvement in jazz education continued and is discussed later. His biography of the Dankworths was published in 1976 and there was a twelve-date

British tour in October 1976 for his new big band. This was followed by brief tours of Hungary and Germany in 1977 and of India in 1979, the latter sponsored by the British Council.

As well as performing *New Conditions* on its 1976 Arts Council-sponsored British tour, the band also premiered a new work, *Symphony of Scorpions*, and featured *British Conversations* (written for the Swedish Radio Big Band) and *Triptych* (another new work first performed in a sextet version in Oxford in February and then with the UMO Big Band in Helsinki in March 1976). It was at the London date of the tour at Ronnie Scott's Club that *Symphony of Scorpions* was recorded for release the following year.[2]

In his 'Timeline', Collier expressed his frustration with both Art Themen and with his agent Harry Paton Evans: 'Problems of Art giving Stan priority and not being able to do a few gigs when Scorpions was written for him. Problems with Harry Paton Evans' office during the tour which fucked up lots of possibilities.' It is unclear what these possibilities might have been. Further insight into the struggles of a jazz bandleader/composer determined to push the boundaries of music are revealed by an incident in Southport.

> Recently in Southport I was hailed from the audience by a gentleman, who after sitting patiently through about ninety minutes of music, wanted to know, 'Could we have some jazz please?' Later in the bar he continued the argument (despite his crushing defeat in a straw poll held from the stage by yours truly), asserting that his ten year old saxophone playing son could make 'noises' better than those of our star performer, Art Themen. Art's other skills as a doctor were almost needed as one apoplectic bandleader was rescued spluttering from his pint of Sam Smith's ('Timeline').

Though he played on *New Conditions*, there is some confusion over when exactly John Webb left the Collier band. It is not clear whether or not he played on the UK tour to support the record in autumn 1976, though he certainly did the Ronnie Scott Club date when *Symphony of Scorpions* was also recorded. However, by the end of that year his place had been taken by Ashley Brown, on Roger Dean's recommendation, although Alan Jackson also played drums in the larger ensemble. Webb is unable to recall the circumstances of his departure, 'I don't remember leaving. I think I was just replaced. The music had become a bit too introverted? I'd had a really good run, and a chance to play with the best musicians around.'

It was clear, nevertheless, that he had enjoyed his time with the band, which he describes as 'really the musical highlight of my life'. And he adds, 'Graham was the perfect bandleader. Amazingly hard working, always lots of gigs, sometimes two or three a day, two schools and a concert in the evening. Very honest. Always good accommodation' (Email Webb/Heining 2015).

In fact, Webb's comments are echoed by most musicians Collier worked with, even if at times he felt taken for granted. Even when the music would not have been their preferred choice ('a bit too introverted' or 'self-indulgent'), whether it was Art Themen, John Webb, Stan Sulzmann or whoever, something in them and in Collier inspired them to give of their best.

* * *

Collier's biography of Cleo Laine and John Dankworth, *Cleo and John*, was published by Quartet in autumn 1976 and one wonders how Collier felt about the divergent opinions of his critics as to his achievements with the book. He gives no clues in his 'Timeline'. Veteran critic Alun Morgan called it 'a surprisingly good book' and gave Collier 'full credit for a tremendous amount of hard work in his researches'. However, he also noted that 'Collier is not above pulling the mat from under their [the Dankworths'] feet, even if he has to use a quotation from someone else to do his hatchet work' (Morgan 1976: 29). Charles Fox, writing in the *New Statesman*, found it 'short on human detail (they come across as guests on a chat show rather than real people) but strong on critical judgements'. Complimenting Collier on his honesty, he acknowledged Collier's misgivings about Laine's then current repertoire and Dankworth's dabbling in third stream music (Fox 1977c).

In a much longer review in *Melody Maker*, Max Jones thought that the effect of Collier's 'anthological' approach – 'building up his biography with the aid of a collection of press cuttings (many from the *Melody Maker*), record details, quotes from the two principals, and mini-interviews with a number of people associated with the couple' – was 'a bit choppy'. At the same time, Jones felt that the approach worked and hung together, offering a 'warts and all' portrait of Dankworth and that though no such 'disfiguring blemishes' emerged in Laine's case, 'the author-compiler doesn't pull too many punches' (Jones 1976: 25).

In fact, one gains the impression that Collier was much taken with Laine, though disliking her then present choice of material, but holds in check a much more negative appraisal of Dankworth. The word 'resentment' is too strong to be used in this case but there is an uncomfortable feeling reading the book of opinions left unexpressed on Collier's part. In the interview with Keith Howes for *Gay News* in 1976 noted earlier, Collier had responded swiftly to a suggestion from Howes that Dankworth and Laine had achieved their success without too much compromise. He replied:

> Well, that's a bone of contention of mine. Dankworth has done a lot for jazz in this country but he has compromised. He said, I think on the Parkinson Show, that he doesn't allow the word 'jazz' to be used on Cleo's billing in the States because it puts people off. She's got so much talent she should be able to sing what she wants but he masterminds her career and tries to put her in certain directions (Howes 1976: 19).

In the same interview, Collier later acknowledged Dankworth's abilities as a film composer: 'He's a supremely good film music writer'. But prompted perhaps by the interviewer, he continued:

> If pushed, people will remember the good things he's done but someone once described John's music as 'cheeky jazz' and I think that's a good name for it because it's not really very deep (Howes 1976: 20).

One may question Collier's assessment of Dankworth's music and doubt that Laine was an unwilling accomplice in some of the more 'middle-of-the road' offerings of her career. Collier is, nevertheless, entitled to his view and it is one that others will share.

Other reviews offered a similar variety of opinions. Barry Conley in *Gay News* clearly enjoyed the book, remarking that it was 'by no means the sycophantic fan magazine type of biography' but an 'honest appraisal of their careers' (Conley 1976). That point was echoed by Kevin Henriques in the *Financial Times*, though Henriques wondered whether 'jazz followers will consider it sufficiently penetrating is another matter' (Henriques 1976: 14).

Finally, the strangest review came from Dave Lee, at one time Dankworth's pianist, in *Punch*. Critics and reviewers can be remarkably lacking in self-awareness and when they leak, they leak by the gallon. That seems to be the case here. What emerges from Lee's review is something personal to him, which appears to be a frustration with both Dankworth and Laine and the musical and artistic choices they have made. This was, in turn, reflected in his opinion of Collier's biography of the couple, which neither tells Lee what he wants to know, nor does it explain quite how, for Lee, their music became so bland. (While Lee does not actually use this word, it does seem to be what he is suggesting.). Lee, in contrast to Henriques, Jones, Conley and others, clearly did find *Cleo and John* sycophantic in its portrait of the couple. He concludes:

> Yes, there ought to be a book about the Dankworths – but the real flesh and blood Cleo and John, not merely a public relations exercise like this (Lee 1976: 596–97).

One wonders if the two subjects were the best choice for Collier's one venture into biography. Responses to Laine and Dankworth, their work and public *personae* are complex and sometimes contradictory. In some they invite awe and admiration, in others envy and mockery. For some, they sold their souls to the devil and mammon long ago. But, for others, their achievements justify every gain, whether personally, financially or socially. No biography of such a couple could please every reader. Their story requires a biographer to get close enough to them as individuals, whilst retaining critical distance, almost to the point of indifference. In fairness, perhaps Collier got as close as he could. Perhaps someone further outside British jazz might have done a more thorough job. At times, for example in relation to his opinions on Dankworth's 'cheeky jazz', there seems to be a gap between the book's manifest and latent content – that is, what is left unsaid (Rycroft 1995: 98–99). This results in a tension in the book that is never satisfactorily resolved.

Just as there had been issues for Collier in his relationship with CUP, a similar dispute would arise for him with Quartet. Collier wrote to John Boothe of Quartet in February 1980 expressing various concerns. In his letter he referred to an inaccurate royalty statement that he received from Quartet in December 1977 in respect of his previous book for the publisher, *Inside Jazz*. He had been told in that statement that he was due £17 for the previous year's sales but, on querying this, the original statement was changed to £228 and he received an apology for the error. Then, late in 1979, he received a negative royalty statement in respect of *Cleo and John*.

Unfortunately, the correspondence in Collier's archive regarding this does not seem to be complete. The February 1980 letter to John Boothe was in response to Boothe's reply to an original letter from Collier raising concern that, apparently, no copies of the book had been sold in the first half of 1979 in Britain or in the USA.

Boothe's subsequent reply was like a red rag to a bull. Collier had apparently referred to a shortfall between books sold and those printed. Given that Boothe's letter acknowledges that there was a discrepancy and given Collier's past royalty statement experience, the reply seems dismissive.

It reads:

> What can I say to satisfy you?
>
> 1. Royalties – this is in the hands of our very understaffed Group Accounts who are currently in the middle of the annual audit. All I can say is that as soon as this is over they will get down to the backlog including the royalty statements and accompanying queries.

2. On the apparent 1400 shortfall: remember we didn't bind all the editions and we currently hold 750 sheets of the text. These are being bound and sold as a paperback in April at £2.50. When the audit is over the Accounts can look into the remaining 650 copies.

Despite its opening salvo – 'Your last letter of December 3, 1979 though being dismissive of a pestering author fell short of being actually insulting' – Collier's letter was, for him, quite measured. There appears to have been no reply and Collier wrote to Quartet's chairman, Mr N. I. Attallah (dated 30 October 1980) threatening to go to the Society of Authors, if the issues were not swiftly resolved. What transpired from all this is unclear. However, the last piece of correspondence on the matter comes from a Juliet Burton of Lawrence Pollinger Limited, Authors' Agents (dated 18 November 1981), advising Collier that rights to *Cleo and John* had reverted to him.

The disputes with CUP and Quartet tell us a lot about Collier. He could be difficult and demanding. When it came to financial issues, he was a terrier. One may note here his background, rich in parental support and encouragement but less so materially. From ordinary beginnings that might have predicted a life just as ordinary, Collier had come a long way. Yet he never seems to have felt secure or at least secure in his position in music. There was always something missing, and even a sense that others were getting something that should have come to him by right of talent and effort. This could, and did, lead to outbursts of petty jealousy. One friend of Collier, who preferred not to be named, said that when they started to get some recognition for their work in the nineties, and told him, his response was one of 'why you and not me?' Mike Gibbs mentions an incident concerning a conference at Leeds in 2011. Gibbs had been invited to give the keynote speech and compose a piece of music to be performed at the conference. Gibbs explained:

> I was offered a commission and workshop by Louise Gibbs and Mark Donlon at Leeds and Louise asked me to give the Jazz Keynote address for the Annual Jazz Conference they have. At that time, Graham had just had his *The Jazz Composer* published. I mentioned this to Louise, suggesting she invite Graham to give a talk on it. She told me they already knew of this, and had in fact already invited Graham to do a talk. But on hearing that I was to be giving the keynote speech, Graham had objected strongly and had declined this invitation.
>
> Graham never said this to me personally, but John [Gill] did in fact tell me that Graham did not consider me a jazz composer. I gleaned that this came from the fact that I was known for all sorts of musi-

> cal endeavours which included pop music, things like The Goodies, writing for Peter Gabriel, Joni Mitchell and others and a lot of my jazz activities as a writer was arranging and orchestration and perhaps my 'tunes' for Gary Burton were only lead sheets. At least, that was my assumption and that Graham's composing was purer, realer.

This was very sad, given their history together, and it does not speak well of Collier. As Gibbs notes generously, 'He died too soon. I always held the position, that as we aged, we'd get to a point we could discuss his stance on my jazz composer status more civilly one day. As we'd originally met while being students at Berklee, we had a sort of brotherly connection that trivial (if he would ever see it that way) disputes couldn't erase' (Email Gibbs/Heining 2017).

We are all capable of such petty jealousies and there is no moral high ground here. These comments do, nevertheless, tell us how insecure Collier seems to have felt inside. There was also perhaps a certain naivety in his dealings with publishers and record companies or, perhaps, he was simply too unrealistic in his expectations. Either way, he seems to have been often disappointed, despite all his achievements.

* * *

1977 began slowly for Collier and he noted in his 'Timeline', 'no work until April...', adding, 'starting to consider giving up bass and playing synths and keyboard – would give me a distance that is impossible as a bass player within the band'. In fact, he would in due course give up the bass with *The Day of the Dead* and subsequent recordings. One bright spot on the horizon was a gift of £1000 towards Mosaic's running costs from Monty Python alumnus, writer and director Terry Jones. It has never been quite clear what the connection was between Collier and Jones, though John Gill suggested that Jones gave the money to enable Collier to record and release a solo album by pianist Howard Riley. That record was called *Intertwine* and came out later in 1977. Roger Dean recalls Terry Jones being present at a band meeting. He notes, 'My impression at the time was that Terry Jones wanted to support Mosaic per se, rather than necessarily specifically Howard but I don't know anything about their possible connection' (Email Dean/Heining 2017).

By then, Collier had sold the Paddington flat and bought another in Nevern Square, Earl's Court. From that point on, life seemed to get busy again. The first big event of 1977 was the premiere of *The Day of the Dead* at the Ilkley Festival in June and this was followed by the expansion of Mosaic with the Howard Riley record *Intertwine*, Roger Dean's *Cycles*, Stan Sulzmann's *On Loan with Gratitude* (a very strong sax and rhythm album) and Collier's own *Sym-*

phony of Scorpions. Then in September, Collier undertook an extended European tour of Germany, Austria and Hungary followed by a session (Collier alone) with the Danish Radio Group later that month.

Ed Speight seems a reliable and amusing guide, as far as the Collier tours around that point were concerned, capturing something of their distinctive flavour:

> [W]e played in Hungary, Debrecen – I can't pronounce it – we played the festival twice, I think... Joe Zawinul was on the bill doing a solo gig, as I recall, and you saw more of Joe Zawinul's arse than you did of him playing (Laughing) because he had these keyboards and synths that had been hired that didn't really work. So, there he was arse in the air plugging things and fiddling around under the keyboards.

He describes the experience as a 'trip and a half going behind the Iron Curtain':

> This hotel which is in the centre of the town or city, it was just like a set for a film of the assassination of Archduke Ferdinand. It was straight out of the Austro-Hungarian empire, a Gypsy band playing and Russian army generals all over the place, all five foot two and round. They were all over the place. Getting into lifts with them. Freaky, wasn't it? I remember talking to the zither player of the Gypsy orchestra. He was an old chap. He would have been about sixty odd or sixty-five then. He must have survived and come through the Second World War and there can't have been many Gypsies who managed to survive that. We were talking to the guys in the band and he said, 'Oh, you're here for the jazz festival are you? Ah, jazz players are you?' And then, he played this kind of Coltrane lick, 'Oh, you mean this kind of thing? Or do you mean like this?' Never make assumptions. Amazing (Interview Speight/Heining 2014).

It was also in this period that Collier made his second foray into musical theatre, writing music and additional lyrics for *Silver Queen Saloon*, a 'Western musical' by playwright Paul Foster. The play had premiered at the experimental, Off-Off Broadway La MaMa Theatre in New York. Collier provided the music or at least the arrangements and additional lyrics for the first performance of the play in Belgium at the Studio Herman Teirlinck in 1977, part of the Hoger Instituut voor Dramatische Kunst in Antwerp.

Such forays into the dramatic arts were not unusual at this time in British jazz. In a way, one can see this as a logical extension of the work of John Dankworth and Cleo Laine in their creation of entertainments using literary themes. This would include, for example, the performance in 1967 in Cardiff and later recording of William Walton's *Façade* (Collier 1976a: 106–107). It would also appear to be a logical outcome of the poetry and jazz movement in Britain (Heining 2012a: 78–81). Further cross-genre collaborations followed. For example, Mike Westbrook worked with Adrian Mitchell on the William Blake play, *Tyger* in 1971 and *White Suit Blues* in 1977 (based on the life of Mark Twain), as well as with John Fox's Welfare State Theatre. Indeed, later theatrical works devised by Mike and Kate Westbrook would include *Mama Chicago* (1978) and *The Ass* (1985).

Between 1977 and 1990, Collier was involved in two stage plays and several radio plays. In terms of his work in theatre, these included *Silver Queen Saloon*, which was also performed at London's Riverside Studios in 1982,[3] and *A Kind of Game*, a new musical drama based on the life of the British-Soviet spy Kim Philby with book and lyrics by David Fisher, was performed first in Barnet in 1980 and again in Manchester at the Library Theatre in 1981.[4] The headline in *The Stage* for *A Kind of Game* ran, 'Barnet aims high with "spy" musical', and the article noted that actor Gary Hope played Philby, while the play was directed by John Sichel, a director of some standing (*The Stage* 1980: 2).[5]

Collier also provided the music for two radio plays. The first of these was broadcast on BBC Radio 3 on 20 September 1988 and was called *Sweet Fat* by Jack Kenny and Peter King. The subject here was an ageing jazz saxophonist on tour once again and seen through the eyes of four people who knew him either casually or intimately. Collier's score was played by Art Themen, Geoff Castle, Ed Speight, bassist Mick Hutton and drummer Ashley Brown. Gillian Reynolds, writing in the *Daily Telegraph*, described the play as 'a triumph' that 'leapt great chasms to capture the peculiar force of all jazz music' (Reynolds 1988: 14), whilst John Marshall in the *Times* noted that the music, 'superb in its own right', was 'woven through the piece with a skill rarely heard' (Marshall 1988).

The second play resulted from a proposal by Collier himself, who first approached Radio 3 in 1985 with the idea of adapting *The Bass Saxophone*, a novella by banned Czech author, Josef Skvorecky. The book came out in English translation in 1980 and in paperback in 1985. Although the idea was well-received, it took until September 1989 for the play to be finally realized and broadcast. The writer commissioned by Radio 3 was Nigel Baldwin, a highly successful playwright for radio and stage. The cast was led by actor John Woodvine, with Art Themen playing bass saxophone on the recording in a group of musicians that included drummer Trevor Tomkins and saxophonist Mike Page. The play was a resounding success and won the prestigious Sony Award for 'Best Radio Drama' in 1990.

Quite why Collier was unable to capitalize on these successes probably has more to do with that combination of luck and patronage – or its absence – needed to succeed in the theatrical world. According to John Gill, one factor might have been that Ned Chaillet, the producer of *The Bass Saxophone*, moved on in the corporation and once a valuable contact is lost the budding playwright or composer often has to start again climbing that greasy pole. Certainly a letter from Graham to one of the senior staff at the BBC regarding payments and fees suggests that dealing with the broadcaster was at times administratively difficult. Collier was also slated to provide the music for a radio production of Shakespeare's *Timon of Athens* but was dropped by the BBC without explanation in favour of another composer. Two other attempts at producing musical dramas came to nothing.

That said, Collier took on each theatre project with typical enthusiasm and full commitment. In many ways, this was one of Collier's most admirable qualities as a person and as a musician. It was not just a willingness to try new things but something more deep-rooted – a need to experiment, a love of free play and a child-like desire to actually see 'what happens if...'. It was also, one suspects, a way of recharging his creative batteries – by shifting his work into a different artistic context, whether in writing about jazz or teaching it to young musicians or by trying his hand in writing for theatre, Collier could examine and test himself and his ideas afresh.

Between 1990 and 1991, Collier made his only two ventures into composing for feature film. The writer and director, David Cohen, approached him to write the music for a film he was making. Cohen was principally a documentary director and producer but also made several other films for television and cinema. Collier worked with him on several documentaries – *Lack of Vision* (1990), *Acceptable Risks?* (1991) and *Forty Something* (1991) – and was used to provide the score for *The Pleasure Principle* starring Peter Firth and Hayden Gwynne (made for general release) and *Northern Crescent* with Ian Hogg and Kulvinder Ghirn (made for television).[6]

Collier clearly enjoyed the experience greatly, although technical problems caused difficulties cuing the music to the film in the case of *The Pleasure Principle*. Financially, the work was quite rewarding, as he was paid something in the region of £10,000 for the feature films and documentaries. Cohen was introduced to Collier by Jan Euden, another producer who knew Collier. Though *The Pleasure Principle* was made originally with Collier's music, circumstances resulted in it being released with an alternative score. Cohen found Collier easy and professional to work with, as he explained:

> I didn't realise at first how distinguished he was but he was very nice. Once he read the script, he did the music and I had written some lyrics, which he set to music. To cut a long story short, I watched him record the music at Air Edel studios – they loved him and gave us an unbelievable deal, realising we didn't have a lot of money.

> Graham was great fun to work with. Knew his onions. He and I got on well for two reasons. First of all, when Palace bought the picture they had done a deal with Warner Brothers, which meant that they wanted the music track re-recorded. So, I had to go to Graham, who behaved like a complete gentleman – John Gill was a bit angry on his behalf. But Graham just said, 'These things happen'.

As a result, there are two musical versions of *The Pleasure Principle*, one with the music Collier had written and the other with music by Sonny Southon.[7] According to Cohen, some of the 'foreign sales of the film and subsequent video and DVD releases contain Graham's soundtrack'. After these problems, Cohen was gracious in providing Collier with several other opportunities to work on several documentaries: 'He had been very generous and I wanted to give him some work in return and he did it off the top of his head. So, my memories of him are nothing but good.' He added, 'In the way of the entertainment business, Graham and I didn't become close, close friends. I moved about quite a bit and, I guess, the last time I saw him would have been in 1993 or 1994' (Interview Cohen/Heining 2017).

So, sadly, there would be no BAFTA or Academy Award for Pte. James Graham Collier to add to his many achievements.

Notes

1. Roger Dean – 'Yes, I think there are Messiaenic connections in *New Conditions* and some later GC things. I don't remember specific conversations about Olivier with Graham. But I'm sure he was aware, and the pieces you mention are appropriate (I know them well)'. At the same time, Dean stresses that, unlike Messaien, Collier strongly resisted the adoption of specific theoretic approaches in his compositional practice (Email Dean/Heining 2016).
2. *Triptych* was recorded at Ronnie's on the same evening as *Symphony of Scorpions*. It was later released as part of the Disconforme reissuing of *The Day of the Dead* in 2000.
3. *Silver Queen Saloon* received a very favourable review from the *Financial Times*' drama critic, Alan Forrest (see Forrest, review of *Silver Queen Saloon*, *Financial Times*, 2 April 1982: 21).
4. Elsie Ashberry remembers seeing *A Kind of Game* in Manchester and meeting Collier and his partner John Gill at the performance.
5. For example, John Sichel had directed Alec Guinness and Ralph Richardson in a BBC production of *Twelfth Night* (1969) and Laurence Olivier, Joan Plowright and Alan Bates in Chekhov's *The Three Sisters* at The National (1970) at Olivier's request.
6. David Cohen's academic background is in Psychology and several of his documentaries including one on Broadmoor, the maximum security psychiatric unit, and another on Soviet psychiatric institutions in the Gorbachev era, draw upon that background. However, he has also worked extensively on feature films such as *The Pleasure Principle*, *Northern Crescent*, *Dead Cool* and *The Bureaucracy of Love* (see https://davidcohenfilm.wordpress.com/film-and-documentary/).
7. Sonny Southon was at the time an up-and-coming female singer-songwriter.

8   The Day of the Dead

For Collier, his most significant musical achievements of the 1970s were the records *New Conditions* (1976), *Symphony of Scorpions* (1977) and *The Day of the Dead* (1978). The last two works owe much to Collier's fascination with the writings of Malcolm Lowry. Collier was not just a fan of Lowry as a novelist but was also intrigued by the literary techniques that he used in his novels. Whether Collier sought to develop similar practices and apply these compositionally or, as John Gill suggested, more conservatively, saw a 'working correlation' between Lowry's approach and his own, is open to discussion. However, there is a strong argument that his reading of the novels influenced him far beyond simply wishing to reference them in his own compositions.

Collier's fascination with Lowry led him to make a pilgrimage to Mexico, the writer's one-time home and the setting for his novel *Under the Volcano*. Collier also joined the Malcolm Lowry Society, presenting a paper at the 1987 International Malcolm Lowry Symposium at the University of British Columbia in Vancouver, where Lowry had also lived at one point. At that conference, Collier was also able to perform *The Day of the Dead*, his major Lowry work, with a group of Canadian musicians. Just how much this meant to him can be seen in his diary entry regarding the event:

> *Day of the Dead* performed at Lowry conference. Gig went well. Andrew Parkin (speaker) excellent; Tom Keenlyside (sax) & Rene Worst (bass) great player and enthusiastic; Ron Johnson (DX7) & Ihor Kukurudza (gtr) good but could do with direction; Bob Murphy (piano) good but less committed and a bit supercilious. Jim McGillveray (percussion & drums) excellent and organised by him. (Sherrill Grace – met his wife at dinner and wife said 'oh, my husband can organise this'...which he did!)...
>
> Standing ovation at end (50-60 Lowry people) 'Made more sense than all the papers...we are told only another novelist could understand Lowry, well, perhaps it's a musician who does'...[1]

One senses Collier's pride at this recognition, coming as it did from academics and Lowry experts. At a superficial level, what Collier found in Lowry's writing is not hard to gauge. Firstly, Lowry loved jazz and mentions musicians such as Bix Beiderbecke, Eddie Lang, Frankie Trumbauer and Joe Venuti in his novels. Secondly, Lowry's prose has a strangely musical and improvisatory quality to it. Thirdly, the construction of Lowry's novels involves sometimes odd juxtapositions, broken passages and themes that end without really concluding only to return later in a different form and peculiar digressions. Such a description could, unsurprisingly, be applied to some of Collier's compositions. In fact, Lowry's key novel, *Under the Volcano* – for fans and for Collier – seems as much composed as written.

The story, such as it is, is set in a small town and province of Mexico on Dia de los muertos or the Day of the Dead near the volcano of Popocatepetl and tells of the last twelve hours in the life of the Consul, Geoffrey Firmin, its main character. It moves backwards and forwards in time, describing the Consul's life history and relationships and his dissolute, alcohol- and mescal-induced state of mind. It is not an easy read.

In his Vancouver conference paper, 'Lowry, Jazz, and *The Day of the Dead*', Collier refers to the 'oblique thinking' and 'freewheeling logic', which he sees as 'moving from connection to connection in a kind of stream of consciousness'. Inevitably, Collier relates this to jazz improvisation. More than that he notes that Lowry attached to himself 'that personal, highly individual look at the world that a jazz musician expresses when he is soloing' (Collier in Grace 1992: 244).

Collier then quotes the phrase 'mosaics of experience', a phrase that, given the name of Collier's fourth album, the name of his record company and the title of this book, seems rather telling. Collier suggests that the phrase has a relevance to jazz and 'is, perhaps, a way of explaining how a jazz musician improvises'. He continues: 'He [Lowry] doesn't usually attempt to build a structure logically, moving from A to Z, through B, C, D etc; he explores his subject in a stream-of-consciousness way, moving from idea to idea until his allotted space is up or he has said all he has to say at this time' (245). Finally, summing up his intention with *The Day of the Dead*, Collier notes that he 'hoped to present a portrait of Lowry and of his Consul, perhaps of all of us in our struggle between good and evil' (248).

One has to ask whether and at what level Collier might have made a more personal connection with Lowry as a person and as an artist. Lowry was one of the great literary drunks of the twentieth century – his state of dissolution hardly corresponded to the more disciplined way in which Collier lived his life. Nevertheless, Collier did relate to that 'personal, highly individual look at the world' that he found in Lowry's work. Referring to *Under the Volcano*, Sven Erik Larsen in his article 'Throw away your mind' argues:

> The Consul is not the main character in the trivial psychological sense, but the main character in the sense that he expounds the conditions of aesthetic creativity in the most extreme sense (Larsen 2004: 61).

It does seem likely that Collier may well have seen parallels with his own compositional approach in the literary techniques of layering, fragmentation and stream of conscious that Lowry used in the novel and elsewhere. Yet, more than that, there did also seem to be an identification at a more unconscious level. In *New Structures*, Collier told Roger Dean, 'I've been trying to write music dramatically all my life and that's what I would say I am: a dramatic composer...the kind of thing I do is to try to paint a picture' (Dean 1992: 170). The creative moment can be an extreme, unsettling and dramatic one and one suspects that Collier related to this aspect in the Consul and in Lowry. Though, here, one would want to add that whereas Lowry's dramatic message is tragic and catastrophic, Collier's is transformative and uplifting, if also at times quite dark. It was perhaps in these aspects of Lowry's work that Collier made so strong an identification with the author and with the Consul.

There are a number of other features of *Under the Volcano* pointed out by Sven Erik Larsen in his article which seem relevant here. Firstly, he writes:

> The text becomes an associative machine that activates the entire cultural context it is part of, but in a way that is not entirely under the control of author, narrator, character or reader (Larsen 2004: 52).

Again, this offers an analogy with Collier's approach to jazz and composition. He trusted his musicians and allowed them considerable latitude. In this, he devolved a significant, though not infinite, measure of control over the shape of the composition to his musicians. Secondly, and perhaps more importantly, Larsen suggests that the book exhibits what in literary theory is referred to as 'intertextuality', that is, the incorporation of different sources and texts into later works of art or literature. Referring to Lowry's references to Dante, Greek myth and the Cabala, he notes that Lowry 're-enacts past texts as present meaning' (52).

Under the Volcano may only move to a limited degree in setting, space and real time but it moves freely between past and present and future. Once more, Collier's writing for jazz ensemble seeks to do something similar. His concept of jazz composition in performance is that it should be in a perpetual state of becoming or, to put it another way, to exist in a state that simultaneously contains its past, present and future. Intertextuality in Lowry's work might involve *Dante's Inferno* and the Cabala. In Collier's case, it involved jazz musicians and composers such as Ellington, Miles Davis and others – and Malcolm Lowry and the abstract artists he so admired. What Collier took from Lowry was a new approach to form and structure, still modular perhaps, but a new way of understanding the relationships between the parts and how form might be built from those relationships.

In his sleeve notes for the original double LP release of *The Day of the Dead*, Collier described his constant re-reading of Lowry's writing, particularly *Under the Volcano*, and his constant discovery of new layers of meaning within the works. He adds that although he had used written texts on several previous occasions, he had been 'wary of contemplating the use of Lowry's words in such a way'. A commission from the Ilkley Literature festival in 1976 combined with the compositional breakthrough represented by *New Conditions* encouraged him to attempt to join the two – Lowry's complex, layered prose together with his own musical approach, which also involved now 'utilising levels and layers, ranging from completely improvised passages to completely written ones with finely controlled gradations between' (Collier 1978b). Once again, this suggests that with both *Symphony of Scorpions* and *The Day of the Dead*, Collier was making a conscious attempt to apply Lowry's literary device, described by Collier as 'the technique of divided attention'. If so, this was his first use of a literary source, not just as inspiration, but in terms of adapting artistic techniques from that medium into musical composition and performance (cf. Lawrence Durrell and *Workpoints*). *The Day of the Dead* is not in any sense a programme work and does not seek to create a narrative from Lowry's writing, works that themselves eschew conventional narrative in favour of a kind of stream of consciousness. Two key sections of the sleeve notes outline Collier's intentions:

> The various levels of *Under the Volcano* (the basic story, the allegory of the world situation in 1938, the mystic or magical symbols scattered through the book, the parallels with Lowry's own alcoholism) plus the references backwards and forwards in time could then be considered a kind of loose parallel to the way my own work had developed.

And, finally:

> What I wanted to achieve was the addition of another layer, a utilisation of the voice *into* the music. This I hope I have done and, in doing so, I have deliberately used what Lowry called 'The technique of divided attention' (Collier 1978b; original emphasis).

In the notes for *Symphony of Scorpions*, Collier repeats that phrase noting that both that work and *The Day of the Dead*, 'explore in musical terms the co-existing levels (both horizontal and vertical) of Lowry's writing, as well as what he called "The technique of divided attention"' (Collier 1977). Setting aside the fact that the term 'divided attention' has a somewhat different meaning in experimental psychology, what it seems is meant by the term in this context is described by Larsen:

> In his introduction to the Signe Plume edition [of *Under the Volcano*], Stephen Spender points to a 'divided attention' in the narrative technique of focalization whoever is carrying the point of view. We are always both inside the mind of the characters and outside, both anchored in the world of sense perceptions and looking into an imaginary world (Larsen 2004: 60).[2]

Much of *Under the Volcano* takes place in the minds of its characters, notably that of the Consul, Geoffrey Firmin. We are never sure whether the actions or events described are real, imagined or whether these are in the past or present. The novel shifts perspective and time to disorientating effect, in particular when we are in the mind of its protagonist. Though Collier attributes the phrase 'divided attention' to Lowry himself, it seems in fact to have been applied to his work initially by Spender (2000).[3] Either way this dual perspective – simultaneously internally reflexive and externally reflective – defines how Collier would approach both *Symphony of Scorpions*, *The Day of the Dead* and, another Lowry composition, *October Ferry*, which appeared on the final side of the album. For reasons that will become clear, the technique works well with the instrumental pieces but less so with the spoken word piece, *The Day of the Dead*.

Reviewing *Symphony of Scorpions* for *Jazzwise* in 2001, I was critical of the music. That opinion has changed significantly. What had seemed then to be a series of disconnected, pan-stylistic episodes, now appears as a far more coherent piece built subtly upon the way in which composer and musicians and improvisation combine to create its form. What appeared then as a marriage of inconvenience between avant-garde and more mainstream jazz, now seems a much braver work that moves far more easily between these reference points than I had originally understood.

The album was recorded in November 1976 at Ronnie Scott's Club along with another piece, *Triptych*. The latter appears only on the Disconforme reissue of *The Day of the Dead*. The original vinyl release of *Symphony* included the additional track 'Forest Path to the Spring', recorded in March 1977. The time span between the recording of *New Conditions* and *Symphony* was just five months and the latter needs to be heard as a companion to *New Conditions*. As Collier wrote in the original sleeve notes,

> Vertically the musical levels used (not always simultaneously) are the usual melody, harmony and rhythm (though these are not necessarily related) as well as written background material, improvised background material from given motifs and solo improvisations, often again from given motifs. Horizontally, one finds a constant referral backwards and forwards to other material.

Collier added that *Symphony of Scorpions* was a much thicker work than *New Conditions* but 'continues the ideas expressed in these pieces as well as exploring and adding several new ones'. Unfortunately, he did not elaborate on what exactly these new ideas were (Collier 1977).

The title comes from Malcolm Lowry's novel *Ultramarine*, where Lowry refers to 'a symphony of scorpions, a procession of flying grand pianos and cathedrals...' Unlike *The Day of the Dead*, however, *Scorpions* should not be heard as programmatic in intention. Art Lange, in a very perceptive review of both the Lowry albums, points out that *Symphony of Scorpions* (though Collier never intended it specifically in that way) is not a symphony at all but instead a concerto with saxophonist Art Themen as its principal soloist (Lange 1979). Seen in this way, Themen becomes the narrator cum protagonist, pursuing both an interior monologue and being engaged in an external dialogue with the other musicians.

It must be said that Themen, like Stan Sulzmann and Pete Hurt, was not enamoured of Collier's music. He states that he was happy to do it because he disliked 'pigeon-holing in music'. However, as he explains, he has never seen music such as Collier's as his forte:

> Most of the time I'm a bebop quartet player. That's not what Graham did but nevertheless I was very happy both musically and socially to be in that environment. But I can't say it was an absolutely gob-smacking experience, one of the best musical experiences I've ever done. I can't say that.

Though he clearly respected Collier a great deal as 'an educator and administrator', Themen contrasts his work with Stan Tracey, itself a remarkable and lengthy association, with his musical experiences with Collier:

> The ingredient, the nub for me is this indefinable swing. Now, if you've got that indefinable sprinkling of stardust, you deserve more respect than somebody who doesn't have that. Now, along those lines, there's strictly no comparison because Stan Tracey – to use that crude jazz expression – could swing like a shit-house door, whereas Graham couldn't swing to save his life.

With regard to *Symphony of Scorpions* specifically, Themen says:

> I suppose I was playing slightly outside my comfort zone. It's very stimulating. In a way, it's a bit of a challenge. But hand on heart, I can't say that *Symphony of Scorpions* or whatever was any different from much of the music I played with Graham. It was interesting but it wasn't what I think I do best (Interview Themen/Heining 2014).

Collier chose his musicians for their individuality, their own special sound and Themen is a highly distinctive soloist. One might take issue with Themen on his point about 'swing' – Collier's music swung when he so chose. In fact, there is just such an example in 'Part 3' of *Symphony of Scorpions*. What is more remarkable is the way that Collier's writing, or rather the settings in which he placed musicians like Themen, seemed to bring out something fresh and new from the players. Collier clearly loved Themen's sound, which is why he wrote *Symphony* as a feature for him. One recalls again his frustration at Themen for missing several performances during the autumn 1976 UK tour for the Contemporary Music Network.

Collier's opinion of Themen is shared by many others, such as Malcolm Griffiths, who also played with Mike Westbrook and Stan Tracey. Griffiths is another Collier alumnus who expresses doubts about the composer's music.

> When I joined Graham's band he had a wonderful tenor player in Art Themen. And Henry Lowther was often there, which was nice. I am not absolutely certain what Graham wanted. All I did when I played with him was improvise with him the way I felt. You were in the band and you were expected to play your thing I suppose. I've only ever played what I felt was right.

Asked how that experience compared with his other musical experiences, Griffiths waxes lyrical about his work with Stan Tracey and Mike Westbrook:

> It was a joy for me to play all those years with Stan Tracey and, similarly with Mike Westbrook, too. In fact, the last album I'm on with Mike, *The Cortège*, is a truly wonderful record with some truly wonderful pieces of music on there. I think the playing of the musicians, it's difficult music and they just play it marvellously. With Stan Tracey, I guess it was his determination to have a damn good rhythm section. If you imagine a cross between Duke Ellington's piano playing and Thelonious Monk. I spent a lot of my career playing in a band with two of the finest tenor players – Art and Don Weller – in the world. I thought they were just stupendous.

Reluctantly, he admitted that he was not as keen on Collier's work.

> I think that's fair enough. I don't know if this is going to tar me in some way but I just thought their music was better. What I will say about Graham was that he was a very good arranger. He knew his business where that was concerned but I preferred playing Stan's music or Mike Westbrook's (Interview Griffiths/Heining 2017).

It is intriguing to hear this from Griffiths – and from Themen and others – and perhaps also paradoxical. Collier wrote for his musicians, for their sounds and personalities. However, he often put them into situations other than those in which they felt most comfortable. And, as Griffiths noted, those musicians were not always clear about his expectations. He may have written for his musicians but this certainly was not true in the same way that it was for Tracey or Westbrook. At risk of over-simplifying the issue, Collier's music was perhaps more a composer's music than a musician's music. If so, maybe that alienated some of Collier's musicians from a sense that they too owned the outcome of the composition.

To return to the piece itself, when Collier talks of co-existing horizontal and vertical levels – in both Lowry's writing and in terms of Collier's musical approach – this is best understood in terms of a certain division of function within the orchestra. This separation is not absolute but it does seem to apply more often than not. In that respect, one can see the rhythm section – bass, drums, percussion – and chordal instruments – piano, guitar, vibes – as dealing primarily with the vertical level. The brass and woodwinds, on the other hand, attend to the horizontal.

'Part 1' of *Symphony* illustrates this well, presenting a series of structured, almost dramatized, events in which Themen's tenor or soprano are engaged by different instruments of the orchestra, either individually or together. The dramatic effect is heightened by use of drawn-out changes in volume and pacing. The roles of John Mitchell, mainly on vibes, and Roger Dean on acoustic piano are central to this effect, though a duel involving trombonist Malcolm Griffiths and Themen with powerful drumming from John Webb offers the section's most exciting episode.

'Part 2' is more pastoral in its mood, albeit eerily so, with Themen's soprano matched by some beautiful, colouristic work from the other horns and from Dean, Mitchell and Webb. It shifts later into an awkward, lopsided Weill-like tune, which Lange, in his review, compares to the writing of Carla Bley and Mike Mantler. The mood shifts once more in 'Part 3', following its fragmentary opening, as the band picks up a Latin groove before moving into a more straight-ahead big band section. The playing from the trumpets of Henry Lowther, Harry Beckett and Pete Duncan is particularly strong, as is Ed Speight's guitar which solos behind Themen's tenor. The overarching feeling in 'Part 4' is once again pastoral, despite one more discordant passage. It concludes with what sounds very much like a *berceuse* or lullaby, albeit one more likely to come from the pen of Weill than Brahms.

'Forest Path to the Spring' rounds off the record. In the paper Collier presented to the Lowry Symposium in Vancouver, Collier quotes from Lowry's novella 'Forest Path':

> One evening on the way back from the spring for some reason I suddenly thought of a break by Bix [Beiderbecke] in Frankie Trumbauer's record of Singing the Blues that had always seemed to me to express a moment of the most pure and spontaneous happiness (Collier in Grace 1992: 244).

As he points out in the paper, he used the first few notes of Beiderbecke's solo in the opening of the composition. The piece is a largely through-composed duet for Themen on soprano and tenor and Speight on classical guitar. It is a delightful ballad feature with Themen at his most romantic.

Barry McRae described the record as 'a joint triumph for the composer Graham Collier and one of our most outstanding jazzmen, Art Themen'. He drew attention to the way Collier, eschewing more traditional accompaniments and backings, made use of 'appropriate counter-melodies or prepared contrapuntal interludes' (McRae 1977d). To place this more firmly in the context of Collier's artistic intentions and the extent to which he sought to mirror Lowry's literary approach, these counter-melodies and contrapuntal interludes represent different layers in the music and, by extension, in the text. Kevin Henriques in the *Financial Times* noted that the music was 'not easily followed at first hearing' but he clearly grasped the composer's aims for the piece, drawing attention to its 'variations in moods, tempos as well as extensive harmonic forays' (Henriques 1977: 3).

Finally, Charles Fox, again taking over Collier's *Gay News* column, showed less enthusiasm for the new record than its predecessor, *New Conditions*. He thought that the 'boogaloo in Part 3' was 'too polite' but that otherwise this was 'a good runner-up to Graham's last LP, which I thought his finest so far' (Fox 1977b: 28).

To date, Collier had released nine albums, each one differing in construction and mood without losing the sense of the composer's personality and *imprimatur*. The last record that Collier would make in the 1970s – and the last one he released prior to *Something British Made in Hong Kong* (recorded in

1985 but released in 1988) was *The Day of the Dead*. The album's release was accompanied by an Arts Council sponsored tour.

Alan Giddings had got to know Collier whilst still at university studying sociology as a mature student. When Giddings finished his degree, Collier recruited him to come and work on his Mosaic label. Giddings would go on to work with a number of organizations in music and other performance arts, including the Jazz Centre Society and the Fairfield Halls. He remembers the tour very clearly and, in particular, the part played by narrator John Carbery.

> Well, Carbery was pissed most of the time (Laughing)... He was very 'actor-ly' and Graham was very used to discussing with band members how he would like to see things interpreted and then taken a bit further on by that person. So, there were always artistic discussions going on because that's how Graham was.

At various points, often decided during the set, Collier would want the music to rise up, overwhelming the narration. This did not sit well with Carbery.

> It was also to do with the whole mayhem of *The Day of The Dead* itself and the music they were trying to create. And he wanted to echo that mayhem and John was very much in that sort of actor-ly way, 'I deliver the words and I want everybody to hear it with complete clarity, dear boy' (Interview Giddings/Heining 2014).

By this point, Ashley Brown had replaced John Webb on drums. As far as it is possible for one person to do so, he combined the roles of Webb and John Mitchell within the orchestra. Brown had been playing in Roger Dean's group and Collier had asked him if he 'would be interested in joining'. Brown explained, 'I think he wanted someone who was interested in playing freely. At the time, I was also using a lot of different percussion instruments that offered a broader range of sound such as gongs and wooden blocks. That was one of the reasons he wanted me in the group.'

Describing what Collier was looking for in terms of how the music would be performed on the tour, Brown noted:

> In a way it was the last knockings of the jazz and poetry movement of the 1960s. John did have a fantastic voice and was perfect for the part of the Consul. The problem is being able to play quietly enough, so there is still music going on behind the voice. Because I played a number of small percussion instruments that was the right approach behind the voice. Graham wanted this wave effect of the Consul being overwhelmed by the insects ticking in the background,

which was my role. The music did go up and down in volume (Interview Brown/Heining 2016).

Others do not remember Carbery being drunk – or sober for that matter – but Alan Wakeman confirms Giddings' impression that Carbery's drinking was an issue, adding, 'I think he was pissed most of the gigs because he was always having arguments with Graham' (Interview Wakeman/Heining 2014). Collier took these things understandably very seriously. Although Alan Giddings (and John Gill) dealt with many of the logistical issues on *The Day of the Dead* tour, responsibility for ensuring that the music was still presented at its best to the audience fell on Collier's shoulders. Throughout his career, Collier would manage every aspect of touring personally, as John Gill noted:

> Graham was the one who organized the hotels, the vans, the transport, the plane tickets – even up to the last tour of the Far East tour that produced *Something British Made in Hong Kong*. He was the person – with me on the phone at home – organising the road stuff. So, he was his own road manager (Email interview Gill/Heining 2015).

That strain could take its toll on Collier's mood. He could be irascible, but then everything came down to him. Alan Wakeman even recalls Collier arguing with, or perhaps 'at', the remarkably even-tempered Harry Beckett:

> I remember funny arguments with Harry Beckett, as well. I think it used to exasperate Graham that he couldn't wind Harry up (Laughing). But Graham was apt to lose his temper about silly things. He had a go at me once and I remember saying something like, 'Well, you shouldn't have been a bass player'. I can't remember what it was about. But Harry usually took the brunt of it all. Funny 'cos he [Collier] built that whole thing around Harry but Harry was the whipping boy in that sense (Interview Wakeman/Heining 2014).

According to Giddings, the gig at Warwick Arts Centre was the best on the tour, with Wakeman playing 'a blinder, absolutely brilliantly'. Prior to the concert, Collier had been 'grumpy' with the saxophonist over some infraction:

> It was the best gig on the tour and at the end of it I went down. I said, 'That was just stunning' and Graham came up and he went, 'I must get grumpy more often'. And he loved it, of course. That was the nature of the man. He was always keen to see musicians go forward and make something bigger and better and that was a great gig that night (Interview Giddings/Heining 2014).

The Day of the Dead also led to a commission for BBC radio to write the music for a dramatization of *Under the Volcano* in 1979. It was clearly a composition that was very close to Collier's heart.

There are two points to note, Firstly, with *The Day of The Dead*, Collier gave up trying to direct the band from the bass – a Mingus-like endeavour if ever there were one and one that required a Mingus-like ability. For this recording, the hugely able and versatile Roy Babbington took over from Collier. After all, Babbington's CV includes stints with Ian Carr's Nucleus, Keith Tippett, Stan Tracey, Soft Machine, Barbara Thompson, Robert Wyatt, Harry Beckett and many others. The second point is a personal one. When it comes to *The Day of the Dead*, I struggle with the record almost as much as I struggle with Lowry's prose.[4]

Reviewing the Disconforme reissue in 2001, I wrote, 'My own view is clouded by an instinctive dislike of "spoken word meets jazz" efforts. Here an actor reads extracts from the work of novelist Malcolm Lowry to some hard-driven post-bop. The result is music that distracts from the spoken text and text that gets in the way of the music' (Heining 2001). Fourteen years later, I stand by much of the review though perhaps not the rather glib description of the music on *The Day of the Dead* and my view of poetry and jazz has mellowed. However, my problem with this particular record - then and now – remains. How does one get a handle on the music, when one is drawn in the first instance so immediately to the words? I suspect that I am not alone in that regard.

Briefly and at risk of over-simplification, in processing spoken language the left hemisphere of the brain is dominant. In processing music, the right hemisphere is dominant. We deal with the combining of music and words most successfully in the context of song or with spoken language and music where the latter follows a predictable and repeating set of patterns. We are as a species already neurologically adapted for language. As anthropologist, Ellen Dissanayake has noted, 'No matter how important lexico-grammatical meaning eventually becomes, the human brain is first organized or programmed to respond to emotional/intonational aspects of the human voice' (Dissanayake 1990, quoted in Storr 1992: 8). This means that not only are we drawn to process language for its semantic content but even more so for its emotional content (see Cooper and Aslin 1994). With *The Day of the Dead*, even when the voice is accompanied by the kind of jazz-rock vamp of "Part 1", one still privileges the voice over the music.[5]

Two critics writing at the time took a similar view to mine. When the work was performed at the Queen Elizabeth Hall in October 1978, critic Max Harrison used the words 'monotony' and 'sameness' to describe the music and he commented, 'Like oil and water, conceptual and non-conceptual arts do not mix well' (Harrison 1978: 19). Art Lange, reviewing the double album for *Down Beat*, went into greater depth in his comments, noting: '*The Day of the Dead* is a much more ambitious undertaking [than *Symphony of Scorpions*], taking greater risks and ultimately falling just short of the mark.' Mentioning Collier's reference to the technique of 'divided attention', he adds, 'One's ears do tend to listen to the meaning of the words before taking note of the parallel musical development, simply because we are trained from birth to do so'. And he continues, 'Unfortunately, concentration on the musical component reveals that Collier's compositional inspiration is not up to the levels of *Symphony*'. In this, Lange supports his argument with reference to what he suggests is a 'dependence upon thematic reference within a variable timbral palette', which, in turn, results in 'an overly subtle, often fragmented flow' (Lange 1979: 21).

To put it another way, two key elements in Collier's compositional armoury are his use of motifs and riffs, on the one hand, and a loose and, at times, elusive, improvisatory framework. As a conductor, when marshalling these resources and techniques alongside others, in a purely musical context, Collier is able to provide the unifying element. Here, a further element – spoken word involving complex and oblique language – is added to that context. The musical choices that Collier makes in *The Day of the Dead* are too broad to support the text. It is worth recalling Ron Atkins' remarks regarding *Wheel of Dreams*, 'Collier is much too sensitive to resort to the gimmicks and the excesses inherent in the form, but I can't help feeling that he has exchanged vulgarity for a kind of polite artiness' (Atkins 1972). A simpler musical approach might instead have reaped greater dividends.

Others have been far more complimentary. Alan Forrest, the literary critic of the *Financial Times*, reviewed the work's premier at the Ilkley Literary Festival, calling *The Day of the Dead*, 'A perfect marriage of words and music, a considerable work, widening the frontiers of jazz and making many earlier experiments with music and the spoken word sound like dilettante dabbling!' (Forrest 1977; see also Forrest 1978). In his *Jazz Forum* review, Kevin Henriques found the music 'directly apposite to the mood or feelings the words convey'. He went on to say that it was not an 'easy 60 minutes of listening', and that it took 'several hearings to appreciate all the finer points of the integration of the music with the words' (Henriques 1979). Barry McRae was slightly more cautious in *Jazz Journal*, describing it as 'a very ambitious attempt to present prose and music together'. And he added, 'In the main it is extremely successful, not because the words are comfortably cushioned, but because one finds one's attention divided almost equally between story and the music' (McRae

1978). And Charles Fox, again taking over Collier's *Gay News*' column, commented, 'Collier keeps control throughout, tingeing, underlining, or setting up exciting contrasts yet always respecting the words [...] All in all, a remarkable achievement' (Fox 1978).

Most recently, Andy Robson writing in *Jazzwise* gave the reissue on BGO Records three stars, though his enthusiastic, excited prose suggests a more generous award.

> Taking Lowry's *Under the Volcano* as his starting point, Collier's music likewise swirls between the deliciously detailed and great spats of open, shattered space for both Themen and Wakeman to rage and revel in. The result is epic, often inchoate, but deliciously carnival-like as befits the coming together of ghosts and the living during *The Day of the Dead* (Robson 2012: 46).

The original LP release of *The Day of the Dead* included on side 4 another Lowry work, *October Ferry*, its title taken from the novella *October Ferry to Gabriola*. On its reissue on CD by Disconforme, three other pieces were included. 'Eridanus' and 'Quanahuac' are, like 'Forest Path to the Spring',[6] duets for Art Themen and Ed Speight and appear largely through-composed. The other track issued by Disconforme was *Triptych*, which was recorded at Ronnie Scott's in March 1977.

October Ferry was first performed in 1977 in Budapest, on Collier's short tour of Hungary and Germany. Although issued as part of *The Day of the Dead* double album, it was recorded six months before the longer work. For that recording, Alan Jackson came in on drums. It is a rousing, dramatic work with a clearly developed internal structure. In just twenty-three minutes, Collier takes the listener through a series of musical moods from its free and pastoral beginnings through riff-laden big band jazz and a 'Basie-into-bebop' section into danceable, large ensemble jazz-rock. More than that, he and his musicians do so seamlessly.

The piece features some particularly fine trumpet, firstly from Henry Lowther – highly melodic and lyrical during its early impressionistic, pastoral passage – and then from Harry Beckett – concise and concentrated as it shifts into jazz-rock. Alan Wakeman and Art Themen both on tenor raise the intensity with successive solos before some beautifully poised bass playing from Roy Babbington and some fine trombone from Griffiths, just as he would say, doing what he does best. It finishes with Roger Dean on electric piano and Speight soloing over a 4/4, rock beat.

October Ferry's concision and coherence contrast markedly with *Triptych*, a work recorded at the same time as *Symphony of Scorpions*. As noted previously, it uses as inspiration three paintings by three abstract expressionist artists – Mark Rothko, Clyfford Still and Hans Hartung. Although Collier does not specify the particular paintings by Rothko, Still and Hartung upon which he draws, his sleeve notes to the Disconforme release offer descriptions that suggest the elements that he wished to reference in his composition. For Rothko, he points to the paintings' 'luminous, floating' quality, adding somewhat curiously, 'The trouble with Rothko lies in portraying static things within a necessarily continuous art like music. Therefore the viewer must move around it!' With Still, Collier notes, 'The theme has it but watch the treatment. The paintings aren't "free" like Pollock but rather controlled wildness.' And for Hartung, he comments on the painter's explosive quality that 'contrasts well with the others'. The key, Collier suggests, involves 'getting the sense of space that parts 1 and 2 have without going into boring riffs' (Collier 2000a). These are clearly 'notes to self'.[7]

When it comes to the composition itself, there is in relation to 'Part 1', the Rothko section, a sense of the music hanging and floating in space. The term 'tone poem' springs to mind, as different musical elements are juxtaposed – Themen's soprano against long brass notes; a trumpet soloing with just guitar accompaniment; a trio of soprano, trumpet and guitar; rumbling percussion with Webb using mallets. Performed entirely *rubato*, the impression is of the music moving around a loosely defined central point, with just a hint of Ellington peering through the mists. At times, the colours Collier evokes – as with Rothko – have a rare depth, a shimmering intensity.

'Part 2' is also out of time. It is more dramatic than 'Part 1' with rising brass choruses and, in the introduction, a free collective improvisation from piano, drums and percussion set against a declamatory brass riff and a counter melody played by the woodwinds, trumpets and single trombone. There are strong performances from Art Themen on tenor, Roger Dean and John Webb. However, the absence now of any real sense of thematic development or movement – two sections each around ten minutes in length feel stretched – becomes an issue. The sense is that, where *October Ferry* had a clear musical trajectory, *Triptych* lacks direction.

The contrast offered by 'Part 3' is immediately striking and even jarring. After a fluttering opening of trills from the brass and woodwinds, we note a time signature (4/4) driven by a solid backbeat from Webb and Roger Dean on electric piano. The music dances, with an attractive loping, almost sleazy feel to it. The horns offer counterpoint, whilst Mike Page, Henry Lowther, Themen and Malcolm Griffiths solo briefly. Here, Collier uses the technique of shadowing, referred to earlier in relation to *Mosaics* and the *Alternate Mosaics*, which he derived in part from New Orleans jazz. The other instruments play embellished or improvised lines behind the main soloist. It concludes with a brief brass chorus. 'Part 3' stands on its own as a piece of big band jazz-rock. However, as to how well it sits with the *rubato* stylings of the first and second sections, is open to question.[8]

Collier did not return to Lowry for inspiration or as a means of stimulating his own compositional thinking. It seems likely that he had by this point succeeded in incorporating those elements of Lowry's literary approach into his work that seemed of most value. However his enthusiasm for the writer continued, as was evidenced by his involvement with the Lowry society. Interestingly, a later work, *Oxford Palms* (2001), would also draw on another novel – William Faulkner's *Wild Palms*. With that composition, Collier would return explicitly to a literary source for artistic and technical inspiration. However, the Lowry phase had been consolidated into Collier's practice by the end of the 1970s.

* * *

Collier's position on the British jazz scene was now pretty well-established. He was accepted by his musical peers and liked by the musicians he chose to play with. His sexuality was not an issue for concern but rather a fact of his life. He was never afraid to express his sexuality and was prepared to offer support to the Campaign for Homosexual Equality and occasionally for other causes. One could not, however, describe him as an activist. One example, when he was willing to lend his more active backing came, in 1979, when he played bass for Tom Robinson's series of solo shows at the Collegiate Theatre, London as part of Gay Pride Week. A recording was subsequently issued by Robinson on Statik Records under the title *Tom Robinson – Cabaret '79*, making this one of Collier's only appearances as a sideman. In fact, when asked by Robinson to be involved, Collier no longer owned a bass. John Gill recalls the event with a certain ironic amusement:

> Having abandoned his bass – in fact, selling it to a friend Marc Meggido[9] – to concentrate on writing and conducting, he took up the bass again at Tom's request, even soaking his fingers in alcohol to harden the tips, and enjoyed the season, apart from the low-level physical violence from the lesbian choir, who targeted him whenever they came onstage as the most obvious symbol of masculinist hegemony in the band and barged him aside! (Interview Gill/Heining, June 2015)

However, in performing with Robinson, Collier was as much helping out a friend as making a personal statement, as John Gill explains:

> Graham always said in any field be it gay rights, nuclear power, the left in general, he wasn't a marcher. He wasn't a joiner. I think he felt that art and engagement had to be separate. He kept his politics away from his art because I think he felt that the two were best left separate. He went on gay pride marches with me, on Anti-Apartheid marches and things like that but he wasn't really a campaigner (Email interview Gill/Heining 2015).

In the earlier interview with Keith Howes for *Gay News*, the writer noted, 'Graham feels strongly that CHE [Campaign for Homosexual Equality] ought to be run more along social lines than political' (Howes 1976: 20). A fair comment perhaps; however, artists also challenge prejudice and promote tolerance through their art and the way they carry themselves. Graham Collier, as he said in several interviews, may have largely avoided in his life and career on the British jazz scene the prejudice frequently encountered elsewhere by gay men and women. Perhaps as he suggested this was as much due to a healthy absence of curiosity and nosiness amongst musicians, writers and fans, as it was due to a still more healthy tolerance.

Despite this general absence of the intrusions of homophobia in the context of his jazz life, there were from time to time incidents – shocking and laughable in equal measure – that clearly indicated that the enjoyment of jazz need not necessarily imply a degree of emotional maturity. At such times, Collier could spring wittily to the fore to challenge homophobia when it crossed his path (see Chapter 9). Amongst his papers, he had kept some correspondence between two homophobic British jazz fans and the ECM label, forwarded to him by the label's Steve Lake. In 1979, whilst reviewing jazz records for *Gay News*, Collier happened to write about Norwegian guitarist Terje Rypdal's album, *Waves*. The record company ECM included a quote from the review in their catalogue, one of which was mailed to a Mr B of West Yorkshire. The recipient was incensed. He wrote to ECM advising the company,

> I don't know if you are aware that *Gay News* is the British newspaper for homosexuals. We British despise homosexuals, and I hope and trust that this insertion (*sic!*) was a mistake. I know that if I were Terje Rypdal I would rather be credited with no reviews than a review by 'Puffs News' (*sic*).

Steve Lake, writer and producer, wrote back on behalf of the company,

> Dear Mr B,
> You do, of course, speak for yourself with your presumptuous (to say the least) statement that 'British despise homosexuals'. I'm British, too, and I don't.

Lake continued,

> Your letter disappointed us. One does hope, however vainly, that music created with sensitivity might be received with a similar sensitivity and openness. Or, to put it another way, we're not interested in making records for any kind of fascist element, whether sexual, racial or political; in fact, this is precisely the opposite of our intention.

This was not the end of the matter, however. Mr B – now of Kent and signing himself 'BA, MA' – delivered himself of a four-page letter in response. He clearly resented the 'dirty slur' implied by Lake's reference to fascism and pointed out that he was, in fact, 'a very right-wing member of the Conservative Party', whilst he presumed Steve Lake to be 'on the extreme left of the Labour Party'. The rest of the letter is in this vein and Mr B makes it clear that not only will he no longer purchase ECM releases but will campaign 'amongst his jazz-loving friends' to discourage them from doing so as well.

One nutter does not an asylum make but another very similar letter, with the same date as Mr B's second missive, also arrived on Steve Lake's desk from a Mr F of Merthyr Tydfil. Mr F wrote that he recently saw the review in *Gay News*, this having been brought to his attention by one of his friends, 'who knows my individual tastes'(!) Mr F was keen to reassure ECM that he was not a 'fascist or a believer in Right-Wing politics' and was 'not an extremist but an ordinary member of the public'. He expressed his fears regarding the breakdown of society and warned that he, too, and many of his friends 'who love and enjoy ECM records' would be 'very disappointed', were ECM's 'mistake' not remedied. He and they would otherwise 'persuade as many people as we can from purchasing your records'.

One can be really confident that these two writers represented only a tiny minority amongst fans of jazz. They wrote their diatribes, after all, nearly forty years ago and much has changed since. However, we will see shortly that at least two established British jazz writers in the eighties felt free and were given free editorial rein to express similar prejudices in print. Still, in some ways, prejudice is easier to combat when it is out in the open and Collier (and others) were more than willing to do so.

Notes

1. Chris Ackerley, one of the participants in the conference, noted: 'I remember Graham and his ensemble playing at the Vancouver conference; it was really a huge coup for Sherrill to get him there' (Email Ackerley/Heining 2015). The paper Collier presented, 'Lowry, jazz and *The Day of the Dead*' (Collier 1992), is included in *Swinging the Maelstrom* edited by Sherrill Grace.

2. Given that Spender was married to Lady Natasha Spender, a concert pianist whose second career was as an academic psychologist – she lectured on the psychology of visual perception at the Royal Academy of Art – it may be that he took the term from her. 'Divided attention' in psychological terms refers to the capacity to attend to more than one input at a time. Kahneman (1973) suggested that a limited amount of attention is allocated to tasks by a central processor. Many factors determine how much attentional capacity can be allocated and how much is needed for each task.

3. Neither Chris Ackerley nor Sherrill Grace, both Lowry experts, recognize the phrase from Lowry's own writings (Email Grace/Heining 2015).

4. I confess that my literary tastes extend more towards literature with a more conventional narrative structure and, though I find Lowry's prose quite beautiful at times, I also find it quite hard work.

5. This is in part due to what is called brain lateralization, that is, the way in which different hemispheres are dominant in different mental and physical activities. The reason we privilege speech over music has both evolutionary and developmental causes. There are different theories about how language originated, with some theorists arguing that music in some form predated speech, while others argue that these emerged as one ability in humans around the same time in our history but later separated into two different functional attributes – with language becoming the vehicle for rational thought and music taking on more symbolic and emotional aspects of communication (Ehrenzweig 1975: 164–65).

6. 'Forest Path to the Spring', as well as being recorded without narration on *Symphony of Scorpions*, is included as part of *The Day of the Dead*.

7. Although *The Day of the Dead* has been reissued by BGO, that reissue does not include *Triptych* or the two shorter duets. These are only available on the Disconforme release.

8. According to correspondence amongst Collier's papers, at one point, it seemed possible that *Triptych* might have been released on the German Vinyl label.

9. Marc Meggido is an improvising bass player, who worked with Roger Dean's group Lysis.

9 The Eighties or 'Graham Collier – The Wilderness Years'

1979 saw the end of the Mosaic label. Since his career began in the mid-sixties, Collier had played many roles on the British jazz scene – bandleader, bassist, composer-arranger, educator, critic, author and record label owner. As noted, Mosaic Records benefited from both Arts Council support and a cheque for £1000 from actor/director Terry Jones. Between 1974 and 1979, Mosaic released five albums by Collier himself, three albums by Roger Dean's Lysis, two by both Howard Riley and Stan Sulzmann and one by the trio Triton with Alan Wakeman, bassist Paul Bridge and drummer Nigel Morris. Sadly, only the Collier, Lysis and Triton records have actually been reissued on CD.

Mosaic Records' brief existence, in practice from 1974 to 1979, had resulted in a remarkable catalogue of adventurous music and Collier was keen to offer opportunities to musicians who had played in his groups and whom he admired. Both Stan Sulzmann and Alan Wakeman were understandably grateful for the opportunity. As Wakeman says,

> Graham offered me a record. He said, he'd got this label going via Terry Jones. I think Howard Riley kicked it off. I think that's where the first idea came from. Terry Jones put up money for Howard Riley to record something.[1]

He had originally planned to record in a quartet with pianist Gordon Beck, bassist Chris Laurence and John Marshall but decided instead to do a trio record with Paul Bridge on bass and Nigel Morris on percussion.

> I got involved with Nigel Morris and so, in fact, Triton was the working band then and I thought it would be a bit mean not to take the opportunity to record it. So, that's why Triton finished up on the label but it was basically Graham saying, 'I'd like you to do your own thing on the label'. And he just gave me... I think £500 was the ball park figure (Interview Wakeman/Heining 2014).

Reviewing the album's CD reissue in 2012, I noted, 'Triton's *Wilderness of Glass* is a saxophone trio set from '78 with Alan Wakeman, bassist Paul Bridge and Nigel Morris on drums. This is vital, visceral music with Wakeman on coruscating form' (Heining 2012b: 28). The record has a marvellous sense of urgency about it, as if the players are losing themselves in that moment of inspiration where nothing else can matter. Much the same could be said of the two Sulzmann records, which makes their absence on CD all the more sad.

> The first was *On Loan With Gratitude*, a quartet with John Taylor, Ron Mathewson on bass and Tony Levin on drums. That was my regular group for almost ten years. We represented the BBC in Molde, Norway for the European network programmes and Charles Fox used one of the tracks, 'GRS', as intro and exit music for his BBC Radio 3 Jazz Programme, called *Jazz Today*. Then, I made a duo recording *'krark'* with a pianist called Tony Hymas, who records mainly for NATO Records these days.

Hymas' worksheet includes names such as John Dankworth and Cleo Laine, Frank Sinatra, Jeff Beck, Jack Bruce, as well as saxophonists Sam Rivers, Tony Coe and Paul Dunmall. Hymas is an incredibly versatile musician, as Sulzmann points out,

> Tony wrote several of the Jeff Beck records and wrote lots of orchestral music as well as being a classical pianist. He is quite a remarkable musician but sort of unclassifiable. So, I was very grateful for the opportunity to make my first recordings as a leader courtesy of Graham (Email Sulzmann/Heining 2015).[2]

Intertwine – Music for Two Pianos, the first of the two Howard Riley discs, involved overdubbing two pianos, whilst the second featured just solo piano. Kevin Henriques, in a review in the *Financial Times*, had questioned whether *Intertwine* could be classed as jazz at all, a comment that he extended to Roger Dean's *Cycles* reviewed in the same piece. He wrote, 'On these two albums Riley and Dean place themselves in that no-man's land between jazz and "straight" contemporary music. Like people in that territory they are isolated from both sides' (Henriques 1977: 3). Whilst others, such as Barry McRae in *Jazz Journal* (McRae 1976b; 1977a; 1977b; 1977c; 1977d), were more open to such approaches to music-making, one suspects that in the conservative world inhabited by much of the British jazz audience it was views such as Henriques' that prevailed. Here one notes that Riley's *Intertwine* and *Shaped – Music for Solo Piano* fall within a period of the pianist's music when it seemed as much influenced by the sonic universe of European art music as by jazz.

The three Lysis records on Mosaic were *Lysis Live*, *Cycles* and *Lysis Plus*, which featured guest Kenny Wheeler. *Lysis Live* and *Lysis Plus* have been reissued on Future Music Records and are still available. *Cycles* featured both solo performances by Dean, a duo with drummer Ashley Brown and a trio with Dean overdubbed on bass, his second instrument. *Lysis Live* was essentially a strong and highly inventive piano trio record with Brown again on drums and with bassist Chris Laurence. However, *Lysis Plus* is even more ambitious in the way it uses other instruments – Kenny Wheeler and John Wallace on trumpets and flugelhorn, Hazel Smith on violins, Geoff Warren on alto saxophone and flute, Brown on drums and Dean himself on piano, bass and vibraphone – and in its development of complex harmonic structures from motivic material, rhythmically and melodically. As with all the releases on Mosaic, these albums offer an entirely fresh perspective on jazz and improvisation.

When his own Mosaic albums were reissued by Disconforme in 2000, Collier wrote in the sleeve notes to *The Day of the Dead* about the players who had recorded with him and made their own albums for Mosaic.

> The musicians involved, as always, gave of their time and talents far beyond the remuneration (if any) we were able to offer. I would like to dedicate these re-releases to them, particularly to guitarist Ed Speight, one of the most under-rated musicians I know, who appears on every one of these records (and all of the others I have released since). As the late Ian Dury said of Ed, 'un musician extraordinaire et un raconteur vraiment bizarre' (Collier 2000b).

Over the years, Collier's own music had followed its own path, which separated it from much of the jazz being made in Britain at the time. It did not fall into the jazz-rock camp or the straight-ahead bag. Collier's big band approach was not that of Mike Gibbs or Neil Ardley and his work fell outside that of free jazz or free improvisation. Although some of the music on Mosaic might have connected with other areas – Howard Riley and to a degree Roger Dean with free improvisation, Triton and Stan Sulzmann with free jazz – the label carried its own individual stamp. It was inevitable, given the difficulties for jazz within the wider music scene in Britain at that time, that the label would need to look further afield if it were to survive.

As we have heard, Alan Giddings was working for Mosaic Records in the late seventies. He explained how Collier made what seemed like a breakthrough for the label with a distribution deal with German company Bellaphon.

> [T]ypical Graham he didn't just sort of take the money and run. He thought, well this would be great. We can invest it in more music, more development, more musicians and so on. And he hired me to see if...on the basis of their...guaranteed contract we could really just develop the record label and get more recordings done because the Bellaphon deal was a guaranteed minimum number of records they would take, which they would distribute particularly through Germany but throughout large parts of Europe at that time.

9 The Eighties or 'Graham Collier – The Wilderness Years' 153

Figure 9. Graham Collier Twelve at The Roundhouse, October 1978. Mosaic Festival. Personnel: Roger Dean (piano), Roy Babbington (bass), Alan Jackson (drums), Paul Nieman (trombone), Pete Duncan, Henry Lowther, Harry Beckett (trumpets), Ed Speight (guitar), Mike Page, Art Themen, Tony Roberts (saxes), Graham Collier (conductor). Copyright Jak Kilby.

The deal with Bellaphon could, indeed should, have ensured the label's survival. It is clear that Collier himself hoped to expand the label's activities. In October 1978, he booked The Roundhouse for a one-day festival for himself and other acts on Mosaic. However, just two months later, he learned that Bellaphon were about to 'renege on their contract' ('Timeline'). With the company failing to meet their contractual obligations, Collier was forced to go to law. According to Giddings,

> Bellaphon were huge distributors at that time but I don't think they really understood anything about contemporary jazz and they realised they were taking all these records which they had guaranteed which in their terms was quite a modest guarantee and they just couldn't shift them. So, for them it was easier to just drop the contract and they did.

The case took until 1984 to be resolved in favour of Mosaic. The only details of sales figures contained in Collier's papers relate to *Darius* and *Midnight Blue*. If these are correct, the former sold around 600 and the latter 400 copies. Assuming this was reflected across sales of other records on Mosaic, then with utmost irony Bellaphon's failure to meet their responsibilities may well have saved Collier financially. He did, apparently in the end, break even. As to whether this would have been the case, were it not for the Bellaphon judgement, is moot. Giddings remembers Collier being 'chuffed that he got a positive outcome but it was, you know, damage limitation. It wasn't the great expansion that he and I had hoped for' (Interview Giddings/Heining 2014).

The big event for Collier in 1979, however, was a tour of India. Not only did it reveal his great strengths as an organizer, it also (in his diary entries and report to the British Council, which had supported it) offers a glimpse into the sometimes curmudgeonly side to his personality.

It took place in January 1979 and was at most levels a success. That it happened at all was astonishing, as Art Themen noted: 'How on earth could somebody get a however many piece band and persuade the British Council to fund that and take us to India? That was an amazing achievement.' And he continued:

> Stan Tracey is a legend and were you to ask me about playing with Stan, I would wax lyrical about how sometimes it levitated and was the most wonderful experience. With Graham, I can't say that but try and get Stan to organise a band to go to India and he wouldn't know where to start. He [Graham] looked like a bank manager. He had authority. He had gravitas. He could persuade people to do that sometimes (Interview Themen/Heining 2014).[3]

The band performed under the name Jazz Musica 12 and featured Pete Duncan, Henry Lowther and Harry Beckett on trumpets, Art Themen, Alan Wakeman and Mike Page on saxes, Malcolm Griffiths on trombone, Roger Dean on piano, Ed Speight on guitar, Roy Babbington on bass, and Ashley Brown on drums. They played at the Calcutta Jazz Festival to an audience of two thousand plus and in Bombay to an audience of a similar size, whilst in Delhi the audience numbered around seven to eight hundred. The final concert was recorded by Air India Radio for broadcast.

Collier's report to the British Council indicates that he also did a couple of lectures on the tour. He found some of the questions 'naïve but not so much, in view of relative unsophistication of audiences there'. Some may find that comment rather patronising and perhaps it reveals too much of Collier's own feelings about the country and the tour. After all, jazz has a history in India going back to the 1920s. At the same time, Collier was evidently aware of the enthusiasm in India for jazz.

Roger Dean describes the experience very succinctly, noting,

> [B]y the time we did that [tour] some of the places we were going to like India were already very clearly part of the jazz diaspora and

> were having international festivals. I think *Jazz Yatra* started about then and was already on the touring circuit for many international musicians. I remember when we went to *Jazz Yatra*, there was a German group sponsored by the German government, Embryo, in the same way that we were sponsored by the British Council. So, it was a mixture of the last remnants of British cultural imperialism plus a genuine jazz diaspora broadening, I think (Interview Dean/Heining 2014).

And Ed Speight echoes the point, adding to it the clear link that could be heard between Indian music and jazz:

> Big audiences. It was well-attended. It was part of a festival in Calcutta. It was very good to get a chance to listen to the local musicians, the classical Indian players – the sitar players and tabla players. You could hear how Coltrane got a lot of ideas. You could see the link between the melodic approach of that form of music with what Coltrane was doing.

Speight's other brief remarks on the tour reference the more mundane elements of life on the road. He is, as ever, an informative tour guide:

> India was quite a revelation. Great food. The only person who got food poisoning was Art Themen. Well, I didn't eat meat the whole time I was there. You didn't need to. Walking through the Calcutta meat market the first day, I thought, 'No!' Mind you, I suppose walking through an abattoir here would put you off (Interview Speight/Heining 2014).

On the other hand, whatever the success of the tour, going by the extract from his diary that he included in his 'Timeline', Collier found it a difficult experience at several levels.

> Interesting to see but so alien in its civilisation, manners, behaviour that I don't feel involved with nor want to be. Their mentality seems to be 'listen to what you say, promise to act on it, then do what they wanted to do all along'... Taj Mahal was absolutely incredible, exceeded one's expectations about ten-fold... Glad I've seen it but would only go back for well-paid work. The band generally behaved very selfishly, wanting to be told everything about 4 times and making no attempt to realise that I am not a band boy at their beck and call. Apart from RD [Roger Dean] and Pete Duncan no-one seemed bothered to offer any help, even when I had a very bad eye... ('Timeline').

In a slightly grumpy report to the British Council, Collier described briefly the three concerts in Calcutta, Bombay and Delhi. However, he reserved most of his comments for the logistical issues and problems on the tour, notably issues with accommodation and concert organization. He might have been a keen and veteran traveller but one is left with the distinct impression that Collier was quite out of sorts throughout the tour.

Figure 10. Jazz Yatra, India, January 1979. Graham Collier, Ed Speight, Geoff Warren.

* * *

In his private life, Collier seems to have been very settled in this period. In 1980, he and John Gill had moved out of Earl's Court and bought a Victorian house in Shell Road in Lewisham. They entertained regularly and film director/producer David Cohen, who visited them at their home on several occasions in the 1990s, described it as a 'kind of slightly chaotic, comfortable, very middle-class home. They were always very hospitable.' Collier and Gill were, by all accounts, very happy there and this was their home until 2000, when they moved to Ronda in Andalucía. In 1983, they began taking holidays on Paxos, Greece. There they made friends with another British citizen, who had a house on the island. When the friend died, they left Collier a half-share on the property, and for many years, Collier and Gill would spend at least a few weeks annually on Paxos.[4]

Reading Collier's papers and talking to friends, one gets the impression that there was often a gap in Collier's emotional world between the private satisfactions of home and relationships and the public dissatisfactions of career. Some of this may be explained by the nature of the artistic life itself. To a degree, this could only be fully lived in the act of creativity – that is, writing or making music itself – or at least engaging with music in some other way, such as teaching. One does not get the sense that Collier was a person who ever quite relaxed, and perhaps it was at those times of inactivity, enforced or simply the result of circumstances, that the doubts crept in.

The feeling that somehow he was not receiving his due persisted for Collier and would even be amplified by changing fortunes in British jazz. In the 1980s, jazz in Britain saw a resurgence. Even major record labels such as Columbia, EMI (through the relaunched Blue Note imprint), Polygram and RCA suddenly began to take an interest in music that they had promoted so abysmally just a decade and a half earlier. Of course, the extent of that interest depended on who one was and how one looked, as much as the actual music. With the exception of veteran Stan Tracey, whose contract was briefly picked up by Blue Note, the musicians who signed on the line were young, good-looking and image-conscious, a situation that reflected similar happenings in the USA.

These labels were, of course, international companies and required sales not just in Britain but across Europe and in the USA as well. In the case of essentially North American concerns such as EMI/Capitol/Blue Note, Columbia and RCA, a further problem arose with British artists signed to these labels. They and their music did not travel to the USA – physically or metaphorically.

Whether in North America, Britain or mainland Europe, these young musicians looked good on album covers and in magazine features. They might, it was felt, be the kind of 'cats' that could turn the fortunes of the music around and finally lay claim to that chimera – a young audience for jazz. Andy Sheppard signed first to Island Records, along with Courtney Pine and the Jazz Warriors. Sheppard would later record for Blue Note but would find himself out of pocket on the deal (Heining 1998b). Trombonist Annie Whitehead recorded for Paladin, a Virgin records' subsidiary, and saxophonist Steve Williamson and trumpeter Guy Barker landed deals with Polygram.[5] The other major big band of the time, Loose Tubes, a band midwifed by Graham Collier, were somewhat cannier. Their first two albums, *Loose Tubes* and *Delightful Precipice*, were released on their own imprint, before their final album of that period, *Open Letter*, came out on the independent EG Records.[6]

That said, the lack of interest shown in those *d'un certain âge*, who did not wear sharp suits or look quite so hot on the cover of *GQ* magazine clearly rankled with Collier, as did a sense that he did not rank with others of his own age amongst jazz critics. For its April 1985 issue, *The Wire* celebrated British jazz and, though he featured in a short piece by Roger Cotterell (Cotterell 1985:

43), Collier's name did not make it onto the front cover alongside the names of Annie Whitehead, Harry Beckett, Mike Westbrook and John Surman. Interviewed by John Wickes a year later, it is evident this 'oversight' still hurt (Interview Collier/Wickes 1986).

This resurgence in British jazz fortunes coincided with an artificial, credit-driven boom in the economy during the period of the Thatcher government between 1987 and 1990. Neither the resurgence, nor the economic boom, which shattered with the recession of 1990, lasted. At the same time, looking back at the period, it is hard not to see the efforts of these major record companies and their executives as inept, firstly, in signing these artists and, secondly, dropping them as soon as the expected sales failed to materialize.

For reasons that will become clear, Collier largely lost interest in making records after *The Day of the Dead*. His only release in the eighties was *Something British Made in Hong Kong*, which came out in 1988.[7] However, *contra* this chapter's intentionally ironic title, he was far from inactive during the decade. He toured, undertook commissions and began teaching at the Royal Academy of Music. Such opportunities came Collier's way because he pursued them, though perhaps the renewal of interest in jazz might also have opened a door or two. As we have said, inactivity was avoided like a curse.

Collier's ability to negotiate with arts bodies continued to be a feature of his career. In 1982, he decided to form a rehearsal band for young musicians. As he later told John Wickes, he was aware that a number of experienced composers – not just himself but others such as Mike Westbrook – had music they had written but which was rarely performed. He saw this as a way of providing an opportunity to bring together players new to jazz and give them the opportunity to develop their skills as performers and writers through exposure to material that would stretch and challenge them. As he said in 2010,

> The band was formed using some money left over from an Arts Council grant as a rehearsal band for the young musicians, who I felt were being denied effective big band experience – for which, read 'NYJO'. Many young players didn't want to join because of the NYJO ethos of louder, higher, faster (Interview Collier/Heining 2010).

Trumpeter Steve Waterman had taken part in the European Youth Jazz Orchestra workshops in London in 1981, where Collier had been one of the guest tutor-composers. Waterman suggests that it was this experience that made Collier realize that 'there were young musicians interested in the kind of music he was writing', which encouraged him to set up the rehearsal band and in which Waterman was one of the regular participants. He added, 'It wasn't just Graham. He was bringing in other composers. I certainly remember Roger Dean coming in and working with us' (Interview Waterman/Heining 2014).

As Collier explained to John Wickes, '[I]t worked for about six months. Then suddenly it seemed to develop a life of its own' (Interview Collier/Wickes 1986). There was a parting of the ways that was at the time quite acrimonious. That rehearsal band, of course, became Loose Tubes.

Quite what went awry is hard to say at this distance in time. Interviewed in 2010, when Loose Tubes' live album *Dancing on Frith Street* was released, both parties had mellowed somewhat in their take on events (Heining 2010). The immediate incident that caused the split seems to have been the band's failure to invite Collier to a gig they had set up. Collier saw this, with some justification, as a snub and one that smacked of ingratitude at the time and money he had invested in the band. However, this particular gathering of young players contained more than its share of strong-minded individuals – people such as Django Bates, Steve Berry, Eddie Parker, Chris Batchelor and Ashley Slater. Quite a few were already connected personally and musically. With hindsight, it was not a case of whether there would be a split between Collier and the band, but rather when.

The signs were there once Django Bates and Steve Berry and others began bringing their own tunes to rehearsals, though Collier was certainly not opposed to this, as Steve Waterman, then a student at Trinity College, explained: 'Graham was very encouraging over allowing people to bring their own pieces in to rehearsals. I don't think he was particularly pushing his own music. He was trying to get everyone to contribute. It was more a collective with Graham being the figurehead pulling it together' (Interview Waterman/Heining 2014).

Waterman has no recollection that the parting between Collier and those who would form Loose Tubes was bitter. Nor did he recall much friction between Collier and Django Bates, Steve Berry and the others. Waterman would, of course, go on to play and record with Collier's big band and smaller ensembles and Collier would also employ him as a trumpet tutor on the jazz degree course at the Royal Academy of Music, which began in 1991.

From the perspective of Steve Berry,

> The stuff we wrote ourselves seemed to take better to us than the stuff that was provided. People were coming in with stuff written for their own bands. I'd be looking at a bass part written for Paul Bridge or Chris Laurence that wasn't written for me, whereas when we wrote things we wrote for Tim Whitehead and our drummer Nic France and so on (Heining 2010: 31).

Roger Dean directed the rehearsal band on several occasions and recalls that these musicians were determined to pursue their own course: 'Yes, I recognise this very well from the sessions I did directing the Loose Tubers. They really did want to do their own thing, which I loved. I see them as jumping head first into fairly post-modern more than avant garde approaches when they got going' (Email Dean/Heining 2017).

Given the time over again, those involved would probably have done things differently. As Collier said in 2010, 'In retrospect, I guess it doesn't matter. As the world sees it, a good band was formed, which helped a lot of musicians become better known and I get a little footnote in the history books!' (Heining 2010: 31). Steve Berry feels it important that Collier receive proper credit.

> Graham's role in the genesis of the band should be acknowledged. Because it was a messy divorce, the band was at pains to excise him from any mention. With hindsight, it obviously should be pointed out that it was due to Graham that it came about at all. He got money from the Arts Council to provide a forum for creative players, who you wouldn't expect to turn up in NYJO. That was his premise and he was entirely right because to us NYJO represented precisely nothing we wanted to do (Heining 2010: 31).

The saddest thing about the affair was that it represented a lost opportunity. Those involved succeeded in creating an impressive and even groundbreaking ensemble. However, the rehearsal and performance orchestra for young musicians – an anti-NYJO as it were – that Collier had envisaged did not result. Collier was hurt by the way the enterprise ended and his enthusiasm for such ventures was dampened, at least for a time, as he told John Wickes:

> I feel a bit of antagonism. It ruined the idea. It can't happen again – not for a few years anyway. You might get some public money if it had turned out successful. I still think there's space for a band of that kind but it won't be me who organises it (Interview Collier/Wickes 1986).

Fortunately, Collier soon had another major project to occupy his time. Towards the end of 1982, with the support of John Cumming and Serious Productions, Collier obtained another grant from the Arts Council to compose a work for a hand-picked orchestra to perform at the Bracknell Jazz Festival. Serious were responsible for programming the festival and their support was crucial. Further to this, Bryan Izzard's Brighter Thoughts film company were to make a documentary of the performance, including interviews with Collier and others conducted by critic Charles Fox. The documentary would later be shown on Channel 4, at that time Britain's newest TV channel and, back then, keen to live up to its public sector broadcasting mandate.

The new work was called *Hoarded Dreams*, its title taken from a book by George Steiner. The title, Collier explained in the programme notes for the festival, seemed 'ideal' for the commission, 'in that it could be used as a springboard for various dreams to be represented in music: a Thatcher-less Britain perhaps, or an Arts Council gift of a Cotswolds' house plus limitless barrels of Fullers'.

Noting that it was the dream of any jazz composer to be able to choose 'a large group of star musicians to perform a long composition written with absolutely no outside restrictions', he explained succinctly his intentions for *Hoarded Dreams*.

> The structure is simple and presents all the musicians in solo situations but situations which are affected strongly by the written framework and the interrelationship between ideas throughout the piece. Essentially, there is a three-way process: the composer was affected by the improvisers; the improvisers will be affected by the writing and we will all be affected by the interplay between all these elements and the overall ambience of the actual performance (Collier 1983c).

Returning briefly to John Gill's earlier comment that Collier was not 'a joiner' and chose to keep his music separate from politics, should not blind us to the fact that he did hold views on such questions and could reasonably be seen as left-of-centre in terms of his political opinions, if somewhat vaguely so. His reference to Thatcher and her policies above was a rare example of him making any kind of political statement, though in an article for *The Wire* in 1985 he would make similar rather general remarks (Collier 1985b).

The Bracknell performance attracted generally favourable reviews. Its subsequent performance as part of the Camden Festival, also produced by John Cumming and Serious, in 1985 and the broadcasting of the Channel 4 documentary shortly before that performance would attract a more negative response in some quarters. However, with the 2007 release of the concert on CD (Cuneiform Rune 252), Collier's achievement with *Hoarded Dreams* now seems a remarkable one.

It is not 'perfect' by any means. In fact, given Collier's approach and his perspective of jazz in performance, one wonders if such a thing might be possible – all compositions are, by that definition, in a simultaneous state of being and becoming. Yet it is a huge, diverse, even sprawling work which by rights should have collapsed under the weight of its own conceit and contradictions. It does not do so. Its architecture, somewhat improbably, holds it together and binds very different performers and performances into something resembling a unitary and satisfying whole. It is interesting to hear what one of the musicians felt at the time and how his view of it was later changed on hearing the recording. Geoff Warren, who played alto sax and flute and was a relative newcomer to the Collier band, recalls:

> At the time I must confess I didn't really understand it. It was very long. The risk was that it became too many episodes because Graham had got too many guys in, fantastic guys, all very, very different.

And he continued:

> It seemed to me at the time to be overlong and lacking form. When the CD – when Graham released it, I relistened to it. I thought, 'This is fantastic'. It was just like a dream, going exactly the way a dream progresses from one episode to another, sort of sliding between one piece and another... I think it's brilliant now but, at the time, perhaps I was too young, too inexperienced (Interview Warren/Heining 2014).

In a sense, Collier's striving to work within and between the twin poles of total freedom, on the one hand, and form and structure, on the other, is significant on a number of levels. Firstly, this is more than a mere desire to blur the boundaries between improvisation and composition. To a certain extent, most jazz does this all the time. What Collier proposes, instead, is a dialectical or dialogic relationship between the two, which exists within the permanent state of tension between the two. The composition, for Collier, like the improvisation, is never final or complete. Secondly, where the approach fails to produce a satisfying outcome on occasion, this is not simply the difference between a good and a poor performance but on the failure of the process. The creative moment requires the tension at its heart to be maintained, with neither composition nor improvisation being ever entirely dominant. In this regard, Collier's approach involves large elements of risk-taking and he is in this respect, therefore, closer to the position of free improvisation than to more straight-ahead jazz practice. The third point concerns the difficulties that Collier's approach and work present in terms of how these are understood and evaluated. Collier's position makes him an outsider. In effect, his work demands to be judged essentially on how successfully he meets his own objectives. In a critical environment that often seemed split between the more or less straight-ahead and the more or less avant garde, that is a big ask.

9 The Eighties or 'Graham Collier – The Wilderness Years' 163

The concert brought together Collier stalwarts such as Ed Speight, Roger Dean and Art Themen, with guests and past associates such as John Surman, Kenny Wheeler, Malcolm Griffiths and Henry Lowther. From (East and West) Germany, the orchestra was joined by trombonist Konrad 'Conny' Bauer, trumpeter Manfred Schoof, saxophonist Matthias Schubert and guitarist John Schröder. Schubert and Schröder were two young musicians whom Collier had met working with the European Youth Jazz project in London in 1981 and who had impressed him greatly.

Other additions included Finnish saxophonist Juhanni Aaltonen, Swedish trombonist Eje Thelin, Polish trumpeter Tomasz Stańko and American trumpeter and Mingus alumnus Ted Curson. The other musicians were from the UK. Geoff Warren was on alto sax and flute, Dave Powell played tuba and Ashley Brown played drums, with Paul Bridge on bass.

In terms of its overall structure, *Hoarded Dreams* contains seven sections, with 'Part 1', the introduction, and 'Part 7', the coda, being quite brief. Geoff Warren's analogy of a dream with a series of semi-connected episodes is a useful one. Another might be of a series of rooms at an exhibition, each room with different content but linked somehow by the artist's imagination.

With *Hoarded Dreams*, Collier utilizes his entire armoury of compositional signatures and techniques. There are interludes of free improvisation punctuated with stabbing riffs and motifs, which then seem to be passed across the orchestra. He would later use this technique (one far from uncommon in symphonic music) to fine effect, most notably on *Charles River Fragments*. There are the inevitable cadenzas, changes of tempo and mood, fluctuations in volume and abrupt endings. Ballads contrast with a fast waltz or with driving jazz-rock or swinging big band jazz, at times with a strong Latin feel. And, perhaps more successfully here than on any of Collier's previous compositions, we hear the deployment of discrete improvising units. In 'Part 2', he features all of his five trumpets – Schoof, Wheeler, Lowther, Stańko and Curson – weaving intersecting melody lines with solos from Lowther, Schoof and, finally, Curson. In 'Part 3', Ed Speight duets, first with Aaltonen on alto on a ballad over glistening orchestral colours and then on a fast-paced waltz with Wheeler. 'Part 4' features the trombones – Bauer, Griffiths and Thelin – with Geoff Warren's flute. This passage is beautifully eccentric with a vaudeville or circus-like quality before the trombones lead a big band section that seems to echo Ellington's 'It Don't Mean a Thing'. And one of the record's many highlights is heard in 'Part 6' with the three tenors of Schubert, Aaltonen and Themen, who are heard as an a cappella trio, then as soloists and finally as a trio but backed by the whole band in a powerful bebop finale to the section.

In addition, the record contains some highly effective and affecting duets, for example between Curson and Brown in 'Part 2', another between Surman on bass clarinet and Stańko in 'Part 5' that has an almost baroque feel to it and later some wonderful interplay between the guitarists in 'Part 6'. This was, as Collier pointed out, a dream band and every single player rises to the occasion, whether it is the tried and tested such as Themen, Griffiths, Wheeler and Surman or the (relative) newcomers such as Warren, Schubert, Schröder or Brown. Ashley Brown, in fact, is a revelation, which, bearing in mind that he came to the orchestra somewhat late in the day, is even more to his credit. He explained:

> With the bigger band, I took over from Alan Jackson. Alan did a rehearsal for *Hoarded Dreams* at the Tramshed in Camden and he got fed up with it. So, I was slipped in to do the actual performance because Alan had been in the big band and I was in the small group (Interview Brown/Heining 2016).

Brown also notes one rather amusing aspect of the concert (and of other experiences he had in large ensembles with Collier). It related to the composer/conductor's 'lazy eye'. It was not always possible for the musicians to know just who Collier was looking at. As he would sometimes look at a player to cue them in to solo or whatever, this could be and was a problem at times (Interview Brown/Heining 2016).

The closing coda ('Part 7') is quite marvellous. It is as if the whole piece has been condensed into its final two and a half minutes. Motifs, riffs, themes and trios and duets are reprised and the main theme of the piece is recalled. Four chords from the horns and a final fifth ends with what sounds like an interrupted cadence. It must have been very difficult to find a way of bringing this huge work to a successful close but it is hard to imagine a better ending to one of Collier's most successful compositions.

But the record's finest moment is also its most controversial. It comes towards the end of 'Part 5' and features Conny Bauer. Writing about the incident a quarter of a century later, Collier noted:

> Reflecting his [Bauer's] usual home in free jazz groups, he played an absolutely staggering, but very long, solo cadenza. It was far too long for the situation, but I could find no sensible way of stopping him, and it was so good that in some ways I didn't want to. But I was aware that, at least as I saw it, he was spoiling the shape of the piece. So, in an attempt to move the piece on, I brought the band in. One critic picked me up on this – in a way rightly, but if I hadn't, I suspect he might still have been playing! (Collier 2009a: 255).

9 The Eighties or 'Graham Collier – The Wilderness Years'

The critic Collier refers to was Dave Gelly, writing in the *Observer*. Gelly pointed out the difficulty faced by the composer in bringing together this diverse collection of players and then, in addition, predicting how each duet or solo or trio might turn out. Gelly continued:

> Sometimes, the guess was brilliant; you couldn't tell where improvisation ended and writing took over. Occasionally, as after a breathtaking cadenza from German trombonist Konrad Bauer, the band's entry stopped the music in its tracks (Gelly 1983: 30).

As Collier was so fond of noting, jazz happens in real time once. Gelly is correct, though he remains sympathetic to Collier's dilemma. In a way, the entry of the band is too much of a contrast initially. By any standards, Bauer's performance is astonishing, as his multiphonics at times have him duetting with himself. However, Collier quickly corrects his initial error by allowing the orchestra a freer rein that then complements Bauer's solo and opens the section out with Stańko joining Bauer.

Of all Collier's compositions, *Hoarded Dreams* is one of the hardest to map and describe. Like the later *Charles River Fragments* from 1994, there is simply so much musical information contained within its seventy minutes. The audience reaction is spontaneous and rapturous, marking one of those transcendent moments in music that follows a massive building of tension before a final release. It might not be 'perfect' but it was a triumph and its availability on CD twenty-four years later makes *Hoarded Dreams* an essential and pivotal work in the Collier canon.

Richard Williams, writing in the *Times*, made comparisons to, at one pole, Gil Evans and, at the other, to Globe Unity Orchestra. He found nothing 'particularly new or original' in the work but felt that it fulfilled its 'function of creating a variety of formats tailored to the best advantage of the individual improvisers'. Devoting much of the review to those same individuals, he concluded by granting that '*Hoarded Dreams* justified its tea-time ovation' (Williams 1983: 16).

John Fordham's review in *The Guardian* was a strange one, indeed. He began by describing Collier's past compositions as 'professional but rather middle-of-the-road'. This, he suggested, accounted 'for the relative frequency with which he is invited to compose them'. His expectations 'focused more on the band than on the work'. Yet, on this occasion at least, 'both thoroughly deserved each other though the orchestrations rarely gave you the feeling that you'd been yanked out of your time and place or been let in on a better way of perceiving it'. This sounds rather reluctant and, yet, Fordham clearly enjoyed the set. He concludes, 'Toward the climax, when Collier set three saxophones yelling demonically at each other against intermittent peals of sound from the brass, this potentially cumbersome outfit was soaring like a glider' (Fordham 1983: 11). That *Evening Standard* critic, Jack Massarik, found the performance a success is more surprising given his preference for bop-derived big band jazz, though his comment that *Hoarded Dreams* 'generated a surprisingly histrionic series of solos from its distinguished cast of 18', could be read more than one way (Massarik 1983: 22).

Charles Fox provided a typically balanced review. He described the performance as 'musical fireworks' and went on to say that the imposition of their personality on such proceedings is 'the aim of the successful jazz composer'. Whilst Fox was not convinced that Collier had achieved that aim entirely consistently, he saw this as 'due to the problems of finding an orchestral vocabulary to encompass the diversity of styles and stances'. He added that there was 'an unselfishness involved in encouraging his sidemen to upstage him' (Fox 1983: 29).

Reviewing the album for *Jazz Review* on its later release, Anthony Troon described the performance as 'staggering' and commented that Collier had taken 'an ensemble of avant garde blowers' and given them 'an inspiring framework of harmony and dissonance from which to launch their challenging statements' (Troon 2007). The reviewer for *Jazzwise* called it 'a monumental piece of music' and asked, 'George Russell, Mike Westbrook, Charles Mingus and Graham Collier – how many other jazz composers could produce something of such epic proportions where both composition and improvisation combine to such powerful effect?' (Heining 2007a: 59). Justifiably, the record was subsequently listed by Brian Morton and Richard Cook amongst their 200 core recordings in *The Penguin Jazz Guide: The History of the Music in the 1001 Best Albums* (Morton and Cook 2010).

Hoarded Dreams' subsequent performance at the Camden Festival in 1985, however, was less positively received, much to Collier's distress. Again with the support of Serious Productions, Collier was able to perform the work in Cologne and the Logan Hall, Camden performance followed this in March 1985. As it happened, Channel 4 decided to show the Brighter Thoughts documentary on 6 March, less than two weeks before the London gig at the Logan Hall. Whether this affected turn-out for the gig for better or worse, according to Jack Massarik, the concert took place before a 'thin' audience (Massarik 1985a).

The concert also featured a new work, *Crystals of Space and Time*. As always with Collier, *Hoarded Dreams* was written with specific individual musicians in mind rather than for a trumpet or saxophone player. Consequently, the need for four replacements for the Cologne and Camden shows required a certain amount of restructuring of the piece, as he explained in an article in an arts magazine prior to the performance in Camden:

9 The Eighties or 'Graham Collier – The Wilderness Years'

Figure 11. Graham Collier and Eje Thelin, *Hoarded Dreams* concert, Logan Hall, Camden, March 1985. Copyright Nick White.

> [A] solo fitted to perfection by Art Themen would not fit Harry Sokal and had to be re-jigged and fitted to the personality of guitarist Terje Rypdal. A hard job but one which comes, as they say, with the territory of being a jazz composer. One of whose main aims is, in Billy Strayhorn's words about Duke Ellington, to ensure that 'the part and the player have the same character' (Collier 1985a).

In terms of the changes, Danish trumpeter Palle Mikkelborg replaced Kenny Wheeler and German saxophonists Michael Pilz and Harry Sokal came in for John Surman and Art Themen respectively. Finally, the brilliant Norwegian guitarist Terje Rypdal took the place of John Schröder.

It is unclear how the audience responded but Barry McRae wrote a favourable review in *Jazz Journal* (McRae 1985), whilst Max Harrison, writing in *Jazz Express*, found the 'improvised solos less satisfying, although they were clearly fully integrated parts of the whole'. He continued: 'The many-sidedness of this jazz was as much a part of its fascination as its large-scale structural ambitions but I suspect that Collier needs to achieve a closer match between his sidemen's personalities and his own' (Harrison 1985). In the *Wire*, Richard Cook's review was negative. He found 'it all so damn stodgy' and described *Hoarded Dreams* as a 'long, sometimes stultifying and occasionally engrossing piece'. He concluded, 'I left feeling too full and knocked about' (Cook 1985: 8).

However, it was two other reviews, one by Derek Jewell in the *Sunday Times* and the other by Jack Massarik in the *Evening Standard*, which really got under Collier's skin. The former was, indeed, somewhat spiteful in tone and said as much about the reviewer as it did about the concert. The other was certainly not favourable but it was actually more measured and one wonders if Collier misread it. Richard Cook's review was, if anything, far more critical.

Massarik's main point seemed to be that what had worked well in the Bracknell sunshine to a rapturous and full house did not perform as successfully on a cold March night before a 'thin' audience in Camden. The problem, as he saw it, was that the piece relied largely on its soloists and, in this context, they had little to fire them to their best work. The tone of the review suggested that he was disappointed (Massarik 1985a).

Jewell's review focuses more on his feelings about 'the vociferous lobby' that 'has been trying to stuff "free" jazz (once avant garde, now long *déjà entendu*) down the public's throats for two decades', than on the music itself, which Jewell found 'drearily gauche' (Jewell 1985: 41).

Sensibly or not, Collier chose to go on the offensive and wrote a full-page article in his defence for the *Wire* attacking Massarik and Jewell. Massarik, who often tended to lead with his chin, then responded via the magazine's letter's page (Massarik 1985b). One suspects that, for all his anger, Collier was deeply hurt by the response of certain critics and that this was compounded by two letters that appeared, one in the *TV Times* and the other in *Jazz Express*.[8] Collier's *Wire* article misrepresented what Massarik was saying in his review. As a result, the article – an attack as much on Thatcherite social and cultural policies, as on Massarik's jazz preferences – actually seems completely over the top. The same points could so easily have been made with less manifest emotion and vitriol and it was this that Massarik then latched onto in his reply rather than its content.

9 The Eighties or 'Graham Collier – The Wilderness Years' 169

> [I] suspect that what really worries Collier about those reviews [Massarik's and Jewell's] is that if his access to public funds dries up, the actual demand for his music might not keep him in manuscript paper. And if that sounds like a lesson in Thatcherite economics, the point is that something really ought to be done to curb the spiralling inflation of Collier's ego (Massarik 1985b: 53).

On balance neither of the two protagonists emerge well from the exchange.

It must be said again that in Collier's case his emotions were always close to the surface. One's sense is of a person easily hurt and roused to anger but also of one whose emotions were more often harnessed positively and directed in terms of his commitment to his art and to his role as an educator. It was almost as if the negative and positive aspects were alternate sources of necessary energy in his make-up. This incident was far from being the only such one in his long career, when wiser counsel might have prevailed. One finds amongst his correspondence a number of letters to publishers, record companies, other musicians and critics that are almost vicious in their tone.[9]

One such example relates to the release on CD of *Hoarded Dreams* and to his relationship with the Cuneiform label. Cuneiform had done an excellent job with the production and presentation of both *Workpoints* and the Bracknell concert. However, the involvement between Collier and the label ended very rancorously in 2009.[10] The reasons for this can best be put down to a clash of expectations. On Collier's part, he had questioned in an email to the label's owner, Steve Feigenbaum, why the label had not used in its publicizing of the album *The Penguin Jazz Guide: The History of the Music in the 1001 Best Albums* accolade of including *Hoarded Dreams* in its core collection of 200 jazz records. Feigenbaum responded angrily and the whole issue descended rapidly into a series of accusations and recriminations, with Collier accusing Feigenbaum of disinterest and Feigenbaum accusing Collier of ingratitude and bad faith. The argument carried out via email escalates over a matter of hours and the limited correspondence available in Collier's archive makes one wonder if there was more to the background of the incident on both sides than first appears. As it stands, it makes for quite bizarre reading. Nor, as we have seen, was this the first occasion when Collier had questioned the level of support he was receiving from a record company or publisher (cf. his correspondence with Cambridge University Press and Quartet).

More surprisingly, Collier could on other occasions show considerable control even where the behaviour of others might be seen as very provocative. It was noted earlier that some jazz fans were no strangers to homophobia. Two jazz writers have also been willing 'to stand up and be counted' for their prejudices. The first of these is Steve Voce, who wrote for many years for *Jazz Jour-*

nal and the second is Jim Godbolt, who edited the *Jazz at Ronnie Scott's* house magazine. The relationship between Voce and Collier, in so far as one existed, was a strange one. Voce continually championed Collier's work, despite his apparent difficulties with Collier's sexuality.

Some years before the *Hoarded Dreams* performances and television documentary, Voce had provoked a minor furore in *Jazz Journal* as a result of his review of an album released on the Stash label, called *AC/DC*, and his subsequent response to criticism from readers. Nearly forty years on, it is hard to imagine anyone writing, or for that matter publishing, such comments as Voce's opening paragraph:

> For God's sake! We've spent 30 years fighting off the image that we're all drug-crazed fiends and now they are trying to make us out to be a load of poofters. Jazz and homosexuality have always seemed almost incompatible. Let's keep it that way (Voce 1977: 56).

Three fans responded in comparatively reasonable tones in the letters' page of the magazine's October issue. As one noted, 'Homosexuality is a fact of life and jazz and blues artists have a habit of singing about facts of life'. The other reader, who chose to identify himself as gay, suggested that Voce had 'finally joined the Whitehouse/Longford brigade'.[11] Another reader described Voce's comments as 'bigoted drivel', which seems as much a statement of fact as one of opinion, particularly in light of Voce's subsequent comments. Any idea that the magazine's editor was merely, if naïvely, treating Voce's views as a matter of free speech is undermined by the headings given on the letter's page – 'In defence of the camp followers of jazz', 'Poof Positive' and 'Low Down'. How they must have sniggered at *Jazz Journal*.

Unashamed in the face of these readers' responses, Voce went on the attack in the February issue in his 'It don't mean a thing...' column. He confessed to surprise at the letters the magazine had received and replied, 'Despite all the much-vaunted "coming out" of homosexuals (I wish they'd go back in) I know of no jazz musician of this particular persuasion'. In response to the likening of his remarks on homosexuality with 'racist comments', he replied that this was 'in very bad taste', continuing, 'Belonging to a race is common to us all, whoever we are, while being homosexual...is obviously not normal'. Finally, he was keen to reassure his readers that he had no wish 'to persecute homosexuals', rather he just did not 'want to know about them'. And just to ensure no misunderstanding, he added, 'Let them get on with it, but don't keep shouting it from the cottage tops' (Voce 1978: 24).

From the above, one wonders if Voce was even aware that Collier was gay. Just to make sure, Collier wrote to *Jazz Journal*, concluding,

9 The Eighties or 'Graham Collier – The Wilderness Years'

> The homo- or hetero- sexuality of individuals is not important in jazz or life in general but what is important is personal freedom. This is surely the very essence of the music and Voce's ill-judged remarks have harmed that principle in a way I never expected to see in the pages of any jazz magazine (Collier 1978a: 78).

The tone is measured and thoughtful, if also direct and unambiguous.

In light of these exchanges, it may surprise readers that Voce continued to support Collier's work. Eight years later, having heard *Hoarded Dreams* broadcast on Radio 3 and having seen the Channel 4 documentary, Voce wrote:

> Collier's work relied heavily upon improvisation and he had a first class group of soloists and sidemen to help him. Some of his music was most delicate, but largely one felt the orchestra had to hurtle to achieve excitement. Let us not detract from the composer, because his methods and objectives seem to be similar to those of Gil Evans – his results are both different and original (1985: 9).

Voce did take issue with one comment made by John Gill in the programme that Collier would never descend to playing Dixieland. Otherwise, Voce's remarks were very supportive of Collier and the music he had witnessed.

Jim Godbolt's comments were another matter altogether. That Godbolt did not like the music is fair enough. His attempts to trivialize the music and musicians with 'witty banter' was really of no matter – it would have been a far greater surprise had he enjoyed it and dispensed with his usual trademark 'wit'. His homophobic comments, however, were something else again. Godbolt wrote:

> There was another commentator, one John Gill, who made a big thing of being Collier's lover and made critical judgement about his man's music. At the end of the show the couple kissed each other on the mouth.

Godbolt made it clear that he would have taken exception, on the grounds of possible bias, to Cleo Laine commenting on John Dankworth's music, though he continued:

> [B]ut, to many, a kiss between John and Cleo would be a lot more acceptable than the male osculation between John and Graham, and Gill being Collier's *inamorato* surely tends to diminish the validity of his critical observations…

He ended his review as follows: 'I wonder, are there are grounds for complaint about *Hoarded Dreams* being advertised as a *jazz* [emphasis original] programme and those uncalled for protestations of gayness in such a context?' (Godbolt 1985: 8–9). The fact that the review tells us more about Godbolt than the targets of his abuse is of scant satisfaction and it would be interesting to know what Ronnie Scott and Pete King thought about Godbolt's comments; this was after all the club's house journal. Collier does not appear to have responded. Perhaps he simply found Godbolt's outburst hysterical, in both common senses of the word.

Notes

1. See earlier comment on the issue from Roger Dean in Chapter 7.
2. The documentation concerning Mosaic is slightly confusing. Arts Council funding appears to have come in 1980 to enable the recording of Stan Sulzmann's *Krark*. Yet, discographies list the album as being released in 1979. I cannot explain this discrepancy. The chronology of events is as accurate as I am able to make sense of it. Some years later, towards the end of Collier's time at the Royal Academy of Music, he began transferring the Mosaic recordings to digital format for possible CD release. However, when his contract with the Academy came to an abrupt end, he left various tapes including Sulzmann's two records behind and was unable to reclaim them. By the time they were discovered ten years later, their condition was such that digital transfer would have been a very costly business (Interview Sulzmann/Heining 2015). Whether or not this explains why the two albums by Howard Riley remain unreleased is unclear.
3. In fact, Stan Tracey did play the Jazz Yatra festival in India on several occasions, once with his eight-piece band, Hexad. Themen's general point remains, however. Tracey was not an organizer and would have relied on others to make the arrangements.
4. It is not entirely clear what happened with the house on Paxos. It is my understanding from Gill that there were difficulties with the other part-owner and that the property needed major renovation. In the end, it seems Collier simply let the place go.
5. Barker relates the difficulties he experienced with Polygram in Heining (1998a).
6. The ill-fated EG Records was set up by David Enthoven and John Gaydon, managers of King Crimson. The two partners invested heavily in Lloyds of London and lost significantly as a result of that company's losses in the 1990s. The legal wrangles surrounding the collapse of EG is one reason why *Open Letter* remains unissued on CD.
7. The company was actually registered in 1975. Though issued on Mosaic in 1988, *Something British Made in Hong Kong* was an afterthought, the company having been wound up in 1984.
8. The first of these was from a Peter Aitken and appeared in the May 1985 issue of *Jazz Express* on page 6 and was a response to the Logan Hall concert. The second was found amongst Collier's papers and was from a Ken Hopley from Manchester. It appeared in the *TV Times* and was a response to the Channel 4 documentary.
9. In Collier's archive, for example, there is one particularly savage letter to a *Melody Maker* critic, Maureen Paton, and another which appeared on that magazine's letters' page attacking Ian Carr, who had been given space in a previous issue to write about Nucleus. There is also some rather angry correspondence between Collier and drummer and improviser Eddie Prévost.

10. The correspondence retained by Collier seems incomplete and, possibly, one-sided. As I am unable to discuss the matter with him, I made the decision not to interview the label's owner Steve Feigenbaum. Because of this, I have limited my comments here to the facts.

11. Mary Whitehouse and Lord Longford were campaigners against 'permissiveness', and spearheaded the national campaign, the Festival of Light. Whitehouse was also founder of the National Viewers' and Listeners' Association (NVLA), through which she led a longstanding campaign against the BBC. In 1977, she initiated a successful private prosecution against *Gay News* for blasphemous libel, which resulted in the paper being fined and its editor, Denis Lemon, receiving a nine-month prison sentence, suspended for two years. Her actions were in response to a poem by James Kirkup published in the magazine, which referred to the sexual fantasies of a Roman centurion confronted with the body of Christ. She said, 'I simply had to protect Our Lord'. Also in 1977, Whitehouse's NVLA gave Jimmy Savile an award for his TV show *Jim'll Fix It*.

10 Pte. James Collier Returns to Hong Kong

Even by Collier's exhausting standards, the 1980s were an incredibly productive decade. Nevertheless, looking from the outside, there was scant evidence for this in terms of recordings. As noted, *Something British Made in Hong Kong*, from 1988, was his only release between *The Day of the Dead* (1978) and *Charles River Fragments* (1995). According to John Gill, Collier had become very disenchanted with the record industry. The major labels were no longer interested, at least not in anyone of his era. His attempts to run his own label had been artistically successful but a nightmare in other respects. What is more, the sheer cost of self-finance and self-release could not be justified in terms of the eventual return – this was, after all, still in the days of vinyl, a more expensive product than CDs.

Yet Collier's work rate continued to be hugely impressive. We have mentioned his involvement in and gestation of Loose Tubes and the monumental *Hoarded Dreams* concert and television documentary. In 1987, *The Day of the Dead* had been performed in Vancouver at the Lowry Conference at which Collier had also delivered a paper. We have also talked about his involvement in musical theatre.

But this barely scrapes the surface of Collier's activities during these years. He conducted performances of his music in Norway, Denmark and Germany on several occasions.[1] And he also arranged existing compositions or completed commissions for a number of other radio big bands, including for the Westdeutscher Rundfunk and Brussels Radio Big Bands. Astonishingly, of these ten or so compositions only *Triptych* has ever been recorded and released (see Chapter 8). This is perhaps another indication of the high quality of Collier's work and how extraordinarily productive he was. He had also worked with and composed for the young musicians attending Eurojazz in 1981, found time for a BBC radio broadcast in 1985 and continued his educational activities. The latter included the designing and establishment of a jazz course at the Sibelius Academy in Helsinki, the commencement of regular teaching involvement at the Royal Academy of Music (from 1986) and, with other musicians and jazz educators, the founding of the International Association of Schools of Jazz. We will examine Collier's work as a jazz educator at greater length in the next chapter.

In addition, the Graham Collier Music toured and performed, with the support of the British Council, in Hungary (1981),[2] Greece (1984), the Far East (1985) and Israel (1986). Finally, what was arguably Collier's most prestigious commission and what he describes as his 'only attempt to work' in the 'third stream' genre came in 1987 (Collier 2009a: 237), when he composed *Plain Song and Mountain Birds* for the WDR Symphony Orchestra and jazz soloists, Ed Speight and Geoff Warren.

Figure 12. Graham Collier Sextet at the British Council circa 1984. Personnel: Graham Collier (conductor), Roger Dean (piano), Geoff Warren (alto), Paul Bridge (bass), Ashley Brown (drums), Ed Speight (guitar), Graham Collier (keyboard). Copyright Jak Kilby.

Turning firstly to the tours Collier undertook in this period, it is worth asking whether such tours would be possible or practical today, thirty years later. So much has changed in that time. In 1981, Hungary was behind the Iron Curtain. In 2017, with its Christian Democrat government pursuing essentially the same austerity economics as other European regimes and with a paucity of festival opportunities for international bands, it is hard to imagine a British band of comparable stature to Collier's being able to tour the country.

With regard to Israel, there are now growing calls for boycott, divestment and sanctions against Israel for its continued and illegal occupation of areas of Palestine and its treatment of the Palestinian Arabs.[3] Whether or not Collier would have supported the boycott is a moot point. However, would such a tour be advisable today given the whole region's instability following the invasions of Afghanistan and Iraq and the eruptions of civil wars in many Middle Eastern states?

By contrast, a tour of India – given funding – would be a distinct possibility today. Whether there would be sufficient interest in a group such as Collier's without British Council sponsorship is another matter. That leaves the Far East. That tour took in the Philippines, Indonesia and Hong Kong. The latter was, of course, returned to the People's Republic of China in 1997. The situation in Indonesia has certainly improved since the ending of the Suharto dictatorship with its massive human rights abuses, including the massacre of nearly one million regime opponents. However, it remains a deeply divided and troubled country and is accused of major rights violations in West Papua.[4] As far as Thailand is concerned, the country has experienced two military coups this century in 2006 and 2014, with the military the effective political power.

When the Graham Collier Music toured the Philippines in 1985, the country was still under the thumb of President Marcos. The dictator was ousted in 1986. In 2017, the current president Rodrigo Duterte, who came to power on an anti-crime ticket, has been conducting a 'war on drugs' that has left nearly five thousand users and dealers dead at the hands of vigilantes and police (Gonzales 2017: 10). In these, and in other respects, the world that Graham Collier negotiated so successfully is now a very different place.

In many ways, the very idea of such tours of exotic, foreign locations seems hugely appealing and, going by the accounts of Geoff Warren and Ed Speight, these were eye-opening experiences. These tours certainly gave glimpses into worlds these musicians would never have experienced on the main European or North American festival circuits. Sometimes what was seen was the harsh underbelly of these countries; at others their charm in a wider world not yet fully globalized. However, when performing in these countries, control over the venues where the group would perform or over the process and management of these tours was largely outside Collier's control. This could and did prove frustrating at times. On a more amusing level, while touring in Greece, the group met a group of Americans in Thessaloniki, as Geoff Warren relates:

> Afterwards we went for a drink with them and it seemed funny. What were these Americans doing in Thessalonica? They were attached to the American Embassy or something but obviously Thessaloniki was right on the border with Yugoslavia which was at that time the other side, as it were. These guys seemed quite sort of important. It seemed quite a high-powered delegation for a little place like that. I remember we were sitting round having a meal afterwards and one of the Americans looked at his watch and Graham did a joke. He said, 'Come in Langley'. And the guy froze.

> He literally froze, like 'Oh, my god! They've realised' (Interview Warren/Heining 2014).

What we might call 'commercial' as opposed to 'cultural' music tours have a different trajectory. Their route is built upon a network of jazz promoters, agents and record companies and takes in only those established clubs, concert halls and festivals on the circuit. These 'cultural' tours sponsored by the British Council were not like that. Not only were the venues often unusual for jazz and sometimes off the beaten track, they frequently involved playing for non-jazz audiences. For example, on the tour of the Far East on several occasions the group played in shopping malls, as Warren recalls:

> I remember Graham had been particularly impressed that we were going into shopping malls, not always places you'd expect to play contemporary music and people were curious and stopping and listening and applauding. I suspect the world wasn't sufficiently globalised at the time for people to expect to hear the pop songs and everything else that came from the west. So, we could actually go there and play our own stuff and people were more open to it. Graham was actually quite happy with that. We were actually playing stuff that might have been considered far out or at least quite spiky and people were willing to listen to it because, you know, if they had been listening to Gamelan the day before they had no preconceived concepts about western harmony or anything. So, we actually found the public quite open to us, whereas in western Europe they might have been more critical (Interview Warren/Heining 2014).

In Greece as well, the tour took the band to little, out-of-the-way places, allowing the musicians to get a sense of life beyond the big cities:

> It was a very interesting, very human tour because they took us round lots of little towns. We did little islands. We did the big places like Athens and Thessaloniki and then lots of little towns right up in the hills. Once again, it was like a band comes into a little town and you get the town hall completely full up because it was an interesting event. We actually got good responses in the little towns because people were open to it, whereas Athens it was part of the concert season of the British Council and half a dozen people turned up and they were more interested in the cocktail party coming afterwards. We worked very hard. They travelled us around in a bus on these mountain roads. Every time you got out, they got out the Metaxa. Even before the gig, there would be a tray of Metaxa brandy before the gig. You had to be a bit careful there (Laughing). And after the

> gig lots of great food. Graham wasn't playing the synth. Roger was quite often using the upright piano that they provided for us, which wasn't always fantastic. So, Roger was actually travelling with a little tuning handle. Before the gig, Roger would tune the piano as best he could. So, it was a bit low level but it was great fun (Interview Warren/Heining 2014).

The impression one gets from the musicians in the band of these British Council tours is generally positive; it is a mixture of the exotic and intriguing and the shocking but fascinating. The oddities and peculiarities that contrast so greatly with other touring experiences at home or in Western Europe – and the food and drink – are frequently noted in their comments, as are social and political issues. It all seems rather jolly. At the same time, going by Collier's 'Timeline', he frequently found it a frustrating business. Then again, as John Gill has pointed out, he was not just the bandleader/conductor/bassist but tour manager and general factotum as well.

Ed Speight described the Far East tour as a 'Herculean' effort to cram in 'as many Far Eastern countries into the shortest period of time', with 'no allowance made for jet lag'. He continued:

> It was just six months or a year before the uprising. Marcos, he went shortly thereafter. The whole of Manila was kind of like the Wild West with army trucks running around, guys with guns. Every supermarket, every major business, bank or whatever had its own armed forces, its own armed guards.

The group stayed in the Manila Hilton in the middle of the red-light district. Jazz musicians see many sides of life but Speight was shocked by what he saw there: 'And you'd see things and think, "Jesus!" People selling their daughters because they didn't have any money' (Interview Speight/Heining 2014). In Indonesia, the band's equipment was 'incarcerated' by the authorities due to bribes not being paid, but the Hong Kong and Thai ends of the tour went to plan with a recording made of the Hong Kong concert.

At the end of the Far East tour, Collier found himself back in Hong Kong for the first time since his army service. The extract from his diary regarding the tour included in the 'Timeline' reads:

> Generally went well but often a mismatch with audiences...we should have got to the musicians more... The real gloom in HK, totally alienated, no idea why I've come all this way for the music to be ignored etc... All very tiring, don't know what would have happened without the Hiltons ('Timeline').

10 Pte. James Collier Returns to Hong Kong

That tour took place at the end of 1985. A few entries later in the 'Timeline' and as a comment on the year overall, Collier notes: 'Some serious depressions and irritations and possibly related stomach illnesses'. At one level, these seem to suggest a weariness with all the responsibility, while, at another, a sense of *ennui* or at least a mismatch between expectation and outcome. As noted, the Hong Kong end of the tour produced Collier's only album of the eighties.

Something British Made In Hong Kong is Collier's least successful album and sits as a rather pallid oddity in the Collier catalogue. The playing is fine and, at times, it feels as if the players – Ed Speight, Roger Dean, Geoff Warren, Paul Bridge, Ashley Brown with Collier on synth – are desperately trying to make 'something' from some slender materials. The music has the feel of a film soundtrack and of incidental music at that. Although the composer speaks in the liner notes in terms of this record as one of his explorations of longer form in jazz, it lacks the coherence of other small group works such as *Mosaics*, *Darius* and *Midnight Blue*.

Geoff Warren's echo-laden flute impresses on the opening 'Midsummer Dawn' but the piece fails to hold the attention. Warren, this time on alto, leads the way on 'Whirligig', supported by strong rhythm playing from Bridge and Brown, as the music shifts between bebop and jazz-rock quite effortlessly. The problem with the album becomes more evident on 'Mist On The Water'. It features Ashley Brown on percussion and, though he plays admirably with an almost Gamelan feel to his performance, the repeated entry of other instruments overshadows rather than shadows Brown's efforts.

Matters improve with 'Queensbury Rules'. A powerful drum solo, punctuated by the other instruments, leads into a wild, swirling performance from the group. There is also some fine bass playing from the late Paul Bridge in a guitar-bass-drums trio with added support from Roger Dean. Ed Speight is outstanding here, his solo a marriage of bebop and rock that is achieved with consummate ease. Sadly, the quieter, more ambient 'Spring Rain' that follows leads to a feeling of dissipation rather than of tension and release. This becomes more acute as this leads into the longest and closing piece, 'Deserted Funfair'. It is all too episodic and one is left with the impression that the dynamic of the whole composition is out-of-kilter. As it is, the record ends not with a bang but rather meanders to a close.

When the album came out in 1988,[5] reviews were far from plentiful but two of these were particularly favourable. Simon Adams, in *Jazz Journal*, felt that Collier's use of the synthesizer extended 'the palette on which he places the improvising and textural resources of the other musicians'. He also clearly appreciated what he saw as the almost impressionistic, pastoral qualities of the music but which he noted 'conceals for further listens a far harder and sharper content' (Adams 1988: 28). Geoff Andrew in *Time Out* noted: 'Rhythms range from thunderous bass riffs (Whirligig) to gently pulsing pastoral (Spring Rain) tones, from squalling sax and spikey guitar to dreamily lyrical flute; throughout, however, Collier's unforced eclecticism and excellent musicianship by all concerned provide a consistently melodic invention' (Andrew 1988: 39).

Stuart Nicholson's brief review in the *Wire* was less enthusiastic and some of his remarks upset Collier quite deeply. He wrote:

> For some reason I've always thought of Graham Collier as the poor man's Stan Kenton. Both somewhat pompous orchestrators who in their time have encouraged the development of young talent, they define their vision of jazz with a somewhat arm's-length quality. *Something British* is a work for sextet written for the Group's Far East tour in 1985. Alternatively, refreshing and stodgy, this is Collier's first album since 1978, and sees him experimenting with synthesisers. Even at its best, with Geoff Warren's alto leading the way, it's a bit prone to wallowing in New Age soundscapes that indulge the leader's new toy (Nicholson 1988: 67).

It is hard to know what the author anticipated by way of a response from Collier to the review. However, some years later Nicholson approached Collier through his partner John Gill to request an interview in connection with the chapter on jazz education for the book that would become *Is Jazz Dead? Or Has It Just Moved to a New Address?* Collier was still upset, not by the review itself but by the comments about and comparisons with Kenton. He declined the interview because, as he said in 2005, he felt that 'life was too short for that' (Interview Collier/Heining 2005).[6]

Such comments aside, one would tend to agree with Nicholson's negative assessment of *Something British*. Fortunately, any notion that Collier's creative juices were running low with the release of what was his weakest album would be completely compounded by the series of records that he would make in the next two decades. Viewed in the context of his career, music such as *Charles River Fragments*, *Winter Oranges* and *Oxford Palms* represent the fulfilment of ambition and potential rather than merely a refinement of compositional technique. Perhaps Collier's remarks in his 'Timeline' tell the story of *Something British* only too well – 'a mismatch with audiences' and the 'real gloom in HK, totally alienated'.

In 1986, as noted, Collier began regular teaching commitments at the Royal Academy of Music. The first performance of the RAM Big Band took place in February and in May Collier conducted the band in a performance of Krzysztof Penderecki's *Actions* with special guests Evan Parker on saxophones, Roger Dean on piano, trumpeter Torbjon Hultmark and Ashley Brown on drums.

What made the event even more significant was that the concert took place in front of the composer himself.

Penderecki had been inspired to compose the piece after hearing Alex von Schlippenbach's Globe Unity Orchestra. According to Evan Parker, the piece had been originally commissioned via J. E. Berendt for the Orchestra. First performances were scheduled for Cologne and at the Berlin Jazz Festival. However, Penderecki did not deliver the score and parts in time for the rehearsal period that had been allowed in Cologne and which were needed for so complex a piece. Therefore, Berendt asked Alex von Schlippenbach, Globe Unity's leader, to get the band to Berlin a day or two early in order to at least play the piece in Berlin. No allowances had been made, however, to pay the band's expenses for a longer stay in Berlin or to pay for the extra work involved. Von Schlippenbach refused. Berendt was, apparently, furious and reprogrammed the performance for the Donaueschingen Festival, as Parker explained:

> When Berendt programmed the piece for Donaueschingen, he invited everyone except Alex to be part of the group assembled to give the first performance. I refused to do it. I learned a lesson about solidarity over that. Somewhere I still have the letter from Berendt urging me very strongly to change my mind. When the performance at RAM came up, perhaps I was asked to be part of it because of the connection with the community of players who did the original performance but at the time I had been very disappointed. If that piece is ever to be played well, it will need more rehearsal time than we had (Email Parker/Heining 2015).

Collier refers to the recording of *Actions* at Donaueschingen and the RAM performance in *The Jazz Composer*. He notes that comparison of the score and recording indicated that 'The band just blew'. He adds: 'What was written seems to have been the honest reaction of a classical composer to what he *heard* [emphasis original] from a band such as Globe Unity Orchestra, but it seems he had little idea how this was achieved.'

Collier had been told by the composer that only five per cent had been actually written, leaving the rest to conductor and performers. He notes, however, that this was not true, pointing out:

> The music requires that the players react to strictly written fragments and achieve its success by its weight of textures, leading to an intensity which one classically influenced observer called 'truly orgasmic'. Our performance, although not of the standard heard in the recording, was, however, much closer to what was written in the score.

At the final rehearsal, Penderecki's only apparent comment was that he thought 'the last chord could be a little longer'. Collier adds: 'Which as I had already indicated to the band, proved that either I was a better conductor of other people's work than I'd ever pretended to be, or that Penderecki, as he had earlier almost admitted, had forgotten the work and was surprised to find it on the programme' (Collier 2009a: 247–48).

The incident is significant because it shows how Collier engaged with music as a process, including where it involved the work of other composers. It further reveals his desire to challenge his charges by placing them in new and unfamiliar situations, posing problems for them to solve to allow them to grow as reflective musical practitioners.

* * *

The tours of Hungary and Greece had been relatively successful. However, the tour of Israel in June 1986 did not go at all well. The audiences were small – this had been expected – but there seems to have been a running issue regarding payment of expenses that Collier believed had been agreed with the tour organizer, journalist and writer, Adam Baruch.[7] Geoff Warren recalls that Collier felt very let down,

> From the moment we got there, we found we were short of money. Everyone was blaming everyone else. The organiser was blaming the British Council. The British Council was saying, 'Look, we paid your flights'. So, basically, we arrived and the day after we arrived we found out we were paying for our own meals and having to stay a week in hotels.

He added: 'I think he later made it up with Adam Baruch, the organiser, because he wrote that piece, "Adam's Marble" for him but at the time Graham was saying, "It feels like I've been shafted by my best friend"' (Interview Warren/Heining 2014).[8]

The situation in Israel at the time was relatively settled. Effectively, the Israeli Defence Forces had driven the PLO from its base in Lebanon, and the bombing by the Israeli Air Force of the organization's headquarters in Tunis in 1985 had been a serious blow to the demands of Palestinians for self-determination. Nevertheless, both Speight and Warren were aware of the tensions in the country and also of differing views between younger and older people on recent events, for example in the Lebanon. Ed Speight's comments seem particularly insightful.

> The thing I noticed then, talking to people of our age group, bearing in mind this was a year or two after the massacres in the Lebanon, in the two refugee camps Shatila and I can't remember the name of the other one[9] – it was where the Lebanese Militias went in and massacred several thousand Palestinians in the refugee camps with the kind of active encouragement from Sharon, who was the general. He caused the downfall of the government of Menachim Begin, who was the premier. And the revulsion caused by that was…[pause] the general impression I got was that the Israelis were saying, 'Look, it's alright if you are being attacked. Of course, you have every right to defend yourself'. Of course. But to do what was done in the name of the IDF in the Lebanon left a great void. It was mainly the younger people who were…who found it repulsive, whereas the older generation were more kind of *que sera* (Interview Speight/Heining 2014).

Geoff Warren also found certain aspects of the tour unsettling and recalls one specific incident, perhaps quite normal in Israel but less so then at home in the UK.

> I remember driving back from Jerusalem to Tel Aviv. We stopped off to get a cup of coffee. And we sat down in this bar and these soldiers walked in and slammed their machine guns down on the table in front of you. It was like living in normal circumstances, living with machine guns and ammunition all the time. You sit down to have a cup of coffee and the guy in front of you has just stuck his Uzi and ammunition down and has his coffee. But I tended to put it out of my mind basically and didn't want to get into that (Interview Warren/Heining 2014).

The year 1987 was an interesting one for Collier, marked by a number of events. On New Year's Day, it was announced officially in the annual honours list that he had been awarded the OBE, Officer of the Order of the British Empire. He makes passing mention to the honour in the 'Timeline', having thrown a party to celebrate on 1 January. ('OBE party: half knew from the media, the other half "you bastard, you should have told us".') He duly attended the Palace to collect the gong in February. Just how much or how little it meant to him is unclear. However, after the ceremony, he took his mother May and brother John to lunch at the Serpentine restaurant in Hyde Park, at that time a rather swanky joint with fabulous views across the park.

In February, he delivered two new pieces commissioned by the Danish Radio Light Orchestra, 'Red Fog at Sunrise' and 'The Mad Kingfisher'. As we have noted, he attended the Lowry Conference in Vancouver and performed *The Day of the Dead* with a Canadian band in May. Then in June that year, 'Eng-

Figure 13. Graham and May Collier following Collier receiving the OBE, February 1987.

lish Bay and North Beach Morning', another new work, was premiered by the Norddeutscher Rundfunk Orchestra and Collier also delivered various workshops in North America. Finally, Collier received delivery of the first copies of his book for jazz students, *Jazz Workshop – The Blues* (1988).

However, perhaps Collier's biggest challenge, at this point in his career, came with the commission for the Westdeutscher Rundfunk Symphony Orchestra that became *Plain Song and Mountain Birds*. The piece brought together a full symphony orchestra with Geoff Warren and Ed Speight as featured soloists. One suspects that the experience of having to write so significant an amount of notational material was quite liberating and that this might in some way be reflected in the work of his later career. It is, nevertheless, difficult to know quite where it fits in Collier's body of work.

Plain Song and Mountain Birds is Collier's one 'third stream' work. As noted earlier, on the whole, he was dismissive of the approach of merging jazz and classical music (see Collier 2009a: 236; Collier 1975a: 64–67). However, in this instance he seems to have grasped the opportunity with both hands. As he pointed out in *The Jazz Composer*, his model for the piece lay in Eddie Sauter's arrangements for strings on the Stan Getz record *Focus*, noting 'It remains the classic lesson in how to use strings in jazz, and how to use jazz when strings are around' (Collier 2009a: 236).

Collier noted also that Sauter's own influences came from Stravinsky and Bartok. In fact, the latter was the more important of the two and it is the angularity of Bartok that gives *Focus* its crucial dynamic and its dramatic sensibility. It is Bartok, as well, that one hears most strongly in *Plain Song and Mountain Birds*, though Collier himself refers to Gregorian chant both in his comments on the work and in its title. This, however, like his allusion to the birds said to roost in the spires of Cologne Cathedral, is probably more a source of inspiration than a direct musical reference point.

Given Collier's reference to Eddie Sauter, it is also important to note that even cursory listens to *Plain Song* and to *Focus* reveal a greater range of dissimilarities than similarities. With *Focus*, the emphasis is very much on fixed tonality. The music emerges simply from each starting point with Getz often soloing over the entire length of each track. *Plain Song*, on the other hand, is episodic though not aleatoric. Furthermore, the mood on *Plain Song* is darker. It is hard, therefore, to point to direct correspondences between the two works. Where these do seem to occur is in certain of the voicings, where I suspect Collier echoes the folk-inflected Bartokian aspects of Sauter's writing.

'Third stream' compositions pose a particular difficulty for critics, as the criteria for judging classical music are different from those that apply to jazz. There are, nevertheless, several quite beautiful moments in *Plain Song and Mountain Birds* where strings combine with Geoff Warren's saxophone and flute or with Ed Speight's guitar. These suggest the potential of 'third stream' music, once pretension is replaced with the desire simply to produce good and interesting music. And there is more than enough in *Plain Song* to make one wish that Collier had been able to pursue similar projects of this kind. The piece is split into five movements linked as so often in Collier's jazz compositions by cadenzas, here from Speight and Warren.

Given the structure and resources of *Plain Song*, much of the 'jazz' to be considered here relates to Speight and Warren, though some of the underlying brass voicings recall Gil Evans. For Ed Speight, it was one of his most memorable musical experiences with Collier. He notes: 'We had nothing written out, me and Geoff. We just had the master score of the piece. I remember the conductor – I can't remember his name – but he did an amazing job translating the whole thing' (Interview Speight/Heining 2014).

Plain Song unfolds slowly. At times, one might wish for something more in the way of thematic development. The sense is less of movement across a musical landscape and more of an unfolding or flowering. There is an absence of fixed tonality. Different sections of the orchestra play seemingly unrelated motifs to each other or to the soloists, and the piece features a simultaneous juxtaposition of soft and harsh musical coloration. At times there is an almost noir-ish, filmic quality to the piece, notably when a duet between Warren on alto and Speight is interrupted twice by discordant strings, recalling both Arnold Schönberg and Bernard Hermann. By contrast, at another point, a duet between Speight and oboe is set against shimmering, gently modulating strings.

At various points, the music threatens to open out but Collier holds the orchestra back. Perhaps this is a flaw in *Plain Song*. Somehow, the tension created by its episodic nature demands fulfilment and release but any such release is only momentary. At this point, it begins to feel somewhat congested. Gradually, however, the orchestra is allowed greater space and in a passage towards the midway point the music builds to a crescendo with tympani and low brass contrasting with piping, vocalized strings behind some free-wheeling alto from Warren. Here, Collier's use of the orchestra is at its most effective from a rhythmic perspective. It is also worth noting that it is here that one notices Eddie Sauter's influence most strongly.

Towards the end, there is some fine writing for lower brass, which contrasts with vocalized strings before a further slow-moving romantic section. This is followed by a building of both tension and volume that then softens as first Warren then Speight play their last cadenzas before the most gentle of cadences, interrupted rather than perfect.

For Geoff Warren, *Plain Song* was 'outside of the general line of development' of Collier's work. With this composition, he notes that Collier was one of three jazz composers commissioned by the West Deutsche Rundfunk Symphony Orchestra but the only one who 'had not fallen into the trap of doing big band writing for a classical orchestra'. He adds, '*Plain Song* was out of the ordinary for Graham because there was (if I remember rightly) hardly any motivic improvisation and no structural flexibility. The orchestra just played straight through with their own conductor. Sort of a one-off experiment, but very interesting' (Interview Warren/Heining 2015).

One would be hard-pushed to describe it as a total triumph but it is more than merely interesting. If ultimately it leaves one dissatisfied, the journey was nonetheless filled with moments of quite lovely music and revealed Collier's ability to deploy different musical resources successfully beyond jazz. The real dissatisfaction is that Collier never had the opportunity to develop his skills in this area with further such orchestral commissions.

The closest he would come to such an opportunity again was in 2001 when he visited Perth, Western Australia and recorded the album *Bread & Circuses* with The Collective, the ensemble formed by trumpeter Adrian Kelly 'to play original music that blended classical and jazz styles, and blurred the boundaries between the two genres' (Email Kelly/Heining 2015). The ensemble might not have been a symphony orchestra. However, in The Collective, Collier found a group of sympathetic musicians who did, in some ways, allow him to explore a similar musical territory.

Notes

1.   These included *Shell View* and *Bodega Bridge* for Trondheim's Bodega Orchestra, February 1980; Danish Radio Big Band, February 1980 – Collier also wrote another piece for the band, *Thames Base* later the same year; WDR Big Band Cologne, April 1980; 'Sad Faced Potter', 'Azure Blues' and 'New Year Song' for WDR Big Band, January 1982; 'Walkabout' and 'September Mist' for WDR Big Band, April 1983; WDR Big Band Cologne, April 1983; Radio Denmark Light Orchestra, January 1984; 'Pebbles Fresh from the Brook' for The Danish Radio Music Workshop Orchestra, July/August 1984; Radio Denmark Big Band, January 1985; 'Red Fog at Sunrise' and 'The Mad Kingfisher' for Radio Denmark Light Orchestra, February 1987; 'English Bay and North Beach Morning' for Norddeutscher Rundfunk Orchestra, June 1987. (N.B. I give above titles of compositions commissioned or played where these have been available in the 'Timeline' or elsewhere.)

2.   The Hungary gig was at the Debrecen Jazzdays Festival in June 1981. The performance of *Ice, the Bright Parrot and the Moon* was paid for by the Hungarian government and was not sponsored by the British Council. It featured a sextet of Roger Dean, Geoff Warren, Ed Speight, Paul Bridge on bass, Ashley Brown on drums and Collier himself on keyboards.

3.   For example, in June 2015 a number of British actors, writers, directors and musicians called upon the UK government to impose sanctions on Israel 'until it abides by international law and ends its occupation of Palestinian land'. These included the film director Ken Loach, actors Sam West, Alexei Sayle, Maxine Peake and Miriam Margolyes, musician Brian Eno, writer Tariq Ali and poet Benjamin Zephaniah (see Palestine News Network, 25 June 2015). The scientist Stephen Hawking has also famously recently declined to attend a conference in Israel (see *New York Times*, 8 May 2013).

4.   See *New Internationalist*, May 2013.

5.   The sleeve notes to the original album release and CD reissue on Disconforme credit the reviews as 1986. This is incorrect.

6.   By contrast, Collier's own remarks about *Is Jazz Dead?* seem quite balanced. He wrote in *The Jazz Composer*: 'An attempt by a British critic to deal with the current dichotomy between American and non-American jazz. It has its moments, but he over-eggs the pudding by ignoring much good American music, and, while praising Norway for its jazz scene, manages to miss much of what's happening elsewhere' (Collier 2009a: 177).

7.   Collier's supplementary report to the British Council is pretty scathing. However, it must be said that the experience did not stop Collier taking a group of RAM students to Israel in 1995 and recording an album with a mixed band of British and Israeli students.

8.   In fact, Collier wrote 'Adam's Marble' for the tour of Israel.

9.   The camps were Shatila and Sabra (see https://popularresistance.org/noam-chomsky-sabra-shatila-massacre-that-forced-sharons-ouster-recalls-worst-of-jewish-pogroms/).

11 Educating NYJO

Collier's commitment to jazz education often seemed as important to him as his work as a composer and performer. Some jazz musicians, not without justification, see teaching – in higher education or privately – as a necessary, monetary distraction from the real thing. Collier, however, was totally convinced that educating the next generation of players was an essential activity for the health and future of the music. He made his position abundantly clear, on many occasions, in the magazine *Jazz Changes* that he wrote and edited for several years. It was an attitude also summed up in an interview in the *Guardian* in 1999. As he explained to writer John Fordham, 'We have a duty to discover and nurture the players who can shift things on' (Fordham 1999).

As noted, this commitment began even before he set sail for Boston (*Luton News* n.d.). And, as early as the 1960s, his emergent philosophy of jazz education already contained elements that would later crystallize into the two phrases that encapsulated his, albeit nascent, performance ethic of jazz – the need to 'move music off the paper' and the belief that 'jazz happens in real time, once'. Even then, he was arguing that jazz education needed to focus on students' capacity to play the music as if they were breathing it. As will be argued later, Collier emphasized the practice aspects of his argument, as opposed to establishing a firmer philosophical basis for it. This is a shortcoming that will be noted in relation to his final book, *The Jazz Composer*.

In 1968, Collier reviewed Bill Russo's book, *Jazz Composition & Orchestration*. In a series of highly critical comments, he wrote, 'What the novice jazz writer is in need of is some guidance towards the art of jazz writing, the differences between jazz and classical musics, the exploitation of these differences and the exploitation of the individualities of jazz musicians' personalities'. This was more than a 'back to basics' response. Here, Collier is referring to what he saw as the essence of jazz composition. His point was simultaneously aesthetic and practical.

Similar considerations encouraged Collier to take jazz into schools and colleges. Those lectures included practical demonstrations by the Collier group. Their aim was to show students, not necessarily musicians themselves, how jazz could be built from certain musical materials but also how exactly the same materials could be utilized to create completely different effects. With older audiences, as David Kennard noted in *Peace News*, the same lectures involved 'demonstrating the basic musical forms on which improvisation is based and showing how jazz composing differs from "symphonic" writing' (Kennard 1968: 11). The emphasis on improvisation and the understanding that this could and should apply to all aspects of performance was at the heart of Collier's educational approach.

Over the decades, Collier taught at summer schools in places as far afield as Barry in Wales, Vancouver and Banff in Canada, Weimar in Germany and Perth in Western Australia. He took his group into schools in Britain and Northern Europe. In 1974, he had persuaded Cambridge University Press to publish *Jazz: A Student's and Teacher's Guide*, along with two LPs giving practical examples relevant to the guide and a rhythm section tape to allow students to practise the exercises included in the book. Collier wanted his teaching to have a concrete, real-world application for students of jazz.

Figure 14. Graham Collier 1975. Photoshoot for *Jazz: A Student's and Teacher's Guide*. Courtesy Cuneiform Records.

Trombonist Mark Bassey, who later played with Collier on *Directing 14 Jackson Pollocks* and on the posthumous *Luminosity* sessions, was still in his teens when he came across the *Jazz: A Student's and Teacher's Guide*. Bassey explained:

> I would have been about fourteen years old and at secondary school, playing trombone but desperately starved of any jazz input. I picked up his book with the cassette and record. I just about wore out the cassette because it had some backings – an introduction to playing a twelve-bar blues. Then there were a few other things. Even at that time, Graham was keen to get away from playing changes. There was one that just had a pulse, starting in C and then moving into this 'time-no-changes' thing. That was quite an early stage for me and a bit more than I could deal with but that was really important for me (Interview Bassey/Heining 2014).

Steve Waterman was another young musician influenced by Collier's writing on jazz. In his case, it was *Inside Jazz* that piqued his interest.

> When I was a student at Brockenhurst College,[1] one of Graham's books was in the music department. This was in the late seventies. I knew nothing about jazz but knew I wanted to play it. My only exposure to the music was through my dad's big band record collection. But reading Graham's book, it really made me interested in hearing things. I remember in particular him talking about the Miles Davis – Gil Evans collaborations and immediately went out and bought *Sketches of Spain*. So, in a way, Graham was an influence on me from the very start through his books (Interview Waterman/Heining 2014).

Collier's ambition for his own music was much the same as his ambition for the young musicians of the future. Much later Collier invited Bassey to do some 'one-to-one' trombone tutoring at the Royal Academy of Music and, as Bassey notes, 'Graham's philosophy was very much about moving things forward'. Such demands sometimes went further than some of his charges felt able to handle or were willing to go. But that belief in the creative potential of individuals was deeply embedded in Collier's attitude to education, which was that it should be about releasing and nurturing the talent that was already present in the student.

As pointed out, Collier had been an active supporter of the London Schools Jazz Orchestra and, later, of National Youth Jazz Orchestra. He had contributed the tune 'Gay Talk' to the orchestra's first, eponymous LP, for which he received the princely royalty payment of £7.62. Collier's NYJO involvement ended early in the seventies. It must be said that Collier disagreed significantly with the educational approach that its musical director Bill Ashton pursued with NYJO and with the music the band made, at least after its first two records.

Whatever Ashton's feelings towards Collier on a personal level, Collier's differences with Ashton seemed to shift over the years, moving from frustration to an active dislike of a person whom he saw as his antagonist. This is evident from comments in letters and other sources in his archive and remarks in his 'Timeline'. In almost all respects, their two personalities and attitudes to jazz and to jazz education could not have been more different. Continuing that feud beyond the grave serves no useful purpose. However, some comment is needed, if only because of the significance of their respective positions in British jazz education.

On balance, it would seem fair to characterize Ashton as a traditionalist in his educational approach, with more or less mainstream tastes in jazz. These tastes were reflected in the music NYJO made. When Ashton was interviewed for *Trad Dads, Dirty Boppers and Free Fusioneers*, his comments regarding freer approaches to jazz were quite scathing and it was clear that he saw these as a dead end and damaging to the music in terms of attracting audiences. With regard to his educational approach, Ashton placed great emphasis on giving young players the opportunity to play together. At base, his belief was that, while some things could be taught in the classroom, the essentials had to be learnt on the stand. As he put it, when interviewed in 2009:

> All jazz classes and courses are if you like short cuts. They can help you because when you see this written, then you can play that. They're not a waste of time but unless you are actually playing with other people, you might as well not bother. Playing in your bedroom will never make you into a jazz player (Heining 2012a: 90).

In the broadest terms, Collier would have agreed with this simple statement. The issue between them was more about what could and should be taught and how the creativity in individuals, indeed in all of us, might be nurtured. At risk of being unfair to Ashton, and he has his many fans in the jazz world not least amongst former pupils, his approach seems to have been essentially practical – place young musicians in the right, structured learning environment, give appropriate and adult instruction and talent will out. He was neither a Jesuit, nor a libertarian.

When it came to jazz education, Collier's approach was predicated on assumptions about the innate creativity of young musicians and the need to challenge them to develop their own musical individuality. Put by way of an analogy, he took the view that learning the language of jazz required more than the 'phrase book' approach that he felt NYJO offered. Throughout, and from early in his career as an educator (this was already evident in his book *Jazz: A Student's and Teacher's Guide*),[2] he emphasized the virtues of improvisation and compositional structures that maximized the potential for spontaneity based on his dictum that 'jazz happens in real time, once'.

There appear to be two distinct models of education involved here. The first is the traditional banking concept of education, so called because knowledge is deposited in the student by the teacher. It is the model of education that many of us will have experienced at school. The teacher–student relationship is essentially that of knowledge versus ignorance. The student learns from the teacher, not vice versa. The second model is the 'problem-posing' or 'dialogic' approach. This describes the relationship between teacher–student very differently, that is, as educator–student and student–educator. Both engage in the learning process seeking knowledge, with the educator's role involving him/her in problematizing the subject under study, as a way of helping all involved in the process to develop a critical understanding and deep appreciation of that subject, whatever it might be. Though the issues are more complex than this being underpinned by different value systems, for our purposes we may usefully see these two approaches as poles on a continuum.[3] If so, then one would argue that Ashton was further towards the traditional end of that continuum, while Collier was more towards the 'problem posing' end (see Freire 1974; 1980).

Over the years, NYJO has helped to develop so many fine musicians, several of whom later played with Collier! However, the earlier discussion of Loose Tubes would indicate that the NYJO/Ashton approach was not for everybody. As Steve Berry, bassist and Tubes' alumnus, pointed out earlier, 'to us NYJO represented precisely nothing we wanted to do'.

We have noted in passing the Eurojazz Seminar for young musicians in London in 1981. Both Collier and Ashton were invited to participate as tutors and contribute compositions. It was an event that revealed clearly the differences between the two men. In a letter to Tony Male, Deputy Director of the Central Bureau for Educational Visits and Exchanges at the Department of Education and Science, Collier described Ashton's teaching and the composition that he had provided as 'badly written Stanza rubbish'.[4] According to a comment on Collier's 'Timeline', Ashton had pre-repaid the compliment by remarking about Collier's contribution, 'Crimson and Saffron', 'The trouble with this sort of music is that no-one can tell if someone plays a wrong note'.

If this smacks of petty squabbling, both men seem to have been in deadly earnest. In all fairness, the basis of their dispute – even allowing for an element of personal rivalry – was ideological. It was about differing opinions as to what jazz is and could be and how young talents might be developed to carry the music on (Ashton) or move things forward (Collier).

On two occasions, their war of attrition spilled over into outright hostilities. The first occasion came in 1993 and focused on a report Collier had written on his 1992 research trip to the USA, funded by the Winston Churchill Memorial Trust, to examine conservatory-level jazz education there and to compare this with Collier's own, wide-ranging experience of European models. (The report will be discussed in more detail shortly.) It is clear from the article, which appeared in *Jazz on CD*, that Collier was talking about diploma/degree level courses (Collier 1993). Ashton, however, came across the article and took exception to Collier's failure to mention NYJO, writing in the orchestra's house journal:

> Talking of education, I spotted somebody in a jazz magazine recently attempting that well-known exercise 'Write two pages comparing British and American jazz education without mentioning the word NYJO'. Not an easy task you may say. The task was achieved by spending most of the article talking about American jazz education which, admittedly, is far in advance of ours. Next assignment, 'Rearrange the following words – *nothing, hiding, to, on, a* – to form a common phrase or saying' (Ashton 1993: 6).

Collier, never one to duck a fight, went straight for the jugular. He makes a number of well-argued and fair comments in a letter to Ashton, pointing out that the article and the report upon which it was based were about 'full-time conservatory-level jazz education'. Although the mode of expression is clearly antagonistic, Collier added with justification that NYJO is far from the last word on jazz education and that many young musicians 'will not go near the band'. Unfortunately, Collier allowed his feelings towards Ashton to intrude and mounts several personal attacks on NYJO's Director. Ashton's reply acknowledges his error and intention to put it right in a following issue of the NYJO magazine, but it reads as if it came from a school-teacher convinced of the rightness of his perspective, concerned to remain dignified whilst castigating firmly an unruly pupil. In other words, it was a red rag to a bull in Collier's case and his reply spits blood.

The second instance was more public. At the 1996 Leeds International Jazz Educators' Conference, held on 3–4 May at the jazz department of the city's College of Music, Collier gave a paper on higher-level degree courses. Ashton queried him from the floor as to whether this was a 'more valid' form of education than that received by the dozens of young jazz musicians who had come through the ranks of NYJO. The exchange began to descend into a 'which of us has done more for jazz education in Britain?' discussion, according to the BBC's Alyn Shipton who was there to make a programme about the conference for Radio 3's *Jazz Notes*. The chair rapidly moved the session on to the next speaker.

After the afternoon's scholarly papers had all been delivered, as a contribution to his programme, Shipton interviewed Collier about his presentation, sitting behind a folding partition at the back of the stage, and then had to vacate the room as an episode of the BBC's 'Jazz Score' quiz was being recorded there immediately afterwards. When the partition was rolled back in front of a full audience for the quiz to begin, it revealed Collier and Ashton locked in a heated argument, in which some witnesses are convinced they came to blows. Red-faced, they quit the stage as the mild-mannered quiz, with the likes of John Dankworth and Digby Fairweather on its panel, began (Email Shipton/Heining, February 2017).[5]

Collier's involvement in jazz education also saw him take an active role in the International Association of Schools of Jazz. He established and edited its quarterly publication, *Jazz Changes*, from 1994–2000, with editorial assistance from John Gill and served as secretary to the Associations' Daily Board for nine years. The IASJ began to come together in 1989 under the initiative of saxophonist Dave Liebman as an alternative organizational voice to the International Association of Jazz Education. As its Chair, Wouter Turkenburg explained,

> It is correct that David Liebman took the initiative to bring together in April 1989 in Rothenburg in Germany a dozen 'head of jazz departments', mainly from Europe and some from the USA, to establish a kind of collaboration. The actual founding of what became the IASJ, the international Association of Schools of Jazz, was done by Graham Collier and me. We designed the Charter and the Bye-Laws, paid for the Notary in The Hague, The Netherlands, and thereby officially founded the organization in 1991. We were the first two official members. After that the IASJ rapidly grew into what it is now: the only worldwide organization for jazz and jazz education. Graham became the Secretary and I became the Chairman (Email Turkenburg/Heining 2017).

The other main international body was the International Association of Jazz Education (IAJE). It was established in the USA in 1968 as the National Association of Jazz Education to promote jazz education, firstly, in North America. It changed its name in 1989 and had expanded its membership to some forty countries by the time of its demise. Given its American origins, it is not surprising that the IAJE was very much based upon an American model of jazz education, which was itself built upon a big band approach to jazz. Liebman, and those who joined him, took the view that there was much more to jazz than this, that 'Jazz has truly become universal. It has largely outgrown its American and black roots to embrace all nationalities.' The founders of the IASJ aimed to build 'a true United Nations of Schools of Jazz'.[6] Somewhat ironically, the IASJ continues to operate, whilst the IAJE was forced to file for bankruptcy in 2009.

Collier attended his first IAJE annual meeting in January 1989 in Los Angeles but was involved in the founding of the IASJ in April that year. Despite early doubts regarding the IAJE, doubts which grew over the years, he attended further conferences and meetings in 1992, 1995, 1996, 1997, 1998, 2000 and 2001. In fact, in 1993, the IAJE gave Collier a 'Certificate of Appreciation' for 'Outstanding Service to Jazz Education'. The following year, Collier expressed his reservations about the IAJE very clearly in the article, 'Jazz education in America'. He wrote:

> In recent years, the IAJE has been attempting to internationalise itself with *a kind of bumbling cultural imperialism somewhat reminiscent of its government's efforts*. There is an almost evangelical edge to this boosterism which grates. It does not seem to occur to Americans in general that people can do a thing well without some American input. And when the subject is jazz, one often feels that because jazz was created there, Americans think they own the copyright (Collier 1994; emphasis added).

This is not some kind of knee-jerk anti-Americanism but rather an example of Collier's belief that jazz education should reflect the broad, ecumenical and unabashedly international church that jazz had become. Collier's research trip to the USA in 1992 was supported by a grant from the Winston Churchill Memorial Trust.[7] The report, rewritten somewhat for the first issue of *Jazz Changes*, is important because it provides, within his critique of much that he observed on his tour, the most coherent statement of his perspective on jazz education. *Contra* Ashton's remarks in *Just Jazz*, Collier argues strongly that American jazz education is not, in any sense, ahead of that in Britain or Europe. The article begins with a quote from an educator interviewed by Collier. It reads, 'In Europe, jazz is still regarded as a noun, while Americans see jazz as an adjective'. The article continues and defines precisely what that statement meant in practice:

> The basic difference however is not between America and Europe, but whether the school is responding to an aesthetic argument – 'It is as worthy of study as Mozart' – or satisfying demand – 'because

there is a market for it'. Many of the jazz schools in America cater to demand. The demand is in two separate areas: what one can call the skilled amateur...and those students wishing to become professional musicians with some skills (jazz as adjective) (Collier 1994: 3).

He notes later that, 'Training the student to make a living from jazz as an adjective in the session world demands different skills than training for jazz as a noun in the club or concert hall' (8).

Two points emerge. Firstly, it is clear that Collier recognized the issue as one that involves ways of being a jazz musician and not just a musician who plays jazz. Secondly, and more obviously, for him, jazz was an 'art' in its own right with distinctive virtues that were as valid as and different from those of classical music. The course that he had, by this point, developed at the Royal Academy of Music was founded on that belief. More than that he believed that any art form had to continue to develop to prosper. This is not about some positivist notion of progress but is based upon a sense of an ongoing dialogue between emerging jazz practice and the jazz tradition.

Collier's remarks in *The Jazz Composer*, on composers and artists as different as Louis Armstrong, Jelly Roll Morton, Duke Ellington, Count Basie, Eddie Sauter, Bill Evans and Miles Davis, demonstrate this emphatically. Collier did not see present-day jazz as an advance on what had been produced in the past by such composers and performers. Rather he saw the work of individuals such as Geir Lysne, Roberto Bonati, Steve Harris, Paul Grabowsky and, of course, himself as carrying the music forward within the spirit and values of its tradition. The music made by the best in the future would not be better than what had gone before – it would serve the music in the present in the same way that, say, Ellington or Miles Davis had served it in the past.

* * *

Collier's belief in the innate creativity of individuals is summed up later in the Churchill report in a reference to his experience at Berklee with Herb Pomeroy. 'I also learned more from Herb Pomeroy than from anyone else, that it was important to be myself: that I had some creative talent and I should develop it come what may. This is the spirit that I believe should be at the heart of any serious jazz programme' (Collier 1994: 8). And at the heart of that creative talent lay a belief in the centrality of improvisation. It is the absence of this belief in the individual, ironically so given America's emphasis on the primacy of individualism, in so many of the courses he observed in the USA that made Collier so critical of much American jazz education in the report. He quotes with relish the President of the IAJE summing up at the 1989 conference: 'at last we have started to talk about improvisation' (Collier 1994: 5).

In Collier's opinion the big band remained an important vehicle for jazz education but the dominance of the model, often with unimaginative charts based largely on the style of the 'Count Basie band of the 1950s' or 'jazzed up version[s] of a current television theme', largely contributed to the ignoring of improvisation in North American jazz education (Collier 1994: 9). Collier's own view of the big band is that it 'should be used as a historical source and [as] a contemporary resource'. He adds that this view was shared by Bill Dobbins at Eastman School of Music, Rochester NY.[8]

At Eastman, big band material aimed for a 'balance between repertoire, recent compositions and student compositions and arrangements', along with charts from composer-arrangers such as 'Quincy Jones, Gary McFarland, Mike Gibbs and myself [Dobbins]' (Collier 1994: 11). In a similar vein, Collier notes that the one high school he visited on his trip, in Penfield NY, had an improvising big band led by Ned Corman. Corman regularly commissioned writers, professionals and graduate students from nearby Eastman to write for his bands (6). These were given by Collier as examples of good big band practice that put improvisation at the centre of the activity.

Collier certainly saw the importance of teaching students about the 'jazz tradition' and its past masters. Nor was Collier in any way opposed to the 'value of practise and technical preparation', as exemplified by musicians such as Michael Brecker and Wynton Marsalis (Collier 1995: 24–25). In fact, he was concerned about what he saw as an over-emphasis on the 'acquiring of technical ability' in jazz education. He expressed his concerns about this very eloquently in *Interaction: Opening up the Jazz Ensemble*. Using an analogy from the teaching of technique in art schools, he quotes artist George Lambert, father of composer Constant Lambert, who described his training as a series of repeated copying exercises until, 'by sheer weight of pigmentation, some sort of imitative quality was achieved'.

Collier continued, 'This is the approach that I feel has dominated jazz education for too long. So often it seems sensitivity is lost and technique – and endurance – are all. This gives a macho bias to jazz and jazz players which has not, I believe, been healthy for the music's development' (Collier 1995: 25). Or as Collier often described it, 'higher, louder, faster'.

In the article for *Jazz Changes*, Collier quotes trumpeter Lester Bowie on the jazz tradition: 'Wynton Marsalis's stress on tradition being so important is mistaken. The real tradition of jazz has always been its quest for individuality' (Collier 1994: 12; see also Collier 2009a: 129). It is the latter vision of that tradition which Collier wanted to teach, not some fixed canon that might be either preserved in aspic and exist as repertoire to be trotted out for well-heeled patrons or to be dipped into as a kind of potpourri of jazz flavours to colour a session for a film or TV show. This belief would at times see him at loggerheads with RAM students, who wished only to play within a certain style. For Collier, jazz was a way of making music rather than a 'genre' or 'style' (see Collier 2009a: 312) – and that, too, should be at the centre of any jazz education programme.

Collier was also concerned about standards and quality. Some might consider his views 'elitist'. However, he believed that the catering for demand – 'the degree business' – evident in North American jazz education was to the detriment of the music. Much of the report is taken up by such concerns. He believed that a significant responsibility of jazz courses lay in preparing students to make a living in the difficult world of jazz. There is a key passage in the article that is illustrative of Collier's thinking:

> [T]o attempt to take on and turn out large numbers of potential jazz musicians leads to an inevitable slackening of standards and an overcrowding of the profession (such as it is) that results in what one can fairly call betrayal of students. I feel I can justify numbers such as the nine in and out we are aiming for at the Academy each year. I would find it difficult to make a case for producing the scores of professional jazz musicians that are produced annually in many colleges both in America and in Europe. As David Demsey[9] says, 'the reality is they teach and play weddings' (Collier 1994: 18)

The follow-up issue of *Jazz Changes* revealed that Collier's thoughts had achieved their purpose, namely stimulating debate. There were letters from Lee Berk, President of Berklee College of Music, pianists/educators Hal Galper and Mark Levine and from music teacher Armen Donnellan of the New School, New York. All were complimentary, if also at times questioning certain specific conclusions in the article.

There was also a longer response from trumpeter Ed Sarath, another board member of the IASJ and programme director on the jazz course at the University of Michigan. In some respects, perhaps as more of an insider compared to Collier's outsider position, Sarath went further in his critique of American jazz education than Collier. If anything the breadth of the second issue of *Jazz Changes* – articles by Hal Galper, David Liebman, two articles on specific aspects of teaching jazz (soloing and rhythm section) and a review of Paul F. Berliner's study of the music *Thinking in Jazz* – served notice that the magazine could, in itself, offer a major contribution to debate on all aspects of jazz education.

Two years later, however, Collier had begun to express doubts about the direction the IASJ was taking and its leadership. Collier might not have been the easiest person to work with. He placed high demands on himself and had high expectations of others. He could be stubborn, particularly when he was convinced he was in the right. At the same time, his descriptions recorded in his 'Timeline' would probably strike a chord for anyone who has been part of an organization or pressure group. Willing horses often get put upon and feel harshly used. However, it is also likely that Collier's expectations were sometimes unrealistic.

Initially, the Royal Academy of Music had effectively funded the magazine, whilst Collier and John Gill had given freely of their time. Many of Collier's expressed concerns focused on the issues of lack of help or financial support from IASJ members or the organization for *Jazz Changes*. However, it also appears that there were issues between Collier and IASJ chair Wouter Turkenburg, and also between Collier and IASJ founder David Liebman.

John Gill did not recall precisely what the disagreements were between Turkenburg and Collier or between Liebman and Collier, though he did remember these taking place. He did, however, suggest that a different philosophy of jazz education was one factor, with Liebman in particular advocating very much an avant-gardist, contemporary emphasis and Collier advocating a greater emphasis on the jazz tradition. 'Graham saw jazz as a continuum', Gill argues, 'going from early New Orleans up to the extremes of the contemporary avant garde. It was about teaching all eras of jazz and nurturing the individual and their ability to play in any format of band be it solo, duo, quintet or big band' (Email correspondence Gill/Heining 2015).

According to Collier's comments in his 'Timeline', by July 1999 and the 10th IASJ Meeting, matters had come to a head, for him, over the funding of *Jazz Changes* and over its function and position in the IASJ. He was also concerned about the organization's relationship with the IAJE, with some in the IASJ favouring closer ties and Collier and others opposing this. He resigned as secretary of the IASJ board and wrote an 'Open Letter' letter to the membership outlining his account of differences between him and Walter Turkenburg.[10] It is clear from his letter that he had been in disagreement with the organization's chairman, for some time – the word he used is 'schism'. Whatever the merits or otherwise of the respective arguments, from that point onwards Collier was effectively side-lined – or had side-lined himself within the IASJ, though he continued to edit *Jazz Changes* until autumn 2000.[11]

Contrary to Gill's recollections, Collier does not mention (in the 'Open Letter' or elsewhere) differences over educational approach, though he may well have had such concerns and may have discussed these with his partner.

In his letter, he does refer to a lack of support and recognition for *Jazz Changes*. Clearly, the magazine and its position within the organization mattered greatly to him. With regard to the relationship between the IAJS and the IAJE, essentially, Collier wanted to restrict collaboration to situations where this was of clear benefit to the IASJ and its members. Though not stated explicitly, it seems that he was worried by the IAJE's desire to 'expand into Europe and the rest of the world, as part of "their mission"'. Again implicitly, he appears to have been anxious that at some stage a merger might be proposed and that this would be on IAJE terms, resulting in the American model of jazz education becoming the dominant one in Europe. Further to this, Collier also refers in his letter to being side-lined by the other board members and to several snubs, in particular, by Turkenburg.

Whether or not Collier's fears were justified is to a certain extent beside the point, as far as Turkenburg is and was concerned. For him, the problem lay in Graham's behaviour and his tendency to leak, by which is meant his difficulties in containing his emotions, in situations where diplomacy was required. Indeed, this had always been a skill that Collier had struggled to acquire and sustain.

Turkenburg disputes much of what Collier wrote in his 'Open Letter', though he acknowledges that there were problems from the outset between Collier and Liebman. He states, 'From the start of the IASJ there were tensions between David and Graham and I found myself in the "in between" position, trying to reduce the tensions, solve the problems, overcome the difference in insights' (Email Turkenburg/Heining 2017).

Collier could be very awkward and stubborn, as Turkenburg points out. At times, containing him must have been quite draining for those placed in such a position. However, Turkenburg gives a specific example of Collier's behaviour and rudeness, which seems to have been the last straw for him and other board members. More importantly, he offers a particular insight into how Collier's behaviour changed at a certain point and a more general one that helps us understand Collier's perception that he was not given sufficient recognition for his efforts and achievements.

The incident that caused Turkenburg concern took place in July 1999 at the annual IASJ meeting, which that year was in northern Spain. Turkenburg explained:

> His position in the IASJ became unsupportable and unsustainable. He was in a state of war with everybody and everyone, including the Berklee School of Music, his alma mater, who had 'stolen' a student off him. In an 'Ongoing Dialogue' during the IASJ Jazz Meeting, with over 40 heads of jazz departments from all over the world at

> one table, he deliberately offended Berklee in a disgraceful way by saying terrible things about the school and the organization.
>
> For more than a decade, I had supported and defended Graham but now a point was reached that I could no longer do this. It was clear that it was better for both the IASJ and Graham that he would leave the organization but it seems that he was not able to do this without 'slamming doors'. On a hot summer's night in Santiago de Compostela, the night before the board elections, I gave him the option to either voluntarily step down as Secretary of the IASJ and become [an] Honorary Member, or to have me give a negative voting advice to the IASJ members in the General Assembly the next day (Email Turkenburg/Heining 2017).

Strangely, going by his remarks in his 'Timeline', it was only at the end of that year that Collier seemed to grasp the significance of his position within the IASJ. Nor does he make any mention of the incident to which Turkenburg refers.

The two other comments that Turkenburg made regarding Collier's personality do ring true in light of Collier's background and history. The first of these concerns a change in Collier that Turkenburg pinpointed to an IASJ meeting in 1997.

> In 1997, I noticed a turning point in the behaviour of Graham Collier. During the annual IASJ Jazz Meeting in Siena, he would go to the beautiful square at five in the afternoon, have a couple of glasses of wine and do 'nothing'. He would just sit there and relax, something he had never done before in his life; he had always worked. He did not allow me or anyone else to come with him. He told me that he started to oversee his life, to see things in a different perspective and felt that some changes had to be made. After that, there was a different Graham indeed. More than before, he, on the one hand, wanted to enjoy life more but, on the other hand, felt that he was under-appreciated, misunderstood, not given the stature he deserved. He was never an easy person but started to become more and more difficult, also in his position in the IASJ. From 1997, he was more thinking about himself and his relationship with John Gill, which was beautiful to see, but, on the other hand, started to get in conflict more and more with his surroundings (Email Turkenburg/Heining 2017).

Turkenburg had clearly picked up on something. In 1996, Collier had decided to bring his association with the Royal Academy of Music to an end, though in practice this took another three or four years, and he and John Gill planned to move abroad. He turned sixty in February 1997 and was reflecting on what he wanted from his future life. However, it was perhaps more complex than Turkenburg was able to ascertain. He is quite right to point out Collier's sense that his work was not given due regard, what some (without wishing to be identified) referred to as a 'sense of entitlement'. However, going by his comments in his 'Timeline', in late 1997 he was actually feeling for the first time that he was valued, including by Turkenburg: 'One factor is the work that has come in – the "recognition" from KHM [Karlheinz Miklin] and WT [Wouter Turkenburg] after Copenhagen that I was on to something that they wanted (although they had had it before!)'

He continued:

> Why the sea change in me though? I suspect it was an attitude of mind prompted by the Miró tile and its philosophy and strengthened by the success of two suites ('Miró Tile' and 'Three Simple Pieces') and three concerts close to each other, plus the facts above. And strengthened too by the decisions made during 96 about finishing with RAM and moving elsewhere. And the feeling that I am now being regarded (by myself as well as others) as a legitimate composer who doesn't need to play an instrument to impress. That what I do is new and educational... I think *Charles River Fragments* was probably a necessary stage to go through but I feel I have found my voice now much more than I did with that. But then my surveys and analyses of my work have always produced highs and lows ('Timeline').

The second point made by Turkenburg is a more general one.

> I hardly talked about this with him but I think that because he came from a 'lower class' and that he worked his way up but never was acknowledged by higher classes or by the high class in the UK, despite receiving the OBE. He was often frustrated. I enjoyed meeting people at dinners and receptions of the IASJ Daily Board I was invited to. He enjoyed the lots of food and the many drinks, never really talking to a lot of people or able to network. The yin-yang worked well for a decade but there came an end to it by 1999 (Email Turkenburg/Heining 2017).

What Turkenburg describes is a sense of always being at a loss, never quite comfortable, constantly needing reassurance but with no amount of praise or reassurance being enough, being a palliative at best. It is sad that, for one with so many achievements to his name, Collier might have felt like this.

There is another issue, however. It can be very hard emotionally to leave something that has been so central to one's life and which is bound up with one's sense of self. A major falling-out, especially where this is seen to result from causes outside oneself, can make leaving so much easier.

Collier's involvement with the IASJ, however fractious it may eventually have become, confirms his standing in the international world of jazz education. The ambivalence and ambiguity that surrounds him, which also seems to have been present in Collier himself, is summed up elegantly by Turkenburg:

> Without Graham Collier, the IASJ would not be what it is now. If he had stayed longer, the IASJ would probably not exist anymore at this moment. It most likely would have collapsed just like the IAJE did in the USA, a few years later. I had great fun being in contact with him over the decade and learned a lot from him. I enjoyed the many phone calls, faxes and mails, the dinners and parties. It was not easy for me to push him out of the IASJ but looking back on the event, it was the best that could happen for me, the IASJ and Graham Collier himself (Email Turkenburg/Heining 2017).

Notes

1. Brockenhurst College is a sixth form college in the New Forest, Hampshire.
2. The fact that the book included a 'play-along' cassette suggests that Collier did think that some work in the bedroom might be useful!
3. In another context, I would argue that the two approaches were based on very different philosophies, themselves based on different understandings of human beings and their place in the world.
4. Letter to Tony Male from Graham Collier, dated 28 November 1981.
5. *Jazz Notes*' report, including Collier's brief interview, was broadcast on 4 June 1996 at 30 minutes after midnight on BBC Radio 3. The edition of *Jazz Score* went out on the BBC World Service on 14 May 1996 (Email Shipton/Heining, April 2017).
6. The quote is taken from the original letter from David Liebman to various individuals from jazz schools, whom he felt were kindred spirits, to see who would be interested in forming a new organization to promote alternative models of jazz education.
7. The Winston Churchill Memorial Trust provides Travelling Fellowships to people regardless of criteria of age, race, creed or disability to travel and undertake research projects. These must be of benefit to a wider community and candidates must show that they are able to disseminate their findings to those working in their field. As Churchill himself put it in Dundee in 1908, 'What is the use of living, if it be not to strive for noble causes and to make this muddled world a better place for those who will live in it after we are gone?'
8. Bill Dobbins, now Professor of Jazz Studies at Eastman, has a remarkable CV. As a pianist he has performed with classical orchestras and chamber ensembles under the direction of Pierre Boulez, Lukas Foss and Louis Lane, and has performed and recorded with such jazz artists as Clark Terry, Al Cohn, Red Mitchell, Phil Woods, Bill Goodwin, Dave Liebman, Kevin Mahogany, Paquito D'Rivera and Peter Erskine. Later in the article, Collier quotes Dobbins again and the latter makes several key points. He says, 'University is now the only way to learn jazz, and is now the only patron of jazz and serious music generally.

It is worthy of study because jazz's artistic level is on a par with that of European music and has been since the time of Louis Armstrong. Jazz is the legitimate continuance of the improvising tradition which formed lots of earlier music.' I particularly like the last point. It suggests that jazz is in some ways the conscience of European art music. He continues, 'But it [jazz] suffers from the worst of both worlds, having to exist without the subvention of classical music or the subsidy of pop' (Collier 1994: 18).

9. David Demsey taught on the Wayne Patterson Course, New Jersey.

10. Ed Sarath sent Collier a thoughtful, supportive email, which is contained in the Collier archive and which suggests that Collier was not alone in his concerns.

11. Within a short space of time, three key elements of Collier's life had come to an end – his involvement with the Royal Academy of Music, the IASJ and *Jazz Changes*. He notes in the 'Timeline', 'This is going to be a strange period – building going on, RAM rumblings and IASJ closings – but I need to use it to get "grounded". The IASJ, Jazz Changes and RAM have been important parts of my life for ten years or so and have all gone sour. I don't feel bad about it, in fact, given the way RAM and IASJ have gone, am relieved that they are finished. The mag, perhaps it will revive itself sometime but I take Ed's point that there is no need to do anything quickly. What will take their place? My own work obviously, and, I guess, a kind of slowing down to enjoy life here, with the sun and the books and CDs and the new house. That should be enough' ('Timeline', July 2000).

12 'Not for any jazz use'

The most important example of Graham Collier's involvement in the teaching of jazz has to be his development and stewardship of the jazz course at the Royal Academy of Music. The course became a four-year, full-time degree in 1991, six years after Collier began teaching at the Academy. Jonathan Freeman-Attwood, the current Principal of the school and who assisted him in setting up the course, suggested that for Collier, 'It was everything coming together. It was his own creative process. It was his writing, his challenge, his own belief in young people, his own desire to be part of the posterity of jazz education.'

The list of alumni from 1991 to 2000, when Collier resigned as Head of Jazz, reads like a 'Who's Who' of present-day British jazz. As Freeman-Attwood commented, 'If you look at the jazz musicians who came out of the Academy in that era, they made a mark very quickly' (Interview Freeman-Attwood/Heining 2015). At times, this aspect of Collier's career has overshadowed his own artistic contribution to jazz. Nevertheless, the fifteen or so years that he was involved with the Academy also served to revive Collier's enthusiasm for music-making and led to changes in his own compositional practice.

Collier began teaching at the Academy in October 1985. As he told John Wickes the following year,

> I've always thought that academies and colleges here should have jazz in them. Somebody told me the Academy might be worth approaching – which I did. Nothing happened for months and months and then they called up and asked, would I go and meet them, and I did. Then they wanted me to prepare some ideas. Then they just offered me a job (Interview Collier/Wickes 1986).

Bearing in mind that the interview with Wickes took place barely a year after Collier had begun at the Academy, he was able to report a huge amount of activity. Anthony Braxton, Michael Garrick, bassist Dave Holland, saxophonist Danny Moss, pianist Brian Lemon, various members of Loose Tubes and Roy Williams had all either done sessions or were, for example, in Garrick's case, contributing more regularly to the programme (Garrick 2010: 129–32).

Before that, however, Collier had been in Helsinki in 1981 at the Sibelius Institute for discussions about a new jazz course. The institute wanted to commission him to design and set up the course but, at this stage, Collier turned them down, considering their suggested fee inadequate. The following year, with a better offer on the table and a good deal of flattery,[1] the parties came to a satisfactory agreement (see Collier 1983a; 1983b). The course that Collier designed for the Sibelius Institute would later provide the basis for the Royal Academy of Music programme.

Collier's arrival at the Royal Academy of Music was not just timely. It coincided with what Jonathan Freeman-Attwood describes as 'part of the *zeitgeist* of the Academy in the late eighties and early nineties'. There was a sense that, 'The UK ought to have one conservatoire that really aimed for the stars and did all those things that the most successful Continental and American conservatoires did'. Collier and Freeman-Attwood got on well together – 'Graham and I just fed off each other' – and they shared a vision and a philosophy. Their aim was to take the best students and help them to become 'more interesting players, more versatile professionals'. Freeman-Attwood used the phrase 'vocational realism' in this context, a phrase that encapsulates so much more than the demand-led and demand-fed model of jazz education that Collier discovered on his American research trip. Freeman-Attwood explains:

> He understood that the point of departure was to get really good jazz players in here and then really make demands of them that would go to make a difference to them initially, then to the institution and ultimately to the world outside (Interview Freeman-Attwood/Heining 2015).

This was, in part, behind the decision to limit the numbers of students to between six and nine a year. Both Collier and Freeman-Attwood feared that a larger intake would result in a loss of focus and some students falling through the gaps. Theirs was a model in pursuit of excellence.

In a very short space of time, the Academy, for an institution of its kind at least, went from being somewhat traditional and hide-bound to opening its doors to a range of music far beyond the classical repertoire. Not only did jazz come in from the cold but commercial music and music theatre as well. That it has adapted so successfully is a tribute to those involved, including Collier and Freeman-Attwood. Nevertheless, there are differences of opinion as to the relationship, certainly in the early days, between the much larger classical music department and the tiny jazz department. Given the Academy's history and the importance of its classical music programme, it would have been surprising if some degree of awkwardness had not characterized the relationship at the outset.

Freeman-Attwood describes it as a 'process of cultural assimilation' and adds, 'I don't think there was a kind of groundswell of prejudice against jazz players'. There was, however, one highly amusing incident that has entered Academy folk-lore. Collier discovered a handwritten notice on a Steinway from one of the classical piano tutors which read, 'Not for any jazz use'. It is uncertain whether the classical tutor was concerned that his or her students might be contaminated by sharing the instrument with their fellow students from the jazz department or whether they were concerned that aspiring jazz pianists might damage it through the sheer ferocity of their playing. Further such examples were, thankfully, few indeed. Yet there remained a certain feeling amongst tutors on the jazz course that they were not truly welcome. Percussionist Trevor Tomkins was one of the tutors brought in by Collier.

> I don't think the powers that be would ever admit it but in real terms it was quite a common feeling amongst most of us jazz tutors – and Graham – that we were the poor relations. It wouldn't be admitted – 'Oh, no, no, no! This is wonderful the course, what it's doing for us...' But in reality... Once, they didn't want to unlock the grand piano and I was going to call the concert off. They wanted us to use this upright and a few days before there was a classical student knocking ten bells of shit out of the thing doing a Beethoven thing. I said, 'None of our jazz players play with that kind of fierceness and strength' (Interview Tomkins/Heining 2014).

The alto saxophonist Martin Speake was also brought in by Collier to teach saxophone at RAM around 1989 and still teaches there. For Speake, establishing the jazz degree course was one of Collier's greatest achievements: 'Those two amazing things he did – the first was being the first jazz musician to get an Arts Council grant and the other was getting jazz into that institution.' Speake's acknowledgement, however, is far from naïve. He is very alive to the difficulties, the 'contrasts' as he puts it, of bringing an improvisational music like jazz into what was, and in some ways still is, traditionally a high art, classical music academy and conservatoire. He argues:

> [T]hey don't understand the music – I'm talking about the institution itself. It's like a smaller version of what's going on in the rest of society in terms of jazz. There is a bit of support but once you find the amount of support accorded classical music or opera, it's miniscule. I always loved this thing Stan Tracey said. He said, 'Jazz is a bit exotic for the English'.

And he adds, 'I kind of liked working with Graham because he was always fighting the corner for the course "against the suits", as he would always say' (Interview Speake/Heining 2014).

Trombonist Martin Gladdish, who was the first student to complete his Masters on the jazz programme at the Academy, also sensed what he described as an 'odd attitude' coming from the classical faculty, 'of it all being quite jolly and fun and, "Hey, Ho! We can leave them in a corner without being terribly serious about it all" (Laughing). So, there was a fair bit of that to battle' (Interview Gladdish/Heining 2015). As a counter or better clarification to this, Jonathan Freeman-Attwood suggests that, as a small department, the jazz course was 'quite ghettoised', adding that this did help the course to 'develop a strong sense of identity' (Interview Freeman-Attwood/Heining 2015). Alyn Shipton, who has taught jazz history at RAM for eight years, suggests that this sense of having to fight one's corner with the more dominant and larger classical department was not just true of jazz but also of other small departments.

The jazz course did not use full-time staff. Even Collier himself was part-time. This enabled him to bring in tutors and teachers from across the music and to ensure that students had a solid grounding in jazz history and its diversity of stylistic approaches. For example, in the late eighties, he brought in the jazz repertory arranger Keith Nichols of the Midnite Follies Orchestra to teach jazz history. Nichols recalls that Collier had originally asked him to direct a project with a group of students who wanted to do a concert of 1920s music. The project was very successful and Collier contacted Nichols again to teach the earlier periods of jazz history. Nichols added, 'I wasn't surprised by Graham's call, because I knew him to be a person of wide musical tastes and very keen on all aspects of jazz, old and contemporary'. A number of 'playing projects' also resulted and Nichols continued to teach at RAM, long after Collier's departure. Nichols explained:

> I never had a cross word with Graham in all the years I worked with him. He supported the history projects wholeheartedly and agreed for me to have guest players perform in the concerts – something that rarely happens now. In those days, there was little interaction between the jazz and classical departments and I never was able to recruit classical players into the jazz concerts in Graham's time – certainly not for want of Graham's trying – it was a state of affairs that existed then and not all that much better now. I never heard any comments about the jazz department from anybody on the classical side. I think this irked Graham a bit. Graham left the content of my lectures and musical playing entirely to me. He respected that I knew what I was doing (Email Nichols/Heining 2014).

Not the all the 'guest' lecturers met with student approval. Pianist Tom Cawley, who studied at RAM from 1994 to 1998, remembered one composition teacher that 'nobody really clicked with'. In general, however, the variety of teachers and teaching benefited the students, as Cawley explains:

> It was really positive. He had assembled some great people there like the aural teacher John Ashton Thomas. He taught aural and transcription, which I teach now at RAM. Everybody loved him... Then there was Trevor [Tomkins] and Jeff [Clyne]. Hugh Fraser – he was a lunatic. He was a breath of fresh air. He would come in occasionally and he was a ball of energy. I enjoyed him (Laughing) (Interview Cawley/Heining 2014).

Although the course did not have a full-time faculty, a small group of musicians did form the core of the teaching staff, as Trevor Tomkins explained:

> Graham used to say that his two right-hand men were me and (bassist) Jeff [Clyne]. Although it was Graham's baby, he got Jeff and I very heavily involved in it. He used to call us three the 'inner sanctum' and later it was Hugh Fraser from Canada who came in and then he built around that (Interview Tomkins/Heining 2014).

Once the degree course was fully established, Collier sought to expand its remit by enabling students to obtain a teaching qualification. He gave this task to Tomkins and trusted him to deliver the programme without interference. Not only was this an innovative development for the jazz course but it had an interesting impact on the Academy as a whole, as Tomkins pointed out: 'I said, "What do you want me to do?" He said, "No! It's your baby. If I didn't think you could do it, I wouldn't ask you. I'm here if you need me. You're in charge".'

Tomkins brought in pianist Nick Weldon to assist and provide an alternative practice model. They created a programme that addressed the principles behind sound educational practice and drew upon the kind of material used in teacher training colleges. The emphasis was heavily practical with the main teaching component involving students in preparing, delivering and analysing teaching sessions. Importantly, the course also brought in classical music students keen to gain the qualification. According to Tomkins, this approach changed after Collier left the Academy and lost the practice focus he had developed (Interview Tomkins/Heining 2014).

Trombonist Hugh Fraser had met Collier in Vancouver, Fraser's home town, when Collier was attending the Lowry conference in 1987. Fraser spent some time in London from 1987 to 1988 and Collier brought him in to do some sessions at the Academy. Once the full-time degree course started, the trombonist would come over to London several times a year to teach there. For Fraser, Collier's ability to manage the bureaucratic politics of academic life allowed those who were there to teach to get on with the job with minimal interference. As he said, 'At least from my point of view, it was very effortless. I could come in there and offer sound educational ideas and have them implemented quickly because it was such a small course'. Fraser was also able to act as an 'interface' between Cuban and American musicians visiting London, as well as 'some of the London guys from other areas' and bring them into RAM. 'Graham was, even then, very positive about having the whole musical arc presented as an educational resource, not just his own special interests' (Interview Fraser/Heining 2015).

However, not everybody saw the regime Collier operated as being quite so open. Some felt that Collier was too keen on presenting his own preferences to the students. Stan Sulzmann was another musician Collier brought into the Academy. Sulzmann related: 'Graham did a good job of administrating the jazz course at the Academy. Unfortunately, I felt he rather pushed his own music onto the students on occasions. He told the students how lucky they were to play his music! I'm not sure this was appropriate.' He added, 'Although, I disagreed with Graham over some things and wasn't in accord with his music, we did get on well as people' (Email Sulzmann/Heining 2015).

Martin Gladdish differs slightly on this point from Sulzmann, suggesting that it was less a matter of Collier's own music and more a case of his own musical and stylistic preferences. Gladdish also notes that Collier could be 'quite sniffy about repertory stuff' (Interview Gladdish/Heining 2015). In fact, conflict emerged in particular with the 1994 intake, which included Tom Cawley, trumpeter Steve Fishwick, drummer brother Matt and others. Steve Fishwick remembered:

> In terms of the approach to teaching, our specific year, the kind of music we were into mainly was the American tradition of jazz and we wanted to follow that line of learning. We wanted to learn it in the proper way of learning music because it was an American, primarily an African-American music... I think quite a few people in our year felt the same way and Graham had a different way of looking at things (Interview Fishwick/Heining 2015).

Tom Cawley noted: 'I think he struggled with our year and I think we struggled with him a little bit... The people in our year were all focused on bop or hard bop, that kind of era. The way of learning it is just to listen to it over and over again, transcribe it, play it as authoritatively as you can'. Collier, on the other hand, 'was into broadening our horizons and suggesting other things, such as free jazz, European jazz, different compositional techniques and I think there was a bit of a clash (Laughing)' (Interview Cawley/Heining 2014).

Martin Gladdish, though not one of that core group, recalled 'quite a few ructions with quite a few students, who had very specific ideas about the sort of music they wanted to play'. Gladdish mentions the Fishwick brothers, who he thought 'very much wanted to be post-bop' (Interview Gladdish/Heining 2015).

Both Fishwick and Cawley felt that Collier's expectations of young players still in their teens were unrealistic. To them, he seemed to be asking them to throw away the music they were passionate to learn and play and produce original music of their own before they had the necessary skills. It is, nevertheless, a point worth noting in Collier's defence that these same students came through any such confrontations to emerge as highly individual and distinctive musicians in their own right. And hindsight allows for a certain mellowing.

Fishwick recognizes that, though he and Collier 'didn't always see eye to eye', Collier never took this personally and he acknowledges that 'Maybe, Graham did foster that kind of critical thinking', and 'you kind of have to create your own work in a lot of ways' (Interview Fishwick/Heining 2015). Now a teacher himself, Tom Cawley feels that it is 'impossible to expect to teach a group of highly talented, highly individualistic and highly motivated brats, essentially, and not expect any conflict (Laughing)' (Interview Cawley/Heining 2014). Yet, in both cases, their memories focus back on the need for a greater emphasis on skills – and, to a certain extent, on structure. The alto saxophonist – and baptist minister – Dan Foster expresses some of this when he says:

> I think Graham's free jazz ethos certainly influenced his leading of the course. Not to say that we played only free jazz. I mean he encouraged us to explore creativity, different areas of improvised music and who we were as individuals – self-expression. This suited me personally rather than being part of a bebop clone production line! The downside of this freedom was that you could get away without really knuckling down and learning the tools of your trade. I came out of the Academy being one of those who got away with this and only really worked on my playing later on (Email Foster/Heining 2014).

On the other hand, saxophonist Amy Gamlen, now based in France, offers a slightly different perspective still. She joined the second year of the course in 1996, having done a year of study at Middlesex University. The university was imposing cuts on students' 'expensive private lessons' and her tutor Martin Speake, who taught at both institutions, suggested she switch to the Academy. Gamlen had her own take on the responses of Tom Cawley, the Fishwicks and others, who were in the year above her. Her recollection is that, 'Graham was dealing with a lot of machismo and immature school hang-up attitudes when I was there'.

> [S]ome of them seemed to feel [they were] still at school with an 'us vs. them' approach – also the 'higher, faster and louder players' – now I realize that they were just trying to boost their own confidence but at the time I didn't really understand it and didn't feel I fitted in...

> All I'll say is that many just wanted the nuts and bolts and didn't want the discussion part – they just wanted to play. Being 'forced' to discuss and sometimes to learn music they didn't like rubbed some up the wrong way but they were a little over-entitled in their attitude and I think it was right to insist everyone participated and had to play in different styles (Email Gamlen/Heining 2014).

As Tom Cawley noted, 'The people whose records we buy, we do so because they are individuals, because they've written something or because they have a new sound'. He now appreciates that that was the challenge that Collier was encouraging them to face. And many of Collier's students have met that challenge with aplomb. Perhaps there were issues, nevertheless, of personal style. Freeman-Attwood describes Collier as 'a pragmatist but also an idealist, I think in many ways, but he was also kind of an autocrat really, so it had to be completely on his terms' (Interview Freeman-Attwood/Heining 2015). Here, Freeman-Attwood is pointing to Collier's passion and self-belief – less firmly grounded than some might have thought – and the complexities of his personality. One might argue that Collier was right to push these students but might also wonder if the experience left some of them feeling unsafe. Being strong individuals, and perhaps already identified as such by Collier, they survived and prospered. Less capable and emotionally resourceful students might not have done so.

Another Collier innovation, inspired again by his experiences at Berklee, was the annual RAM student CD. All of the students and staff interviewed saw this as a very positive experience. During his time at RAM, Collier acted as midwife to seven CDs made by different groups of students each year. The opportunity allowed students to learn how to work in the studio and how to present their work in that context to best effect; as Freeman-Attwood points out, this enabled the students to learn that 'controlling adrenalin in the studio is very different from live performance' (Interview Freeman-Attwood/Heining 2015). It was all part of the responsibility that Collier believed the Academy had, not just to train musicians but to help prepare them for careers in the real world as jazz musicians.

Each year students submitted compositions and performed these for their peers and staff. From these discussions, Collier would make a final decision as to what to include, the aim being to create a coherent CD. These seven records contain in total more than eighty tracks and feature some impressive young musicians, already revealing the potential Collier saw in them to a wider audience. At times, one hears the mature article. At others, one hears young players still finding their way.[2] However, one cannot imagine any lover of jazz being disappointed by any of these CDs and most would be surprised that many of these players and composers were barely out of their teens.

The first CD, *Spirits Rising*, came out in 1994. Being the first such foray into recording, it featured compositions by Hugh Fraser and Collier, as well as compositions by pianists Christian Vaughan and Peter James, vocalist Lisa Millett, violinist Christian Garrick, and saxophonists Stephen Main and Matthew Morris. Collier's thirty-four minute suite, *One By One the Cow Goes By*, was composed for the RAM Big Band's appearance at the 1992 Camden Jazz Festival. It is an interesting composition in its own right. However, Collier also uses the piece as an illustration of his approach to composition in his book *Interaction: Opening up the Jazz Ensemble* (Collier 1995).

The piece is in six movements and there is a strong emphasis on form. 'Part One' is described as a *rubato* ballad, though for much of its length it is in 4/4, with elegant, poised solos from Stephen Main on soprano and Patrick White on trumpet. The other horns provide what Collier calls a 'soft carpet of sound over which the soloists can improvise and play their given melodies' (Collier 1995: 88). 'Part Two' opens with a simple vamp from the piano over which guitarist Nick Goetzee solos. Different sections are cued in, first the low horns, then gradually the other instruments each with their own melody line. Collier builds tension by randomly bringing in different riffs – or 'shout motifs' (Collier 1995: 90). Christian Vaughan solos next, followed by Hugh Fraser both accompanied by a bass pedal in C from Jon Noyce on electric bass. This section fades slowly with Fraser's trombone shadowed by soprano sax.

'Part Three' could so easily have been a challenge, as the horns play without any rhythm or pulse stated or implied, but is successfully realized. The music is created from several motifs that are built up separately to create a series of layers that shimmer delicately before piano and guitar create a simple bridge into 'Part Four'. This unfolds first into a collective improvisation from the orchestra, which swiftly transforms into a sumptuous big band waltz with intertwining solos from Dan Foster on alto and Matt Colman on trombone, who then solos with just the rhythm section. From time to time, the other horns play a refrain behind the soloists. The solos end suddenly but the shift into 'Part Five' is beautifully executed. Jon Noyce improvises around a motif provided by Collier, whilst the horns provide a softly-voiced but rich, textural backcloth. As Matthew Morris on baritone and Christian Garrick on violin solo together, the volume rises with the addition of the orchestra playing slightly out-of-tempo. A brief drums and percussion duet between Matthew Skelton on drums and Jon Machin on congas leads into an Afro-Cuban section, whilst Main plays a piping series of phrases on soprano. Noyce again provides a strongly inflected bass pedal, as David Holt solos on trombone, with periodic interjections from the lower horns. The music builds to a crescendo as other horns are added to the mix. When guest Steve Waterman begins his solo, there is a sudden jolt of electricity. It would be a show stealing moment in any company but there is something else going on here. Collier is using the orchestra almost percussively, creating a kind of shuffle in the background, something that becomes even more obvious once Main begins his soprano solo. The piece ends with a simple coda from Main.

There is so much going on here that begins to suggest a new direction in Collier's compositional approach. It is not that he has jettisoned what he has achieved so far. Rather there is a new economy and a greater sense of flow between the different parts evident in *One By One the Cow Goes By*. One gets the same impression of a shift in Collier's compositional practice from a recording made two years later with a group of students in Israel.

Following his difficult experiences on tour in Israel in 1986, Collier returned, on a trip organized by Adam Baruch, to Israel in February/March 1995 with a group of six students from the Academy to work with some Israeli students from Rimon School of Jazz and Contemporary Music in Ramat HaSharon, near Tel-Aviv, Israel.

Two close friends of Collier's and Gill's – Don Busby and John Lucarotti, whom they knew from holidays in Paxos – had died in November 1994. Collier flew to Israel shortly after on IASJ and Royal Academy business, presumably finalizing arrangements for the students' visit. From comments in his 'Timeline', it is evident that Collier was feeling very low before and during the trip. He noted, 'I felt like a zombie for many days and went off to Israel in a very depressed state' ('Timeline').

He had planned to record with the RAM and Rimon students while in Israel and was working on two pieces, one *Adam's Marble* (originally written in 1986 on the previous Israel tour with his band) and the other an entirely new work. He wrote in his 'Timeline', 'I had finished the piece to complement Adam's Marble and had decided to call it Bright as Silver (a reference to the sun – which with the Med was what I saw as linking John L and Don). So it was appropriate that I did get it finished and titled before the event.'

The RAM students were pianist Peter James, saxophonist Stephen Main, bassist Mihaly Biggs, trumpeter Patrick White, trombonist Matt Colman and drummer Russell Morgan. The group spent ten days in Tel Aviv with nine students from the Rimon School of Jazz and Contemporary Music (NB Names in Appendix 1 'Discography'). Any differences of opinion between Collier and Baruch arising from the previous Collier Music tour were clearly set aside and the visit produced an excellent CD featuring these young players with special guest veteran Israeli clarinettist Harold Rubin. The album, *Adam's Marble*, came out in 1995 on Baruch's Jazzis label and featured three Collier compositions – 'Aberdeen Angus', 'Adam's Marble' and 'Bright as Silver (for Don & John)'. The title track and 'Bright as Silver' provide the meat of the record, and feature some remarkably mature performances that belies the youth of these musicians.

Figure 15. Graham Collier and students – Israel RAM/Rimon collaboration, March 1995.

The two longer pieces from Collier are indicative of the direction in which his compositional approach was moving. However, the version of 'Aberdeen Angus' is well-executed with two beautifully poised solos from Patrick White first on trumpet and then switching to flugelhorn. It is a performance that reveals Collier's ability to draw something new and of the moment from older material and is a precursor to something that Collier would do on a grander scale with the retrospective piece *Forty Years On* from *Directing 14 Jackson Pollocks* in 2004.

'Bright as Silver' opens the record. It seems to be a composition in three movements. The first is primarily a blowing vehicle for the band; the second is a ballad, somewhat more open-ended and impressionistic, built around a quartet of instruments; the third largely reprises the first, albeit with a reference back to the ballad section, here with the whole orchestra.

It begins with a fine solo from Rubin's clarinet, combining jazz and Israeli folk influences but in a thoroughly contemporary style. There are also strong performances from Yiftach Kadan on guitar and from the two soprano saxophonists Stephen Main and Daniel Frankel, who solo after Rubin. However, one of the most impressive musicians on display is pianist Peter James. His chording, both comping behind soloists or bridging moments between solos, is sonorous and dramatic and when he opens the second section it is with charming delicacy and almost classical lyricism. The emphasis throughout is on keeping the solos short and crisp, an approach that differs somewhat from Collier's usual more open-ended approach, and the charts for the horns are full of attack and purpose.

The quartet in the second section is made up of James with Eldad Tsabari on flute, Mitchell Rosen on tenor and Mihaly Biggs on bass. Here, James plays a series of related melodies that seem barely suggested by the compositional material but which are just right. Collier never tired of stressing to students, following Miles Davis in this respect, that less was often more. James gives a perfect example of this. The music then opens out, leading into a solo from Boris Malkovsky on synthesizer. Synthesizer solos are not to everyone's taste but in Malkovsky's hands it provides one of the highlights on the record. The tightness of both the rhythm section and the horns is particularly impressive, especially in players so young. The music is light, warm and sunny. Collier varies when he brings the horns in, and for how long, to add tension and drama and creates a sense of increasing forward momentum, even though the actual pace has not altered. The section closes with a lovely clarinet coda from Rubin. James introduces the final *rubato* ballad section of 'Bright as Silver', which expands slowly, joined first by Rosen on tenor, then Main on alto and finally the whole orchestra. This is a pleasingly confident performance, not least given that the band had just a few days to rehearse. The music rises and falls as effortlessly as breathing and closes with a gentle fade.

Adam's Marble begins ominously with what sounds like chords drawn from Malkovsky's synthesizer. A brief duet between flute and soprano follows, before guitar and percussion enter. The piece at this point hangs out of time in the air. The volume builds as other members of the orchestra enter, improvising freely. The moment passes, leaving flute and piano alone before drums and electric bass pick up a tight funk groove. The other instruments alternate freely, contributing stabbing riffs. There is no sense of movement, more a marching on the spot. Piano and soprano duet with James playing a kind of counterpoint to Frankel's sax before the piece shifts into a ballad section with the addition of some beautiful flugelhorn from White. White solos, first, over rhythm accompaniment and is then shadowed by one of the saxes. Biggs' bass introduces a simple riff, which is swiftly picked up by the band and is transformed into a bebop-tinged big band section. Main solos briefly on alto, shadowed by the horns, before a percussion duet from Russell Morgan and Shahar Haziza that is punctuated by the horns and by solo trombone. The full ensemble returns for a short Basie-like interlude, before a return to the opening melody with James, Biggs and Kadan on guitar and then Frankel on soprano. James is again particularly impressive in his ability to create beautiful counter melodies to the soprano.

Adam's Marble shifts pace again, now into a slow samba rhythm but with some witty and clever slightly out-of-time playing from the horns. Uri Shamir's electric bass is strong and confident in the subtly shifting, shuffle rhythm he maintains, alternating bars of short and long notes. The section ends abruptly and returns to the opening *rubato* section, first with flute and piano and with electric bass playing gently in the background, then with soprano to the fore. Once more, the piece fades like a wisp.

Adam's Marble is not perhaps a first-rank Collier recording, though Ken Rattenbury reviewing the record in *Crescendo & Jazz Music* (Rattenbury 1996) described it as 'quintessential Collier'. Perhaps there is a sense that Collier does not quite trust his young musicians to allow these compositions to breathe in the way he would with more experienced players. However, at the same time, this might be justified in the fact that it allows for a contained and coherent series of statements that might not have been the case, had too much latitude been granted. What is, however, interesting from the perspective of Collier's later work is that, like *Charles River Fragments* which came out the previous year, there is a greater emphasis on form. It is as if *Hoarded Dreams* followed the logical trajectory established by *New Conditions* and *Symphony of Scorpions* and brought that journey to a close. The experiences since, perhaps including that of writing *Plain Song and Mountain Birds*, heralded a new phase.

Collier might have been feeling low emotionally and physically prior to and during the period in Israel. However, his comments in the 'Timeline' show quite how unhappy he was and are quite scathing about his Israeli hosts, revealing both his level of frustration and a lack of tact on his part. Writing about the affair from the perspective of the RAM students, Collier is happy that it went well and was a successful learning and social experience. He commented: 'Certainly they got a lot out of it in terms of friends and exposure to different country and mentality! Musically too they had to learn to deal with the recording studio and the pressures of time in terms of listening to playbacks and endless debates about which take is better.' However, he added that he was tired most of the time and concerned that he 'wasn't cutting some of it musically (not well enough prepared in some cases)'. However, he felt he had no reason 'to be ashamed of the music', adding later, 'the concerts worked and there was enough "acclaim" for my music to make me feel happy'.

He also referred to what he saw as a long running feud between Adam Baruch and another member of the Rimon faculty, as well as to another member of staff, whom he felt interfered constantly. Nor did Collier like the fact that the school was a long way from the facilities of a town. He did not like the food and found everything expensive. He remarked, 'Maybe it is age..., maybe I came tired and never got over it... There is no doubt though that this is a tiring process anyway and that there is a lot of angst around in this country which certainly doesn't make it any easier'. However, two things that Collier wrote stick out in this section of the 'Timeline'. Firstly, he commented: 'Decided that the problem, my problem?, with the Israelis is there is a basic middle eastern/Med. inefficiency, alongside an apparent Western attitude and a refusal to admit that they, the individual, could possibly be wrong.'

A level of disorganization and poor communication had dogged his group's 1986 tour. Whether his comments reflected accurately that experience and his experience in 1995 is beside the point. It is remains a rather bald and bold statement and arguably a sweeping generalization.

The second point is more questionable still and relates to a letter he had sent to the RAM students prior to the trip, 'which warned the students about the Israeli aggressive side'. A RAM student had left their copy behind and it had come to the attention of Rimon staff. At an IASJ meeting later in 1995, one of the Rimon lecturers bearded Collier on the issue. Collier wrote:

> 'After all we did for you' she said, with scant regard for chronology, or her aggressive side in (as an obvious example) reading this letter, discussing it with others, and then challenging me on it! I asked if she'd ever been on an El Al plane but she seems determined to be the victim, so I shouldn't expect too many invitations from her!

(There was no sign of side from any of the Israeli students – all keen to know what was happening.)

There are things one thinks; there are things one says and, sometimes, there is a necessary divide between the two. And then there is what one records for posterity. In the words of one of the most twee and trite of popular songs, 'Sorry seems to be the hardest word'.

* * *

Before continuing the discussion of Collier's career as an educator, it is useful to examine *Charles River Fragments* in some detail because it can be seen as a pivotal work in the final flowering of Graham Collier as a composer. It also offers an opportunity to consider how the experience of working at RAM may have impacted on Collier's later work as a composer. It resulted from an Arts Council commission and was performed by what Collier now referred to as The *Jazz* Ensemble at the London Jazz Festival in May 1994. Originally issued on Hugh Fraser's Boathouse Records, *Charles River Fragments* was reissued on Jazzprint in 2003. It features both the ten-section title piece and a shorter work, 'The Hackney Five', dedicated to the Palmer family, close friends of Collier and John Gill. *Charles River Fragments* itself refers to the river that runs through Boston and is dedicated to both Charles Mingus and Collier's mentor, Herb Pomeroy.

'The Hackney Five' had previously been performed by the RAM big band and Roger Dean recalls playing it in other Collier groups prior to that. On this performance, it opens with a simple but strong motif on electric bass from Dudley Phillips. This motif is, in turn – as with *Hoarded Dreams* and *Plain Song*, for example – passed around the orchestra with different sections forming and alternately playing the motif or improvising around it. In common with other Collier compositions, he includes both freer sections and others performed over a strong, anchoring rhythmic pulse. Throughout the piece John Marshall is given considerable freedom both in keeping time but also in creating forward momentum.

A fine band is peppered with Collier alumni such as Ed Speight, Marshall, Henry Lowther, Art Themen and Geoff Warren and (relative) newcomers such as Steve Waterman, Chris Biscoe and Mark Lockheart. Roger Dean had moved, by then, to Australia and was unable to make the concerts, though he would, in the future and settled 'down under', travel from Australia to play with Collier's bands. His place was taken by Pete Saberton. Solo duties on 'The Hackney Five' are taken by Hugh Fraser on trombone and Waterman on trumpet and are precisely fitted to the musical background. The pace is constant throughout but tension is built and released by changes in volume. Different elements, motifs or riffs are constantly brought together in new formations and collisions. Phillips and Marshall are crucial to the success of the piece, providing a constant flowing but varying rhythmic accompaniment, with Andy Grappy's tuba a key voice within the orchestra and piping reeds a recurring feature in this performance. 'The Hackney Five' returns appropriately to the introduction and fades. One could almost describe the piece as the essence of Collier.

Charles River Fragments itself is divided into ten 'Parts', which occur non-sequentially. (The order is 'Part 4', 'Part 7', 'Part One', 'Part 8, 'Part 3', 'Part 5', 'Part 9', 'Part 2', 'Part 6, 'Part 10'.) In addition, the notes refer to ten 'Fragments', presumably motifs, riffs and so forth. There is also a main melody, which appears at the beginning and at the close, but which also seems to relate to the various 'Parts'.

There are terminological issues in describing and analysing extended works in jazz, which are compositions that rely on specific compositional elements or devices to create a strong, coherent sense of thematic development. Collier was certainly not the only jazz composer to seek to resolve the difficulties that extended form posed to the jazz composer. Others including George Russell, Roberto Bonati, Maria Schneider, Geir Lysne and Barry Guy spring to mind. However, on the whole, more common in the music are the jazz suite (for example, a performance bringing together a number of differing compositions around a literary or political theme – Duke Ellington, Mike Westbrook, Carla Bley, John Dankworth, Ian Carr, Kenny Wheeler) and the jazz tone poem (shorter, internally coherent pieces – Gil Evans, Ellington again, Gerry Mulligan, Bob Brookmeyer, Gary McFarland, Tomasz Stańko).

On the one hand, the critic-writer is almost forced to use terminology derived from classical music theory. On the other hand, she/he should not forget that, even in classical music, the idea of a symphony based upon the sonata form of four or five contrasting movements and variations is not the only game in town. Interestingly, Geoff Warren says of 'The Hackney Five', '[I]t is one of the most amazingly, perfectly structured pieces I have ever played or conducted. It has a system all of its own with the progression of entries and exits. And it works as jazz. It has a symmetry that reminds me of Webern!' (Email Warren/Heining 2015).

The jazz composer has to decide how to balance the written with the improvisational. However, the responses of jazz composers to that dilemma have been largely idiosyncratic. Firstly, classical music builds upon a well-established academy culture, a situation that (until recently at least) does not apply to jazz. Secondly, jazz composers have tended to write for the individual voices of their musicians, rather than compose for an (at point of composition) anonymous orchestra, ensemble or quartet. It is worth suggesting that, in this regard, jazz composers may, in practice, have more in common with composers using aleatoric approaches than with composers of the nineteenth-century romantic and late romantic traditions.

As I have already suggested, *Charles River Fragments* seems to have been informed by Collier's experience of composing and performing *Plain Song and Mountain Birds* in Germany and *One By One the Cow Goes By* and *Adam's Marble* in Israel. From one perspective, *Charles River* is a transitional record. However, from another, one senses the beginnings of a qualitative change in Collier's approach and it is reasonable to assume that his teaching involvement at RAM was one factor in that change process. It also appears that, following *Plain Song*, Collier had developed greater skill and confidence in using what might be called 'flexible form' as opposed to 'open form' compositional approaches.

However, it must be stressed that – despite the absence of recordings between *Something British* and *Charles River* – Collier continued to compose and work with his small six-piece group. As Geoff Warren points out, 'After the "drought", Graham is moving towards the *Jazz* Ensemble (12-13 piece) as his standard unit, which he would be conducting from the rostrum, not from a second keyboard. I feel that from here the flexible structure (i.e. changing the order of movements) has its real beginning' (Email Warren/Heining 2015). Warren's point – that Collier always seemed to be able to take something forward from each experience – is a good one. Now, those experiences were leading to a first step along a new path.

Roger Dean concurs with Warren's points. However, he refers back to *New Conditions*, which he argues 'involved a substantial dissolution of tonality and a removal or diminution of references to traditional forms such as blues (essentially tonal) or modal forms (a relative of tonality). After this, there was more of a return to those forms'. However, he also notes that, 'Graham became more fluent at handling the soloist/group improv/compositional continuum' (Email Dean/Heining 2015).

Charles River Fragments is in many ways a massive undertaking, almost comparable in scale to *Hoarded Dreams*. It opens with the main melody which passes around the instruments in the orchestra, sometimes played exactly, at others with variation. As with *Plain Song*, Collier holds the orchestra back rather than opening the music out, as it moves from the 'Main Melody' to a bass cadenza from Phillips. Here, however, the technique is much more successful because any delay is only brief before the orchestra and Themen on bass saxophone for 'Part 4' (memories of the Josef Skvorecky radio play, perhaps) pick up what sounds remarkably like a rhumba. Themen makes light of the unwieldy instrument, as the lower brass underpin the bass saxophone with trumpets and other woodwinds playing a counter melody. This opening section sets the scene for what is to follow, with certain techniques being reused in different guises at various points.

For example, Collier uses the orchestra to thicken (a word Collier uses several times to describe the process in *The Jazz Composer*) the sound behind Ed Speight, as he begins his solo in the second section ('Part 7') and later behind Art Themen on tenor in the third section ('Part One'). Another favourite technique, used throughout is to split the horns – higher and lower brass – and have each play different melodies behind a soloist. The orchestral playing behind Themen's solo in 'Part One' illustrates this perfectly. And again, as was the case in 'Part One' and with *Plain Song*, a melody is passed across the orchestra at the opening of the fourth section ('Part 8'). And, of course, Collier's favoured bridging cadenza is deftly deployed at several points.

Much of the music is in 4/4 and quite often danceable, a very fast quick step in the third section, another slower rhumba in section four prior to a fine funky blues with Lockheart on tenor in 'Part 8'. Collier does include *rubato* sections and others featuring freer ensemble playing. Perhaps the finest solo on the record, and some of the strongest writing in the piece, comes with Waterman's trumpet on the *rubato* ballad section in 'Part 3' over some Spanish, Gil Evans-influenced orchestral scoring. However, freer, out-of-time elements are fewer here and deployed with greater caution and economy than in previous Collier compositions.

'Part 5' features a solo from Marshall, with Collier using the horns like a Greek chorus to provide a rumbling commentary or sharp sonic blasts that affirm or declaim. Biscoe's baritone sax solo in 'Part 9' – Biscoe only played twice with Collier, here and some years later on the short *Jackson Pollocks* tour in 2004 – is, as ever with him, poised and elegant. The backing here is beautifully simple, accompanied for much of its duration just by a simple pedal from Phillips' bass and the gentle tapping of Marshall on the rim of his snare. 'Part 2' opens with a free collective improvisation from the horns before a Basie-like big band section and a Tyner-esque solo from pianist Pete Saberton with occasional percussive, atonal flourishes. A lovely, lyrical passage follows from Saberton alone, until he is joined by Warren on flute. *Charles River Fragments*, in all its variety, now finds the space for a ballad in 4/4, performed with finesse from Warren to fine accompaniment from Saberton.

There is a slight sense of disappointment at the way that the moment passes so abruptly with a further free section from the other instruments. 'Part 10', however, features some strong and very rhythmic soprano from Themen set against an intriguing and complementary arrangement for the rest of the band. It ends with the return of the opening melody, a rather subdued ending and perhaps something of an anti-climax.

Returning to questions of terminology, *Charles River Fragments* defies traditional expectations as to how music in longer works, jazz or classical, should unfold. Arguably, the closest parallels to what Collier was trying to achieve lie outside jazz and in twentieth-century classical music, in particular post-war music, in terms of the overall shape and division into movements and the episodic nature of what occurs in those movements. With regard to the former, the most obvious parallels might be Messiaen's *Turangalila-Symphonie* and his *Des canyons aux étoiles...*, the 'symphony' being in ten movements of varying lengths and *Des canyons* in twelve. A further example would be Gunther Schuller's *Seven Studies on Themes of Paul Klee*. In relation to the episodic quality of the piece, the most obvious parallel would be Webern. First performed in 1913 but revised in 1928, *Six Pieces for Large Orchestra, Op. 6* is in six movements and lasts just 13 minutes. At no point does the whole orchestra play together. His *Symphony, Op. 21* (1929) is in two movements, the first lasting seven and a half minutes and the second two and a half. All of these depart from both the sonata form of introduction, exposition, development, recapitulation and coda and from the four or five movement symphony of sonata or allegro, adagio, minuet or scherzo followed by a further allegro, rondo or sonata.

As ever, Collier was seeking a flexible form within which he could work, whereby different elements and sections could be spontaneously deployed at his, the conductor's, discretion. This is what he meant by his maxim, 'Jazz happens in real time, once'. Clearly, the improvisational aspect of what he was seeking lay outside the work of Messaien, Webern, Boulez or whoever. However, it is intriguing how far his solution parallels developments in twentieth-century straight music. Whether *Charles River Fragments* represents the ending of one phase, as Collier himself seemed to suggest in his 'Timeline', or a consolidation or a step towards the next phase is open to question. One suspects that it represented the latter, though subsequent works in the main would be less detailed, shorter and less cluttered. But what Collier had achieved with this composition was, as Roger Dean points out, a greater fluency and flexibility in his ability to deploy his resources in performance (Email Dean/Heining 2015).

* * *

Whatever Collier's successes at the Academy – in 1994 this was recognized when the school made him an Honorary Member of the Royal Academy of Music – his time there was marred by the circumstances surrounding his departure. In 1999, he decided to give up his post and move to Spain with John Gill. Jonathan Freeman-Attwood was Vice-Principal at the time and remembers Collier coming into his office. 'He said he was resigning and he was literally in tears', Freeman-Attwood recalls. 'I said, "This is a huge surprise, a shock. Why?" He said, "Because I feel I've done all I can". He was going to live in Spain and he wanted to do other things' (Interview Freeman-Attwood/ Heining 2015).

According to Martin Speake, Collier had hopes that the saxophonist might succeed him:

> When he left, he recommended me to take over as Head of Jazz there and I went to an interview. I did a terrible interview and realised I was saying all the wrong things. I was saying that I wanted to continue as he was doing and they didn't want to hear that. That was my impression and that they'd almost decided. Gerard Presencer did it after that (Laughing).

The appointment of Gerard Presencer, a very fine trumpeter, but with limited teaching experience was to some a surprising choice for the post. As Speake says, without rancour, 'The thing about the Academy – and they said this to me – they try things out. They do make in their own way quite bold decisions. They're very conservative but then all of a sudden the decisions they make in who they appoint are quite radical' (Interview Speake/Heining 2014).

Once the appointment of Presencer had been decided, however, the Academy made another 'radical' decision. Instead of letting Collier sail off into the setting sun, the then Principal Dr Curtis Price offered him a post as an International Consultant and Adviser to the jazz course at an annual salary of £10,000. The letter from the Director of Finance and Personnel, Jan Whitehouse, was dated 23 August 1999 and defined the role as being 'a roving ambassador for the course, international recruiting, some group/class-based work' and 'ongoing advice to Gerard Presencer', who had been appointed as Collier's successor.

In fact, according to Freeman-Attwood, Collier was not invited back to teach at the Academy. An earlier letter from Dr Price, dated 7 June 1999, to Collier had made the initial offer. However, there was a subtle difference between the two letters. The first, from Dr Price, stated, 'It is expected that this appointment will be reviewed annually until you reach retirement age'. The second from Jan Whitehouse reads, 'This appointment will initially be for one year and will be reviewed during spring 2000'. The latter is apparently normal practice at the Academy and results from difficulties in predicting funding in the longer term. However, Collier understood from the first letter and from prior conversations that the post was his as long as he felt able to continue. It seems probable that the difference in wording resulted from a 'tidying-up' by the personnel department of the open-ended arrangement implied in the Principal's letter. Either way, it proved a recipe for miscommunication and no one at RAM took responsibility to clarify issues with Collier.

Early in May 2000, Collier received a letter terminating the contract from Whitehouse. This came out of the blue, as far as Collier was concerned. It had been felt in some quarters that Collier had overstepped his advisory role in March 2000 but Collier had understood that any such difficulties had been resolved. To say the least, Collier was deeply hurt at the way his contract was terminated and his closest colleagues, Trevor Tomkins, Jeff Clyne and Martin Speake, clearly believed he had been poorly treated (Interview Tomkins/Heining 2014; Interview Speake/Heining 2014). For fifteen years, Collier had made a substantial contribution to the Academy and its jazz course. By any standards, the fact that Collier was not contacted personally by the Principal, even by phone, to advise him of the decision seems rather shabby.

Collier sought a meeting with the Principal. However, this did not result in any change in the Academy's position and he sought legal advice, only to be told that such action was unlikely to succeed. In frustration, Collier publicly severed his connections with the Academy and returned his HonRAM Award – 'the highest honour which can be awarded to musicians who have not attended the Royal Academy of Music'. The school's jazz course was largely his creation and that fact alone should have given those involved pause for thought and cause, perhaps, for regret. That Collier's name featured prominently in the Academy's course material for the 2000/2001 intake and that his name remained on the Academy's website, despite requests that it be removed, was surely a 'cock-up' rather than anything more devious. Inevitably, however, it added insult to injury and made for an interesting news item in the magazine *Private Eye* (2002).

It must be stressed that the Academy and the jazz course have long recovered from any difficulties from this era. The current Head of Jazz, trumpeter Nick Smart, continues to build upon his predecessor's achievements and the course is justifiably highly regarded in all circles. At the same time, one may suggest that the departure of Trevor Tomkins and Jeff Clyne from the Academy a few years later could also have been better handled.

The current principal, Jonathan Freeman-Attwood, prefaces his comments on the affair by noting, 'This is kind of my predecessor's territory but my understanding is as follows... What should have happened was that Graham should have been given a fantastic, enormous, bloody great party and everybody in the world invited to come and see him off into the sunset with the greatest celebration of a great head of department'. Instead, he describes what followed with careful diplomacy, as 'messy and unfortunate', and adds, 'One conclusion to draw from this unhappy episode is the unnecessariness of it'. With vehemence but also with sadness, Freeman-Attwood continues: 'It [the consultant post] was full of so many levels of contradictions that what was a well-meaning idea ends up being a right royal fuck-up, actually. I think he was toyed with – unintentionally – and I think it brought out the worst in everybody and everything' (Interview Freeman-Attwood/Heining 2015).

Notes

1. 'There's no-one in Finland at this time who could set it up. No one with the knowledge and the imagination.' And '[We] would be honoured if I did the job for them. Must be in demand all over Europe, even in the US...' 'Timeline', June 1982.

2. I provide a list of tracks and recordings and personnel in Appendix 1, as well as a list of RAM-Collier alumni in Appendix 4.

13 The Last Suites

We have already suggested that *Portrait*, *Darius* and even *Midnight Blue* involved a retracing of steps in order to discover a way forward (see Chapter 5). To some extent, *Charles River Fragments* could be seen as almost a laboratory work, an experiment to see what could usefully be retained and what left behind. It remains an intriguing and fascinating work. At the same time, there are moments in it that feel rather cluttered – particularly for a composer whose ethic could be described as 'less is often more'.

With the Lowry records, Collier had spoken of different levels within the compositions and he develops the idea further in his final book, *The Jazz Composer*. In using the term, he meant to distinguish between the different musical events that can be brought to bear within a composition. These may be, most obviously, 'supporting levels' – that is, events that add depth and richness to the main event or level, i.e. the soloist or main melody or theme. This might be a riff, a chord sequence directly related to the melody or a rhythmic pulse or any combination of these. However, what had begun to concern Collier was the way in which alternative, independent levels might be introduced to add contrast but more importantly create a division of attention in the listener.

In this respect, Collier was, no doubt, developing ideas that had been prompted by his reading of Malcolm Lowry's *Under the Volcano* and other novels. However, he also refers more specifically to a musical influence, the Miles Davis track, 'Vonetta', from the album *Sorcerer* (1967). The contrast between the main ballad and the 'quasi-military rolls' on drummer Tony Williams' snare drum creates a sense of tension, as if the ballad is about to 'be ripped apart at any moment'. Collier adds, 'The realisation that Tony Williams seems to be in a parallel universe in the recording of 'Vonetta' was the springboard for my thoughts on this area of the music' (Collier 2009a: 298). Collier acknowledges that within the context of classical music such techniques are used widely, if obviously pre-planned. His point is, however, that these same techniques might be used compositionally (i.e. prefigured as in his later *Vonetta Factor*) or improvised (i.e. signalled or autonomously generated at the time of a performance).[1]

With these comments in mind, the music that followed *Charles River Fragments* evidenced a new economy and coherence. In 1997, Collier was given the opportunity to perform a series of concerts in different London venues as part of the London Jazz Festival featuring his band, now called The *Jazz*

Ensemble, which also introduced two RAM students in saxophonist Steve Main and trombonist Matt Colman. The CD that resulted – *The Third Colour* (Jazzprint 2003) – took its title from a remark by art critic Clement Greenberg that 'line' was 'the third colour that exists between two other areas'. What Collier took from this is more important than what Greenberg meant by the comment, namely that, 'This aptly describes my aim to find the third colour between what is written and what is improvised' (Collier 2003).

The Third Colour CD is a double album featuring four pieces – *Three Simple Pieces*; *Shapes, Colours, Energy*; *The Miró Tile*; *The Third Colour*.[2] Collier has written quite extensively on each of these works in *The Jazz Composer*. The first of these features four soloists on the three sections – the first slow, the second walking-pace (it is actually slower than it first appears), the third faster. Collier notes that there are 'no obvious connections' between the movements (Collier 2009a: 267).

'One' is a ballad performed by Steve Waterman using a familiar theme-solo-theme pattern but played loosely. The orchestra frames Waterman's solo quite beautifully, providing a rich harmonic backcloth that rises and falls, whilst John Marshall's drumming lends additional, subtle textures. There is just a hint of a waltz towards the end. 'Two' features a solo from Ed Speight over a repeating pedal from Roger Dean. Here, Collier uses a newly favoured technique contrasting the higher and lower horns consecutively. Marshall and bassist Andy Cleyndert provide a strong, driving but fluid pulse, what Collier calls 'an open-form repetitive rhythmic pattern' (Collier 2009a: 267). On 'Three', Art Themen's tenor solo opens with a loose rhythmic accompaniment in 4/4 before a dramatic entrance from the orchestra that presages a fast-paced sax and rhythm section with periodic interjections from the other horns entering from oblique angles and, at times, working according to a different rhythmic pattern. The previous reference to this as a kind of Greek chorus is particularly apt here. The pace slows dramatically leading to a solo from Marshall, punctuated by long notes from the horns before an abrupt ending. *Three Simple Pieces* is a contained and controlled example of jazz composition in performance. In fact, that impression continues throughout *The Third Colour* CD.

Shapes, Colours, Energy is in five movements. 'Shapes' is a ballad in free time featuring the whole orchestra but led by Hugh Fraser's trombone. Fraser is shadowed at various points by one of the trumpets, probably Waterman. A similar attention to different levels can be heard in 'Energy' where Marshall's drum solo is supported and punctuated by two different interjections from the horns, one in the upper register and the other in the lower. This use of contrast between the lower and higher register horns was becoming a major feature of Collier's work. Speight introduces the third movement, 'Shapes & Colours', which becomes a duet with Main on soprano backed gently by Cleyndert and Marshall. Main's tone has an almost flute-like quality that is highly distinctive. Colman enters for a beautifully lyrical trombone solo that caresses the melody with softly voiced brass gradually increasing in volume, an example of what Collier calls the supporting level. In 'Energy Squared', Roger Dean picks up a solid riff, as Geoff Warren comes in on alto. This section is a fine piece of post-bop, which features trills, discordant runs from the piano and electronic sounds from Dean's synthesizer. The orchestra now contributes a riff based on two bar-length notes; this contrasts rhythmically with the sax and rhythm accompaniment. Oren Marshall solos next on tuba, his long notes and slurs driven along by some fine rhythm playing from Cleyndert and John Marshall, along with fills from the horns. Fraser's solo begins over a steady pulse, which disintegrates before the return of the horns playing a two-note riff. It closes with the whole ensemble on 'Colours', a short feature which seems to echo but not reprise the first movement. Here, texture – or textural improvising – is the key.

Much of *The Miró Tile* is performed *rubato*, notably the opening sections to 'Mud 1', 'Mud 2' and 'Mud 3', making it one of Collier's more abstract, even freer-sounding pieces. Even where a strong pulse is evident, on 'Mud 2', during Karlheinz Miklin's tenor solo, and 'Ed 1', a feature for Speight and Warren on alto, Collier mixes free time and more obviously rhythmic passages. His main concerns seem to lie with texture and the contrasting colours provided by the levels of individual solo voice and orchestra. 'Mud', in some ways, offers a good analogy for the often densely layered orchestral level. The voices of Ed Sarath on flugelhorn (an IASJ colleague and friend), Miklin (another IASJ colleague), Speight, Dean on both acoustic piano and marimba-like electronic keyboards, Warren and Marshall, by contrast, provide sharp, bright colours. 'Ed 2' involves Sarath, largely alone but with some wonderfully dark orchestral fills. Finally, lower brass and synthesizer take us into 'Mud 4', a feature for John Marshall. A fanfare swells behind the drums and it feels as if Marshall is being lifted by the orchestra. It closes with a delightful coda from an unidentified soprano saxophone.

By contrast the six-part piece, *The Third Colour*, is a work that seems to span different periods from Collier's career. The first five sections are described as 'Grooves', with the final section 'Out Blues'. The groove feel is at times reminiscent of *Down Another Road*, although these dissolve swiftly into moments of collective free improvisation that recall *New Conditions*. Further to this, both solo cadenzas and unusual instrument pairings abound. The new element, here, involves the way Collier is creating new textures and harmonies by combining instruments across the orchestra in intriguing ways. As he notes in *The Jazz Composer*, 'The discovery that I could group instruments, and therefore possible textures, by range rather than instrumental group, and that, where possible, I could even seat the players in a way that would maximise this effect, was very liberating in terms of texture' (Collier 2009a: 294). This is mainly evident here with what Collier calls in the notes 'The low hornes', a grouping of Art Themen on bass sax, Hugh Fraser on bass trombone, Oren Marshall on tuba and Andy Cleyndert on bass. The parallel here with George Russell, who also used this approach, is intriguing, given Collier's dislike of Russell's music (Heining 2009: 291). A further parallel might be Barry Guy: both Collier and Guy use/used a modular approach as jazz composers.

Even though Collier, at times, seems reluctant to let a 'groove' settle for any length of time, the general impression is of music driven by a strong rhythmic pulse. In this, it is perhaps his most 'traditional' big band work. Quieter passages intersect with powerful, rhythmic ones. Volume is built up as one of the instruments solos, only to fall away again. What makes it different is the way the orchestral resources are deployed. Collier really gives the listener the sense of something quite organic, even mammalian that breathes. The playing and solos, in particular from Marshall and Cleyndert, Dean and Waterman, are excellent. However, the whole feels so much greater than the different elements that it contains. It is actually incredibly simple in structure, yet with a truly live, spontaneous feel to it.

The Third Colour itself was also given an American premiere in New York in March 2003 at the Elaine Kaufman Center by the Manhattan New Music Project, along with another work *Oxford Palms*. (The latter will be discussed shortly.) The concert also featured compositions by Norwegian composer-pianist Jon Balke and Irish composer Roger Doyle. Collier had just turned sixty-six and his obvious appreciation at the recognition seems to have been coloured by a generalized sense of frustration, ennui and even malaise. Collier commented in his 'Timeline' entry:

> The gig – it happened because I was there. Paul Nash who is a bit of a twat was making 'suggestions' as to how it could be improved to me and the musicians at one of the two [sic] rehearsals (another one was added with two horns missing) rather than getting on with it. His main points of issue were the opening of OP ('it's too dry', 'how does it fit in with the rest of the piece'...!!!) and the solo horn at B1 ('it needs some harmonic colouring'...!!! 'Your music will be better if you do this'...!!!) And all this when he hadn't understood – or read at all as far as I could see – the notes I'd sent with 3C.

He concluded:

> The gig was enjoyable in many ways but it could have been much improved if there had been sufficient rehearsal time to make some instrumental changes (rather than following the suggestions I'd made before knowing the musicians) and to spend some time on specific parts. But the musicians and audience seemed to enjoy it. Tom Varner is great and there was a really good alto solo in OP. Gene Perla messed the start of Out Blues up and the violinist's idea of interpreting a melody was – always – to play the first three notes a few times and then play the rest of the notes straight! But it was my New York conducting debut! ('Timeline')

These remarks do more than reveal the curmudgeonly side to Collier's character. They perhaps also suggest a man still able to enjoy life and work but one for whom no amount of acknowledgement can ever quite compensate for the feeling that they were being short-changed in some way. None of this diminishes Collier's music or achievements. It is simply sad that those achievements and recognition received were not enough. If one song might describe this aspect of Collier's personality, it would surely be Leiber and Stoller's 'Is That All There Is'.

* * *

Having given up his post of Head of Jazz in autumn 1999, and at that point starting his year as 'roving ambassador' on behalf of the academy, Collier and his partner, John Gill, continued with their plan to settle in Spain. They moved into their house in Ronda in Andalucía at the end of January 2000. It had taken some time to get the place just as they wanted it, adding a second floor to a single storey building. Saxophonist and educator, Issie Barratt, visited regularly and describes the property as an 'an amazing two-floor house with a terrace that looked down into the Ronda Gorge' (Email Barratt/Heining 2017).

With a small pension, the need to continue working was both a financial consideration but primarily an artistic one. If Collier's work rate slowed somewhat in the last decade of his life, compared to many in his field he was a positive workaholic. He released three further CDs with a fourth, *Luminosity*, recorded posthumously with an orchestra of Collier alumni. In addition, he completed and published his most extensive written work on jazz in *The Jazz Composer*. Nor did the travel bug desert him and he continued to tour and lecture during these years.

As 2000 began, Collier seemed quite positive about the future and almost evangelical about what he might do to disseminate his ideas on jazz and jazz composition. As he wrote in the 'Timeline', he had 'enough work (with RAM consultancy) to fill in the year and it seems that I now ought to be thinking seriously about who I can write for...' He concluded his comments with the following: 'The re-release of the first 5 vinyl records on CD and the reaction Third Colour is getting are signs that people are beginning to realise what I am about. I suspect this next year will lead to some changes in my attitudes to things (already has in terms of the IASJ) and this could well affect the magazine.'

By April, however, the 'RAM consultancy' had gone sour and, by July, Collier had resigned from the board of the IASJ. Perhaps the best way to describe the impression left by comments from the 'Timeline' is that he clearly felt bitter and very angry with both RAM and with certain IASJ colleagues. At the same time, one senses a certain relief at being able to let go and have space for himself and for John, as Wouter Turkenburg has suggested. His difficulty, however, was that to let go meant accepting, what was for him, the unacceptable. Anything could become personal for Collier and when it came to the recognition (or perceived lack thereof) of him, his work and his efforts, it was intensely personal. One senses that, for him, letting go meant the other side won or got away with it and that this somehow diminished him. Yet Collier did try to look forward and keep working and growing both musically and as an, increasingly peripatetic, educator.

Despite the rawness of the situation at the Academy, this did not stop the premiere in June 2000 of a new work, *Bread & Circuses*, with the student big band including James Allsopp, Ivo Neame (more often heard on piano these days with the trio, Phronesis) and Simon Allen on reeds and Gwilym Simcock on piano. Collier noted that this and the performance and recording of *Winter Oranges* with the Danish Radio Jazz Orchestra (DRJO) were the highlights of his year.

With regard to Collier's involvement with the DRJO, astonishingly, this had begun in 1968. As noted previously, he was the first British jazz composer to work with the orchestra. Even more amazing was the fact that between 1968 and 1992, during the period Erik Moseholm was in charge, Collier completed thirty-five commissions for the orchestra and big band.

The two performances and recording of *Winter Oranges*, along with 'Part One' and 'Part Two' of *Three Simple Pieces*, were a great success. That fact, however, did not stop a typically gruff Collier comment in the 'Timeline' regarding the DRJO – 'Band fine once they know what could be done although there were some odd moments and their clock watching is a bit annoying!'

Winter Oranges was recorded at the Copenhagen Jazzhouse in November 2000. The title piece is a four-part suite. However, the album opens with *Three*

Simple Pieces, 'Part One' and 'Part Three'. The take on 'Part One' here is more formally structured but less slow-moving than that on *The Third Colour* CD. The drums are also less prominent than was the case with the original version. Here, the emphasis is on the ballad moving slowly in two time, with few (if any) *rubato* passages. The feel is elegiac and it contains a poised and elegant performance on flugelhorn from Thomas Fryland with strong support from pianist Nikolaj Bentzon. 'Part Three' is altogether wilder, building to a series of climaxes when the other horns enter to join tenorist Tomas Franck and the rhythm section. The way that drummer Søren Frost and percussionist Ethan Weisgard combine is particularly effective. Yet somehow the feeling here is of a well-drilled big band cutting loose without quite the spontaneity of Collier's hand-picked ensembles. One might miss the slower build and that sense of a wayward, argumentative Greek chorus from the horns of the original take. However, as Collier points out in the sleeve notes, his aim for any composition involved the capacity to make it afresh each time it was played.

With *Winter Oranges*, the extent to which the four movements – 'Blue Spring', 'Eggshell Summer', 'Tinted Autumn', 'Winter Oranges' – relate to each other is not entirely clear. It was composed in Ronda and takes its title from the old orange tree on the terrace of the couple's house, which provided them with 'Fresh orange juice throughout our first winter' in Andalucía. Each movement stands easily on its own and yet gains from the contrast when brought together with the other three sections. Collier notes that each section has certain autobiographical connotations, representing his own trajectory as a composer. As such, each movement becomes increasingly open and, for want of a better term, 'free' (Collier 2001).

'Blue Spring' has a certain Gil Evans-like quality. It begins with a series of *rubato* passages featuring a fine trio of Michael Hove on soprano, Steen Hansen on trombone and Henrik Bolberg on flugelhorn. The contrasting textures offered by the three horns is quite lovely. A more straight-ahead section follows with Hove on soprano with rhythm section but this is disrupted magnificently, as Collier brings in the rest of the orchestra playing in the same time signature but just out of sync with the soloist. This is repeated as Hansen solos on trombone, growls and slurs aplenty, before the music slows dramatically with the return of Hove, shadowed here by Uffe Markussen's bass clarinet, as the section comes to a sombre close.

The second section, 'Eggshell Summer', is available in another version on a CD by saxophonist George Haslam's Meltdown Big Band on Slam Records.[3] It begins gently and out-of-time with pianist Bentzon, drummer Frost, Weisgard on percussion and bassist Thomas Ovesen pitted against a series of long, slightly discordant notes from the horn section. In fact, the way Collier uses the two percussionists on the whole record recalls the highly textural playing of John Mitchell and John Webb on *Symphony of Scorpions* and *New Conditions*. This leads into a duet between Bentzon and flautist Nicolai Schultz that is brought to a close with a crescendo from the whole ensemble. A further, remarkably ethereal duet follows with guitarist Anders Chico Lindvall and Ovesen on bass. Collier builds tension by holding the band back, delaying the anticipated opening out of the music.

It finally opens out into a jazz-rock, funk groove led by Lindvall's guitar with rhythm and some strong support play from Bentzon and Frost. Here, the riffing from the horns directly complements solo and rhythm to fine effect and the pacing is superb. In fact, George Russell used David Fiuczynski and later Mike Walker in similar ways with his Living Time Orchestra.[4] A slower, dirge-like passage with trumpet, bass clarinet and Hove now on clarinet leads into a delicate flute that recalls birdsong from Schultz.

Ovesen's bass solo begins 'Tinted Autumn' against a pedal from the piano. The ensemble provide additional colours – chiming guitar, descending bass clarinet, a repeating pattern from the higher register horns. The emergence of Bolberg's trumpet has much of that sense of drama and excitement that both Harry Beckett and Steve Waterman so often brought to Collier's music. The composer notes that the piece 'pits the energy of the large jazz group against that of the soloist and allows me to be a creative conductor' (Collier 2001). This seems to confirm the sense that 'Tinted Autumn' is pieced together live from musical fragments and beautifully so. Collier sets up a veritable tussle between the trumpeter and the band over a boiling rhythm section with some fine guitar effects from Lindvall. If the sense at the outset was of late September sunshine, the mid-section is of late October storms.

It closes abruptly but leads immediately into 'Winter Oranges'. The opening to the final movement is one of the finest moments in any Collier record. Four ascending notes played individually by alto, soprano, trumpet and bass clarinet lead to a brief quartet from the same instruments and then a cadenza from Markussen on bass clarinet. The other instruments shadow Markussen before an uncredited trumpet cadenza, I suspect, from Bolberg. The whole band opens the music out somewhat mournfully behind Markussen. Vincent Nilsson's trombone makes the next statement accompanied by Axel Windfeld's tuba, bass clarinet, bass, percussion and guitar. Two sudden entrances by the horns are characterized by dramatic crescendos before Collier brings things to a lumbering close.

Winter Oranges is one of Collier's most successful extended pieces. It has a coherence in its overall structure that allows it to move through a series of quite distinct and different episodes. It is very successful in creating a series of different moods appropriate to its journey across a life and it has a concision and strong sense of purpose and movement. Finally, it is played sympathetically by a fine band, with each musician rising to the occasion.

The Meltdown version of 'Eggshell Summer' was a studio recording made in January 2001 with Collier conducting, a few months after the Danish premiere. This take is altogether wilder and looser. It features the wordless vocals of Alison Bentley, in place of the flute of Nicolai Schultz, which completely changes the textural character, and Bentley's performance is highly affecting and personal. Later, the jazz-rock section from the Danish record is given a more traditional big band reading.

Meltdown was the brainchild of baritone saxophonist George Haslam. It began in the nineties and brought together musicians from different areas – classical, rock, folk and jazz – with Haslam inviting various people to compose music for the band. With Arts Council support, Haslam commissioned Collier and he composed *Oxford Palms* for the band. The piece had its first performance in Oxford, England at the Jacqueline du Pré Music Building on 27 May 2001. Though Meltdown never recorded the piece, it was subsequently played and recorded by the Australian ensemble, The Collective, in Perth in September 2001.

Haslam explained that Meltdown used a number of Collier pieces in rehearsal, though they did not play these in public:

> We had quite a few pieces of Graham's in the library – 'Aberdeen Angus', 'Under The Pier', 'Three Simple Pieces'. However, the only one we recorded was 'Eggshell Summer'. The only other one we played in public was *Oxford Palms*.

Haslam described Collier as 'very easy to work with', adding, 'I'd only met him once or twice before he felt like a friend. There were no difficulties at all. Very amicable.' Asked how the band found Collier's approach to conducting the ensemble, he replied:

> No one said anything about it being difficult. They said it was a very interesting experience. Looking at the score of *Oxford Palms*, it wasn't the sort of piece you can just sit down and play. It's all free, a lot of improvising both solo and collective. Graham would stand at the front and just direct what sections to play, where to play in the score and who should be playing it and improvising. Some of the members of the band hadn't had any experience before of this type of directing or organising the music but no one ever said anything about it being difficult, not to me anyway. They maybe found it a bit challenging sometimes.

However, Collier's 'lazy eye' presented a minor challenge, as Haslam explained:

> I remember him standing before us and pointing and it wasn't always clear where he was pointing. Every conductor who you work with in orchestras or big bands has their own way and you have to get used to their way of doing things. Sometimes, there would be a little bit of confusion because you were trying to take in what was on the page in front of you and you were trying to watch what he was doing with his hands and eyes, of course. Let's just say that at times it wasn't too clear (Interview Haslam/Heining 2017).

* * *

The sense that emerges from the 'Timeline' for this period is of a man taking stock but also very active in his own life. And there was much to look forward to, not least a trip to Western Australia for workshops organized by the Western Australia Academy of Performing Arts. As a recently graduated student of the Academy, trumpeter Adrian Kelly was introduced to Collier. Kelly had recently formed The Collective and, as Kelly explains,

> [A] couple of performance opportunities came up. So, I offered our services to Graham. I think the idea of working with such a unique group of people appealed to Graham and his music appealed to us. I forget who suggested that we record the performance, but it was fortunate that we did, as I think it was a really rewarding experience for all and it was great to be able to document it (Email Kelly/Heining 2015).

Given that The Collective included both jazz and classical musicians, Kelly's comments about rehearsals offer useful insights into Collier's methods. Kelly recalled:

> A lot of it was talking about the approach to the music and conceptual concepts, particularly for some of our more classically-based performers. Then there was a matter of Graham learning about how we played and improvised, so he was familiar with the forces he had to work with as he directed the performance, and the ensemble learning about how Graham delivered his cues so we could respond well in performance. We also worked out which members would be featured in which piece. I think the unique instrumentation of the group gave Graham options that he did not often have, so it was important for him to spend time hearing the orchestration possibilities. The actual written material was not difficult for the ensemble to learn (Email Kelly/Heining 2015).

Kelly was particularly enthusiastic about the way Collier allowed 'the performer's individuality to come through whilst retaining compositional control of structure, and also how to integrate improvisation into all elements of a composition and not just in "solo sections"'. Another important aspect that Kelly took from Collier was the encouragement 'to improvise and "personalise" the written material – almost as though the notations were a guide' (Kelly/Heining 2015).

Collier was in Perth working as an arranger and composer with Australian saxophonist Graeme Lyall, whilst also undertaking some teaching responsibilities. The opportunity to work with The Collective seems to have been a fortunate accident rather than anything pre-planned. He had arrived in Perth in good spirits but a few days later suffered severe stomach pains. A visit to the local university medical centre resulted in some tests, including a Barium enema and a diagnosis of diverticulitis. Collier wrote with evident frustration in the 'Timeline': 'Meanwhile – and for 10 days – its [*sic*] antibiotics and painkillers, sleeping a lot, liquid diet and no booze'. A matter of days later, however, he noted,

> As has happened before – with jetlag, which in some ways this has resembled – there was a definite point (late Saturday) when I suddenly felt Normal, 'as though my brain had returned to me' as I called it. Having been out for an interview and then wandering around Perth after lunch I felt that I'd had enough and came back and slept – but then that's getting to be normal – and as of now I feel ok again.

When the opportunity to work with The Collective occurred, Collier had with him two recent compositions, *Bread & Circuses* and *Oxford Palms*. *Bread & Circuses* had been written for a proposed educational documentary dealing with his methods of composition and was first workshopped at the Royal Academy of Music and subsequently in Mannheim, Germany. It seems that the documentary never materialized. *Oxford Palms* was loosely inspired by the form of *Wild Palms*, a novel with two interlocking ideas written by William Faulkner, whose home town was Oxford, Missouri. As Collier explained in the sleeve notes for the *Bread & Circuses* CD, the work's own 'two interlocked ideas' involve 'a blues form and ballad melody which come together at the end'. *Oxford Palms* provides yet another example of the way that Collier used a literary model to inform his compositional practice.

The title track is more complex in structure. It involves three distinct introductions, which 'serve to introduce the motifs and ideas of the composition'. These are followed by three sections – 'Ballad 1', 'Clapping' and 'Pattern 1'.

Though Collier notes that these can be played in any order, this is their order on the record. 'Interlude' follows as a bridge between the two halves of the piece and is in turn followed by 'Pattern 2', 'Ballad 2', 'Blues' and, finally, 'Coda'. As noted, Collier was no fan of what he saw as 'third stream music' and, yet, this album finds the composer in territory that is itself mapped by both jazz and classical music. In that respect, The Collective both in its aesthetic – essentially a new music co-operative – and make-up – strings combined with 'jazz' instrumentation – offered the perfect vehicle for such explorations.

This is some of Collier's finest and most evocative work and amongst the very best performances of his music. Its introduction seems to hold its different elements in an elegant tension, as strings, woodwinds, brass and percussion move around first one motif before the piano introduces a second. There is no fixed tonality here, though the music is not atonal in the sense sometimes understood colloquially, i.e. cacophonous or unapproachable. There is a sense of mystery conveyed here in the combining of brass, saxophones and strings with gentle washes of percussion rising and falling in volume. However, some may search in vain for a recognizable ballad form. Later, Collier's skill in deploying the different resources available is evident as he brings in first euphonium, then marimba and alto enter, with the latter freely interpreting the motif before the piano and the whole orchestra join. Altoist Graeme Blevins gives a particularly strong solo here, as the music opens out.

The pacing is carefully chosen to create contrast, as when Jeremy Greig's trombone moves slowly against a modulating backcloth provided by piano, marimba, drums and bass. This builds very slowly into one of those near-Spanish tunes, that so often seem to surface in Collier's work, drawing no doubt on his love and respect for Gil Evans. The entry of the brass and strings broadens the textures as this section progresses at a slow-ish march before slipping out of tonality and time, as it rises towards its solemn conclusion.

Collier might have subtitled the piece, 'Themes and Variations'. An instrument or group of instruments states a motif or theme and this is then modified by one of the soloists or by the whole orchestra or sections of it. This is something that Collier has done often in the past. What makes *Bread & Circuses* different lies in the possibilities that The Collective's instrumentation offer. The textures that emerge are both unusual and vary from the delicate to the sumptuous. More than that, it creates intriguing patterns and shapes that are quite unexpected. It is almost tempting to suggest that *Bread & Circuses* might be Collier's minimalist masterpiece, for it moves more by subtle changes in its inner workings than by a more elaborate and traditional notion of thematic development.

Oxford Palms offers a major contrast. It begins with 'Picky Blues and Ballad One', a typically fragmentary introduction. A solo blues cadenza follows on soprano from Lindsay Vickery, a performance marked by Vickery's unusual but intriguing sound on the instrument. This leads into 'Open Blues and Ballad Two', as drums and percussion pick up the pace. Here, three saxophones – Blevins on alto, Vickery on soprano and Lee Buddle on baritone – solo against the riffs provided by the band. There is a sense that the trio and ensemble are at odds, as if playing to a different rhythm. The tune accelerates and rises to a crescendo, only to be followed quite crisply by a drop in pace and volume.

Vickery's soprano introduces the ballad section over marimba and then enters into a duet with Buddle's baritone. A series of quite lovely chords are picked up by the orchestra in response. It is notable that Vickery plays alone, whilst the orchestra comes in behind Buddle. 'One Note Blues and Ballad Three' opens with a vamp softly played by the trombones, quickly joined by Steve Richter's percussion. A new counter riff emerges from the woodwinds and both build in volume, as leader Adrian Kelly's trumpet becomes more in evidence. It falls away, then leaving essentially just Vickery on soprano and piano, rhythm and strings to lead into the third ballad section.

This section is taken *rubato* with some highly impressive work from Vickery before it settles very briefly into a more standard ballad form. Kelly introduces 'Clapping Blues and Ballad Four', his tone on trumpet taut and edgy. As the other brass join stating the riff, the volume increases before a further riff emerges from the woodwinds. Once more it fades and a duet between Blevins and Vickery begins. Yet behind the ballad one still hears the brass playing the blues riff of the first part of this movement. The effect is eerie but strangely comforting and any tension is only partially relieved in the final chord and its imperfect cadence.

Collier journeyed on to Sydney, meeting John Gill there and staying with Hazel and Roger Dean. He also met up again with Mike Nock, whom he had known at Berklee, and pianist/composer Paul Grabowsky, of whom Collier was a great admirer. Two performances with local musicians in Sydney and Manly also ended well. All in all, Collier seems to have enjoyed the trip, though it was somewhat marred by his digestive problems. The year ended well with a concert at Dartmouth College in New Hampshire and a lecture in New York. In addition, Collier signed contracts for the release of CDs of *Winter Oranges*, *The Third Colour*, *Bread & Circuses* and the reissue of *Charles River Fragments* with British company Jazzprint.

Over the next couple of years, Collier kept working and travelling. There were further health niggles and the tone of remarks in the 'Timeline' seems dissatisfied and 'grumpy' at times but bright and enthusiastic when things went to plan. The year 2004 seems to have been one of mixed fortunes with the highlights being concerts in Birmingham and at the London Jazz Festival, which resulted – eventually – in the release of *Directing 14 Jackson Pollocks*, a double CD taken from a performance at the Purcell Room in November 2004. Its title came from a friend of a friend. After hearing the concert, she remarked, 'His laid back attitude was totally at odds with the full frontal sound of the music. He appeared to casually stroll the stage, giving directions to these fantastic musicians by hand signals... It was a bit like someone directing 14 Jackson Pollocks' (Collier 2009b). Given that Pollock was Collier's favourite painter, he clearly loved the attribution. The concert featured a wholly new composition, *The Vonetta Factor*, commissioned by Birmingham Jazz, and *Forty Years On*, a suite built upon earlier Collier pieces such as 'Aberdeen Angus', 'Mackerel Sky' and *New Conditions*.

Figure 16. Graham Collier, Purcell Room, London Jazz Festival, November 2004. *Directing 14 Jackson Pollocks*.

Reviewing the concert for *The Times*, writer Alyn Shipton was decidedly unimpressed. The review also covered the White Foundation World Saxophone Competition and the performance by Carla Bley's quartet, The Lost Chords, which had taken place earlier on the same day. In a telling introduction to his comments on Collier's Purcell Room set, Shipton wrote, 'There had been equally high hopes for the return to the Purcell Room of the veteran British composer Graham Collier after a long period abroad'.

The problem for Shipton lay more with *Forty Years On* than with *The Vonetta Factor*. Noting that Collier's 'best compositional moments happen when his long, loping melodic lines emerge from the ensemble or when chunky backing riffs build into thrilling climaxes', Shipton argued that 'none of the ten movements in his suite had enough space to develop'. He continued:

> Most players seemed to have the instruction 'Go completely bonkers now!' written on every solo. Only the flautist Geoff Warren, the bassist Jeff Clyne and the trombonist Fayyaz Virji showed some restraint among a torrent of screeches, honks, wails and howls.
>
> Fortunately Collier's new commission, *The Vonetta Factor*, showed more compositional restraint, or maybe just the effects of exhaustion from his previous suite. With more reflection, increased space for solos and a jaunty swaying climax, it proved to devastating effect that less is more (Shipton 2004).

John Fordham's *Guardian* comments were more favourable, though he gave the concert only a three-star review. Fordham clearly agreed with Shipton in respect of *The Vonetta Factor*, noting that:

> Collier is a composer who puts the creativity of his soloists first. Here at the Purcell Room, the writing was arrayed in compact clusters with acres of space in between for the soloists to weave intricate countermelodies. The finale, a new Birmingham Jazz commission called *The Vonetta Factor*, represented the process at its most rigorous.

Fordham's comments on *Forty Years On* were brief: 'This ran from free-collective thrashes, past a trombone soloing against a tuba and out into swing with a slurred blues for Ed Speight's guitar'. With *The Vonetta Factor*, he drew particular attention to the contrast between 'a brooding drum tattoo, a brain-jangling burst of electronics from keyboardist Roger Dean and imaginative breaks from trumpeters Steve Waterman and Harry Beckett, trombonists Mark Bassey and Fayyaz Virji, and reed players Art Themen, Chris Biscoe and James Allsopp'. He concluded, 'The jostling lines that Collier's music intertwines got tangled at times, but the reasons he has been such a force in British jazz were clear enough' (Fordham 2004).

My own recollection of the concert, confirmed for me by the CD, is different from that of Alyn Shipton. *The Vonetta Factor* is clearly the more significant event compositionally but *Forty Years On* seems packed with some fine moments of wit, excitement and charm. The concert opened with the playing of an extract from Harry Beckett's solo from 'Aberdeen Angus', itself from Collier's first album *Deep Dark Blue Centre*. The humorous intent of the device was obvious and continued on the suite's opening section, 'Between a Donkey and a Rolls Royce', in the braying duet between Gideon Juckes on tuba and Mark Bassey on trombone. A similar witty intention seemed present in the duet between trumpeter Alex Bonney and James Allsop on bass clarinet set against a more or less swinging traditional big band arrangement on 'An Alternate Eggshell Summer'. The concert had concluded with an encore and reprise of 'Mackerel Sky', which had been included in *Forty Years On* but with different soloists, once again a moment that offered a warm, cheeky ending to the evening.

It would be fair to say that with *Forty Years On*, Collier seems to have paid more attention to the separate parts of the suite than to the way in which these might hang together. However, its purpose was more to explore a career in the music and an approach based on the notion that 'jazz happens in real time, once'. There are strong and empathic duets between Dean and Warren on flute on 'Ryoanji', a piece inspired by the philosophy underpinning the Japanese garden, and between Virji and Trevor Tomkins on 'An Alternate Aberdeen Angus'. Elsewhere, Biscoe's baritone solo on 'Between a Donkey and a Rolls Royce' and his alto on 'An Alternate New Conditions and Some Out Blues' are powerful and challenging statements from one of Britain's finest musicians. The same can also be said of the performances of Themen on tenor and Waterman on trumpet on a brooding 'An Alternate Third Simple Piece'. At times, the textures the band achieved recalled Gil Evans, notably on 'Mackerel Sky, an alternate blues' and on 'An Alternate New Conditions and Some Out Blues', while the rhythm section of Dean, Speight, Clyne, and Tomkins, depping for an indisposed John Marshall, play with a loose, limber flow throughout.

Reviewing the CD for the *All About Jazz* website, Nic Jones commented specifically in relation to *Forty Years On*, 'The music throughout is unsurprisingly febrile and the level of engagement with the moment is never in any doubt'. In respect of *The Vonetta Factor*, Jones noted:

> Again the ensemble produces a performance almost in defiance of the number of musicians deployed, such is its deft touch with the material at its disposal, although the flow of the music is anything but seamless. Instead a kind of impetus stems from the music's very discontinuities, with the heat Chris Biscoe generates on baritone sax amounting to a gradual sea change. After it, things are animated, although only for a passage, before the inimitable trumpeter and flugelhornist Harry Beckett again demonstrates why he's played such a key role in Collier's music over the years (Jones 2009).

Anthony Troon, writing in *Jazz Journal*, was similarly effusive, commenting:

> Once again, Collier's remarkable vision as a composer and Machiavellian mixer of the musical maelstrom comes arrestingly to the fore. In some ways, his act of composition is to choose his pyrotechnical players, light the blue touch paper, and let them soar and make sparks...the sum of these two CDs illustrates a talent long recognised as unique in world jazz by those who relish the art of the unpredictable (Troon 2009: 21).

The Vonetta Factor, however, is in some ways one of Collier's strangest compositions. Inspired by the strange juxtaposition of martial drumming and a jazz ballad on Miles Davis' 'Vonetta' from the *Sorcerer* album (a point we have already noted and which Collier refers to at length in *The Jazz Composer*) it extends that idea into the very fabric of the composition itself. As a result, it seems to sound different every time one hears it. This is primarily because of its episodic nature or, as Jones notes, its 'very discontinuities'.

Its most surprising juxtaposition comes at around four and a half minutes when a big band riff gives way to Dean's keyboard, which recalls one of Stockhausen's electronic pieces, such as *Kontakte* or the earlier *Étude Concrète*. The interjections of the horns and Trevor Tomkins' drums merely add to the strangeness of the episode. Elsewhere, ballad sections and pastoral moments are preceded by a loping big band theme. Moments of free blowing intersect with more straight-ahead passages. At another point, led by Biscoe's baritone, the music becomes increasingly wilder and freer. However, rather than descend completely into chaos, the music shifts into a swinging, big band section. The music is tense and edgy, even during its pastoral moments, because Collier refuses to let anything settle for long, a fact illustrated in its conclusion where a brief reprise of the opening theme is broken up by a series of rising, stabbing choruses.

If the whole point was to explore musically the potential of strange juxtapositions in a jazz context, something perhaps more common in contemporary classical music (think Stockhausen or Boulez), then it has been surprisingly successful. At times, one feels that it should collapse under the weight of its own conceit. That it does not do so may well be as much a tribute to the band and their levels of concentration as to the composer himself. The sense one gets of *The Vonetta Factor* is of collage or, alternatively, the 'cut-up' technique used by writers such as William Burroughs and Brion Gysin. Strange and disparate elements and materials are brought together by the artist to create new layers of meaning or sense. It works but does so in its own disorienting way.

The concert was the last occasion that Collier would perform his music with a band that he had assembled personally. This thought lends a poignancy to the occasion but time and again the feeling is that the band, the Collier stalwarts at least, were truly doing it for him.

The album also includes a second take of *The Third Colour* from that issued originally. Because the motivic material Collier uses for each of the 'grooves' is the same, the architecture of the piece changes little, if at all. However, what happens within that structure is altered by the use of different instruments and soloists. These create new possibilities and fresh colours. In some ways, forced to choose, one might just opt for this version over the original.

The year 2005 seems to have been a slow one, though 2006 made up for this to a certain extent. Collier notes in the 'Timeline':

> Concentrating more on the website and general promotion of the royalties side of things, realising that gigs aren't coming as they used to, and starting to think that perhaps semi-retirement has arrived, or will soon, and that I can live with the roses of reading, listening etc. All in all, I'm pretty happy and content, although as always, more money and gigs would help.

During the year, he finished *The Jazz Composer* and he spent much of March and April in the USA and Canada, undertaking a workshop for Hugh Fraser and road-testing *The Blue Suite* at the University of Victoria. However, health concerns seemed to loom ever larger with liver problems and hypertension. The next year was Collier's seventieth and he had high hopes for it in terms of a celebratory tour. This perhaps was something of a let-down, certainly in terms of the UK. In the end, all that he was able to organize was a date with the Derby Youth Orchestra with Harry Beckett as guest soloist and, through Frank Griffiths (Head of Jazz), a concert with student musicians at Brunel. Collier had received a considerable amount of support over the years from the British jazz establishment. Despite this, it was evident that he felt let down on this occasion, which given his contribution to the music one can understand.

A series of concerts in Holland with local musicians in Arnhem and Amsterdam and a four-day workshop in Malmö, as well as work in Switzerland later in the year did, however, offer some compensation for any such disappointment. Collier summed up his northern European sojourn, including the trip to the UK, quite optimistically:

> All in all I did have a good time on the trip, made some good music, met many old friends and made some new, made a small profit and had time off in Barcelona, Amsterdam and London – not forgetting Bremen which was a good hang (which cost €700 or so). I didn't do as much as I had hoped, but age and tiredness inevitably affected

what I could do. *But this is an indication of what I should be doing* [original emphasis].

Once again, however, there is a strong sense of *ennui* creeping in:

> On a personal level, it is obvious that I am not doing as much work as I think I should be. Part of the reason is age, part lost contacts (IASJ, IAJE etc), but perhaps the biggest part is that I don't think the world cares. I think that part of my general disillusionment is that jazz is being mislabelled in a big way and that those of us who want to change it are being ignored, kept out of the mainstream…
>
> *Disillusionment is a good way of expressing how I feel.* This is expressed in the JC book, which I have said is a kind of culmination of my life's work, and its publication is one of the planks of my wanting to… stop? Get out? Slow down? *In a sentence: I am more and more disillusioned with the state of jazz today, and feel that I have done my bit and should let my work speak for itself* [original emphasis]

Saxophonist Issie Barratt had known Collier and Gill since the mid-nineties in London. She had been a regular visitor to their Lewisham home and subsequently to their house in Ronda. She had really enjoyed her visits to Ronda but had also noticed over the years Collier's growing dissatisfaction.

> They loved it there! We loved it too….and it was so easy to visit as Malaga's only 3 hours away and then we'd get a lovely lift with a local taxi driver. It was a fabulous time. I went every year. Graham began to get really confrontational and angry. I was the new head of jazz at Trinity College of Music and Graham was feeling ignored by the UK. It was hard to see. John remained jolly, however, and we always had a great time (Email Barratt/Heining 2017).

Early in 2008, Collier and Gill moved from Spain to the Greek island of Skopelos, hoping to make Collier's pension from RAM stretch a little further. They were fortunate in getting out of Spain before the 2008 economic crash and settled into life on this quiet, verdant and friendly island in the Aegean. Their many happy holidays on Paxos helped make the move an attractive proposition. Both Collier and Gill loved the sea – they had originally considered moving to the Balearics – and Gill was a keen sailor, though he never owned his own boat. However, Barratt said they both began to voice concerns about the situation in Ronda:

> They began to say Ronda was changing – McDonalds moved in and they felt it was a bit homophobic, but the economy was also something to do with it with Graham living off his pension and savings.

> Also, John was writing a book on Greece and Graham went with him – he fell in love with the Sea and said it was where he wanted to spend his last years. Economically, Greece seemed at the time a better option than Spain. The latter had already started its recession. None of us saw Greece's crash further down the line (Email Barratt/Heining 2017).

The move was a success and both Collier and Gill seemed to have been happy on Skopelos. The town itself had some excellent restaurants and nice shops. Their house was quite lovely. There was no garden but the balcony looked out across other white, stucco houses to the sea. It was comfortable, warm in winter and cool in summer, and there was space for both men to work.

Collier continued to compose and write and devoted quite a lot of time to 'blogging'. Whenever he came across a composer or musician who he felt was taking the music forward he would champion their cause. He had with Gill's help set up his own website called *Jazz Continuum* and reviewed CDs by such composers and players on his site. The Italian composer and bass player, Roberto Bonati, was one artist with whom Collier seems to have felt a strong connection, primarily in terms of Bonati's wide-ranging artistic vision. In the early 2000s, he had contacted Bonati by email to compliment him on his album, *A Silvery Silence*, which like several Collier works had a literary inspiration, in this case, Melville's *Moby Dick*. Bonati was touched by the contact, as he explained:

> It was about 2003. He said, 'I like your record very much and I write a review on my website *Jazz Continuum*'. It was so tender and very humble in the way he was presenting himself and I was very happy because I knew very well who he was and I had some of his books. They were very inspiring to me. So, I write back and say, 'Of course, I know you and know your work and I am very interested in what you write both as a composer and as a critic'...

> I found his ideas about this music an inspiration. What he said about how you can combine composition and improvisation made much sense to me. So, when he contacted me and said he liked my music and I read what he wrote about my record *A Silvery Silence* – the one inspired by the *Moby Dick* novel – it meant so much.

They began a regular correspondence and, in September 2009, Bonati invited Collier to do a workshop at the Arrigo Boito Music Conservatory of Parma, where Bonati is Head of Jazz, and a subsequent performance with his students at the ParmaJazz Frontiere Festival in November 2009. Both were very successful by all accounts and Bonati noted that the students derived a great deal from working with Collier. This is evident from the film of the concert they performed with Collier conducting that November.[5] As well as several shorter pieces, Collier was able to perform *The Blue Suite* once more with what appears to have been an unusual line-up going by his notes in the 'Timeline'.

> Tenor sax and clarinet, tenor sax and alto sax and soprano sax, trumpet, clarinet and bass clarinet, violin (classically trained), 2 female singers, guitars 2-3 from 7 (used all 5, I think), piano and keyboards *players alternated*, double bass, electric bass, 2 drummers [original emphasis].

Bonati was clearly very moved by Collier's support and encouragement for his work and added, 'In his book, he speaks so well of me, which is kind of embarrassing. He writes about all these musicians and then he writes about me and nobody knows who this guy is' (Interview Bonati/Heining 2015).

The experience seems to have left a major impression on Bonati and the bassist-composer subsequently composed and performed a work in Collier's honour, following his death in 2011.

Towards the end of 2009, Collier completed a lifetime ambition by visiting the Galapagos Islands. In comparison with the previous years, 2010 proved busier for Collier with concerts in Denmark and Sweden and attendance at Jazzahead in Bremen. At the same time, the pace of his life had slowed down considerably even when set against the earlier years following his separation from the Royal Academy of Music. He kept busy writing and 'blogging' and was still in the market for work. It was on a holiday in Crete with Gill in September 2011 that Collier was taken ill one night. He died of heart failure on Friday 9 September. It was quick, relatively painless but quite unexpected.

Notes

1. I am grateful to Roger Dean for helping to clarify this point. Dean, of course, used a not dissimilar approach with his group LYSIS in the 1980s.

2. *Three Simple Pieces* was written for Collier's 60th birthday concert at the Royal Academy of Music in 1997. *Shapes, Colours, Energy* was commissioned by the Arts Council. First performed at the Banff jazz school in Canada, Collier notes that it was inspired by the setting, including the 'implied energy' of the school itself. *The Miró Tile* was first performed at the Bruckner Conservatorium in Linz, Austria in 1996. Finally, *The Third Colour* was commissioned by the London Jazz Festival for performance at the 1997 festival.

3. 'Eggshell Summer' is to be found on *Meltdown* (SLAMCD 243).

4. David Fiuczynski on, for example, *Uncommon Ground* and *Electronic Sonata for Souls Loved by Nature – Events XI-XV* from *The London Concert* (1990) Label Bleu LBLC6527/8; Mike Walker on *It's About Time* and *Living Time* from *It's About Time* (1995) Label Bleu LBLC6587.

14 Legacy

If we date Collier's professional career from his return to the UK and formation of his first band around 1964 and see the posthumous *Luminosity – The Last Suites* from 2014 as his swan song, we have a half-century of creative activity across a number of fronts. Together these form Graham Collier's legacy.

In those fifty years he made, including the *Adam's Marble* album, seventeen records. In addition, two key works – *Workpoints* and *Hoarded Dreams* – were released some years after their performance. Bearing in mind that Collier, with the exception of *Something British Made in Hong Kong*, took a recording sabbatical from 1979 (*The Day of the Dead*) to 1994 (*Charles River Fragments*), this achievement is all the more remarkable. More than that, during those years, Collier wrote over one hundred compositions, including many extended works, for small and large ensembles, including music for films, theatre and radio drama. More than forty of these have never been recorded, or, if recorded for radio broadcast, have never been released. A large, perhaps the largest, part of this book has been devoted to an appreciation and also a critical examination of that body of work.

However, Collier had so many roles in the music that it is important to try and understand those other parts of his legacy, as an advocate for jazz and as a theorist of jazz aesthetics. He was active throughout his career as an educator and pioneer of jazz education, spending some fifteen years teaching at the Royal Academy of Music. In addition, he was an active member of the IASJ, editing and writing much of the content of its magazine, *Jazz Changes*. His importance in this respect is unassailable. We can also characterize Collier as a jazz activist, who sought to promote jazz as an art music and as one of the two main artistic developments of the twentieth century, the other of which would be film. In this regard, as a writer and critic Collier wrote for a number of publications but more significantly he produced seven books on jazz. It is an astonishing catalogue of creative activity by any standards.

Collier's work in all these fields was so interconnected that it is sometimes hard to evaluate these activities separately. Reading Collier's papers, a lot emerged that one would have anticipated but even this invariably became more nuanced. Other aspects of his life and character came to light that were more surprising. Collier could be awkward and difficult, whilst also charming and amusing in greater measure.

He thought very deeply about jazz, art and culture and was passionate in defending his own views on these questions. He could be relentless in pursuing publishers and record companies, who were – in his view – slow in meeting their contractual obligations. He could also be very combative and even spiteful. There were more than a few occasions in his life when greater reflection might have resulted in caution and an equally or more successful outcome.

But in the main, those he worked with liked him and respected him; even those he antagonized by his behaviour have good words to say about him. What is immediately apparent is how much of himself Collier invested in all aspects of his work and life.

In terms of his musical legacy, Collier drew on a broad understanding and appreciation of other musics in his work as a composer and musician. For example, he drew upon rock and jazz-rock throughout his career and this led to some intriguingly strange juxtapositions at times, for example at the end of *New Conditions*. Certain records by the Graham Collier Music, notably *Darius* and *Down Another Road*, bear comparison sonically and texturally with the work of Ian Carr's Nucleus. In some ways, this was a sign of the times and reflected the approaches that, inspired by developments in rock music and by Miles Davis, some jazz musicians were exploring. It is fair to say that, over its career Nucleus took this further than Collier, who seemed to integrate aspects of rock music into his work whilst moving away from what might be called jazz-rock. For Collier, rock and jazz-rock were resources and possibilities to be deployed for particular compositional and performance purposes, not ends in themselves. Remember, here, his written instruction to drummer John Webb – 'free rock'.

In terms of classical music, that there are sometimes parallels between the way jazz musicians and classical composers work should not surprise us. The making of music, in particular when it comes to composition, is a kind of problem-posing and problem-solving activity. Within any musical approach or genre, some of these problems may generalize to other musics but some will be specific to that approach or genre. The creative composer concerned, as Collier was, with taking the music forward progresses by experimentation and challenge. Music becomes a question of 'what if?' rather than a matter of 'what next?' or 'how?' The key question specific to jazz, as we have argued throughout, focuses on the relationship between what is improvised and what is composed. Perhaps this is the main contribution that jazz has made and can make to twentieth- and twenty-first-century music. Not only did Collier apply this problem-posing approach to himself and his own work but he sought to develop that same critical/reflective approach in his students. This is central to his philosophy and performance ethic of jazz.

We may note parallels in Collier's notion of the improvising conductor with other musicians, notably George Russell, Lawrence 'Butch' Morris and John Zorn. Collier compares his way of working with that of Morris in *The Jazz Composer* (Collier 2009a: 249–50, 271). The most intriguing aspect of this is that these jazz composer-conductors have each developed that side of their work in ways that are specific to their own *modus operandi*. Such idiosyncrasy extends to the compositional process as well. Jazz composers tend to work in isolation from each other, and their work largely (though less so these days) develops outside the academy. We may talk of certain big band styles with reference to Count Basie. We may talk of a music sounding 'Ellingtonian' or even note Gil Evans as an obvious influence upon it. But we rarely speak of music sounding Bley-like, Collier-like, Brookmeyer-like, Thad Jones-like, Gibbs-like or Westbrook-like. And that is not because these composers are 'also-rans' but a reflection of the situational context in which the jazz composer works.

Perhaps the closest parallel to Collier's way of working was that of George Russell, though there are also similarities between Collier and Barry Guy in their use of modular approaches to composition. Collier did not like Russell's music, though one wonders if he had listened to *Electronic Sonata, Othello Ballet Suite, Vertical Form VI* or *The African Game* (Collier 2009a: 252–53, 313; Heining 2009: 291). The differences between their work are clear. For one thing, Russell's music is much stronger and more powerful rhythmically. Russell's harmonic sense was very strong and he would start with a basic jazz chord but then build layers upon it that would transform it pantonally into something far wider and richer. One does not hear that in Collier's music. Where he uses a modal approach the sense is more that the harmonies are stretched across a musical canvas, rather than stacked in layers. With Russell, to use his own terminology, the form is vertical. It is also the case that much in Russell's music which sounds improvised is actually written. In fact, *Vertical Form VI* is largely through-composed. With Collier, form is horizontal. That said Collier's music has far more freedom in it for the musicians and not just the soloists. The written compositional elements are, as noted time and again, only a starting point.

There are differences too in the way that one experiences form and detail as a listener in relation to their music. With Russell, in most instances, one hears the form first and discovers the detail later. With Collier, it is the other way round. One hears the detail and discovers the form through subsequent and, in some cases, repeated listening. To use an analogy that relates to Collier's love of fine art, Russell always takes you to one room in a gallery but allows you to experience every aspect of its contents afresh on each visit. Collier, on the other hand, takes you through every room in the place but on another tour will take you by another route entirely.

Saxophonist Chris Biscoe played with Collier on three or four occasions, including on *Charles River Fragments* and the *Jackson Pollocks* CD. He also played extensively with George Russell and Mike Westbrook. Asked what he saw as the differences between the three bandleader/composers, he responded:

> [M]y first thought was that the main driving force behind Graham's writing was the integration of composition and collective improvisation, while Mike Westbrook's concerns centre more on orchestral colour, harmony and structure. George Russell's greatest strength, I suppose, was his extraordinary approach to rhythm.
>
> However, on listening again [to *Charles River Fragments*], I find it difficult to reconcile my hazy memory of Graham directing and moulding the band, introducing and layering motifs, with what I hear. On the CD, the performance seems to be a series (suite, if you will) of solos. The structure of each solo is determined collectively, but there is far less a sense of big-band collective improvisation than I remember (Email Biscoe/Heining 2014).

The distinction between Collier and Westbrook is a valid one. The point about Russell's approach to rhythm is also pertinent. That layering of rhythms like an African drum choir is a continent – and a hemisphere – away from Collier's use of rhythm (Heining 2009: 291). However, Biscoe's last point is intriguing. Certainly, some musicians who played with Collier struggled to make sense of the whole, given the fragmentary experience of working in the band. At times, as with Geoff Warren's earlier remark about hearing *Hoarded Dreams* on CD, re-listening brought the relationship between detail and structure into focus. Biscoe seems to be saying that, for him, the reverse was true. By contrast, despite the detail of Russell's work and the demands it placed on musicians, its strong rhythmic sense was its foundation if not its structure. This is a key difference in outcome, at least, even though certain of their working methods were closer than might otherwise appear the case.

Both also used their own gestures to change what actually occurred in performance. In Russell's case, this could involve altering the order in which things happened but mostly how long particular musical events lasted. With Collier the potential for moving musical elements around was far more extensive. Of more significance, however, is their use of a similar method of constructing their compositions. They built their compositions through bringing together a series of elements which were in some ways discrete and distinct. It was the process of bringing these elements together that created the musical work. This is different from the way many composers work, for example beginning with a melody, harmonizing it, exploring its potential through a series of variations or through the use of counter-point and counter-melodies. To use another analogy from fine art, had they been painters, Russell would have been a 'Rothko' and Collier a 'Jackson Pollock'. Even more intriguingly, on stage they used similar ways of positioning the musicians. There are diagrams by both that show how they avoided the traditional big band practice of grouping by instrument and replaced this with something they related directly to the role played by individuals in the composition. And both valued individuals and individual voices. There is a quote from one musician, guitarist David Fiuczynski, who played with Russell, of which Collier would have approved. He said:

> He could be very hard if something was played incorrectly but I'll never forget that when we were playing things correctly and he was frustrated, he was like, 'You've got the notes together. Screw the notes. I can care less about the notes. You have to say something' (Heining 2009: 263).

Sadly, I was never able to play *The African Game* or *Othello Ballet Suite* or *The London Concert* for Collier and discuss these works with him. However, I would have stressed how Russell layers different riffs one upon another on *The London Concert* version of *Electronic Sonata* and how the playing of the horns contrasts with the rest of the music, most notably because they are playing out of time with the other instruments. I would have drawn attention to the abrupt shift in pace, mood, tempo and textures around eight and a half minutes led by Pete Hurt's bass clarinet and the ensemble *rubato* section that develops from this. I would have pointed to the way Russell talks of 'Events' in relation to *The African Game* and how these seemed to be constructed from fragments, riffs and motifs in a way not so dissimilar from Collier's own practice in terms of outcome, if not in relation to how this is achieved. Finally, I would have suggested that Russell achieves on *Othello Ballet Suite* a music that is episodic and abstract which explores similar sonorities to his own work. And Collier would still probably have disagreed with me!

A further parallel lies in the fact that both Collier and Russell sought to theorize the music, though they did so in very different ways, beginning from different standpoints and with different intentions. Russell's Lydian Concept is primarily concerned with musical theory, the building blocks of the music and jazz (Russell 2001). His ideas do have philosophical implications but these are undermined somewhat by his references to mysticism, his misunderstanding of the relationship between music and physics and his misreading of musical history (Heining 2009: 306–315). Where Russell starts with musical theory,

Collier begins with philosophy, even if this is not fully contextualized within a broader philosophical or theoretical frame. Collier's concerns lie firstly with aesthetic values, though also with the expressive, performance aspect of these. Further, to the extent that he is arguing that this is how things should be, there is an additional normative, ethical purpose to his writing on the subject.

Collier spoke often of his vision of jazz, both in *The Jazz Composer* and other works but also in interviews and articles. His ideas about jazz form, performance and the primacy of improvisation in jazz were well-articulated and constituted, as I have suggested, a nascent jazz aesthetic. There is much jazz to which Collier took great exception. But his tastes were also very catholic. On the one hand, he rejected music that he saw as dogma masquerading as tradition, that is, the neo-conservatism of the Marsalis brothers and their like. As Miles Davis once remarked, and as Collier quotes, 'Didn't I do it good the first time?' (Collier 2009a: 112). And he rejected what he saw as the repertory approaches of big band writers such as Sammy Nestico, Thad Jones, Jim McNeely and others.

However, he would not necessarily have denied George Russell, Sun Ra and Thelonious Monk, artists he simply did not get, their place in the canon of the jazz tradition. On the other hand, the jazz artists whose work he valued covered a wide spread of approaches and styles. He admired people such as Geir Lysne, Paul Grabowsky, Roberto Bonati, Tom Cawley, Corey Mwamba, James Allsopp and Steve Harris and his group ZAUM, as well as others such as Carla Bley, Michael Mantler, Evan Parker and Globe Unity Orchestra. What these very different individuals have in common is a commitment to moving jazz forward or, to use Collier's term once again, 'off the paper'. All too often in the jazz world the differences between what might be 'good' as opposed to 'bad' jazz are put down to matters of personal preference. Collier went further than this in *The Jazz Composer*, seeking to outline a theory of jazz in performance, that is, how the whole performance and not just the 'solos' might be informed and infused (and enthused!) by improvising. One might not agree entirely with his views or always enjoy the results in terms of their outcome in his compositions but he challenges one to respond and engage with the argument.

Collier's view of jazz was that it was an art form, valid in its own right and on its own terms. He believed that it should not try to ape classical music in producing works that combined the worst aspects of both but should seek to establish the legitimacy of its own tradition and history and its unique emphasis on improvisation. In a sense, his work as a composer could be said to concern itself with the dialectical relationship between composition and improvisation. These concerns were at the heart of all his activities. With hindsight, it is no surprise that he was the first jazz musician to obtain an Arts Council grant or the first to establish a full-time jazz degree course in the UK. Collier did more than anyone to position jazz as an art music in Britain. And he and his music benefited significantly from the numerous commissions and Arts Council and British Council grants that supported his recordings, tours and writing. This was not a matter of self-interest but a consequence of and just reward for his efforts. So doing, he opened the door for so many others. In this, Collier was representative of a trend. He did not, however, cause or create it but this remains in some degree a part of his legacy.

As suggested already, the opening up of funding to jazz and other 'fringe' arts has to be understood in the context of post-war political, as well as cultural, activity. Viewed politically and socially, during these years, there existed in Britain, and elsewhere in Europe, a balance of forces in this country and elsewhere, something that has since been lost. In the fifties through to the seventies, the democratic left was a force to be reckoned with, trades union membership was very high and unions were well-organized. At the same time, there was no widespread desire for a more radical transformation of society and there was arguably a corresponding acceptance amongst sections of the ruling class that some forms of state provision and regulation were, following the disasters of the twenties and thirties, no bad thing. It was a situation in which social democratic ideas and values could be seen to hold sway or at least a certain currency. Most importantly, part of that zeitgeist was a desire for the democratization of the arts, paralleled by moves towards wider citizen participation in social, political and cultural life. These were years of optimism.

Following the awarding of Collier's Arts Council grant, British jazz found itself for the first time able to call upon two regimes for support. The first was the music business of record companies and promoters, which might be described as the regime of accumulation. The second was the regime of (state) patronage. As the major record companies lost interest in jazz and became increasingly focused on quick returns on investment, so jazz became more reliant on the regime of patronage. However, just as it competed unequally within the music business with pop, rock and classical music, so too it remained the poor relation of high art classical music and opera. That this is also an issue of class should be apparent (see, for example, Johnson 2002; Lopes 2002).

Collier had every reason and every justification to press the case for state funding of jazz and its status as art. Jazz musicians and fans pay their taxes too! Within the 'social/liberal democratic' consensus of those times, it seemed hard to imagine the golden goose would not continue to lay golden eggs and for jazz and other fringe arts to receive an ever fairer share. Sadly, all things do not remain equal and now the barbarians are not just at the gates, they hold the citadel.

Social democracy foundered on the rock that was once the Bretton Woods Agreement. That agreement, reached between the Allied nations in 1944 and accepted in the post-war settlement of hostilities between the Allies and the Axis powers, sought to avoid the kind of economic crises that had blighted the inter-war years and had led to the rise of fascism. It required national governments to maintain a link between their gross domestic product and the value of their currency. Effectively, this meant that manufacturing capital was tied to finance capital and vice versa. Richard Nixon's decision to float the dollar in 1971, the so-called 'Nixon Shock', removed its link to the gold standard and began the modern era of neo-liberal economics and the effective separation of finance from manufacturing, which was the effective cause of the 2008 crash. National governments are more and more subject to the fluctuations of the financial markets and their capacity to exercise economic controls are further limited by the free movement of finance capital that has followed deregulation (Wade 2006; Glyn 2006). This is the reality that now faces liberal and social democratic parties in the North Atlantic economies (Fraser 2013).

In this context, what prospect is there now that marginal arts such as jazz will get their fair share of arts funding? Even if they were to do so, it would be taken from an ever-dwindling pot. What is more, the legacy of arts funding for jazz is less one of increasing acceptance of jazz as art but rather its greater marginalization. State funding requires trusted bodies and key individuals to press the case for jazz. It needs 'professional' jazz advocates – promoters, broadcasters, writers, arts professionals and even friendly politicians. French cultural philosopher Pierre Bourdieu describes such processes as a competition to acquire cultural capital within a field, capital that may then be translated if successful into other forms of capital, such as finance or influence (Bourdieu 1993; 1998). Such processes create their own elites.

One of the long-term consequences of positioning jazz as an art form and fostering its reliance on state and other regimes of patronage has been the rise of just such an elite. That elite not only speaks for British jazz but, like the liberal/social democratic politics that spawned it, says, 'Leave it to us'. This is a backwash effect of what the writer Paul Lopes has called 'the rise of a jazz art world', of the positioning of jazz as an art form (Lopes 2002). One might suggest that the need now is not for advocacy but activism – and activism that understands that there can be no cultural equality without social and economic equality. However much one might agree with Collier that jazz is a major art form, deserving of state support as a social and cultural good, his analysis fails ultimately because it has no political perspective beyond liberalism. To say this is not to blame Collier, decry his efforts or diminish his legacy, but rather to understand the unravelling of jazz advocacy of this kind.

In fairness, despite Collier's aim of and success in positioning jazz as an art music, it must be acknowledged that he was only too aware of the complexity of the issues facing jazz, falling as it does between the stools of state and other funding and the music business. Much of the chapter 'Deepening the game' in *The Jazz Composer* is devoted to these questions. He writes: 'It could be argued that the "crisis in jazz" is not lack of record sales, lack of audiences, but that sales *per se*, audiences *per se*, are seen as important' (Collier 2009a: 150). He goes on to quote guitarist Derek Bailey on the contradictions and compromises imposed by both the worlds of accumulation and patronage on jazz and other avantist musics, contradictions that it is necessary to find ways of resisting. He goes on to argue: 'The whole marketing and packaging (what we could call Americanising) of jazz implies that there is an audience we should be looking for, rather than an art we should be working within'. Before anyone cries 'elitist', let us be clear that such a charge can only be justified if Collier – and Bailey – were arguing that this music is so rarefied and difficult that only a minority of individuals could possess the necessary sensibility of mind and soul to appreciate it. That is what 'elitist' means and it is not what Collier is saying. It is not elitist to ask people to make the effort to hear, to see, to think, to feel rather than accept passively or gladly what the regime of accumulation is willing to sell them. More than that, it is at these points that aesthetics takes on a political or at least a transformative hue (Bhaskar 1991).[1]

Further, at another level, in his proselytizing on behalf of jazz and his efforts in taking jazz into schools and colleges, Collier recognized that creativity and the capacity to appreciate and value art was an essential human characteristic and that recognition is itself a transformational ethic. In some ways, even more than his recordings, if Collier's writings on jazz were to encourage others to re-evaluate their own practice in terms of what the underlying values of the music might be, then that would be a remarkable legacy, indeed.

At the same time, it must be said that *The Jazz Composer* is not without its shortcomings or critics. Collier approached Francesco Martinelli, a lecturer and archivist at Siena Jazz University, in the hope that Martinelli might translate the book into Italian and publish it as part of the university's series of books on jazz. Martinelli sums up both the strengths and problems with *The Jazz Composer* very concisely, when he notes:

> I said I wasn't interested. My aim is to provide a frame of reference for Italian jazz students with a complete panorama of the subjects we touch upon. So, we try to select the best biography of Charlie

> Parker, the best Django biography. So, while for me, it was very interesting reading *The Jazz Composer* and hear his thoughts about improvisation and composition and how they can work together, at the same time it was extremely personal as a point of view. He just picked those cases he was interested in and never mentions several of the most important figures in European jazz. In my opinion, you can't avoid mentioning Alex von Schlippenbach, Barry Guy, Peter Kowald, Maarten Altena, Kenny Wheeler and Bruno Tomasso in Italy. It is a very intellectually stimulating book but it doesn't have the kind of broad vision of the subject that we look for in the translations we publish (Interview Martinelli/Heining 2016).

The book was also turned down by the consulting editor for Equinox Publishing for very similar reasons. John Gill described the book as 'a kind of mission statement' and it is certainly that. Collier obviously saw it as something more definitive. It stands as an important part of his legacy and is a brave attempt to *begin to* expound a philosophy and aesthetic of the music. Sadly, Collier's own strong opinions blinded him to ideas and music that might actually have refined and broadened his argument and, even in some cases, supported it.

We have seen on many occasions that Collier valued individual voices, taking his cue from Ellington and Miles. His music needed his musicians to speak in their own tongue to make it come alive. He believed greatly in personal expression and sought to communicate this to his, sometimes reluctant, students. But this is not the exultation of the individual found in bourgeois culture and it certainly does not deny the individual as within totalitarian, collectivist cultures. His music was, after all, about the relationship between the composed and the improvised, the composer and his musicians. It emphasized improvisation and spontaneity over production and reproduction and – apart from brief moments – did so on the fringes of the dominant culture. In essence, this is an alternative model of individualism that is perfectly compatible with socialist and anarchist critiques. It is a musical praxis, which stresses the potential of co-operative values, of experimentation and creativity and which suggests that the individual may ultimately find their highest form of expressive value within the collective and in the contribution they may make to a shared musical world.

Questions of aesthetic – and ethical – value lie at the very heart of an art form. And the study of aesthetics has similarities with the study of ethics in that both are concerned with finding objective, contextual ways of attributing value (Dewey 2005). Collier might well have been concerned not to place his art at the service of politics and keen to maintain that separation. But in locating improvisation and, therefore, processes of change at the centre of his aesthetic, Collier is drawn into questions of value that go beyond art in suggesting that the creativity and the creative life are valid in their own terms beyond commerce. And he was very aware of this issue. In chapter 7 of *The Jazz Composer*, 'Why would we want to repeat it?', Collier includes a quotation from a letter by Malcolm Lowry:

> Why can I play it over and over again? As many times as a Beethoven quartet, save that I am not going to compare the two, since jazz isn't music perhaps so much as a form of expressionism, maybe actually more analogous to literature or poetry, than music. But where the heck, in what passage or movement of prose can I find the selection, the discipline, unselfishness, spontaneity, freedom, and final concision, and form of this darn thing? As well as the chaos, mournfulness, despair? These qualities ought to be in prose, this rhythm ought to be manifest in any interpretation of the modern world: but it simply isn't (Collier 2009a: 127).

This is a concise and articulate statement of what might constitute an aesthetics of jazz, but also in its reference to the modern world it is an ethical statement too. To return to the quote from Bill Evans used by Collier earlier, the whole quotation of which we have previously used only the first sentence, is similarly instructive in terms of Collier's jazz aesthetic:

> Jazz is not a what, it is a how. If it were a what, it would be static, never growing. The how is that the music comes from the moment, it is spontaneous, it exists in the time it is created. And anyone who makes music according to this method conveys to me an element that makes his music jazz (Collier 2009a: 312).

Collier himself writes of 'preserving the soul of jazz'. At its heart, the kind of aesthetic he proposes is an essentialist one. For all the limitations that such an idealistic position may involve, it is nonetheless one that he seeks to justify continually with reference to examples in practice and which he demonstrated in his own work. He writes succinctly: 'Preserving the soul of jazz is not a matter of notes, but of philosophy' (Collier 2009a: 129). This is a very clear recognition of a key point about jazz, one that is all too often overlooked and one that offers a radical message. Never mind, 'It don't mean a thing if it ain't got that swing'. It don't mean a thing, if its core virtues and values are not understood and, in some shape or form, conveyed in the music and by those who speak on its behalf. Bill Evans was right: jazz is a 'how' or at least should be. Unfortunately, too much of what passes for jazz or is presented as such is now a 'what'. Evan Parker, in an interview some years ago, expressed this confusion in an intriguingly elliptical manner. He was referring to the point in the sixties where artists such as AMM, the Spontaneous Music Ensemble, Mike

Westbrook and others were considering how to take their music forward. He suggests the view that, in its current usage, the word 'jazz' is a recipe for confusion and for clashes of expectations.

> In all those cases, those people are thinking, 'Okay. What's the next step? Where are we going?' It's a dynamic and it has to be going somewhere. Otherwise, it becomes static and ossified and classicised which has happened with... in fact, I doubt that the use of the word 'jazz' does anybody any favours to describe some of these things. [At a festival] this week in Portugal, the 'jazz word' was everywhere and it's a source of confusion for people because everybody knows what jazz is – the trouble is they don't all agree with one another. The real problem arises when people's expectations are not met. They've gone to the trouble to come to a thing because it was called 'jazz'. The thing that sends a chill through my heart is when I see outside a wine bar or a pub a blackboard that says, 'Jazz every Wednesday'. Like, that's all people need to know. That's it. The problem is that people come for what they expect and it isn't what they find (Interview Parker/Heining 2012).

The answer to that confusion cannot be purely definitional, a Marsalis-like canonization of the jazz tradition, a practice of exclusion of anything than does not fit that narrow definition. The answer must be ecumenical and based on a clear understanding and exposition of a jazz aesthetic. As Collier also notes, 'The sanctity of the jazz performance is a result of improvisation, and leads, inevitably, to the truism that jazz happens in real time, once' (Collier 2009a: 129). But these are not mainstream cultural values. They are not about a product, a style or a genre. They reflect something more organic and, I suspect, that this is why the music advanced by Evan Parker or Keith and Julie Tippett(s), on the one hand, or by Graham Collier or Mike Westbrook, on the other, does not easily find and hold an audience in the regime of accumulation that is the music business. If you cannot define what it is, how on earth can you market it? And if it were a 'how', then it cannot be about reproduction, which is at the heart of regimes of accumulation. Followed to its logical conclusion, this leads us into uncharted waters – those very waters in which those above and younger artists like James Allsopp and Tom Cawley, others such as Roberto Bonati, Alex von Schlippenbach, Geir Lysne, Myra Melford, Marilyn Crispell, William Parker or Roscoe Mitchell (and many others) choose to swim. It requires a different approach to that of commerce or the current regime of patronage.[2]

Sadly, Collier never fully explores the implications of his arguments about and on behalf of jazz. He never elaborated these points into a grounded statement of aesthetic and even ethical values, though the normative thrust of his writing suggests that at some level he saw the question in those terms. This is a difficult issue and, perhaps, one beyond the scope of this biography. However, followed to its logical conclusion, Collier's argument takes us into the heart of what jazz is, that is, its essential nature and how that relates to other musical arts. It is true that Collier went to some lengths to differentiate jazz from classical music and saw jazz as a 'how' rather than as a 'what'. At the same time, he concentrates more on the practical implications of what he is arguing for the performer or composer rather than the implications of the philosophical issues his arguments raise. These go far beyond matters of definition and would require examination of jazz as a cultural practice against other cultural practices, for example European art music. Indeed, to do so would require the interrogation of what Australian academic Bruce Johnson describes as the 'epistemological frame' and 'aesthetic frame' that supports European art music but which disadvantages jazz and other non-high art musics. As Johnson argues, 'The gatekeepers – traditional musicology, the forms and practices that it has canonised as the aesthetic and moral apogee of music, and the policies and attitudes arising from these – are in turn the music agents of Enlightenment epistemology'.

Johnson suggests that within that frame there is a 'fixation on product rather than process' and he continues:

> The more comfortably any cultural practice can be incorporated into such a model, the more privilege it will enjoy... [I]n the general category of 'music' jazz is less conformable than conventional art music to the dominant episteme, and that some practices associated with particular styles are even less so than others (Johnson 2002: 100).

Johnson draws extensively on Foucault in making these points, essentially locating his arguments in the discourses of power and knowledge. However, similar conclusions could be reached from the perspective of critical theory. Herbert Marcuse, for example, in *The Aesthetic Dimension: Toward a Critique of Marxist Aesthetics* (1978/2003) seeks to develop an aesthetic framework that sees art as functioning as the critical conscience of society. This idea allows both for the autonomy of the art work, that is, it allows it to exist outside and independent from that which it observes, and it privileges, to an extent, form over content. In this he departs from 'vulgar' Marxist notions that it is the social content of a work that makes it revolutionary or political. As he notes:

> The critical function of art, its contribution to the struggle for liberation, resides in the aesthetic form. A work of art is authentic or true not by virtue of its content (i.e., the 'correct' representation of social conditions), not by its 'pure' form, but by the content having become form (Marcuse [1978] 2003: 8).

Following this line of argument in respect of jazz and the ideas about it that Collier expresses forces us to consider the culturally critical aspects of jazz vis à vis other musical arts and allows us to understand why jazz might struggle to gain access to the 'dining room of funding, recognition and support', to use Johnson's telling phrase (Johnson 2002: 100). Indeed, Johnson would question whether locating jazz as a 'high-art' music, which appears to have been Collier's aim, is in itself desirable. Furthermore, merely stating that jazz is a radical and fundamentally different art form does not tell us why this is so or how this is so, beyond establishing the primacy of improvisation within it. It does not consider what this means in the broader context of values and ideas about art, nor does it examine the wider implications this may have for our critical understanding of dominant ideas and values about art and of how the artistic act of creation or indeed human creativity are understood and valued in capitalist society. Stating that jazz is an art form deserving equal status with classical music does not explain why it is not accepted as such or even denied such a status. To understand this requires the location of our debate within a discussion of ideology, power and knowledge.

From a more liberal perspective, Collier might equally have located his ideas within a more idealistic philosophical framework based on the Kantian notion of the sublime. Discussing Kant's *Critique of Judgement*, Nicholas Garnham argues that, for Kant, art was 'a mode of cognition that bridged the sensual and rational sides of humans'. Arguing against post-modernist and social constructivist approaches to art, Garnham notes:

> One way of resisting this reduction of the aesthetic to the social and ideological is to return to the Kantian argument for the autonomy of the aesthetic and for the positive political and moral evaluation of art as both a mode of cognition and a practice that stems from them (Garnham 2000: 155).

Such an approach could arguably have led Collier either in the direction of the social democratic ideas of Pierre Bourdieu or towards those of the Frankfurt School of Marcuse and Adorno.

Another option might be to ground Collier's ideas within the kind of philosophical/psychological tradition represented by American philosopher John Dewey and humanistic psychologists influenced by his ideas such as Carl Rogers ('the good life') or Abraham Maslow ('self-actualization'). This would emphasize the transformative potential of experience and of the creative act and potential in all human beings. Like Garnham (and Marcuse and others of the Frankfurt School) this perspective presupposes elements of choice, voluntarism, creative engagement and the exercise of judgement by the perceiving subject, as well as by the artist/producer themselves, and raises questions that are both aesthetic and ethical (Kirschenbaum and Henderson 1996; Maslow 1954). Collier's arguments would certainly fit within each of these philosophical frameworks, grounding his arguments beyond the subject itself, i.e. jazz as an art form. Without such a basis, the sense left by Collier's writings, and philosophizing, on jazz is of a need to plant these in better soil.

This is a radical message, indeed. Collier may have kept his political views and his art separate but the aesthetic values he espoused and their practical expression in his music surely contradict the values of mainstream culture quite profoundly. To use Jacques Rancière's definition of 'politics' as actions that transgress or challenge the dominant order (he uses the word 'police' to describe the activities of the established order), jazz, or at least that jazz Collier advocates, can be seen as such a transgression (Rancière 2011).

* * *

Collier's final musical legacy lay in two records – both double CDs released by John Gill after his partner's death. The first was *Relook*, a fine compilation reaching back to Collier's Berklee days with the recording made there of 'The Barley Mow' and including thirty-eight minutes of unreleased material. The second was the posthumous recording of Collier's last two suites. It was, of course, a Collier album *sans* 'the lad himself'. But it succeeded in expressing the values and virtues of his music and his contribution to jazz.

Reviewing *Luminosity* for the *All About Jazz* website, I wrote:

> A new work, posthumously released and recorded – how many of those can there be in jazz. *Luminosity* features two late works by composer Graham Collier brought to realisation through the efforts of his partner, author John Gill, and aided by conductor Geoff Warren. To say this record is a fine valediction is a statement infused with regret. These two compositions reveal just how much music Collier still had to offer.
>
> Fortunately, Gill and Warren were able to bring together a band that is packed with Collier alumni. In fact, pretty much everyone on this album has at some point played his music and, in some cases – John Marshall, Art Themen, Ed Speight, Roger Dean, Steve Waterman and Warren, himself – the association goes back several decades (Heining 2014).

The record featured two suites, *The Blue Suite* and *Luminosity*. The first of these had received its premiere in 2007, Collier's seventieth year, in Holland with the ArtEZ Big Band and further part and full performances had followed at Brunel

University in London and in Parma. The piece had also been performed by another student ensemble in Arhus in 2010. *Luminosity*, however, was never performed in Collier's lifetime.

The *Luminosity* CD is intriguing in so many respects, not least musically. The two suites draw upon different Collier obsessions. *Luminosity* is inspired by the work of abstract painter Hans Hofmann, whilst *The Blue Suite* owes its debt to Miles Davis' *Kind of Blue*, which was for the composer the defining example of his own belief that 'Jazz happens in real time, once'. Given that it was recorded posthumously, one had to wonder how Collier's absence as conductor had affected the outcome. Clearly, had he been there, he would have made different choices from those made by Geoff Warren. However, Warren succeeded quite remarkably in taking on the compositional materials left by Collier to create two works that were both distinctive and coherent and which bear their composer's own personal stamp. In fact, both works seem in these readings to be as approachable and accessible as anything Collier has written. After all, was not Collier's main thrust in all his work the belief that the composer should trust his musicians?

Both works here use certain Collier trademarks. Written material is used both as a source for a musician's solo and to inform the improvisation in some other way, texturally, harmonically or simply in terms of the mood. Each suite opens with a loosely structured and more or less freely interpreted movement which resurfaces in the middle and at the end of the suite. With *The Blue Suite*, this is called 'Kind of Sketchy' – an obvious reference to *Kind of Blue* and *Sketches of Spain*. With *Luminosity*, the linking piece is called 'Orchestral Dominances'. These short sections serve to integrate the other movements but also serve as a commentary on the work as a whole.

There is a conscious referencing throughout *The Blue Suite* to Miles Davis' recordings, a kind of doffing of a cap, as with 'Kind of Sketchy' and its vaguely Spanish feel reminiscent of the famous Davis/Evans collaboration. However, even more important to Collier is the imperative to make jazz from the simplest materials, which was how he understood *Kind of Blue*. And there are other echoes perhaps – the brooding long notes of James Allsopp's bass clarinet, hinting at Bennie Maupin's contribution to *Bitches Brew* on 'Kind of Sketchy' and Steve Waterman's bravura trumpet recalling Miles himself on 'All Kinds'. The first part of *The Blue Suite* offers a taster of each of the different sections that will be given expanded readings later in the work. This approach does not only give the work a sense of structure; it also exposes the very architecture of the work for the listener.

The next section allows for more expansive soloing and adds 'Kind of Freddie' (a reference to 'Freddie Freeloader'). When the full versions make their appearance, they do so not so much as old friends but as old friends seen in a new light. Art Themen's tenor solo on the second 'Kind of Green' is set up by Roger Dean's delicate piano and emerges with all the fractured romanticism of which Themen is so capable. Ed Speight's solo guitar on 'Kind of Freddie' then leads into the beautifully voiced, loping big band theme. Allsopp's bass clarinet is again strategically placed to add a darker, ironic colour to the piece. Roy Babbington's bass opens the return of 'Kind of So What' before a stabbing brass riff appears along with the tune's original melody and some particularly strong playing from Graeme Blevins on tenor and from Mark Bassey, who improvises freely on trombone over a subtly shifting rhythm section, his solo punctuated by that same brass riff. 'All Kinds' follows with a solo from John Marshall and a staccato but strongly rhythmic solo from Waterman and some acerbic alto from Andy Panayi before the final reprise of 'Kind of Sketchy'.

Luminosity is organized on similar lines. The ensemble, riff-led, almost Basie-like 'Orchestral Dominances' bookends first 'Yellow Hymn' and Above Deep Water' and then 'Jardin D'Amour' and 'Blue Monolith'. Each of the main sections begins with a brief *cadenza* or duet – Trevor Tomkins and Marshall on percussion on 'Yellow Hymn', Babbington on 'Above Deep Water', Panayi on flute duetting with Speight on 'Jardin D'Amour', Dean with Tayloresque flourishes on 'Blue Monolith'. Each tune is then expanded to allow for a series of three or four solos.

The opening of 'Yellow Hymn' with its Satie-like theme might well be one of the most beautiful things Collier ever wrote. It unfolds into an ensemble piece noteworthy for some graceful trumpet from Martin Shaw set against some perfectly poised comping from Dean. Themen's soprano is suitably serpentine, whilst Speight's chiming guitar melody seems to sit inside the rhythms of Babbington, Marshall and Tomkins only in turn to be enveloped by the brass and woodwinds. By contrast, 'Above Deep Water' is menacing and dark in its opening before shifting pace and opening out with Panayi's alto against two contrasting riffs from different sections of the horns. The mood shifts dramatically at various points – a romantic piano trio interlude and a brief descent into chaos. If there are two instrumental colours that stand out on both suites, it would be Panayi's flute – notable on both 'Kind of Sketchy' and 'Kind of Green' – and Allsopp's bass clarinet. The flute opens 'Jardin D'Amour', whilst bass clarinet closes the movement. But what is most striking is how these improvisations intertwine and seem so integral to the splendidly lyrical composition. The same must be said of 'Blue Monolith'. It begins like a kind of freeform *Rhapsody in Blue* with Dean's piano before a Basie-ish riff sets in offering ample space for the contributions of both Blevins and Waterman. The horn interjections also recall both Basie and Ellington but the way that Waterman and Blevins duet – trading phrases and crossing swords – is responsible for one of the finest big band moments on *The Last Suites*. With Collier, it was first and always about the music and that is ultimately his legacy – whether in education, writing or composing. *Luminosity* is simultaneously a valediction and a vindication.

I concluded my *All About Jazz* review:

> Both suites unfold elegantly through a series of contrasting moods that are shaped artfully by – and shape artfully – the contributions of the musicians. The thought that this music could be heard again but differently is one to ponder. The likelihood that that probably won't happen is quite poignant. That said, if epitaph there must be, *Luminosity* is an exceptional commemoration of a creative life well and boldly lived (Heining 2014).

Notes

1. 'If one is in the possession of a theory that explains why false consciousness is necessary, then one can pass immediately, without the addition of any extraneous value judgment, to a negative evaluation on the object that makes such consciousness necessary and to a positive evaluation on action rationally directed at removing it' (Bhaskar 1991: 155–56).

2. If Graham Collier – and those other artists who swim against the tide – had a theme song, then it surely would be Gil Scott-Heron's 'The Revolution Will Not Be Televised' – 'The revolution will not be televised/Will not be televised/Will not be televised/Will not be televised/The revolution will be no re-run brothers/The revolution will be live'. In contrast, I suggest that the theme song of the British jazz establishment including its print media would be the Bee Gees' 'Stayin' Alive' – 'Life goin' nowhere, somebody help me/Somebody help me, yeah/Life goin' nowhere, somebody help me, yeah/I'm stayin' alive/Ah, ha, ha, ha, stayin' alive, stayin' alive/Ah, ha, ha, ha, stayin' alive'.

Bibliography

Adams, S. 1988. "Review of *Something British Made in Hong Kong*." *Jazz Journal* (April): 28.
Allen, C. 2011. "Graham Collier - Interview by Clifford Allen, January 16th 2011." http://paristransatlantic.com/magazine/interviews/collier.html
Andrew, G. 1988. "Review of *Something British Made in Hong Kong*." *Time Out*, 20–27 January: 39.
Ashton, B. 1993. *News from NYJO* (Autumn): 6.
Atkins, R. 1972. "Graham Collier at the Shaw Theatre." *The Guardian*, 11 May: 12.
—1976. "The jazz hustlers." *The Guardian*, 16 October: 8.
Bhaskar, R. 1991. "Social theory and moral philosophy." In *Philosophy and the Idea of Freedom*, 145–61. Oxford: Blackwell.
Bird, C. 1967a. "A whole scene going at Barry." *Melody Maker*, 26 August: 6.
—1967b. "How I learned to stop worrying and live with the avant garde." *Melody Maker*, 16 December: 6.
—1972. "Review of *Wheel of Dreams*." *Melody Maker*, 24 June: 58.
Blain, B. 1968. "Truly a great performance by Collier's Dozen." *Morning Star*, 18 July: 2.
Bostrell, P. 1973. "Love and all that jazz." *Lunch* 20 (May): 4–6.
Bourdieu, P. 1993. *The Field of Cultural Production*. Cambridge: Polity.
—1998. *The State Nobility: Elite Schools in the Field of Power*. Cambridge: Polity.
Bowlby, J. 1967. *Child Care and the Growth of Love*. Harmondsworth: Pelican.
Brown, R. 1970. "Review of *Songs For My Father*." *Jazz Journal* (August): 29.
—1971. "Review of *Mosaics*." *Jazz Journal* (June): 34.
—1972. "Review of *Wheel of Dreams*." *Jazz Journal* (June): 14–15.
—1973. "Jazz views of Shakespeare." *Jazz Journal* (June): 8–9.
—1974. "Review of *Inside Jazz*." *Into Jazz* (February): 39.
Brown, S. 1974. "Jazz and the philistines." *Punch*, 23 January: 141.
Carr, I. [1973] 2008. *Music Outside: Contemporary Jazz in Britain*. London: Latimer.
Carroll, J. M. 2007. *A Concise History of Hong Kong*. Plymouth, MD: Rowan & Littlefield.
Carter, J. 1970. "Review of *Songs For My Father*." *Crescendo* (July): 29.
Christie, I. 1964. Review of Graham Collier Septet debut, Woodstock Gallery (Collier archive).
Clayton, J. 1968. "Jazz festival." *Birmingham Post*, 4 September: 8.
Clayton, P. 1968. "Patronage stomp." *Sunday Telegraph* 14 July, 24.
Cockburn, C. 1973. *The Devil's Decade*. London: Sidgwick & Jackson.
Collier, G. 1963. "Forcing ground for talent." *Crescendo* (April): 35–36.
—1965. "Review of *Basie Picks the Winners*." *Crescendo* (December): 15.
—c. 1967. "The Collier Sextet in schools" (Collier archive).
—1968a. "Concert programme notes for *Contrapuntal Forms*." July 1968.
—1968b. *Radio Times*, 4 July: 41.
—1968c. Sleeve notes to *Down Another Road*, Fontana SFJL 922.

—1970a. Sleeve notes to *Songs For My Father*, Fontana 6309006.
—1970b. Notes to *Smoke Blackened Walls And Curlews*.
—1973a. *Inside Jazz*. London: Quartet.
—1973b. Sleeve notes to *Portraits*, Saydisc SDL244.
—1974. Report to British Council, 13 November.
—1975a. *Jazz: A Student's and Teacher's Guide*. Cambridge: Cambridge University Press.
—1975b. *Compositional Devices*. Berklee: Boston.
—1976a. *Cleo and John: A Biography of the Dankworths*. London: Quartet.
—1976b. Sleeve notes for *New Conditions*, GCM761.
—1977. Sleeve notes for *Symphony of Scorpions*, GCM773.
—1978a. Letter to *Jazz Journal*, May 1978: 78.
—1978b. Sleeve notes to *The Day of the Dead*, GCMD783/4.
—1983a. "Jazz in Finland: An exclusive report from Graham Collier." *Set to Music*, January/February: 7.
—1983b. "Jazz in Finland: Graham Collier sends his second exclusive report." *Set to Music*, March/April: 6.
—1983c. Programme notes for *Hoarded Dreams*, Bracknell Festival, 20 June.
—1985a. "Updating the Dream", c. February 1985 (Collier archive).
—1985b. "Brave New World? A personal opinion by Graham Collier." *Wire* 15 (May): 8.
—1988. *Jazz Workshop: The Blues*. London: Universal.
—1992. "Lowry, jazz, and *The Day of the Dead*." In *Swinging the Maelstrom: New Perspectives on Malcolm Lowry*, ed. S. Grace, 243–48. Montreal: McGill-Queens University Press.
—1993. "Jazz goes to college." *Jazz on CD* (August): 39–40.
—1994. "Jazz education in America." *Jazz Changes* 1/1 (Spring): 2–18.
—1995. *Interaction: Opening up the Jazz Ensemble*. Mainz: Advance Music.
—2000a. Sleeve notes to reissue of *The Day of the Dead*. Disconforme Disc 1975 CD.
—2000b. Sleeve notes to Disconforme release of *Midnight Blue*. Disc 1972 CD.
—2001. Sleeve notes to *Winter Oranges*, JPVP126CD.
—2003. Sleeve notes to Jazzprint release of *The Third Colour*, JPVP129CD.
—2005. Sleeve notes to *Workpoints*, Cuneiform RUNE CD 213/214.
—2009a. *The Jazz Composer: Moving Music off the Paper*. London: Northway.
—2009b. Sleeve notes to *Directing 14 Jackson Pollocks*, Jazzcontinuum CD.
Conley, B. 1976. "Cleo – an honest appraisal." *Gay News*.
Cook, R. 1985. "Graham Collier International Band (*Hoarded Dreams*)." *Wire* 15 (May): 8.
Cooke, J. 1967. "Review of *Deep Dark Blue Centre*." *Jazz Monthly* (August): 23–24.
Cooper, R. C., and R. N. Aslin. 1994. "Developmental differences in infant attention to the spectral properties of infant-directed speech." *Child Development* 65/6 (December): 1663–677.
Cotterell, R. 1985. "Graham Collier: composer." *The Wire* 14 (April): 43.
Crescendo. 1966. "New Collier Side-man." *Crescendo* (June): 3–4.
Dawbarn, B. 1969. "Review of *Down Another Road*." *Melody Maker*, 30 August: 19.
Dean, R. T. 1992. *New Structures in Jazz and Improvised Music since 1960*. Milton Keynes: Open University Press.
Dewey, J. 2005. *Art as Experience*. New York: Perigree.
Ehrenzweig, A. 1975. *The Psychoanalysis of Artistic Vision and Hearing*, 3rd ed. London: Sheldon.

Fahey, B., and G. Collier. 1963. "Two views of Kentonia." *Crescendo* (December): 4–5.
Farbey, R. 2010. *The Music of Ian Carr: A Critical Discography*. London: Farbey.
Faulkner, W. 1991. *Wild Palms*. London: Picador.
Feather, L. 1964. "Review of *Jazz in the Classroom VII*." *Down Beat*, 5 December: 24.
Fordham, J. 1973. "Review of *Portraits*." *Time Out*, 24 August: 45.
—1974. "Review of Stan Tracey *Alone at Wigmore Hall* and Graham Collier Music *Darius*." *Time Out*, 13 December: 47.
—1983. "Bracknell Jazz Festival." *The Guardian*, 4 July: 11.
—1999. "Jazz Week" (interview with Graham Collier). *The Guardian*, 26 May: 15.
—2004. "Graham Collier." *The Guardian*, 19 November.
Forrest, A. 1977. "Authors baht 'at" (review of Ilkley Literature Festival). *Financial Times*, 21 June: 4.
—1978. "The Day of the Dead" (review of QEH performance). *Financial Times*, 20 June: 17.
Fox, C. 1967. Sleeve notes for *Deep Dark Blue Centre*. Deram.
—1968. "Themes and solos." *New Statesman*, 22 March: 392.
—1969a. *Jazz in Perspective*. London: BBC.
—1969b. "Review of *Down Another Road*." *Gramophone* (November): 849–50.
—1970. *Jazz Today*, 16 June. BBC Radio 3 broadcast.
—1973. "That Shakespearean rag." *New Statesman*, 18 May: 742.
—1977a. "Jazz notes" (review of *New Conditions*). *Gay News*, 24 March–6 April: 28.
—1977b. "Review of *Symphony of Scorpions*." *Gay News*, 6-19 October: 28.
—1977c. "What a lark." *New Statesman*, 28 January: 132.
—1978. "Review of *The Day of the Dead*." *Gay News*, 21 September–4 October: 34.
—1983. "Sleight-of-hand" (review of Bracknell Jazz Festival). *New Statesman*, 8 July: 29.
Fraser, N. 2013. "A triple movement?" *New Left Review* 81 (May–June): 119–32.
Freiberg, M. 1963. Sleeve notes to *Jazz in the Classroom Vol VIII*. Berklee Records 8.
Freire, P. 1974. *Education: The Practice of Freedom*. London: Writers and Readers Publishing Cooperative.
—1980. *The Pedagogy of the Oppressed*. Harmondsworth: Penguin.
Garnham, N. 2000. *Emancipation, the Media, and Modernity*. Oxford: Oxford University Press.
Garrick, M. 2010. *Dusk Fire: Jazz in English Hands*. Reading: Springdale.
Gelly, D. 1983. "Just Jazz" (review of Bracknell Festival). *Observer*, 10 July: 30.
Gibbs, M. 1962. Sleeve notes to *Jazz in the Classroom Vol VII*. Berklee Records 7.
Glyn, A. 2006. *Capitalism Unleashed: Finance, Globalization and Welfare*. Oxford: Oxford University Press.
Godbolt, J. 1985. "Free and gay." *Jazz at Ronnie Scott's* (May/June): 8–9.
Goldberg, J. 1980. *Jazz Masters of the Fifties*. Boston: Da Capo.
Gonzales, I. 2017. "Duterte's bloody war continues apace." *New Internationalist*, January/February: 10.
Grace, Sherrill, ed. 1992. *Swinging the Maelstrom: New Perspectives on Malcolm Lowry*. Montreal: McGill-Queen's University Press.
Green, B. 1968. "Money for improvising." *Observer* review, 24 March: 32.
Harrison, M. 1978. "Graham Collier" (review of *The Day of the Dead* – QEH). *The Times*, 4 October: 19.

—1985. "Graham Collier International Big Band" (review of Camden Festival). *Jazz Express* (April): 15.
Haskins, C. 1989. "Kant and the autonomy of art." *Journal of Aesthetics and Art Criticism* 47/1 (Winter): 43–55.
Hazell, E. 1995. *Berklee: The First Fifty Years*. Boston: Berklee Press.
Heining, D. 1998a. "A very honourable guy." *Avant* 8 (Summer): 36–37.
—1998b. "Learning to wave." *Avant* 9 (Autumn): 6–7.
—2001. "Review of *Midnight Blue/Darius/New Conditions/The Day of the Dead/Symphony of Scorpions/Something British Made in Hong Kong*." *Jazzwise* (November): 46.
—2005. "Parallel universe." *Jazz UK* 64 (July/August): 16–17.
—2007a. "Review of *Hoarded Dreams*." *Jazzwise* (February): 59.
—2007b. "Big it up." *Jazzwise* (February): 36–38.
—2009. *George Russell: An American Composer*. Lanham, MD: Scarecrow.
—2010. "A dance to the music of time." *Jazzwise* 146 (October): 30–32.
—2012a. *Trad Dads, Dirty Boppers and Free Fusioneers: British Jazz 1960–1975*. Sheffield: Equinox.
—2012b. "Review of *Triton*." *Jazz UK*. August/September: 28.
—2014. "Review of *Luminosity* CD." *All About Jazz*, 14 November. https://www.allaboutjazz.com/luminosity-by-duncan-heining.php
Henriques, K. 1975. "Academic blues." *Financial Times*, 9 October: 3.
—1976. "Cleo, John and Coltrane." *Financial Times*, 13 November: 14.
—1977. "Review of *Symphony of Scorpions, Intertwine, Cycles, On Loan with Gratitude*." *Financial Times*, 27 October: 3.
—1979. "Review of *The Day of the Dead*." *Jazz Forum* 60 (April): 49.
Holden, L. 2003. *Vauxhall Motors and the Luton Economy 1900–2002*. Martelsham: Boydell & Brewer.
Hollis, P. 1997. *Jennie: A Life*. Oxford: Oxford University Press.
Houston, B. 1967. "Collier – an arranger of care and skill." *Melody Maker*, 1 July: 11.
Howes, K. 1976. "Graham Collier: Keith Howes meets the gay 'jazz composer of the future'." *Gay News*, 23 September–6 October: 19–20.
Hyder, K. 1973. "Collier: hustler supreme." *Melody Maker*, 13 October: 20.
James, M. 1970. "Review of *Songs For My Father*." *Jazz Monthly* (October): 12–13.
Jenkins, H. 1979. *The Culture Gap: An Experience of Government and the Arts*. London: Marion Boyers.
Jewell, D. 1967a. "School of surprise: Jazz LPs reviewed by Derek Jewell." *Sunday Times*, 1 October: 41.
—1967b. "British Bull Year." *Sunday Times*, 3 September: 28.
—1968. "World asunder" (review of *Contrapuntal Forms*). *Sunday Times*, July: 48.
—1975. "Conversation piece" (review of *Café Blues* and *Midnight Blue*). *Sunday Times*, 7 December: 39.
—1985. "Music in the name of jazz." *Sunday Times*, 24 March: 41.
Johnson, B. 2002. "Jazz as cultural practice." In *The Cambridge Companion to Jazz*, ed. M. Cooke and D. Horn, 96–113. Cambridge: Cambridge University Press.
Jones, M. 1976. "Married to jazz." *Melody Maker*, 11 December: 25.
Jones, N. 2009. "Graham Collier: *Directing 14 Jackson Pollocks*." *All About Jazz*, 11 August.

Kahneman, D. 1973. *Attention and Effort*. Englewood Cliffs, NJ: Prentice-Hall.
Kendall, P. M. 1973. *The Art of Biography*. London: George Allen & Unwin.
—2013. Biography entry in *Encyclopaedia Britannica*. http://www.britannica.com/EBchecked/topic/65924/biography
Kennard, D. 1968. "Getting jazz organized." *Peace News*, 19 April: 11.
Kington, M. 1967a. "Jazz in the open air." *The Times*, 14 August: 5.
—1967b. "Jazz to enjoy at home." *The Times*, 26 August: 7.
—1967c. "Award for jazz composer." *The Times*, 7 September: 8.
—1968. "Jazz work on a large scale." *The Times*, 19 March: 11.
Kirschenbaum, H., and V. L. Henderson. 1996. *The Carl Rogers' Reader: Selections from the Lifetime Work of America's Pre-eminent Psychologist, Author of On Becoming a Person and A Way of Being*. New York: Houghton Mifflin.
Kyaga, S. *et al*. 2012. "Mental illness, suicide and creativity: 40-year prospective total population study." *Journal of Psychiatric Research*: 1–8.
Lange, A. 1979. "Review of *Symphony of Scorpions/The Day of the Dead*." *Downbeat*, 22 March: 20–21.
Larsen, S. E. 2004. "Throw away your mind." In *Reinventions of the Novel: Histories and Aesthetics of a Protean Genre*, ed. K.-M. Simonsen, M. Ping Huang and M. Rosendahl Thomsen, 49–64. Amsterdam/New York: Editions Rodopi B.V.
Lee, D. 1976. "The Dankworth saga." *Punch* (October): 596–97.
Lopes, P. 2002. *The Rise of a Jazz Art World*. Cambridge: Cambridge University Press.
Lowry, M. 1990. *Under the Volcano*. London: Picador.
Lucklin, B. 1973. "Jazz on the dole." *New Society* 6 (December): 610.
Luton News. 1963. "Luton man to tour with Jimmy Dorsey." 18 April: 1.
—n.d. "Graham (jazz arranger) is set for states." (Collier archive).
Marcuse, H. [1978] 2003. *The Aesthetic Dimension: Toward a Critique of Marxist Aesthetics*. London: Beacon.
Marshall, J. 1988. "Review of *Sweet Fat*." *The Times*, 19 September: 20.
Maslow, A. 1954. *Motivation and Personality*. New York: Harper.
Massarik, J. 1983. "Sing along with Bobby – and they did." *Evening Standard*, 5 July: 22.
—1985a. "Difficult dreams." *Evening Standard*, 19 March: 26.
—1985b. Letter to *Wire*, issue 17 (July): 53.
Mathieu, B. 1964. "Review of *Jazz in the Classroom Vol VIII*." *Down Beat* 24 (September): 25–26.
McLean, I. 1961. "Berklee bound." *Jazz News*, 25 February: 16.
McRae, B. 1973. "Review of *Portraits*." *Jazz Journal* (September): 28.
—1976a. "Review of *Midnight Blue*." *Jazz Journal* (January): 29.
—1976b. "Review of *Lysis Live*." *Jazz Journal* (December): 26.
—1977a. "Review of *New Conditions*." *Jazz Journal* (July): 41.
—1977b. "Review of *Cycles*." *Jazz Journal* (October): 41.
—1977c. "Review of *Intertwine*." *Jazz Journal* (October): 52.
—1977d. "Review of *Symphony of Scorpions*." *Jazz Journal* (October): 40–41.
—1978. "Review of *The Day of the Dead*." *Jazz Journal* (September): 36.
—1985. "Camden Jazz Week" (review of *Hoarded Dreams*). *Jazz Journal* (May): 22–23.
Melody Maker. 1971. "Mean, moody and magnificent" (review of Montreux Jazz Festival), 26 June: 24, 34, 41.

Morgan, A. 1967. "Review of *Deep Dark Blue Centre*." *Gramophone* (August): 133.
—1971. "Review of *Mosaics*." *Gramophone* (November): 923.
—1976. "Cleo and John – a biography of the Dankworths." *Jazz Journal*, October: 29.
Morton, B., and R. Cook. 2010. *The Penguin Jazz Guide: The History of the Music in the 1001 Best Albums*. London: Penguin.
Murph, J. 2010. "Rhapsody in rainbow: jazz and the queer aesthetic." *Jazz Times*, 1 December. https://jazztimes.com/features/rhapsody-in-rainbow-jazz-and-the-queer-aesthetic/
Newman, B. 1947a. "The Ideographic Picture," taken from the catalogue for an exhibition of Abstract Expressionist art at the Betty Parsons Gallery, New York.
—1947b. "The first man was an artist." *Tiger's Eye* 1 (October): 59–60.
Nicholson, S. 1988. "Review of *Something British Made in Hong Kong*." *Wire* 50 (April): 67.
O'Reagan, J. 2009. Sleeve notes to BGO Reissue of *Darius/Midnight Blue/New Conditions*, BGOCD895.
Pearce, D. 2013. *Dizzy Gillespie Was At My Wedding*. Richmond, UK: Bill Scott & Iain Hannah.
Priestley, B. 1968. "Graham Collier." *Jazz Monthly* (May): 13.
—1982. *Mingus: A Critical Biography*. London: Quartet.
Private Eye. 2002. "Educashun news." *Private Eye* 1045, 11 January: 7.
Race, S. 1963. "Review of *Jazz in the Classroom VII*." *Crescendo* (December): 20.
Rancière, J. 2011. *The Politics of Aesthetics: The Distribution of the Sensible*. London: Continuum.
Rattenbury, K. 1996. "Review of *Adam's Marble*." *Crescendo & Jazz Music* (August/September): 20.
Reynolds, G. 1988. "Review of *Sweet Fat*." *Daily Telegraph*, 20 September: 14.
Robson, A. 2012. "Review of *The Day of the Dead*." *Jazzwise* (February): 46.
Russell, G. 2001. *Lydian Chromatic Concept of Tonal Organization*. Brookline, MA: Concept.
Rycroft, C. 1995. *Critical Dictionary of Psychoanalysis*. London: Penguin.
Shipton, A. 2004. "Alyn Shipton at the South Bank." *The Times*, 23 November.
—2007. Sleeve notes to BGO Records reissue of *Down Another Road*, *Songs For My Father* and *Mosaics*. BGO CD767.
Speake, M. 2010. Interview with Pete Hurt. https://www.martinspeake.com/pete-hurt
Spender, S. 2000. "Introduction." In *Under the Volcano*, ed. M. Lowry, vii–xxvi. London: HarperCollins.
The Stage. 1980. "Barnet aims high with 'spy' musical." 10 April: 2.
Storr, A. 1992. *Music of the Mind*. London: HarperCollins.
The Sun. 1967. "Jazz grant." 31 August.
Temperer, B. 1974. "Review of *Portraits*." *Coda* (December): 16–17.
Tomkins, L. 1964. "Review of Graham Collier Septet debut Woodstock Gallery." *Crescendo* (May): 26.
Troon, A. 2007. "Review of *Hoarded Dreams*." *Jazz Review* (June/July): 30.
—2009. "Review of *Directing 14 Jackson Pollocks*." *Jazz Journal* (October): 21.
Vacher, P. 2011. "Michael Garrick Obituary", 15 November. https://www.the guardian.com/music/2011/nov/15/Michael-garrick
Voce, S. 1975. "76 trombones." *Jazz Journal* (April): 20.
—1977. "Gay jazz releases." *Jazz Journal* (August): 56.
—1978. "Mincing with some barbecue." *Jazz Journal* (February): 24.
—1985. "It Don't Mean a Thing." *Jazz Journal* (June): 9.

von Bertalanffy, L. 1973. *General Systems Theory*. Harmondsworth: Penguin.
Wade, R. 2006. "Choking the south." *New Left Review* 38 (March–April): 115–27.
Walters, M. 1971. "Supplying the musical bricks." *Sounds*, 27 March.
Webb, F. 1994. *A History of Hong Kong*. Harmondsworth: HarperCollins.
Welch, C. 1967. "Graham Collier Big Band." *Melody Maker*, 29 July: 4.
—1978. "Review of *New Conditions*." *Melody Maker*, 7 January: 18.
Wickes, J. 1999. *Innovations in British Jazz*. Chelmsford: Soundworld.
Wilkinson, E. 1939. *The Town that was Murdered*. London: Left Book Club.
Williams, M. 1970. *The Jazz Tradition*. Oxford: Oxford University Press.
Williams, R. 1970. "Strong solos on Collier's slight themes." *Melody Maker*, 13 June: 26.
—1971. "Collier loosens up." *Melody Maker*, 8 May: 11.
—1972. "Collier's new music." *Melody Maker*, 18 March: 16.
—1973. "Collier's confection" (review of *Portraits*). *Melody Maker*, 28 July: 42.
—1983. "Review of Bracknell Festival 1983." *The Times*, 5 July: 16.
Wilmer, V. 1968. "Review of *Workpoints*." *Down Beat*, 16 May: 36–37.
Wordie, J. 2016. "What sparked Hong Kong's Double Tenth riots." *South China Morning Post*, 7 October. https://tinyurl.com/2025663-riots.

Mosaics **Interviews and Correspondence**

Ackerley, Chris. Email interview, 16 April 2015.
Ashberry, Elsie. Interview, 21 August 2014.
Barratt, Issie. Email interview, 2 January 2017.
Bassey, Mark. Interview, 20 November 2014.
Beckett, Harry. Interview, August 2008.
Betjeman, Paul. Email correspondence, 22 February 2015.
Biscoe, Chris. Email interview, 7 September 2014.
Bonati, Roberto. Interview, 1 October 2015.
Brown, Ashley. Interview, 8 December 2016.
Burton, Gary. Email interview, 29 July 2014.
Castle, Geoff. Interview, 31 August 2014.
Cawley, Tom. Interview, 21 November 2014.
Cohen, David. Interview, 10 January 2017.
Collier, Graham. Interview, June 2005.
Collier, Graham. Email correspondence, 1 December 2008.
Collier, Graham. Interview, January 2009.
Collier, Graham. Interview, August 2010.
Dean, Roger. Interview, 14 July 2014.
Dean, Roger. Email correspondence, 31 July 2015.
Dean, Roger. Email correspondence, 20 December 2016.
Dean, Roger. Email correspondence, 15 April 2017.
Evans, Nick. Email interview, 9 October 2014.
Findikoglu, Emin. Email interview, 29 January 2015.
Fishwick, Steve. Interview, 23 March 2015.
Foster, Dan. Email correspondence, 17 November 2014.
Fraser, Hugh. Interview, 1 June 2015.
Freeman-Attwood, Jonathan. Interview, 17 March 2015.
Gamlen, Amy. Email interview, 17 November 2014.
Gibbs, Mike. Interview, 7 August 2014.
Gibbs, Mike. Email correspondence, 22 January 2017.
Giddings, Alan. Interview, 3 October 2014.
Gill, John. Email correspondence, 13 August 2014.

Gill, John. Email interview, 15 January 2015.
Gill, John. Email correspondence, 2 February 2015.
Gill, John. Interview, 12 March 2015.
Gill, John. Interview, 19 June 2015.
Gill, John. Email correspondence, 5 December 2016.
Gladdish, Martin. Interview, 16 March 2015.
Gojkovic, Dusko. Email interview, 23 September 2014.
Grace, Sherrill. Email interview, 16 April 2015.
Griffiths, Malcom. Interview, 14 January 2017.
Haslam, George. Interview, 10 January 2017.
Hiseman, Jon. Interview, 19 November 2016.
Kelly, Adrian. Email interview, 14 March 2015.
Marshall, John. Interview, 5 August 2014.
Martinelli, Francesco. Interview, 28 July 2016.
Naylor, Hattie. Interview, 24 January 2017.
Nichols, Keith. Email correspondence, 13 November 2014.
Parker, Evan. Interview, September 2012.
Parker, Evan. Email correspondence, 15 May 2015.
Riordan, Pte. Paddy. Interview, 19 August 2014.
Roms, Dr Heike. Email interview, 12 February 2015.
Shipton, Alyn. Email correspondence, 26 February 2017.
Shipton, Alyn. Email correspondence, 26 April 2017.
Speake, Martin. Interview, 13 October 2014.
Speight, Ed. Interview, 27 August 2014.
Sulzmann, Stan. Email interview, 29 March 2015.
Sydor, Bob. Interview, 3 January 2017.
Themen, Art. Interview, 20 November 2014.
Tomkins, Trevor. Interview, 9 September 2014.
Turkenburg, Wouter. Email interview, 19 January 2017.
Wakeman, Alan. Interview, 8 September 2014.
Wakeman, Alan. Email correspondence, 17 February 2015.
Warren, Geoff. Interview, 9 August 2014.
Warren, Geoff. Email correspondence, 31 July 2015.
Waterman, Steve. Interview, 6 October 2014.
Webb, John. Email interview, 29 March 2015.

Appendix 1

Graham Collier Discography

N.B. only original and most recent catalogue numbers are given. All compositions Graham Collier unless otherwise stated.

Key for abbreviations: alto flute (afl), alto saxophone (as), baritone saxophone (bs), bass (b), bass clarinet (bcl), bass guitar (bg), bass trombone (btb), cello (clo), clarinet (cl), composer (comp), conductor (cond), drums (d), electric bass (el-b), electric piano (el-p), electronics (elec), euphonium (euph), flugelhorn (flhn), flute (f), french horn (frhn), guitar (g), keyboards (ky), leader (ldr), marimba (mar), narration (narr), oboe (ob), percussion (perc), piano (p), soprano saxophone (ss), synthesizer (syn), tenor saxophone (ts), trombone (tb), trumpet (t), tuba (tba), vibraphone (vib), violin (vn), viola (vla), voice (v).

Graham Collier Septet – *Deep Dark Blue Centre* (DML 1005/SML 1005/BGO CD 822).

Blue Walls (b) (Charlie Mariano), El Miklós (a), Hirayoshi Suite (b), Crumblin' Cookie (b), Conversations (a), Deep Dark Blue Centre (a).

(a) Graham Collier (b), Kenny Wheeler (t, flhn), Mike Gibbs (tb), Dave Aaron (as, f), Karl Jenkins (bs, ob), Philip Lee (g), John Marshall (d). Rec. 15 and 18 January 1967.

(b) Harry Beckett (t, flhn) replaces Wheeler. Rec. 24 January 1967.

Graham Collier Sextet – *Down Another Road* (Fontana SFJL 922/ BGO CD767).

Down Another Road, Danish Blue, The Barley Mow, Aberdeen Angus, Lullaby for a Lonely Child (Jenkins), Molewrench.

Graham Collier (b), Harry Beckett (flhn), Stan Sulzmann (as, ts), Nick Evans (tb), Karl Jenkins (ob, p), John Marshall (d). Rec. 21–22 March 1969.

Graham Collier Music (Featuring Harry Beckett) – *Songs For My Father* (Fontana 6309006/BGO CD767).

Song One (Seven-Four), Song Two (Ballad), Song Three (Nine-Eight Blues), Song Four (Waltz in Four-Four), Song Five (Rubato), Song Six (Dirge), Song Seven (Four-Four Figured).

Graham Collier (b), Harry Beckett (t, flhn), Alan Wakeman (ts, ss), Bob Sydor (ts, as), John Taylor (p), John 'Chick' Webb (d). Guests: Tony Roberts (ts), Alan Skidmore (ts, ss), Derek Wadsworth (tb), Philip Lee (g). Rec. 19–21 February 1970.

Graham Collier Music (Featuring Harry Beckett) – *Mosaics* (Phillips 6308051/BGO CD767).

Mosaics – Part One: Theme 1, Part Two: Themes 4, 2 and 3, Part Three: Themes 4 and 6, Part Four: Themes 2 and 8.*

Graham Collier (b), Harry Beckett (t, flhn), Alan Wakeman (ts, ss), Bob Sydor (ts, as), Geoff Castle (p), John 'Chick' Webb (d). Rec. The Torrington pub, London, 8 December 1970.

Graham Collier Music (Featuring Harry Beckett) – *The Alternate Mosaics* (BGO CD822).

The Alternate Mosaics – Part One: Theme 1, Part Two: Theme 2, Part Three: Theme 6, Part Four: Theme 8.

Graham Collier (b), Harry Beckett (t, flhn), Alan Wakeman (ts, ss), Bob Sydor (ts, as), Geoff Castle (p), John 'Chick' Webb (d). Rec. The Torrington pub, London, 12 December 1970.

Graham Collier Music – *Portraits* (Saydisc SDL244/BGO CD 822).

And Now For Something Completely Different Part One, And Now For Something Completely Different Part Two; Portraits 1.

Graham Collier (b), Dick Pearce (flhn), Pete Hurt (as), Ed Speight (g), Geoff Castle (p), John 'Chick' Webb (d). Rec. 16–17 November 1972.

Graham Collier Music – *Darius* (Mosaic GCM741/BGO CD895).

Darius Part One, Part Two, Part Three, Part Four; New Dawn.

Graham Collier (b), Harry Beckett (t, flhn), Derek Wadsworth (tb), Ed Speight (g), Geoff Castle (p), John 'Chick' Webb (d). Rec. 13 March 1974.

Graham Collier Music – *Midnight Blue* (Mosaic GCM751/BGOCD895).

Midnight Blue; Adam; Cathedra.

Graham Collier (b), Harry Beckett (t, flhn), Derek Wadsworth (tb), Ed Speight (g), Roger Dean (p), John 'Chick' Webb (d). Rec. 17 February 1975.

Graham Collier Music – Jazz Lecture Concert (Resources of Music 0521 205638).

History; Improvisation; Instruments & Individuality; The Complete Performance (*Darius* Part One only).

Graham Collier (b), Harry Beckett (t, flhn), Derek Wadsworth (tb), Ed Speight (g), Roger Dean (p), John 'Chick' Webb (d). Rec. 1975.

Graham Collier Music – Jazz Lecture Concert (Resources of Music 0521 205638).

Improvising From a Basic Motif (Over a Tapped Pulse); More Complex Improvising From A Basic Motif (Over A Pedal Note And Pattern); Several Musicians Using a Pre-Arranged Form To Illustrate Simple Arrangements And Motif Improvising; Improvising From A Basic Motif Over A Basic Blues Progression; Chordal Improvising (Including Passing Notes) Over A Basic Blues Progression; Several Musicians Playing Short Pre-Arranged Riffs And Answering Solo Fills On A Basic Blues Sequence; Chordal Improvising (With Passing Notes) Over a Common Bass Pattern; Chordal Improvising On A Common Popular Song Sequence With Backings And Riffs Made Up By The Other Musicians; Illustration Of Imaginative Small Group Arranging. Opening to Portraits 1; Improvising Using Three Scales Commonly Used Over A G7 Chord; Improvising Using The Dorian Mode; Improvising On Blues With A Complex Time Structure – 'Song III'; Improvising On Contemporary Harmonies – '*Mosaics* II'; Improvising On 5/4 Blues; Group Mood Improvisation on 'Ghosts'; Group Freely Improvising With No Pre-Conceived Structure; Soloist Indicating In His Cadenza Which Option He Wishes To Take.

Graham Collier (b), Harry Beckett (t, flhn), Derek Wadsworth (tb), Art Themen (ts), Alan Wakeman (ts, as), Ed Speight (g), Roger Dean (p), John 'Chick' Webb (d). Rec. 1975.

Graham Collier Music – *New Conditions* (Mosaic GCM761/BGOCD895).

New Conditions Introduction, *New Conditions* Part 1&2, *New Conditions* Part 3, *New Conditions* Part 4, *New Conditions* Part 5&6, *New Conditions* Part 7, *New Conditions* Part 8, *New Conditions* Finale.

Graham Collier (b), Harry Beckett, Henry Lowther, Pete Duncan (t, flhn), Malcolm Griffiths (tb), Alan Wakeman, Art Themen (ts, ss), Mike Page (as), Ed Speight (g), Roger Dean (p), John 'Chick' Webb (d), John Mitchell (perc). Rec. 2–3 June 1976.

Graham Collier Music – *Symphony of Scorpions* (Mosaic GCM773/ BGO1028).

Symphony of Scorpions; Forest Path to the Spring.

Graham Collier (b), Harry Beckett, Henry Lowther, Pete Duncan (t, flhn), Malcolm Griffiths (tb), Art Themen (ts, ss), Tony Roberts, Mike Page (saxes), Ed Speight (g), Roger Dean (p), John 'Chick' Webb (d), John Mitchell (perc). Rec. 7 November 1976. (NB 'Forest Path to the Spring' rec. Ronnie Scott Club, 10 March 1977).

Graham Collier Music – *The Day of the Dead* (Mosaic GCMD 783/4/DISC 1975 CD/BGO1028).

Sides 1–3: *The Day of the Dead* – Parts 1&2, Part 3, Part 4, Part 5, Part 6, Parts 7&8.

Side 4: *October Ferry* (original double LP release).
Add *Triptych*; Eridanus, Quanahuac (Disconforme CD release).

Graham Collier (comp, cond), John Carbery (narr), Harry Beckett, Henry Lowther, Pete Duncan (t, flhn), Malcolm Griffiths (tb), Art Themen (ts, ss), Alan Wakeman (ts, ss, bcl), Mike Page (as, f), Ed Speight (g), Roger Dean (p), Roy Babbington (b), John 'Chick' Webb (d), John Mitchell (perc) – Alan Jackson replaces Ashley Brown 'Part 5' only. *The Day of the Dead* and *October Ferry* rec. March/April 1978. 'Eridanus' and 'Quanahuac' rec. 10 March 1977. *Triptych* rec. Ronnie Scott Club, 10 March 1977.

Graham Collier Music – *Something British Made in Hong Kong* (Mosaic GCM 871).

Midsummer Dawn, Whirligig, Mist on Water, Queensbury Rules, Spring Rain, Deserted Funfair.

Graham Collier (comp, ky), Geoff Warren (as, ss, f), Ed Speight (g), Roger Dean (p), Paul Bridge (b), Ashley Brown (d). Rec. December 1985.

Graham Collier/The Jazz Ensemble – *Charles River Fragments* (Boathouse Records BHR004/Jazzprint JPVP123CD).

The Hackney Five; *Charles River Fragments* – Main Melody/Fragments 1-4 repeated/Part 4, Fragments 5 to 7/Guitar Cadenza/Part 7, Fragments 8 to 1 into Part One/Fragments 2 to 8 into Part 8, Fragments 9 to 3 into Part 3, Fragments 4 to 5 into Part 5, Fragments 6 to 9 into Part 9, Fragments 10 to 2 into Part 2, Fragments 3 to 6 into Part 6, Fragments 7 to 10 into Part 10 and Main Melody.

Graham Collier (comp, cond), Henry Lowther, Patrick White, Steve Waterman (t), Hugh Fraser (tb), Bill Mee (btb), Andy Grappy (tba), Art Themen, Mark Lockheart (saxes), Chris Biscoe (bs, cl), Geoff Warren (as, f), Ed Speight (g), Pete Saberton (p), Dudley Phillips (b), John Marshall (d). Rec. 15 May 1994.

Graham Collier/The Jazz Ensemble – *The Third Colour* (ASC CD 28/Jazzprint JPVP129CD).

Three Simple Pieces – One, Two, Three; *Shapes, Colours, Energy* – Shapes, Energy, Shapes & Colours, Energy Squared, Colours; *The Miró Tile* – Mud 1, Mud 2, Mud 3, Ed 1, Ed 2, Mud 6; *The Third Colour* – Groove 1, Groove 2, Groove, 3, Groove 4, Groove 5, Out Blues.

Graham Collier (comp, cond), Ed Sarath (flhn), Steve Waterman, Simon Finch (t), Hugh Fraser, Matt Colman (tb), Oren Marshall (tba), Karlheinz Miklin, Art Themen, Steve Main (saxes), Geoff Warren (as, f), Ed Speight (g), Roger Dean (ky), Andy Cleyndert (b), John Marshall (d). Rec. November 1997.

Graham Collier & The Danish Radio Jazz Orchestra – *Winter Oranges* (Jazzprint JPVP126CD).

Three Simple Pieces – Part One and Part Three; *Winter Oranges Suite* – Blue Spring, Eggshell Summer, Tinted Autumn, Winter Oranges.

Graham Collier (comp, cond), Anders Gustafsson, Benny Rosenfeld, Thomas Fryland, Henrik Bolberg, Thomas Kjærgaard (t, flhn), Vincent Nilsson, Steen Hansen, Kim Aagaard, Ingerid Annette Huseby (tb), Axel Windfeld (btb, tba), Ulfe Markussen (ts, cl, bcl), Tomas Franck (ts, ss), Michael Hove (as, ss, cl), Nikolai Schultz (as, ss, f), Flemming Madsen (bs, bcl), Anders Chico Lindvall (g), Nikolaj Bentzon (p), Thomas Ovesen (b), Søren Frost (d), Ethan Weisgard (perc). Rec. 17 November 2000.

Graham Collier & The Collective – *Bread & Circuses* (Jazzprint JPVP131CD).

Bread & Circuses; *Oxford Palms*.

Graham Collier (comp, cond), Adrian Kelly (t, ldr), Lucy Fisher, Stephanie Dean (vn), Martin Payne (vla), Jenny Tingley (clo), Jeremy Greig, Kieran Hurley (tb), Matthew Savage (euph, tb), Lindsay Vickery, Graeme Blevins, Lee Buddle (saxes), Grant Windsor, Tom O'Halloran (p), Phil Waldron (b), Steve Richter (perc, mar), Hans Drieberg (d, perc). Rec. September 2001.

Graham Collier Dozen – *Workpoints* (Cuneiform Rune 213/214).

CD 1 Deep Dark Blue Centre, The Barley Mow; *Workpoints* – Part One, Part Two, Part Three, Part Four.

Graham Collier (comp, b), Harry Beckett, Kenny Wheeler, Henry Lowther (t, flhn), Chris Smith, Mike Gibbs, John Mumford (tb), Dave Aaron (ts, as, ss, f), John Surman (bs, ss, bcl, p), Karl Jenkins (bs, ss, ob, p), Frank Ricotti (vib, perc), John Marshall (d). Rec. March 1968.

CD 2 *Live in Middelheim* – Little Ben, Under the Pier; Darius – Part One, Part Three, Part Four, Part One Reprise; Clear Moon, Mackerel Sky.

Graham Collier (b), Harry Beckett (t, flhn), Art Themen (ts, ss), Ed Speight (g), Roger Dean (p, elec p), John Webb (d). Rec. August 1975.
(Released 2005.)

Graham Collier – *Hoarded Dreams* (Cuneiform Rune 252).

Graham Collier (comp, cond), Kenny Wheeler, Henry Lowther, Manfred Schoof, Tomasz Stańko (t, flhn), Malcolm Griffiths, Conny Bauer, Eje Thelin (tb), Dave Powell (tba), Art

Themen, (ts, as), Juhanni Aaltonen (ts, as), Matthias Schubert (ts, ob), John Surman (bs, bcl), Geoff Warren (as, f), Ed Speight, John Schröder (g), Roger Dean (ky), Paul Bridge (b), Ashley Brown (d, perc). Rec. 2 July 1983.
(Released 2007).

Graham Collier – *Directing 14 Jackson Pollocks* (jazzcontinuum GCM2009).

Forty Years On – Between a Donkey and a Rolls Royce, An Alternate Aberdeen Angus, An Alternate Ryoanji, An Interlude, An Alternate *New Conditions*, and Some Out Blues, An Alternate Eggshell Summer, Mackerel Sky, an alternate blues, An Alternate Low Circus Ballad, An Alternate Third Simple Piece.

The Vonetta Factor – The Vonetta Factor, The Vonetta Conclusion; An Alternate Mackerel Sky; *The Alternate Third Colour* – First Grooves, Second Grooves, Third Grooves, Out Blues. *Forty Years On, The Vonetta Factor* and 'An Alternate Mackerel Sky' rec. November 2004. *The Alternate Third Colour* rec. November 1997.

Forty Years On, The Vonetta Factor and 'An Alternate Mackerel Sky' – Graham Collier (comp, cond), Alex Bonney, Harry Beckett, Steve Waterman (t, flhn), Mark Bassey, Fayyaz Virji (tb), Gideon Juckes (tba), Art Themen (ts, ss), James Allsopp (ts, bcl), Chris Biscoe (bs, as), Geoff Warren (as, ss, afl), Ed Speight (g), Roger Dean (p, ky), Jeff Clyne (b), Trevor Tomkins (d).

The Alternate Third Colour – personnel and recording date as for *The Third Colour*.

Graham Collier (with musicians from the Royal Academy of Music & Rimon School of Jazz and Contemporary Music) – *Adam's Marble: Jazz in Israel Vol. 25* (Jazzis 1025).

Bright as Silver (for Don & John), Aberdeen Angus, *Adam's Marble*.

Graham Collier (comp, cond), special guest soloist Harold Rubin (cl), Patrick White (t, flhn), Matt Colman, Rafi Malkiel (tb), Mitchell Rosen (ts), Stephen Main (as, ss), Eldad Tsabari (f), Yiftach Kadan (g), Ron Bet-Sira (elec p), Peter James (p), Boris Malkovsky (syn), Mihaly Biggs (b), Uri Shamir (bg), Shahar Haziza (d), Russell Morgan (d, perc). Rec. March 1995.

Graham Collier – *Luminosity – The Last Suites* (jazzcontinuum 2014).

The Blue Suite: Kind of Sketchy/Kind of So What/Kind of Green/All Kinds/Kind of Sketchy/Kind of Green/Kind of Freddie/Kind of So What/All Kinds/Kind of Sketchy.

Luminosity: Orchestral Dominances (in)/Yellow Hymn/Above Deep Water/Orchestral Dominances/Jardin D'Amour/Blue Monolith/Orchestral Dominances.

Geoff Warren (cond), Mark Bassey (tb), Steve Waterman, Martin Shaw (t), Jonathan Williams (fhn), Andy Grappy (tba), Art Themen (ts, ss), Graham Blevins (ts, cl), Andy Panayi (as, f), James Allsopp (bcl), Ed Speight (g), Roger Dean (p, elec p), Roy Babbington (b), John Marshall (d), Trevor Tomkins (perc). Rec. June 2013.

Compilation

Graham Collier – *Relook* (jazzcontinuum 2012).

Down Another Road, The (Berklee) Barley Mow, Crumblin' Cookie, An Alternate *Workpoints*, Song Three Live (Excerpt), *Mosaics* (Excerpt), The Alternate *Mosaics* (Excerpt), Adam, Aberdeen Angus, *New Conditions* Part 4, Forest Path to the Spring, *Symphony of Scorpions* Part 2, *The Day of the Dead* (Melange), *Hoarded Dreams* Part Two, *One by One the Cow Goes By*, The Hackney Five (Excerpt), *The Third Colour* Groove 2, *Oxford Palms* Open Blues and Ballad, The Vonetta Factor (opening), An Alternate Aberdeen Angus.

Personnel as for album release. See above except – 'The (Berklee) Barley Mow' – Dusko Gojkovic (t), Mike Gibbs (tb), Richard Iannitelli (as), Sadao Watanabe (f), Gary Burton (vib), Mike Nock (p) – other uncredited. Rec. 1963. *One By One the Cow Goes By* – Steve Waterman, Gabriel Garrick, Patrick White, Sean Griffith (t), Hugh Fraser, Matthew Colman, David Holt (tb), Bill Mee (b, tb), Dan Foster, Matt Stewart, Stephen Main, James Scannell, Matthew Morris (saxes), Nick Goetzee (g), Peter James (elec p, t, tb), Christian Vaughan (p), Jon Noyce (b), James Scannell (as), Matthew Skelton (d), Tom Hooper, John Machin (perc). Rec. 1993.

* The original LP lists the titles of *Mosaics* differently. In the biography, I have used those that relate to the recent BGO CD release. On the LP, these are given as: Side 1: Piano cadenza (including Theme 1), Theme 1 (ensemble) and flugelhorn solo, Duet flugelhorn and soprano and soprano cadenza, Theme 2 (soprano and rhythm) and soprano solo, Drum cadenza (including Theme 2) into Theme 3 (ensemble); Side 2: Flugelhorn cadenza (including Theme 4) Duet bass/flugelhorn, Theme 6 (ensemble) and tenor solo (Sydor), Tenor cadenza and tenor duet, Piano cadenza into Theme 2 (piano and rhythm), Flugelhorn solo over Theme 8 in tenors. (NB Titles are given as on original LP.)

Appendix 2

Compositions

N.B. In alphabetical order with works recorded highlighted in bold. This list was taken from Graham Collier's now defunct website, Jazzcontinuum, with certain additions.

'Aberdeen Angus' (1967) *Down Another Road* (album included in first Beat Goes On (BGO) compilation). Included in *Back to the Bus: Babyshambles* (a compilation of tunes listened to on the Babyshambles tour bus). Different versions were recorded on *Adam's Marble* (also used on the CD accompanying *Interaction*), and as 'An Alternate Aberdeen Angus' on *Directing 14 Jackson Pollocks* (2003).

'Adam' (1974) *Midnight Blue* (album included in third BGO compilation).

'Adams Marble' (1986) *Adam's Marble.*

'Alexandria Quartet' (1965/6) A suite for Big Band and voices inspired by Laurence Durrell's novels. Unrecorded partially because Durrell's agent told Graham in no uncertain terms that he would not allow his words to be used in such a composition.

'And Now for Something Completely Different' (1971) *Portraits* (album included in second BGO compilation).

'Azure' (1982) Written for and performed by the Westdeutscher Rundfunk Big Band/Orchestra, January 1982. Began life as one of three linked pieces to be called 'Rings of Sound'. The other pieces were 'Crimson' and 'Colour of Bronze'.

'The Barley Mow' (1962) *Down Another Road* (album included in first BGO compilation). Recorded in a different version on *Workpoints*. The *Workpoints* version was included in *The Cuneiform Story* compilation (a Jazz Italia cover-mount CD).

'The Bass Saxophone' (1989) Music for a BBC adaptation of Josef Skvorecky's novella for a production which won the Sony Drama Prize of that year.

'Bird' (1995) Music for Radio Three Drama by David Halliwell.

'Blue Spring' (2000) *Winter Oranges.*

'The Blue Suite' (2006) *The Last Suites.*

'Bodega Bridge' (1980) Written for and performed by Trondheim's Bodega Orchestra, February 1980.

'Bread & Circuses' (2000) *Bread & Circuses*; 'Ballad One' was included in *Forty Years On, Directing 14 Jackson Pollocks* (2003) as 'An Alternate Low Circus Ballad'.

'Bright as Silver (for Don & John)' (1994) *Adam's Marble*.

'British Conversations' (1975) Commissioned by Swedish Radio for their Big Band and performed in Stockholm in 1975. 'Clear Moon' and 'Mackerel Sky' have been used as separate items and are listed elsewhere.

'Burbling for Bob' – Written for and performed by Radio Suisse Normande, June 1970–January 1971 (N.B. Radio Suisse Normande is based in France).

'Café Blues' (1975) Unrecorded. Inspired by Carson McCullers' novella *Ballad of the Sad Café*.

'Cathedra' (1974) from *Midnight Blue* (album included in third BGO compilation).

'Charles River Fragments' (1994) *Charles River Fragments*.

'The Chief of Rostrums and the Domino Woman' (1979) Recorded but unreleased. Portraits of two minor characters in Malcolm Lowry's *Under the Volcano*.

'Children of Adam' (1973) Performed at the Cockpit Theatre, January 1973, for a concert, *Fanfare for Europe*, to celebrate UK entry into the Common Market.

'Clear Moon' (1975) (From *British Conversations*).

'Colour of Bronze' (1982) Began life as one of three linked pieces to be called 'Rings of Sound'. The other pieces were 'Crimson' and 'Azure Blues'. 'Colour of Bronze' was formally commissioned by the Milton Keynes Festival, February 1982. Also performed by Collier sextet for BBC *Jazz Today*, broadcast March 1982.

Contrapuntal Form (1968) Commissioned by Harlow Festival. Inspired by five sculptures in the town.

'Conversations' (1967) *Deep Dark Blue Centre* (album included in second BGO compilation).

'Conversations with Magic Stones' (1990) Unrecorded. Inspired by a Barbara Hepworth sculpture seen in St. Ives, Cornwall.

'Crimson' (1981) Began life as one of three linked pieces to be called 'Rings of Sound'. The other pieces were 'Colour of Bronze' and 'Azure Blues'. Unclear but likely that this became

'Crimson & Saffron' written for Eurojazz 81 – European Community Youth Jazz Orchestra. December 1981.

'Crimson & Saffron' (1981) See above.

'Crowley's Carol' (1970/1971) – written and performed by Radio Suisse Normande, June 1970–January 1971 (N.B. Radio Suisse Normande is based in France).

'Crumblin' Cookie' (1964) *Deep Dark Blue Centre* (stereo version of album included in second BGO compilation). Included in two compilations by whatmusic.com: *Trailer Happiness, Velvet Voodoo*, and *New Tokyo International Jazz Airport meets whatmusic.com*.

'Crystals of Space and Time' (1985) Unrecorded suite written to complement a performance of *Hoarded Dreams* at the Camden Jazz Festival in 1985.

'Danish Blue' (1968) *Down Another Road* (album included in first BGO compilation).

'Darius' (1974) *Darius* (album included in third BGO compilation); Parts 1, 3 & 4 only, recorded in a different version on *Workpoints* CD and on **Graham Collier Music** – Jazz Lecture Concert – Part One only (Resources of Music 0521 205638)

'The Day of the Dead' (1977) *Day of the Dead* (album included in fourth BGO compilation).

'Deep Dark Blue Centre' (1966) *Deep Dark Blue Centre* (stereo version of album included in second BGO compilation). Recorded in a different version on *Workpoints*.

'Deserted Funfair' (1985) *Something British Made in Hong Kong*.

'Down Another Road' (1967) *Down Another Road* (album included in first BGO compilation). 'Recorded in a new version 2005 on *Seven's and Eight's* by Nostalgia 77, which had over 6,000 plays on their MySpace page. In 2007 Universal Japan released this track as part of a 2 CD compilation by DJ/Producer Jazztronik. Although I was pleased at the inclusion, it was a blatant breach of my copyright. When I complained they paid compensation, but took the album off the shelves... And despite many requests they have failed to produce royalty statements or even a copy of the CDs! (This is one episode in a long-running fight with Universal to get them to acknowledge that I was reassigned the rights to three of my early albums in 1996. The full story will be carried elsewhere in due course.)' (Extract from Collier's Jazzcontinuum website, which is no longer active.)

'Eggshell Summer' (2000) *Winter Oranges*. Recorded in a new version by George Haslam's *Meltdown* in 2001. A different version, 'An Alternate Eggshell Summer', was included in *Directing 14 Jackson Pollocks* (2003).

'El Miklos' (1966) *Deep Dark Blue Centre* (stereo version of album included in second BGO compilation).

'English Bay and North Beach Morning' (1987) Commissioned and performed by Norddeutscher Rundfunk Orchestra, June 1987.

'Eridanus' (1977) Guitar and saxophone duo added to *The Day of the Dead* when Disconforme issued it as a double CD. Not included in the fourth BGO compilation version.

'Facets' (1973) Performed at the Cockpit Theatre, January 1973, for a concert, *Fanfare for Europe*, to celebrate UK entry into the Common Market. Described in 'Timeline' as 'a new composition for Europe'.

'Five Characters in Search of a Volcano' (1979) Recorded but unreleased. Inspired by five minor characters in Malcolm Lowry's *Under the Volcano*.

'Forest Path to the Spring' (1977) *Symphony of Scorpions* (album included in fourth BGO compilation).

Forty Years On (2003) A relook at some pieces written during Collier's career recorded on *Directing 14 Jackson Pollocks*. Most sections mentioned elsewhere on this page.

'Four Pieces for Paul Klee' (1989) Four saxophone quartets inspired by Paul Klee paintings. Published by Advance. Unrecorded, but MP3 files available.

'From Acorns' (2007) Unrecorded. Commissioned by Derby Jazz for performance by Harry Beckett and the East Midlands Jazz Orchestra.

'From Nine to Infinity' (1998) Commissioned by the IASJ for their ninth jazz meeting. Recorded on *IASJ Gala Concert*.

'Go West' (1968) Originally 'Song Nine' from *Songs for My Father*. Recorded on *Flare Up* by Harry Beckett.

'Grown Men' (1984) Unrecorded. Written for the rehearsal band which later became *Loose Tubes*.

'The Hackney Five' (1985) *Charles River Fragments*. The track was also used in the CD accompanying *Interaction*.

'Hirayoshi Suite' (1966) *Deep Dark Blue Centre* (stereo version of album included in second BGO compilation).

Hoarded Dreams (1983) Issued 2007 on Cuneiform.

'Hong Kong Suite' (1958) Unrecorded. Written while in Hong Kong with the British Army.

Ice, the Bright Parrot and the Moon. Commissioned by the Debrecen Jazzdays Festival in June 1981.

'In the Tavern of his Birth' (1978) Conceived as a companion piece to *The Day of the Dead*, premiered early in 1978 and performed again at *The Day of the Dead* concert at the Queen Elizabeth Hall in October 1978.

'It's Been So Good' (1975) Performed by Collier sextet with addition of Norma Winstone for BBC, broadcast July 1975.

A Kind of Game (1979) Musical about Kim Philby with David Fisher.

'Latin Brown' (1970/1971) Written for and performed by Radio Suisse Normande, June 1970–January 1971 (N.B. Radio Suisse Normande is based in France).

'Little Ben' (1975) *Workpoints*.

'Luminosity' (2010) *The Last Suites*. A suite, playable in any order, inspired by paintings by Hans Hofmann.

'Mackerel Sky' (1975) (From *British Conversations*). Two different versions, 'Mackerel Sky', appeared on CD 2 of *Workpoints* and 'An Alternate Mackerel Sky' was included on *Directing 14 Jackson Pollocks* (2003).

'The Mad Kingfisher' (1987) Commissioned and performed by the Danish Radio Denmark Light Orchestra, February 1987.

'The Magic Ride' (1969) Music for a documentary on the building and maiden voyage of the QE2.

'Memories Arrested in Space' (2007) Six saxophone quartets inspired by Jackson Pollock paintings from 1947. Published by Advance. Unrecorded, but MP3 files available.

'Mescalusions' (1985) Unrecorded as yet.

Midnight Blue (1974) *Midnight Blue* (album included in third BGO compilation).

'Midsummer Dawn' (1985) *Something British Made in Hong Kong*.

The Miró Tile (1996) *The Third Colour*.

'Mist on Water' (1985) *Something British Made in Hong Kong*.

'Molewrench' (1968) *Down Another Road* (album included in first BGO compilation).

Mosaics (1971) Recorded live in London in three different performances. One was chosen for *Mosaics* (album included in first BGO compilation). Two tracks from another version were first issued on *Elastic Jazz: Sketches Of Britain*, a compilation of British jazz from the 60s and 70s and later issued in full as *The Alternate Mosaics* in the second BGO compilation.

New Conditions (1975) *New Conditions* (album included in third BGO compilation). 'An Alternate New Conditions' (part 6 only) was included in *Forty Years On, Directing 14 Jackson Pollocks*' (2003).

'A New Dawn' (1973) *Darius* (album included in third BGO compilation), and used in the CD accompanying *Interaction*.

'New Fire' (1980) Commissioned for Greenwich Festival, based on 'New Fire Festival of the Aztecs'.

'A New Three Chord Trick' (1983) Commissioned by TV South for the Berkshire Youth Jazz Orchestra.

'New Year Song' (1982) Written for and performed by the Westdeutscher Rundfunk Big Band/Orchestra, January 1982.

'Northern Crescent' (1990) Music for a television drama.

October Ferry (1977) *Day of the Dead* (album included in fourth BGO compilation).

'An Odyssey' (1973) Written for an expanded ensemble – Collier, Ed Speight, Geoff Castle, John Webb, Dick Pearce, Brian Smith, Alan Skidmore, Art Themen, Harry Beckett, Kenny Wheeler, and unnamed cellist. Performed at the Institute of Contemporary Arts, August 1973, and Cockpit Theatre, October 1973. Included 'A New Dawn' – see separate entry.

One by One the Cow Goes By (1991–92) Written for the Royal Academy of Music Big Band. Recorded on *Spirits Rising* (RAM records). Sections of this recording were used in the CD accompanying *Interaction*.

'The Other Side' (1970) Recorded on *Flare Up* by Harry Beckett.

Oxford Palms (2001) Commissioned by George Haslam for Meltdown's performance at the Oxford Contemporary Music Festival. Inspired by the two interlocking ideas of William Faulkner's *Wild Palms*. Recorded by The Collective, Perth, Australia, released as *Bread & Circuses*.

'Pebbles Fresh from the Brook' (1984) Unrecorded. Commissioned by the Danish Radio Music Workshop Orchestra.

Plain Song and Mountain Birds (1988) Unrecorded. Commissioned by West Deutscher Rundfunk for a concert by their Orchestra, with soloists Geoff Warren (flute and saxophone) and Ed Speight (guitar).

'Portraits' (1972) *Portraits* (album included in second BGO compilation).

'Portraits II' (1972) Written for John Webb.

'Postal Order from my Grannie' (1974) Songs written for a musical with Mike Naylor.

'Quanahuac' (1977) Guitar and saxophone duo added to *The Day of the Dead* when Disconforme issued it as a double CD. Not included in the fourth BGO compilation version.

'Queensbury Rules' (1985) *Something British Made in Hong Kong.*

'Red Fog at Sunrise' (1987) Commissioned and performed by the Danish Radio Denmark Light Orchestra, February 1987.

'Rings of Sound' (1981) Unrecorded. See under 'Crimson' for details.

'Rolli's Tune' (1968) Recorded by Harry Beckett's band as 'Rolly's Tune' on *Flare Up* and included on *Impressed with Gilles Peterson*, a compilation of British jazz from the 1960s and 70s, which also included 'Lullaby for a Lonely Child' from *Down Another Road* (composed by Karl Jenkins). On his website Jazzcontinuum (no longer active), Collier commented, '[This] was the first example of Universal not asking my permission before using a track which I owned the rights to'. Also used as part of the background score to *The Long Firm* (BBC Television).

'Rosemary for Remembrance' (1973) Commissioned by The Globe for Shakespeare birthday celebrations. Hamlet connection. Linked to 'Sherris for Valour'.

'Ryoanji' (1973) inspired by the Japanese Garden in Kyoto. Recorded in two different versions as part of the book/CD package *Interaction: Opening Up the Jazz Ensemble* (Advance). 'An Alternate Ryoanji' was included in *Forty Years On, Directing 14 Jackson Pollocks* (2003).

'Sad Faced Potter' (1982) Written for and performed by the Westdeutscher Rundfunk Big Band/Orchestra, January 1982.

Sea, Sky and Down (1973) Commissioned by Southern Arts for Worthing Festival of Literature. Prose by R. H. Jeffries, poetry by Ted Walker.

'September Mist' (1983) Written for and performed by the Westdeutscher Rundfunk Big Band/Orchestra, April 1983.

Shapes, Colours, Energy (1995) *The Third Colour.*

'Shell View' (1980) Written for and performed by Trondheim's Bodega Orchestra, February 1980.

'Sherris for Valour' (1973) Commissioned by The Globe for Shakespeare birthday celebrations. Linked to 'Rosemary for Remembrance'. Falstaff portrait.

'Silver Queen Saloon' (1977) Songs for play written by Paul Foster. Part commissioned by Antwerp Theatre and John Calder.

'Six Possible Pictures' (1986–87) Unrecorded. A suite for Big Band looking at the history of jazz through a contemporary composer's eyes.

Smoke Blackened Walls and Curlews (1970) Commissioned by Bradford festival, words by Ted Hughes, Edward Carpenter, J. B. Priestley, Mrs Gaskell.

Songs for My Father (1970) Seven songs recorded for *Songs for My Father* (album included in first BGO compilation).

'Spring Rain' (1985) *Something British Made in Hong Kong.*

'Suite Sandy Brown' (1969) Written for a concert with Sandy Brown. Derived from 'Sweet Georgia Brown'.

'Sweet Fat' (1988) Music for play by Jack Kenny and Peter King commissioned by BBC Radio Three.

Symphony of Scorpions (1976) *Symphony of Scorpions* (album included in fourth BGO compilation).

'Thames Base' (1980) Written for Danish Radio Big Band, featuring Niels-Henning Ørsted Pederson.

The Third Colour (1997) *The Third Colour.* Recorded in a different version as 'The Alternate Third Colour' on *Directing 14 Jackson Pollocks* (2003). 'Out Blues' from 'The Third Colour' was also included in *Forty Years On, Directing 14 Jackson Pollocks.*

'The Third Road' (1968) Recorded on *Flare Up* by Harry Beckett, also on three separate albums by Ted Curson who added lyrics – and retitled it 'Lin's Garden' – when they worked together in Hamburg. The albums – with no lyrics and varying degrees of composer credit – are *I Heard Mingus*, *'Round about Midnight*, and *Travelling On*.

Three Simple Pieces (1997) 'Parts 1-3' *The Third Colour*; 'Parts 1 and 2' recorded in a different version by the Danish Radio Jazz Orchestra on *Winter Oranges*. 'Part 3' was included in *Forty Years On, Directing 14 Jackson Pollocks* (2003) as 'An Alternate Third Simple Piece'.

'Three Solid Gs' (1992) Unrecorded. Commissioned by Graz, Austria City Council for performance at the IASJ Conference.

'Tinted Autumn' (2000) *Winter Oranges.*

'To The Boathouse' (1999) Composed for the Vancouver and Victoria International Jazz Orchestras.

'Trigon Blues' (1970/1971) Written for and performed by Radio Suisse Normande, June 1970–January 1971 (N.B. Radio Suisse Normande is based in France). 'Trigon Blues' may be a reference to Lynne Chadwick's sculpture in Harlow which inspired one of the sections on the 1968 commission *Contrapuntal Forms* in 1968.

Triptych (1976) Big Band suite inspired by three painters including Mark Rothko and recorded on the same night as *Symphony of Scorpions*. Added to *The Day of the Dead* when Disconforme issued it as a double CD. Not included in the fourth BGO compilation version.

'Ultramarine' (1979) South East Arts Commission. Title (only) from Malcolm Lowry.

'Under the Pier' (1973) *Workpoints*. Two different versions were used in the CD accompanying *Interaction*.

'Under the Volcano' (1979) Dramatic Music for BBC adaptation produced by John Tydeman. Adapted from *The Day of the Dead* music.

The Vonetta Factor (2004) *Directing 14 Jackson Pollocks*.

'Walkabout' (1974) Originally a song in 'Postal Order from My Grannie'. Performed by the Westdeutscher Rundfunk Big Band/Orchestra, April 1983.

Wheel of Dreams (1970–72) Multi-media self-portrait, commissioned by Camden Festival. For Norma Winstone, cello, seven-piece band, pre-recorded voice tracks and projections on three screens. Words drawn from a variety of sources including Conrad Aiken, Walt Whitman, W. H. Auden and Michelangelo.

'Where Will They Put the Blue Plaque Now?' (1970) 'Last piece written in my London flat before they knocked it down' (quote from Jazzcontinuum website, no longer active).

'Whirligig' (1985) *Something British Made in Hong Kong*.

Winter Oranges (2000) Commissioned by The Danish Radio Jazz Orchestra. Recorded on *Winter Oranges*. All sections mentioned above as separate items.

Workpoints (1968) *Workpoints*. Released 2005 on Cuneiform Records.

'World Turned Upside Down' (1974) Some songs for a proposed jazz opera with Mike Naylor.

Appendix 3

Graham Collier BBC Radio Broadcasts

1965 BBC Light Programme, 13 September, *BBC Jazz Club*. Broadcast by Graham Collier Septet shared with Joe Harriott Quintet and the Mike Carr Trio.

1966 BBC Light Programme, 17 April, *The Jazz Scene*. General review of jazz scene. Graham Collier Septet and Ronnie Scott Quintet with Mark Murphy.

1967 BBC Home Service, 4 August, *Jazz at Night*. Various performers including Graham Collier Septet.

1967 BBC Light Programme, *The Jazz Scene*. General review of jazz scene. Graham Collier Septet and Ed Faultless Trio with Art Themen.

1968 BBC Radio Three, Wednesday 10 July. Graham Collier Dozen perform *Workpoints*. Graham Collier (comp, b), Kenny Wheeler, Harry Beckett, Henry Lowther (t), Mike Gibbs, Chris Smith, John Mumford (tb), Dave Aaron (as), John Surman (bs, bcl), Karl Jenkins (bs, p), John Marshall (d), Frank Ricotti (vib, perc).

1968 BBC Radio One, 10 January, *Jazz Club*. Performances by Graham Collier Septet, Tony Lee Trio and Don Rendell–Ian Carr Quintet.

1968 BBC Radio One, 3 July, *Jazz Club*. Performances by Graham Collier Septet, the Alan Haven Duo and the Art Ellefson Sextet.

1969 BBC Radio One, 16 February, *Jazz on One*. Graham Collier discusses the jazz scene.

1969 BBC Radio One, 19 March, *Jazz Club*. Performances by Graham Collier Sextet, the Gordon Beck Trio and the Alan Skidmore Quintet.

1969 BBC Radio One, 20 December, *Jazz Club*. Performances by Graham Collier Sextet (with Art Themen and Harry Beckett) and the Ed Faultless Trio.

1969 BBC Two, Tuesday 7 October, *Jazz Scene at the Ronnie Scott Club*. Graham Collier Music play selections from *Down Another Road*. Graham Collier (b), Harry Beckett (flhn), Nick Evans (tb), Stan Sulzmann (saxes), Karl Jenkins (p, ob), John Marshall (d).

1970 BBC Radio Three, 31 August, *Jazz in Britain*. Graham Collier Music perform 'Where Will They Put The Blue Plaque Now'. No other details.

1970 BBC Radio Three, 4 May, *Jazz in Britain*. Graham Collier Music.

1970 BBC Radio Two, 13 May, *Jazz Club*. Performances by Graham Collier Music featuring Harry Beckett and Bobby Breen with the Colin Purbrook Quartet.

1970 BBC Radio Two, 2 November, *Jazz Club*. Graham Collier Music featuring Harry Beckett and Sandy Brown and the Harold McNair Quartet.

1971 BBC Radio Three, 11 January, *Jazz in Britain*. Graham Collier Music play *Mosaics*. No other details.

1971 BBC Radio Three, 5 July, *Jazz in Britain*. Graham Collier Music perform *Smoke-blackened Walls and Curlews*. John Carbery narrating. No other details.

1971 BBC Radio Two, 4 October, *Jazz Club*. Programme from Montreux Jazz Festival including performance of *Mosaics* by Graham Collier Music.

1971 BBC Radio Two, 7 June, *Jazz Club*. Graham Collier Music and the Pat Smythe Trio.

1972 BBC Radio Two, 26 June, *Jazz Club*. Graham Collier Music and the Tony Milliner Sextet.

1973 BBC Radio One, 1 July, *Sounds of Jazz*. Graham Collier Music and the Tommy Whittle Quintet.

1973 BBC Radio Three, 12 January, *Jazz Workshop*. Graham Collier Music perform 'And Now For Something Completely Different'. No other details.

1974 BBC Radio One, 14 July, *Sounds of Jazz*. Graham Collier Music perform Ellington's 'Love You Madly' amongst other titles.

1974 BBC Radio Three, *Jazz in Britain*. Graham Collier Music perform *Darius*. No other details.

1975 BBC Radio Two, 17 August, *Sounds of Jazz*. Graham Collier Music and the CDM Trio. GCM perform, with addition of Norma Winstone – 'Little Ben', 'It's Been So Good', 'Clear Moon', 'Small Change'.

1976 BBC Radio Three, 22 March, *Jazz in Britain*. Graham Collier Music.

1976 BBC Radio Two, 5 December, *Sounds of Jazz*. Graham Collier Twelve.

1977 BBC Radio Three, 8 February, *Music in Our Time*. Graham Collier Music perform extracts from *New Conditions*. No other details.

1977 BBC Radio Three, 31 October, *Jazz in Britain*. Graham Collier Music perform extracts from *The Day of the Dead*. No other details.

1978 BBC Radio One, 23 April, *Sounds of Jazz*. Graham Collier Twelve and Morrissey/Mullen.

1978 BBC Radio Three, 20 January, Repeat of *Lifelines: Music in Principle*.

1978 BBC Radio Three, 26 June, *Jazz in Britain*. Graham Collier Music perform extracts from *The Day of the Dead*. No other details. (Probably a repeat broadcast)

1978 BBC Radio Three, 4 August, *Lifelines: Music in Principle 2: Fascinating Rhythm*. Graham Collier discusses rhythm from a jazz musician's point of view and Keshav Sathhe demonstrates its uses in Indian music.

1978 BBC Radio Three, 6 November, *Jazz in Britain*. Graham Collier performs *October Ferry* featuring Henry Lowther, Harry Beckett, Pete Duncan (t), Paul Nieman (tb), Art Themen, Alan Wakeman, Tim Whitehead (ts, ss), Ed Speight (b), Roger Dean (p), Jeff Clyne (b), Ashley Brown (d).

1979 BBC Radio Four, 9 March, *Under the Volcano*. Radio play with music by Graham Collier.

1979 BBC Radio Three, 10 September, *Jazz in Britain*. Graham Collier Music performs 'The Chief of Rostrums' and 'The Domino Woman'.

1980 BBC Radio One, 23 November, *Sounds of Jazz*. Graham Collier Big Band perform 'Ultramarine', 'Walkabout', 'Bodega Bridge'.

1981 BBC Radio Three, 13 April, *Jazz in Britain*. Graham Collier Music perform 'New Year Song'. No other details.

1982 BBC Radio Three, 29 March, *Jazz in Britain*. Graham Collier Music (sextet) perform 'Colour of Bronze'.

1982 BBC Radio One, 25 July, *Sounds of Jazz*. Alex Gregory Quintet and Graham Collier Music.

1983 BBC Radio One, 17 July, *Sounds of Jazz*. Don Weller Quintet and the Graham Collier Big Band perform 'September Mists I, II, III', 'Azure Blues'.

1983 BBC Radio Three, 9 May, *Jazz in Britain*. 'Ice, the Bright Parrot and the Moon'. Graham Collier (syn), Geoff Warren (as, f), Ed Speight (g), Roger Dean (p, vib), Paul Bridge (b), Ashley Brown (d).

1984 BBC Radio Three, *Music Weekly*. Arts review. Graham Collier talks about the 'composer's role in jazz'.

1984 BBC Radio Three, 19 March, *Jazz Today*. Graham Collier Music (Mark Woods depping for Ed Speight) perform 'Lakka'.

1984 BBC Radio Three, 30 October, *Magnum Opus*. Repeat of *Hoarded Dreams* from Bracknell Festival.

1985 BBC Radio Three, Wednesday 22 May. Graham Collier *Midnight Blue*. Programme a tribute to Barnett Newman.

1985 BBC Radio Three, Wednesday 29 May. Graham Collier 'Adam' and 'Cathedra'. Programme a tribute to Barnett Newman.

1985 BBC Radio Two, 8 December, *Sounds of Jazz*. Pete Hurt Orchestra and Graham Collier Music (ten-piece band) perform 'Mescalusions'.

1986 BBC Radio Three, 7 January, *Jazz Today*. Graham Collier Music featuring Graham Collier (ky), Steve Waterman (t, flhn), Mike Mower, Mark Lockheart (ts, ss), Geoff Warren (as, ss, f), Steve Mulligan (bs, bcl), Ed Speight (g), Roger Dean (p, ky) Paul Bridge (b), Ashley Brown (d, perc).

1987 BBC Radio Three, 13 April, *Jazz Today*. Graham Collier Music featuring Graham Collier (syn), Geoff Warren (ss, f), Ed Speight (g), Roger Dean (p, DX7), Mick Hutton (b), Ashley Brown (d/LA Toys).

1987 BBC Radio Two, 11 October, *Sounds of Jazz*. Graham Collier Big Band.

1988 BBC Radio Three, 16 September, *Sweet Fat*. Radio play by Jack Kenny and Peter King. Music composed by Graham Collier and performed by Art Themen (ts, ss), Ed Speight (g), Geoff Castle (p), Mick Hutton (b), Ashley Brown (d). Repeated 27 March 1990.

1989 BBC Radio Three, 29 September, *The Friday Play*. Repeat of *The Bass Saxophone*.

1989 BBC Radio Three, 31 December, *The Bass Saxophone*. Radio play based on novel by Josef Skvorecky. Repeated 19 June 1990.

1992 BBC Radio Two, 26 February, *Jazz Parade*. Graham Collier interviewed by musician and broadcaster Digby Fairweather.

1994 BBC Radio Three, 11 June, *London Jazz Festival*. Graham Collier and The *Jazz* Ensemble perform *Charles River Fragments*. Personnel as for CD.

1995 BBC Radio Three, 22 July, *Studio Three: Bird*. Radio play by David Halliwell with music by Graham Collier performed by Art Themen (as), John Horler (p), Jeff Clyne (b), Trevor Tomkins (d).

1997 BBC Radio Three, Saturday 22 November, *Impressions*. Graham Collier and The *Jazz* Ensemble. Live recording London Jazz Festival. Personnel as for *The Third Colour* CD. Interview with Graham Collier.

1997 BBC Radio Three, 1 March, *Impressions*. Graham Collier interviewed by Brian Morton.

2001 BBC Radio Three, 20 October, *Jazz File: Teaching Jazz*. Alyn Shipton asks if it is possible to teach jazz. 'Avril Dankworth, Michael Garrick and Graham Collier remember the first British attempts to integrate jazz and education'.

2004 BBC Radio Three, 1 December, *Performance on 3*. London Jazz Festival. Music from Brad Mehldau, Graham Collier and his Celebration Band, Gilad Atzmon and Gwyneth Herbert.

2005 BBC Radio Three, 15 April, *Jazz on 3*. Graham Collier and The *Jazz* Ensemble perform *Forty Years On*. Personnel as for *Directing 14 Jackson Pollocks* CD. Interview with Graham Collier.

2009 BBC Radio Three, 5 December, *Jazz Library*. Graham Collier interviewed by broadcaster, author and musician Alyn Shipton.

Appendix 4

Royal Academy of Music Collier Alumni

N.B. The following list was compiled from RAM Graduation Year Books and Academy Jazz Student CDs prepared during Graham Collier's tenure as Head of Jazz. Any alumni not included will rest assured that they have been protected from inclusion by the Data Protection Act 1998.

Adam Goldsmith (guitar)
Amy Gamlen (saxophone)
Andrew Kuc (guitar)
Andrew Tolman (bass)
Anesha Blair (voice)
Bob Knight (drums)
Borre Molstad (tuba)
Chris Hutchings (drums)
Christian Garrick (violin)
Christian Vaughan (piano)
Christopher Higginbottom (percussion)
Daniel Foster (saxophone)
David Beebee (piano)
David Holt (trombone)
Dimitrios Vasilakis (saxophone – postgraduate studies 1991)
Duncan Mackay (trumpet)
Edward Benstead (trumpet)
Gareth Lockrane (flute)
Hannah Vasanth (piano)
Henry Collins (trumpet)
Ian Price (saxophone)
Ivo Neame (saxophone)
James Allsopp (saxophone)
James Fenn (guitar)
James Knight (saxophone)
Jeremy Brown (bass)
Joe Aukland (trumpet)
John Dickson (trumpet)
John Dowell (saxophone)
Jon Machin (drums)
Jon Noyce (bass)
Jonathan Thomas (bass)

Julian Cox (bass)
Kathleen Willison (voice)
Mark Lloyd (drums)
Martin Gladdish (trombone)
Matt Colman (trombone)
Matt Fishwick (percussion)
Matt Stewart (saxophone)
Matthew Morris (saxophone)
Matthew Skelton (drums)
Michael Feltham (trombone)
Mick Ball (trumpet)
Mihaly Biggs (bass)
Naomi Barker (saxophone)
Nicholas Dover (saxophone)
Nicolas Goetzee (guitar)
Ollie Hayhurst (bass)
Osian Roberts (saxophone)
Owen Rodgers (saxophone)
Patrick White (trumpet)
Paul Booth (saxophone)
Peter James (piano)
Richard Ashmore (trombone)
Richard Cross (trombone)
Rob Taggart (piano)
Robert Dowell (trombone)
Robert Knight (percussion)
Robert O'Neale (piano)
Sally Knight (trombone)
Samuel Mayne (saxophone)
Sean Griffith (trumpet)
Simon Allen (saxophone)
Stefan Heckel (composition)
Stephen Corley (piano)
Stephen Main (saxophone)
Steve Fishwick (trumpet)
Thomas Caris (guitar)
Thomas Hooper (percussion)
Tim Febey (trombone)
Tim Smart (trombone)
Tom Cawley (piano)
Tom Hooper (drums)
Tom Mason (bass)
Trevor Walker (trumpet)
Werner Kristiansen (guitar)

Index

Key for abbreviations – Beat Goes On records (BGO); Cambridge University Press (CUP); Danish Radio Jazz Orchestra (DRJO); International Association of Jazz Education (IAJE); International Association of Schools of Jazz (IASJ); London Schools Jazz Orchestra (LSJO); National Youth Jazz Orchestra (NYJO); Royal Academy of Music (RAM)

'A Kind of Game' (Musical about Kim Philby with David Fisher) 128, 130 n.4
'A New Dawn'
   Darius LP 103, 107
Aaltonen, Juhanni (saxophonist) – *Hoarded Dreams* 163
Aaron, Dave (saxophonist)
   Deep Dark Blue Centre LP 36, 38–40
   Workpoints 45
'Aberdeen Angus'
   Adam's Marble CD 215–16
   Down Another Road LP 52–53, 55
   Forty Years On suite 240–42
Abse, Danny (poet) 94
'Adam'
   Midnight Blue LP 109–11
Adam's Marble
   CD 215–17, 248
   composition 182, 187 n.8, 214, 221
Adorno, Theodor (philosopher) xiv, 261
Aiken, Conrad (author) 92
'Alexandria Quartet'
   Lawrence Durrell/title of *Workpoints* 44
Allen, Simon (saxophonist/RAM student) 232
Allsop, James (saxophonist/RAM student)
   Forty Years On 241–42
   Luminosity CD 263–64
Ambrose (band leader) 7
AMM 259
'And Now for Something Completely Different'
   Portraits LP 85, 89 n.9
Anderson, Paul F.
   Collier car accident USA 2, 5–26
Ardley, Neil (composer)
   approach to composition 120, 152
Armstrong, Louis (trumpeter) 62, 78, 196, 204 n.8
Arts Council of Great Britain 113, 235, 247 n.2
   Charles River Fragments 219
   first jazz musician to receive Arts Council grant xii, 1, 41–43, 49, 207, 254
   funding for Mosaics label 116, 150, 172 n.1

   funds rehearsal band/Loose Tubes 158, 160
   Hoarded Dreams 160
   New Conditions tour 121
   The Day of the Dead tour 140
   under Jeannie Lee/Lord Goodman 71 n.1
Ashberry, Elsie (cousin)
   recollections of Collier family 1–5, 130 n.4
Ashton, Bill (NYJO)
   disagreements with Collier xii, 97, 191–95
   educational approach 191–92
   Eurojazz 1981 192–93
   Just Jazz, NYJO house journal 193
   Leeds International jazz Educators' Conference 1996 193–94
   on free jazz 191
Ashton Thomas, John (RAM teacher of aural skills) 209
Auden, W. H. (poet) 92
Austin, Larry (composer) 97
Australia/Perth
   recording of *Bread & Circuses* 186

Babbington, Roy (bassist)
   CV 142
   Jazz Yatra/India 154
   Luminosity CD 264
   October Ferry 144
   replaces Collier in orchestra 142
Bailey, Derek (guitarist) 76, 84, 256
Baldry, Long John (singer) 35
Balke, Jon (pianist) 230
Barker, Guy (trumpeter) 157, 172 n.5
'The Barley Mow'
   Down Another Road 54
   Jazz in the Classroom VII/Relook CD 17, 23–24, 26 n.2, 262
   John Marshall contribution to 53
   Workpoints CD 44, 46
Barratt, Issie (saxophonist/educator) 231, 245–46
Barry Summer School 34–36, 48 n.6, 53, 63, 189

Bartók, Béla (composer) 185
Baruch, Adam
　Adam's Marble CD (see under title)
　Israel tour 182
　RAM/Rimon collaboration 214–15
Basie, Count (bandleader)
　influence on Collier 55–58, 60–61, 144, 196–97, 217, 222, 250, 264
Bass Saxophone, The
　radio drama/Sony Drama Prize 128–29
Bassey, Mark (trombonist)
　Collier's educational approach 190
　Luminosity 264
　on *Jazz – A Student's and Teacher's Guide* 190
　Vonetta Factor 241–42
Batchelor, Chris (trumpeter)
　Loose Tubes 159
Bates, Django (pianist/composer)
　Loose Tubes 159
Bauer, Konrad (trombonist)
　Hoarded Dreams 163–65
BBC 87, 129, 173 n.11, 174
　BBC Third Programme 42, 70, 103
　Jazz Club 31, 33, 104
　Jazz Notes 69, 194, 203 n.5
　Jazz Today 69, 151
　Sweet Fat 12
　Under the Volcano 142
Beck, Mike (drummer) 29–30
Beckett, Harry (trumpeter) 32, 36, 38, 50–51, 53, 71 n.4, 80, 86, 142, 153, 234
　British Conversations 111
　Collier school tours 62
　Darius 106–107
　Deep Dark Blue Centre 37, 39, 48 n.7
　Derby Youth Orchestra 244
　Down Another Road 53–55
　easy-going attitude of 141
　Flare Up 64, 82
　Globe Playhouse Trust Concert 103
　Jazz Yatra/India 154
　John Webb on Beckett 67
　Memories of Bacares 118
　Mosaics/The Alternate Mosaics 74–78
　New Conditions 118
　October Ferry 144
　on Collier 65
　on The Old Place 32–33
　recruits Geoff Castle 73
　returns to Collier 105
　Songs For My Father 64, 67–68
　Symphony of Scorpions 139
　Vonetta Factor/Forty Years On 241–42
　The Wire 158
　with Stan Tracey 120
　Workpoints 45–46
Bee Gees 265 n.2
Beiderbecke, Bix (trumpeter)
　Malcolm Lowry admiration of 132, 139
Bellaphon (German record distributor)
　Mosaic Records deal with/breach of contract/settlement 152–54
Bennett, Richard Rodney (pianist/composer)
　wins second prize in Berklee competition 12, 14 n.2
Bentzon, Nikolaj (pianist)
　Winter Oranges 233–34
Berendt, Joachim (journalist/promoter)
　commissions Penderecki's *Actions* for Globe Unity Orchestra 181
Berk, Lawrence (founder Berklee College)
　origins of Berklee 16–17
　Recording Band' 21
Berk, Lee (educator)
　Berklee named after 16
　President of Berklee 198
Berklee College of Music 9, 28–29, 38, 48 n.9, 55, 72, 126, 200, 239, 262
　Berklee International Octet 17
　Berklee Press/*Compositional Devices* 96, 101
　Collier first British student xii, 91
　Collier *Jazz News* article on 14
　Collier later derogatory remarks on 200–201
　Collier on studying at 15–16
　Down Beat competition 12
　fellow students at 17
　Gary Burton on 19
　Herb Pomeroy at 16, 19–22, 196
　Jazz in the Classroom LPs 17, 21–24, 212
　Paul Betjeman on 22–23
Berry, Steve (bassist)
　Loose Tubes 159–60, 192
Betjeman, Paul
　shares flat with Collier 22–23
Biggs, Mihaly (bassist/RAM student)
　Adam's Marble CD 216–17
　Israel trip 214
Bigler, Heinz (saxophonist)
　wins first prize *Down Beat* competition 12, 17
Biscoe, Chris (saxophonist)
　Charles River Fragments 219, 222
　compares Collier and Mike Westbrook 251
　Directing 14 Jackson Pollocks CD 241–43

Blevins, Graham (saxophonist)
   Bread & Circuses CD 238–39
   Luminosity CD 264–65
Bley, Carla (composer) xiii, 138, 220, 240, 253
Blodwyn Pig 12–13
'Blue Spring' (*Winter Oranges*) 233
Bluesology 35
Blue Suite, The
   Luminosity CD 244, 247, 262–64
Bolberg, Henrik (trumpeter)
   Winter Oranges 233–34
Bonati, Roberto (composer/Head of Jazz, Parma) xiii, 220, 259
   Collier admiration of 196, 246, 253
   invites Collier to Arrigo Boito Music Conservatory of Parma 2009 246–47
Bonney, Alex (trumpeter)
   Directing 14 Jackson Pollocks CD 242
Boulez, Pierre (composer) 120, 203 n.8, 223, 243
Bourdieu, Pierre (philosopher) 255, 261
Bowie, Lester (trumpeter)
   on Wynton Marsalis 197
Bowlby, John (child psychiatrist) 28
Bracknell Jazz Festival
   Hoarded Dreams 112 n.9, 160–61, 168–69
Bradfield, Colin (saxophonist) 29–30
Braxton, Anthony (saxophonist/genius) 205
Bread & Circuses 61, 186, 232, 237–39
Brecker, Michael (saxophonist) 197
Bretton Woods Agreement
   shaping of North Atlantic economies post WWII 255
Bridge, Paul (bassist) 159, 163
   Hungary gigs 187 n.2
   Something British Made in Hong Kong 175, 179
   Triton trio 150
'Bright as Silver (for Don & John)'
   Adam's Marble CD 214–16
'Brighter Thoughts (film company)
   Hoarded Dreams documentary 160–61, 166, 170
   homophobic reaction to 171–72
'British Conversations' 111, 121
British Council
   sponsors Collier tours 105, 112 n.7, 121, 154–56, 175–76
Brontë, Charlotte 70
Brookmeyer, Bob (trombonist/composer) 106, 220, 250
Brown, Ashley (drummer) 128
   Hoarded Dreams 163–64
   Hungary gigs 187 n.2
   Jazz Yatra/India 154
   Lysis Live 152
   Lysis Plus 152
   on Collier 'lazy eye' 164
   on *The Day of the Dead* 140–41
   Penderecki's *Actions* 180
   replaces John Webb 121, 140
   Roger Dean *Cycles* 151
   Something British Made in Hong Kong 175, 179
Brown, Pete (poet/musician) 94
Brown, Sandy (clarinettist)
   Review of *Inside Jazz* and *Music Outside* 100–101
Brubeck, Dave (pianist/composer)
   Collier view of 96
Brussels Radio Big Band 174
Brymer, Jack (clarinettist) 14 n.1
Buddle, Lee (saxophonist)
   Bread & Circuses 239
Burch, John (pianist) 48 n.6
Burton, Gary (vibraphonist)
   Collier on 20
   on Berklee 16–17, 19
   on Collier 17–18, 21, 24, 112 n.4, 126

'Café Blues' 111
Camden Jazz Festival
   performance of *Hoarded Dreams* 1985 167–69
Campaign for Homosexual Equality (CHE) 113–14, 146–47
Carberry, John (actor)
   drinking 140–41
   Sea, Sky and Down 95
   Smoke Blackened Walls and Curlews 70
   Wheel of Dreams 94
   The Day of the Dead 140–41
Carpenter, Edward (socialist/early gay activist) 70
Carr, Ian 47, 81, 172 n.9, 220
   Barry Summer School 34, 48 n.6
   Globe Playhouse Trust concert 102–103, 112 n.4
   Music Outside: Contemporary Jazz in Britain 1, 49, 71 n.5, 96, 100
   Nucleus 53, 106, 142, 249
Carr, Mike (organist) 31, 41
Castle, Geoff (pianist)
   Darius 106
   Globe Playhouse Trust concert 103
   joins Collier 73

Montreux Jazz Festival 79–80
Mosaics/The Alternate Mosaics 73–78
Nucleus 65, 107–108
on 'Gay Talk' 63
on Collier/NYJO 63
Portraits 85
private lessons with Collier 29, 72–73
Sweet Fat 108
'Cathedra'
    Midnight Blue 109–10
Cavelli, Pierre (guitarist) 51
Cawley, Tom (pianist/RAM student)
    Collier admiration of 253, 259
    differences with Collier 210–12
    on RAM 208–209
Chadwick, Lynne (artist) 50
Channel 4
    Hoarded Dreams documentary 161, 166, 171, 172 n.8
Charig, Mark (trumpeter) 35
Charles River Fragments 60, 163, 165, 173, 202, 217, 219–23, 227, 239, 248, 251
China 11, 176
Clayton, Peter (journalist/presenter)
    Jazz Notes 69
Cleo and John 111, 122–25
Cleyndert, Andy (bassist)
    Third Colour 228–30
Clyne, Jeff (bassist) 9
    at RAM 209, 225
    Directing 14 Jackson Pollocks 241–42
Cohen, David (film producer) 70, 129–30, 156
Cohn, Al (saxophonist) 41, 203 n.8
Coleman, Ornette (saxophonist) 57, 61, 96
Collective, The
    Bread & Circuses 186–87, 235–39
Collier, Elizabeth May (mother) 1–2, 4, 27, 183–84
Collier, Graham
    abstract art/interest in 50–52, 92–95, 109–10, 145, 252, 263
    and New Orleans jazz 45, 55–56, 60, 145, 199
    as author (see under individual titles)
    Ashton, Bill/NYJO
        Collier relationship with xii, 97, 191–95
        differing educational approach 191–92
    Berklee
        Collier first British student xii, 91
        Collier/studying at 15–16
        Down Beat competition 12
        later criticism of 200–201

compositional approach 64, 98–100, 133–35, 214, 216–17, 220–21
philosophy of jazz/performance aesthetic xiii, xiv, 42, 64, 69–70, 93–94, 96, 98–100, 109, 188, 195–96, 248, 253, 255–62
compositions (see under individual titles)
Davis Miles/admiration of 14, 96, 134, 190, 196, 257
    influence of *Kind of Blue* on Collier 40, 54–57, 216, 263
Ellington, Duke/influence of 16, 55–56, 69, 86–87, 98–99, 104, 113, 118–19, 134, 145, 163, 167, 257, 264
Evans, Gil/influence on Collier 16, 55–56, 69, 86–87, 98–99, 104, 113, 118–19, 134, 145, 163, 167, 257, 264
family relationships
    Collier, Elizabeth May (mother) 1–2, 4, 27, 183–84
    Collier, Jack (father) 2–6, 8, 13, 27, 65
    Collier, John (brother) 1, 4–6, 12, 183
foreign tours 108, 175–76
    Far East 175
    France 116
    Germany/Austria/Hungary 127
    Germany/Switzerland France 105
    Greece 175
    Holland/Belgium 82
    Hungary 175
    Hungary/Germany 121, 144
    India 121, 154–56
    Israel 175, 182
health/mental/physical
    depression xi, 90–91, 111–12 n.1, 88, 179
    gall bladder 85
    'lazy eye' 1, 164, 236
    physical health 155, 237, 239–40, 244
jazz education
    Finland/Sibelius Academy 174, 205–206, 226 n.1
    IAJE/IASJ (see under IAJE/IASJ)
    jazz in schools 62–64, 82, 122, 188, 256
    RAM (see under RAM)
Gill, John, relationship 104, 114, 116, 156, 171–72, 201
literature/interest in 42, 70, 92–95, 111, 127–29, 131–36, 139, 146, 237
Loose Tubes 157, 159–60
Mingus, Charles/influence of 33, 43, 55–56, 59–61, 69

Mosaic Records (see under Mosaic Records)
recordings (see under individual titles)
sexuality 18, 113–15, 122, 147
   homophobia 50, 147–48, 169–72, 245
Skopelos/Greece 9, 245–46
Spain/Ronda 9, 156, 224, 231, 245–46
'Third Stream' 97–98, 122, 175, 184–85, 238
UK tours 42, 44, 47, 50, 62, 103–104, 116, 118, 137, 140–41
Collier, Jack (father) 2–6, 8, 13, 27, 65
Collier, John (brother) 1, 4–6, 12, 183
Colman, Matthew (trombonist/RAM student)
  Israel trip/*Adam's Marble* CD 214
  Spirits Rising CD 213
  The Third Colour CD 228–29
Coltrane, John (saxophonist) 61, 69, 77, 110, 127, 155
Composers' Guild 83
Compositional Devices 96, 101
Contrapuntal Forms 50–52, 71 n.4, 92–93
'Conversations'
  Deep Dark Blue Centre 39
Corman, Ned (musician/educator) 197
Crispell, Marilyn (pianist) 259
'Crumblin' Cookie'
  Deep Dark Blue Centre 39, 53
'Crystals of Space and Time' 166
Cumming, John (producer)
  Serious/*Hoarded Dreams* 160–61
Cuneiform Records
  Collier argument with label owner 169
  Hoarded Dreams 161
  Workpoints CD 42, 44, 46, 108, 112 n.6, 112 n.9
CUP
  dispute with 101–102, 169
  Inside Jazz 101
  Jazz: A Student's and Teacher's Guide 96, 189
Curson, Ted (trumpeter)
  Hoarded Dreams 51, 163–64

'Danish Blue'
Danish Radio Light Orchestra 183, 187 n.1
Dankworth, John (saxophonist/composer) 41, 51, 80, 104
  Cleo and John 111, 120, 122–25
  Collier opinion of 122–23
  $1,000,000 Collection 51–52
Darius 84, 103–108, 110, 116, 153, 179, 227, 249

Davis, Miles (trumpeter) 37, 58, 249, 253
  and 'shadowing' 60
  Collier admiration of 14, 96, 134, 190, 196, 257
  influence of Davis/*Kind of Blue* on Collier 40, 54–57, 216, 263
  'Vonetta' (*Sorcerer*) 227, 243
The Day of the Dead 93, 95, 111, 126, 130 n.2, 131–35, 140–44, 148 n.1, 149 n.6, 149 n.7, 152, 158, 174, 183, 248
Dean, Elton (saxophonist) 35
Dean, Roger (artist)
  cover for *Mosaics* 80, 114
Dean, Roger (pianist/composer) 140, 149 n.9, 150, 153, 172 n.1, 175, 219, 239, 247 n.1
  and Mosaic/*Lysis Plus* 151–52
  compositional shift with *New Conditions* 108–109, 130 n.1, 221
  Forty Years On 242
  harmonic freedom *Darius* 106
  Hoarded Dreams 162–63
  Hungary 1981 tour 187 n.2
  Jazz Yatra/India 154–55
  Loose Tubes 159–60
  Luminosity 262, 264
  Mosaic/*Cycles* 126, 151–52
  Mosaic/*Lysis Live* 118, 151–52
  New Conditions 118
  New Structures in Jazz and Improvised Music since 1960 74, 106, 108–109, 133
  October Ferry 144
  on *Charles River Fragments* 223
  on *Midnight Blue* 110
  on use of modular structure *Mosaics/Portraits* 74
  on *Workpoints* 47
  RAM/Penderecki's *Actions* 180
  recommends Ashley Brown 121
  replaces Geoff Castle 108
  Something British Made In Hong Kong 175, 179
  Symphony of Scorpions 138
  The Third Colour 228–30
  The Vonetta Factor 241, 243
  Triptych 145
Debussy, Claude (composer) 56
Deep Dark Blue Centre
  'Deep Dark Blue Centre' 40, 44, 46, 54
  LP 28–29, 36–41, 48 n.7, 52–53, 56, 61, 71 n.4, 74, 84, 241
Demsey, Dave (musician/educator) 198, 204 n.9
Derby Youth Jazz Orchestra
  concert with Collier 2007 244

'Deserted Funfair'
  Something British Made in Hong Kong 179
Desmond, Paul (saxophonist) 14
Dewey, John (philosopher) xiv, 257, 261
Directing 14 Jackson Pollocks
  Forty Years On 216, 240–43
  Vonetta Factor 227, 241–43
Disconforme (Spanish record company) 48 n.7, 93, 130, 135, 140, 144–45, 149 n.7, 152, 187 n.5
Dissanayake, Ellen (anthropologist) 142
Dobbins, Bill (musician/educator) 197, 203 n.8
Doig, Sally (artist) 50
Donnellan, Armen (musician/educator) 198
Dorsey, Jimmy
  'Ghost' band/Collier tours with 25–26
Down Another Road 70
  'Down Another Road' 53–54, 71 n.4
  LP 51–56, 72, 84, 229, 249
Down Beat
  Berklee scholarship competition 12–14
  International Jazz Critics Poll 41
Downes, Bob (musician) 9, 80, 92, 97
Doyle, Roger (composer) 230
DRJO 1, 54, 127, 187 n.1, 232–35
Duncan, Pete (trumpeter) 153
  Jazz Yatra/India 154–55
  New Conditions 118
  Symphony of Scorpions 139
Durrell, Lawrence (author)
  Collier's use of term 'workpoints' 44
  refuses permission for use of extracts of *Justine* 44, 48 n.12
Dury, Ian 66, 152

'Eggshell Summer'
  Directing 14 Jackson Pollocks 242, 247 n.3
  Meltdown 235
  Winter Oranges 233
'El Miklos'
  Deep Dark Blue Centre 38–39
Elastic Jazz – Sketches of Britain 77, 88 n.3
Elgar, Edward (composer) 54
Ellington, Duke (pianist/composer) xiii, 6, 20, 44, 61, 196, 220, 250
  Collier arrangement 'Star-Crossed Lovers'/ *Jazz in the Classroom* LP 23–24
  influence on Collier 16, 55–56, 69, 86–87, 98–99, 104, 113, 118–19, 134, 145, 163, 167, 257, 264
  Mike Westbrook and 119
  Mingus and 59–60
  Stan Tracey and 137

'Eridanus'
  The Day of the Dead (Disconforme) 144
Eurojazz 1981/European Community Youth Jazz Orchestra 158, 163, 174, 192
Evans, Bill (pianist)
  Collier admiration of 99, 196, 258
  with George Russell 78
Evans, Gil (composer/arranger) 37, 61, 190, 220, 250
  Collier's admiration of 14, 57
  influence on Collier 55, 58–59, 118–19, 165, 171, 185, 222, 233, 238, 242, 263
Evans, Nick (trombonist)
  Barry Summer School 35–36, 63
  Down Another Road 54–55
  'Down Another Road' 53–54
  joins/leaves Collier 36, 53, 65
  touring/school concerts 62, 86, 109
Evans, Pat (saxophonist)
  Barry Summer School 34, 36
  LSJO 48 n.5

Faulkner, William
  Wild Palms/Oxford Palms 237
Findikoglu, Emil (pianist)
  Berklee 24
Fisher, David (playwright)
  A Kind of Game 128
Fishwick, Matt (drummer/RAM student) 210–11
Fishwick, Steve (trumpeter/RAM student) 210–11
Fiuczynski, David (guitarist) 234, 247 n.4
Flamingo (night club) 41
'Forest Path to the Spring'
  The Day of the Dead (Mosaic) 135, 139, 144, 149 n.6
Formerly Fat Harry 67
Foster, Dan (saxophonist/RAM student)
  on RAM/Collier 211
  One By One the Cow Goes By 213
Foster, Paul (playwright)
  Silver Queen Saloon 127
Fox, Charles
  Deep Dark Blue Centre sleevenotes 28, 36, 40
  Hoarded Dreams interviewer 161
  Jazz in Perspective 99, 151
  Jazz Today 69
  takes over Collier's 'Jazz Notes'/*Gay News* column 117–18, 139, 144
Fox, John (Welfare State Theatre)
  with Mike Westbrook 92, 128

France, Nic (drummer)
 Loose Tubes 159
Franck, Tomas (saxophonist)
 Winter Oranges 233
Frankel, Daniel (saxophonist/Rimon student)
 Adam's Marble CD 216–17
Frankfurt School xiv, 261
Fraser, Hugh (trombonist/educator) 244
 Boathouse Records/*Charles River Fragments* 219
 meeting Collier 209
 Spirits Rising CD 213
 teaching at RAM 209–10
 The Third Colour 228–30
Freeman-Attwood, Jonathan (Principal RAM)
 Collier's departure from RAM 224–26
 on Collier at RAM 205–208, 212
 RAM Jazz CDs 212
Freire, Paulo (educator) 192
Frink, Elizabeth (artist) 50
Frost, Søren (drummer)
 Winter Oranges 233–34
Fryland, Thomas (trumpeter)
 Winter Oranges 233

Galper, Hal (pianist/educator) 198
Gamlen, Amy (saxophonist/RAM student)
 on Collier at RAM 211–12
Garnham, Nicholas (writer) 261
Garrick, Christian (violinist/RAM student)
 Spirits Rising CD 213–14
Garrick, Michael (pianist/composer) 52, 61, 205
 poetry and jazz 94
 Travelling Jazz Academy/jazz in schools 62, 71 n.7, 87
Gaskell, Mrs. (author) 70
Gay News 123
 blasphemy trial 173 n.11
 Collier 'Jazz Notes' column xii, 117–18, 139, 144
 Gay News interview 18, 114, 122, 147
 homophobic reaction to 'Jazz Notes' column 147–48
General Systems Theory xiii
Gertburg, Hans (producer) 51
Getz, Stan (saxophonist)
 Focus LP 184–85
Gibbs, Mike (composer/trombonist) 24, 32, 51, 61, 197, 250
 and Berklee 16
 and rock music 80–81
 Collier jealousy of 125–26
 Collier on Gibbs 20
 'El Miklós' 38–39, 48 n.9
 Gibbs' compositional approach 152
 Globe Playhouse Trust concert 102–103, 112 n.4
 International Jazz Octet (founder member) 17
 Jazz in the Classroom Vol VII sleevenotes 23
 joins Collier 32, 36, 38
 on Collier at Berklee 17–18
 on Herb Pomeroy 20–21
 Pete Hurt compares Gibbs/Collier 86
 Workpoints 45
Giddings, Alan (arts management)
 Mosaic Records 152–54
 on *The Day of the Dead* 140–41
 recruited by Collier 140
Gill, John (author) xi, 15, 17, 125, 141, 156, 172 n.4, 180, 201, 214, 239
 Collier and business 116, 141, 174, 178
 Collier death 247
 Collier/army life 10, 12, 91
 Collier/depression 90
 Collier/family 2, 5–6
 Collier/politics 146–47, 161
 Collier/Third Stream music 98
 Collier's attitude to sexuality 50, 113–14
 death xii
 disagreement with Wouter Turkenburg 199
 Hoarded Dreams 171
 Issie Barrett on 245–46
 Jazz Changes 194, 199
 Luminosity 262
 meets Collier 113
 Mike Naylor and family 104
 Mosaic Records 126
 move to Ronda 201, 224, 231
 move to Skopelos 245–46
 on *The Jazz Composer* 257
 relationship with 114, 116
 Relook compilation 26 n.2, 262
 shared interest in literature 48 n.12
 theatre/film 128–30
 Tom Robinson concert 146
 use of literature/art as model for compositional approach 92–93, 131
Gladdish, Martin (trombonist RAM student)
 on Collier at RAM 208, 210–11, 215
Globe Playhouse Trust concert 103, 112 n.2
Globe Unity Orchestra 165, 253
 Actions/Penderecki 181
'Go West'
 Harry Beckett *Flare Up* LP 64, 82

Godbolt, Jim (writer)
    homophobic review of *Hoarded Dreams*,
        Channel 4 documentary 171–72
    Jazz at Ronnie Scott's 170
Goetzee, Nick (guitarist/RAM student)
    Spirits Rising CD 213
Gojkovic, Dusko (trumpeter)
    Berklee 17
    Collier on Gojkovic 18
    on Collier 18
Grabowsky, Paul (pianist/composer)
    Collier admiration of 239
Grace, Sherrill (academic)
    Lowry conference 131–32, 139, 148 n.1,
        149 n.3
Graham, Kenny (saxophonist/composer) 51–
    52
Grammar schools 7, 91
Grappy, Andy (tubist)
    Charles River Fragments 220
Green Howards xi, 9–14
Greenberg, Clement (Marxist art critic) 228
Gregorio, Conrado (saxophonist)
    Berklee/ International Jazz Octet 17
Greig, Jeremy (trombonist)
    Bread & Circuses 238
Griffiths, Frank (saxophonist/Head of Jazz
    Brunel) 244
Griffiths, Malcolm (trombonist) 109
    compares Collier/Tracey/
        Westbrook 137–38
    Hoarded Dreams 163–64
    Jazz Yatra/India 154
    New Conditions 118
    October Ferry 144
    Symphony of Scorpions 138
    Triptych 145
    with Collier 86, 120
Guy, Barry (bassist/composer) xiii, 119–20,
    220, 230, 250, 257

'The Hackney Five'
    Charles River Fragments CD 219–20
H.M.S. Hampshire
    Graham Collier Music play for crew and
        officers 105
Hancock, Herbie (pianist) 53, 56, 81
Hansen, Steen (trombonist)
    Winter Oranges 233
Harlow Festival/Sculpture Park 50, 52, 71 n.3,
    71 n.4, 92
Harmon, Adrian (guitarist) 70
Harriott, Joe (saxophonist/composer) 31, 48
    n.11, 57

Harris, Steve (drummer)
    AUM/Collier admiration of 196, 253
Hartung, Hans (artist)
    Triptych 93, 145
Haskins, Casey (writer) xiv n.1, 110
Haslam, George (saxophonist)
    Meltdown Big Band commissions *Oxford
        Palms* 235–36
    records 'Eggshell Summer' 233, 235
Hayes, Tubby (saxophonist) 48 n.11, 52
Haziza, Shahar (percussionist/Rimon student)
    Adam's Marble CD 217
Hepworth, Barbara (artist) 50, 52
Herman, Woody (clarinettist/bandleader)
    'Early Autumn'/Collier arrangement 14
Hermann, Bernard (film composer) 186
Heycock, Wyndham (principal/Barry Summer
    School) 48 n.6
'Hirayoshi Suite'
    Deep Dark Blue Centre 37, 39
Hiseman, Jon (drummer) 29
Hoarded Dreams 60, 112 n.9
    Camden Jazz Festival performance/
        reception 165–69
    CD/Bracknell Festival 161–66
    Channel 4 documentary 170–72
    (see also under Massarik, Jewell, Collier,
        Voce, Godbolt)
Hoffmann, Hans (painter)
    inspiration for *Luminosity* 263
Holland, Dave (bassist) 205
Holloway, Laurie (pianist/composer) 70, 112
    n.5
Holt, David (trombone/RAM student)
    Spirits Rising CD 214
homophobia 50, 147–48, 169–72, 245
homosexuality
    Campaign for Homosexual Equality 113–
        14, 146–47
    Sexual Offences Act 1967 71 n.2
Hong Kong
    Collier in 8–10, 14
    Double Tenth Riots 11–12
    (see also under Collier: foreign tours)
Horovitz, Michael (poet)
    poetry and jazz 94
Hove, Michael (saxophonist)
    Winter Oranges 233–34
Hughes, Ted (poet) 70
Hultmark, Torbjon (trumpeter)
    Actions/RAM 180
Hungary (see under Collier: foreign tours)
Hurt, Pete (saxophonist)

on Collier's music 51, 86–87, 136
Portraits 85–86, 89 n.9, 103, 252
Hutton, Mick (bassist)
   Sweet Fat 128
Hymas, Tony (pianist)
   Stan Sulzmann LP *'krark'* 151

Iannitelli, Dick (saxophonist)
   Berklee 23–24, 26 n.2
Ilkley Literature festival
   The Day of the Dead premiere 126, 134, 143
Incus Records 84
India Tour/Jazz Yatra (see under Collier: foreign tours)
IAJE 245
   awards Collier 'Certificate of appreciation' 195
   bankruptcy 195, 203
   Collier's reservations regarding 195–97, 199–200
   founding of 194
IASJ 204 n.11, 214, 218, 229, 232
   Collier and 194, 245, 248
   dispute with 199–203, 232
   founding of 174, 194–95
   Jazz Changes and 96
Inside Jazz 18, 124
   discussed 96–101
   Steve Waterman on 190
Interaction: Opening up the Jazz Ensemble
   and musical aesthetics xiii, 96, 197
   musical examples 213
International Jazz Sextet/Octet (Berklee) 17
Israel
   RAM/Rimon student School collaboration/*Adam's Marble* CD 214–19
   (for Israel tour see under Collier: foreign tours)

Jackson Brothers
   funding of *Deep Dark Blue Centre* 36, 52
Jackson, Alan 'A.J.' (drummer) 50, 121, 153
   replaced by Ashley Brown 164
   The Day of the Dead 144
Jackson, Jack (bandleader/disc jockey) 36, 48 n.8
James, Peter (pianist/RAM student)
   Adam's Marble CD 214, 216–17
   Spirits Rising CD 213
'Jarrow Crusade'
   and Labour/TUC 2–3
Jazz: A Student's and Teacher's Guide 96, 189

and musical aesthetics 192
dispute with CUP 101–102, 169
Jazz Illustrations cassette 96
Jazz Lecture Concert 96, 108
   Mark Bassey on 190
Jazz Centre Society 81, 140
Jazz Changes
   Collier and IASJ 199–200, 204 n.11
   Collier USA research trip report 195–98
   Collier view of jazz education 188
   IASJ house journal 96, 194, 248
The Jazz Composer: Moving Music off the Paper 97, 125, 181, 187 n.6, 231, 244
   and musical aesthetics xiii, 96, 99–100, 188, 253, 256–62
   jazz/classical differences 98
   on own compositional approach 222, 227–28, 230, 243, 250
   references to musicians 56–58, 60, 184–85, 196, 253
Jazz Notes (BBC) 69, 194, 203 n.5
Jazz Today (BBC) 69, 151
Jazz Warriors 157
Jazz Workshop (Hamburg) 1, 51
Jazz Workshop: The Blues (book) 96, 184
Jeanette Cochrane Theatre 32
Jenkins, Hugh (Arts Minister) 71 n.1
Jenkins, Karl (musician/composer) 50–51, 62–63, 71 n.4
   Barry Summer School 35
   Deep Dark Blue Centre 38–40
   Down Another Road 53–55
   joins Collier 36
   leaves to join Nucleus 65
   Workpoints 43, 45–46
Jewell, Derek
   negative review of *Hoarded Dreams* 1985 concert and Collier's response 168–69
Johns, Terry (French horn) 29–30, 36
Johnson, Bruce (author/educator) 260–61
Johnson, Ron (synthesizer)
   The Day of the Dead/Lowry conference 131
Jones, Elvin (drummer) 65
Jones, Quincy (composer/arranger) 197
Jones, Terry (writer/actor/director)
   financial support for Mosaic Records 126, 150
Jones, Thad (trumpeter) 58, 117, 253
Juckes, Gideon (tubist)
   Directing 14 Jackson Pollocks 242

Kadan, Yiftach (guitarist/ Rimon student)
   Adam's Marble CD 216–17
Kai-Shek, Chiang (politician) 11

Kant, Immanuel (philosopher) xiv n.1, 110, 261
Keenlyside, Tom (saxophonist)
   The Day of the Dead/Lowry conference 131
Kelly, Adrian (trumpeter)
   Bread & Circuses 239
   Collier as composer 236–37
   director of The Collective 186
Kenny, Jack and King, Peter (playwrights)
   Sweet Fat 128
Kenton, Stan (bandleader) 6, 14, 26 n.1
   Collier compared to by Stuart Nicholson 180
Kinsey, Tony (drummer)
   poetry and jazz 94
Klooks Kleek (night club) 41
Knepper, Jimmy (trombonist) 62
Kramer, Timothy (cellist) 94
Kukurudza, Ihor (guitarist)
   Day of the Dead/Lowry conference 131

Labour Party 3, 37, 148
Laine, Cleo (singer) 52, 127, 151, 171
   Cleo and John 111, 122–24
   Collier admiration for 122–24
Laing, R. D. (psychiatrist) 100
Lake Steve (ECM producer)
   response to homophobic correspondence 147–48
La MaMa (theatre group) 127
Lancaster, Jack (saxophonist) 12–13
Lang, Eddie (guitarist) 132
LaPorta, John (saxophonist/educator)
   Berklee 17, 19
Lateef, Yusef (saxophonist) 41
Laurence, Chris (bassist) 70
Lee, Jeannie (Arts Minister) 71 n.1
Lee, Phil (guitarist) 29–30
   Deep Dark Blue Centre 36, 38–40
   recruits John Marshall 33
   Songs For My Father 65, 67
Leeds International Jazz Educators' Conference 1996 125, 193
Lemon, Brian (pianist) 205
Leonhart, Jay (bassist/songwriter)
   Berklee 17
Lerner and Loewe (composers)
   'On The Street Where You Live' 74
Levine, Mark (pianist/educator) 198
Liebman, Dave (saxophonist) 198
   Collier disagreement with 199–200
   IASJ founding of 194–95, 203 n.6
Lindvall, Anders Chico (guitarist)
   Winter Oranges 234

'Little Ben' 104, 112 n.6
Little Theatre Club 32
Lockheart, Mark (saxophonist)
   Charles River Fragments 219, 222
Logue, Christopher (poet)
   poetry and jazz 94
London Jazz Festival
   Charles River Fragments 219
   Directing 14 Jackson Pollocks 240–42
   The Third Colour 227–28, 247 n.2
London Musicians' Co-operative 81
London Schools Jazz Orchestra (see under NYJO)
Loose Tubes 174, 192, 205
   beginnings as rehearsal band/separation from Collier 157, 159–60
   recordings 157
Lopes, Paul (author) 255
Lowe, Dave (trumpeter) 29–30
Lowry, Malcolm 142, 144
   inspiration for Collier 92–93, 131–36, 139, 146
   Lowry and jazz 131–32, 139, 253
   The Day of the Dead/Lowry Conference 131, 148 n.1, 149 n.3, 174, 183, 209, 227
   (for Lowry recordings see under *The Day of the Dead*/*Symphony of Scorpions*/*October Ferry*)
Lowther, Henry (trumpeter) 137, 153
   Charles River Fragments 219
   Hoarded Dreams 163
   Jazz Yatra/India 154
   New Conditions 118
   October Ferry 144
   Symphony of Scorpions 139
   Triptych 145
   Workpoints 42, 45
Luminosity 93, 190, 231, 248, 262–65
Lunch
   Collier interview 114–15
Luton
   Collier desire to leave 8
   Collier family and 1–6
   Luton Grammar School 6–9, 15, 27
   Vauxhall Motors 3, 5, 9, 13
Lysne, Geir (composer) xiii, 220, 259
   Collier admiration for 196, 253

'Machau Interlude'
   composition written for *Down Beat* competition 14
Machin, Jon (percussionist/RAM student)
   Spirits Rising CD 214

'Mackerel Sky'
   Directing 14 Jackson Pollocks 240, 242
Mahavishnu Orchestra 81
Main, Stephen (saxophonist/RAM student)
   Adam's Marble CD 214, 216
   Spirits Rising CD 213
Malkovsky, Boris (synthesizer/Rimon student)
   Adam's Marble CD 216–17
Mantler, Mike (trumpeter/composer)
   Collier admiration of 138, 253
Marcos, Ferdinand (dictator) 176, 178
Marcus, Steve (saxophonist)
   Berklee 17
Marcuse, Herbert (philosopher) 14, 260–61
Mardin, Arif (record producer)
   Berklee/friendship with Collier 17, 24, 26 n.4
Mariano, Charlie (saxophonist)
   'Blue Walls' on *Deep Dark Blue Centre* 37–38
Markussen, Ulfe (saxophonist)
   Winter Oranges 233–34
Marquee (night club) 31, 41
Marsalis, Wynton (trumpeter) 197, 253, 259
Marshall, John (drummer) 48 n.6, 50–51, 71 n.4, 150, 242
   Charles River Fragments 220
   Collier and gigs 61
   Deep Dark Blue Centre 37–39, 43
   Down Another Road 53–55
   'The Hackney Five' 219
   joins Collier group 33–34, 36
   joins Nucleus 65
   Luminosity 262, 264
   on Collier bass playing 66
   The Third Colour 228–30
   Workpoints 45–46
Marshall, Oren (tubist)
   Shapes, Colours, Energy 229–30
Martinelli, Francesco (author/academic)
   turns down *The Jazz Composer* project 256–57
Maslow, Abraham (psychologist) xiv, 261–62
Massarik, Jack (journalist)
   negative review of *Hoarded Dreams* 1985 concert and Collier's response 168–69
Maupin, Bennie (saxophonist) 263
McCullers, Carson (author) 111
McFarland, Gary (composer) 57, 197, 220
McGillveray, Jim (percussionist)
   Day of the Dead/Lowry conference 131
McGregor, Chris (pianist/bandleader) 32, 65
McLear, Joe (saxophonist) 29–30
McNair, Harold (saxophonist) 41

McNeely, Jim (composer/arranger)
   Collier criticism of approach 58, 253
Melford, Myra (pianist) 259
Melody Maker
   'Jazz Poll' 41, 48 n.11
Messiaen, Olivier (composer) 119–20, 130 n.1, 223
Michelangelo (artist) 92
Middelheim Festival
   Workpoints CD 108, 112 n.6, 112 n.9
Midnight Blue 74, 84–85, 93, 108–11, 116, 153, 179, 223
'Midsummer Dawn'
   Something British Made in Hong Kong 179
Mikkelborg, Palle (trumpeter)
   Hoarded Dreams 1985 performance 167
Miklin, Karlheinz (saxophonist)
   IASJ 202
   Third Colour CD 229
Miller, Harry (bassist)
   Ogun Records 84, 118
Miller, Hazel (label owner)
   Ogun Records 84, 118
Millett, Lisa (vocalist/RAM student) 213
Mingus, Charles 62, 142, 163, 166
   Charles River Fragments dedicated to 219
   Collier group compared to 33, 43, 55–56, 69
   influence on Collier 59–61
   Workpoints and 45
'Mist on Water'
   Something British Made in Hong Kong 179
Mitchell, Adrian (poet/playwright) 128
Mitchell, John (percussionist)
   New Conditions 118–20, 234
   Symphony of Scorpions 138, 234
Mitchell, Roscoe (saxophonist/composer) 259
'Molewrench'
   Down Another Road 53, 55
Monk, Thelonious (pianist/composer) 78, 137
   Collier dislike of 57, 253
Montgomery, Marion (vocalist) 70, 112 n.5
Montreux Jazz Festival
   Collier group at 79–80, 82
Moore, Barbara (singer) 29–30
Moore, Henry (artist) 50
Morgan, Russell (drummer/RAM student)
   Adam's Marble CD 215, 217
Morris, Lawrence 'Butch' (composer) 250
Morris, Matthew (saxophonist/RAM student)
   Spirits Rising CD 213–14
Morris, Nigel (drummer) 150
Morrissey, Dick (saxophonist) 52

Morton, Jelly Roll (pianist/composer) xiii, 69, 196
Mosaic Records
   Alan Giddings and 140, 152–53
   Arts Council and 116, 150, 172 n.1
   Collier establishes own label 84, 104, 116
   deal with Bellaphon/collapse of label 152–54
   expansion 118, 126
   recordings on 150–52, 172 n.2, 172 n.7
   Roundhouse festival 153
   Terry Jones and 126, 150
Mosaics 48 n.7, 52, 72–77, 79–81, 84–85, 107, 114, 145, 179
   The Alternate Mosaics 77–78, 145
Moss, Danny (saxophonist) 205
Mulligan, Gerry (saxophonist/composer) 220
   Collier admiration for 14, 57
Mumford, John (trombonist)
   Workpoints 45
Murphy, Bob (pianist)
   The Day of the Dead/Lowry conference 131
Musicians' Co-operative 81
Mwamba, Corey (vibraphonist)
   Collier admiration of 253

Nash, Paul (Director Manhattan New Music Project) 230–31
National Jazz Federation (NJF) Festival 31, 41
Naylor, Hattie (playwright) 104
Naylor, Mike (playwright/songwriter)
   'Postal Order from my Grannie' and 'World Turned Upside Down' 103–104, 112 n.5
Neame, Ivo (saxophonist/pianist/student at RAM) 232
Nestico, Sammy
   Collier criticism of approach 58, 253
New Conditions 61, 111, 114, 131, 134, 217, 229, 234, 249
   'An Alternate *New Conditions*' 240, 242
   as 'Third Stream' 98
   Collier compares with *Symphony of Scorpions* 135–36
   compared with Westbrook *Citadel/Room 315* and Tracey *Salisbury Suite* 119–20
   genesis of 116–17
   Messiaen and 119, 130 n.1
   reception 117–18, 139
   Roger Dean on 47, 108–109, 221
   UK tour 116, 121
New Orleans Jazz
   Collier references to 45, 55–56, 60, 145, 199
Newman, Barnett (artist) 109–10

Nichols, Keith
   Midnite Follies Orchestra/RAM 208
Nilsson, Vincent (trombonist)
   Winter Oranges 234
Nixon, Richard
   'Nixon shock' 255
Nock, Mike (pianist/student at Berklee) 239
Noyce, John (bassist/RAM student) 213–14
Nucleus (see under Carr, Ian)
NYJO/LSJO 29, 48 n.5, 50
   Collier and Bill Ashton xii, 97, 191–93, 195
   Collier recruits from 63, 85
   'Gay Talk' 63, 82, 97, 190–91
   Loose Tubes and 158, 160, 192

October Ferry 135, 144
   Collier on 93
   compared with *Triptych* 145
Ogun Records 84, 118
Old Place, The (see under Ronnie Scott's Club)
One by One the Cow Goes By
   Spirits Rising CD 213–14, 221
Order of the British Empire
   Collier awarded 4, 183–84
Ovesen, Thomas (bassist)
   Winter Oranges 233–34
Oxford Palms 180
   Bread & Circuses CD 237, 239
   commissioned by George Haslam/Meltdown 235
   inspired by William Faulkner 146
   New York premiere 230
Oxley, Tony (drummer) 9, 63, 80, 105
   Incus 84

Page, Mike (saxophonist) 128, 153
   India Jazz Yatra 154
   New Conditions 118
   Triptych 145
Panayi, Andy (saxophonist)
   Luminosity CD 264
Park Lane Group 111
Parker, Charlie (saxophonist) 6, 59
Parker, Eddie (flautist)
   Loose Tubes 159
Parker, Evan 47, 253, 258–59, 88 n.3
   and performance of Penderecki's *Actions* 180–81
   Incus 84
Parker, William (bassist) 259
Parkin, Andrew
   narrator *Day of the Dead* Lowry conference 131

Pearce, Dick (trumpeter) 89 n.10
  joins Collier 63, 85
  Portraits 85–86
'Pebble Fresh from the Brook' 187 n.1
Penderecki, Krzysztof (composer)
  RAM performance of *Actions* 180–82
Petersen, Jack (guitarist/educator)
  Berklee 17, 19
Philby, Kim (MI5/KGB agent)
  A Kind of Game 128
Philippines/President Marcos/martial
  law 176, 178
Phillips, Dudley (bassist)
  Charles River Fragments 219–22
Pilz, Michael (saxophonist)
  Hoarded Dreams 1985 performance 167
Pine, Courtney 157
Plain Song and Mountain Birds 97, 175, 184–
  86, 217, 219, 221–22
Pollock, Jackson (artist) 252
Pomeroy, Herb (trumpeter/educator)
  Charles River Fragments dedication 219
  Collier on 16, 20, 22, 196
  Gary Burton on 19
  influence on Collier 28–29, 55, 196
  Mike Gibbs on 20–21
  Recording Band/*Jazz in the Classroom* 21–
    23, 212
Portraits 48 n.7, 84–87, 88 n.8, 94, 103, 105, 107
  Roger Dean on 74
'Postal Order from my Grannie'
  (musical) 103–104
Powell, Dave (tubist)
  Hoarded Dreams 163
Presencer, Gerard (trumpeter)
  takes over as Head of Jazz/RAM from
    Collier 224
Prévost, Eddie (drummer) 172 n.9
Price, Curtis (principal/RAM) 224
Priestley, J.B. (author) 70
Private Eye 225
Pyne, Chris (trombonist) 9

QE2/music for documentary 70, 82, 88 n.6
'Quanahuac' 144
Quartet Books
  Cleo and John 122
  Collier dispute with 101, 124–25
  Inside Jazz 96, 101
'Queensbury Rules'
  Something British Made in Hong Kong 179

Radio Denmark Big Band 187 n.1
Radio Denmark Light Orchestra 187 n.1

Radio France – *New Conditions* 116
Radio Suisse Romande 82
RAM 228, 237, 245, 247 n.2
  and *Jazz Changes* 199
  annual student recording 22, 212–14
  departure from 201–202, 204 n.11, 208,
    223–26, 232, 247
  RAM big band 180–82, 212–14, 219
  RAM/Rimon collaboration 187 n.7,
    214–19
  reception by classical tutors 91, 206–208
  teaching philosophy at xi, 21, 90, 104,
    158–59, 172 n.2, 174, 190, 196, 198,
    206–214, 248
Rancière, Jacques (philosopher) 262
Ravel, Maurice (composer) 56, 59
Rendell, Don (saxophonist) 34, 36, 48 n.6, 48
  n.11, 291
Rendell–Carr Quintet 48 n.6, 48 n. 11, 291
Richter, Steve (percussionist)
  Bread & Circuses 239
Ricotti, Frank (vibraphonist) 50, 53, 71 n.4
  joins Collier 41, 63
  Workpoints 42–43, 45
Riley, Howard 32, 80
  Mosaic/*Intertwine*/*Music for Solo
    Piano* 126, 150–52, 172 n.2
Riordan, Patrick 'Paddy'
  Green Howards/Hong Kong 9–11
Roberts, Tony (saxophonist) 153
  Songs For My Father 65, 68
  Workpoints 51
Robinson, Tom
  Tom Robinson – Cabaret '79, Collier
    performs with 146
Robson, Jeremy (poet)
  poetry and jazz 94
Rodin, Auguste (artist) 50
Rodrigo, Joaquín
  Concierto de Aranjuez 59
Rogers, Carl (psychologist) xiv, 261
'Rolli's Tune'
  Harry Beckett *Flare Up* LP 64
Rollins, Sonny (saxophonist) 78
Roms, Professor Heike (academic) 34, 48 n.6
Ronnie Scott's Club
  Jazz at Ronnie Scott's (house journal) 170
  Symphony of Scorpions/*Triptych* 121, 135,
    144
  The Old Place 32–33
Rosen, Mitchell (saxophonist/Rimon student)
  Adam's Marble CD 216
Ross, Annie (vocalist)
  Globe Playhouse Trust concert 103

Rothko, Mark (artist) 93, 145, 252
Rubin, Harold (clarinettist)
    Adam's Marble CD 215–16
Rubin, Ron (bassist) 70
Ruegg, Matthias (composer/arranger) 78
Russell, George (composer) xiii, 220
    and Westbrook 119
    as conductor 250
    Collier dislike of 57, 253
    Collier/Russell compared 37, 166, 239, 250–53
    use of cadenza 78
    use of guitar compared with Collier 85, 89 n.8, 234
Russo, Bill (composer/arranger) 14, 188
Rutherford, Paul (trombonist) 9
'Ryoanji'/'An Alternate Ryoanji'
    Forty Years On 242
Rypdal, Terje
    Collier review of *Waves* in *Gay News* 147–48
    Hoarded Dreams 1985 performance 168

Saberton, Pete (pianist)
    Charles River Fragments 219, 222
Saldahna, 'Dizzy' Sal (pianist)
    Berklee student 17
Salisbury, The (gay pub) 114
Santini, Ray (tutor at Berklee) 48 n.9
Sarath, Ed (trumpeter/educator)
    IASJ 198
    supportive of Collier 204 n.10
    The Third Colour CD 229
Sauter, Eddie (arranger)
    influence of *Focus* on *Plain Song and Mountain Birds* 57, 184–86, 196
Saydisc (label)
    Portraits 84, 88 n.7
Schillinger method 14, 16
Schneider, Maria (composer) 220
Schönberg, Arnold (composer) 186
Schoof, Manfred (saxophonist)
    Hoarded Dreams 163
Schröder, John (guitarist)
    Hoarded Dreams 163–64, 167
Schubert, Matthias (saxophonist)
    Hoarded Dreams 163–64
Schuller, Gunther (composer) 97, 223
Schultz, Nikolai (flautist)
    Winter Oranges 234–35
Scott, Ronnie (saxophonist/club owner) 172
Scott-Heron, Gil 265 n.2
'Sea, Sky and Down' 95
Shamir, Uri (bassist/Rimon student)
    Adam's Marble CD 217

Shapes, Colours, Energy 247 n.2
    The Third Colour CD 228–29
Share Robert (Berklee Provost)
    Recording Band 21–22
Shaw, Martin (trumpeter)
    Luminosity CD 264
Sheppard, Andy (saxophonist) 157
Shipton, Alyn (author/broadcaster) 208
    BGO sleevenotes 54, 72
    Leeds International Jazz Educators' Conference 193–94, 203 n.5
    on *Forty Years On* 240–41
Sibelius Academy
    basis for RAM degree programme 206
    Collier designs jazz degree programme 174, 205–206
Silver Queen Saloon 127–28, 130 n.3
Simcock, Gwilym (pianist/RAM student) 232
Sims, Zoot (saxophonist) 41
Skelton, Matthew (drummer/RAM student)
    Spirits Rising CD 214
Skidmore, Alan (saxophonist) 79–80, 92, 103
Songs For My Father 65, 67–69, 71 n.9
Skvorecky, Josef (author)
    The Bass Saxophone 128, 221
Slater, Ashley (trombonist)
    Loose Tubes 159
Smart, Nick (Head of Jazz/RAM) 225
Smith, Brian (saxophonist) 65, 71 n.8, 103
Smith, Chris (trombonist)
    Workpoints 45, 53
Smoke Blackened Walls and Curlews 70–71, 92
Soft Machine 65, 81, 142
Sokal, Harry (saxophonist)
    Hoarded Dreams 1985 performance 168
Something British Made in Hong Kong 139, 141, 158, 172 n.7, 174, 179–80, 221, 248
Songs for My Father 29, 52, 64–69, 72, 79–80, 85
Sony Drama Prize
    The Bass Saxophone 128
Soukop, Will (artist) 50
Speake, Martin (saxophonist/educator)
    Collier at RAM 207, 211, 224–25
    interview with Pete Hurt 86–87
Speight, Ed (guitarist) 103, 111, 112 n.9, 153, 187 n.2
    Charles River Fragments 219, 222
    Collier and John Gill 114
    Collier tours 127, 176, 178, 182–83
    Collier tribute to 152
    Darius 107
    Forty Years On 241–42
    Hoarded Dreams 163

India Jazz Yatra 154–56
joins Collier 85
Luminosity CD 262, 264
New Conditions 118
October Ferry 144
on Collier bass playing 66
Plain Song and Mountain Birds 175, 184–86
Portraits 85
role in Collier groups 30, 59, 85, 89 n.8
Something British Made in Hong Kong 179
Sweet Fat 128
Symphony of Scorpions 139
The Third Colour CD 228–29
Spender, Stephen
on Malcolm Lowry 135, 149 n.2
Spontaneous Music Ensemble 259
'Spring Rain'
Something British Made in Hong Kong 179–80
Stańko, Tomasz (trumpeter) 220
Hoarded Dreams 163–65
Steam Records 84
Stevens, Jack (saxophonist)
Berklee International Jazz Octet Recording Band 17
Stevens, John (drummer) 9
Little Theatre Club 32
Still, Clyfford (artist) 93, 145
Stockhausen, Karlheinz (composer) 243
Strayhorn, Billy (composer/arranger) 56, 60, 167
Collier arranges 'Star-Crossed Lovers' 23–24
Sulzmann, Stan 71 n.4
critical of Collier's music 51, 122, 136
Down Another Road 53–55
Hoarded Dreams 163–64, 167
joins Collier 50, 63
Mosaic/On Loan With Gratitude/'krark' 126, 150–52, 172 n.2
on Collier at RAM 210
replaced by Alan Wakeman 62
Surman, John (saxophonist) 32, 51, 81–82, 92, 158
Workpoints 42–43, 45
Sweet Fat (radio play) 128
Sydor, Bob (saxophonist)
Collier/LSJO 63
joins Collier 63, 65
Mosaics/Alternate Mosaics 73–75, 77–78, 80
Songs For My Father 68–69
Symphony of Scorpions 61, 93, 118, 121, 130 n.2, 131, 134–37, 143–44, 149 n.6, 217, 234

Taylor, John (pianist) 51
On Loan with Gratitude 151
replaced by Geoff Castle 72
Songs For My Father 65, 67–69
Terry, Clark (trumpeter) 106, 203 n.8
'Thames Base' 187 n.1
Thelin, Eje (trombonist)
Hoarded Dreams 163, 167
Themen, Art 86, 111, 153
Charles River Fragments 219, 221–23
critical of Collier's music 51, 122, 136–38
Directing 14 Jackson Pollocks CD 241–42
Globe Playhouse Trust concert 103
Hoarded Dreams 163–64, 167
Jazz Yatra/India 154–55, 172 n.3
Luminosity CD 262, 264
New Conditions 118, 120
October Ferry 144
Sweet Fat 128
Symphony of Scorpions/written for 121, 136–39
The Day of the Dead 144
The Third Colour CD 228, 230
Triptych 145
'Third Road'
Harry Beckett *Flare Up* LP 64, 82
The Third Colour CD
Shapes, Colours, Energy 228–29, 247 n.2
The Miró Tile 93, 202, 228–29
The Third Colour 228–30, 247 n.2
The Third Colour (*Forty Years On*) 61, 232, 235, 239, 243
Three Simple Pieces 202, 228, 247 n.2
Third Stream (see under Collier)
Three Simple Pieces 202, 247 n.2
The Third Colour CD 228
Meltdown 235
Winter Oranges 232
'Tinted Autumn'
Winter Oranges 233–34
Tippett, Keith (pianist/composer) 65, 142, 259
Arts Council grant 47
Barry Summer School 35
compositional approach 120
Tippetts, Julie (vocalist/lyricist) 259
Tomkins, Trevor (drummer/educator)
and RAM 207, 209
Collier/Tomkins departure from RAM 225
Directing 14 Jackson Pollocks CD 242–43
establishes teaching diploma at RAM 209
Luminosity CD 264
The Bass Saxophone 128
Torrington, The (jazz venue/pub) 72, 88 n.1